Votes and Violence

Why does ethnic violence break out in some places and not others? More important, why do some governments try to prevent antiminority riots while others do nothing, or even actively encourage attacks? This book answers these questions through a detailed study of Hindu-Muslim riots in India, as well as case studies of Ireland, Malaysia, and Romania. It shows how electoral incentives at two levels interact to explain both where violence breaks out and, more importantly, why some states decide to prevent mass violence and others do not. While developing this electoral incentives model, the author shows why several alternative explanations for ethnic violence – focusing on town-level social and economic factors, the weak capacity of the Indian state, or India's alleged lack of "consociational power sharing" – cannot explain the observed variation in Hindu-Muslim riots.

Steven I. Wilkinson is Assistant Professor of Political Science at Duke University, where he has taught since 1999. He has traveled extensively in India since his first visit there in 1989. He has been awarded fellowships from the Harvard Academy for International and Area Studies, the Columbia University Society of Fellows in the Humanities, and the Harry Frank Guggenheim Foundation.

Cambridge Studies in Comparative Politics

General Editor

Margaret Levi   *University of Washington, Seattle*

Assistant General Editor

Stephen Hanson   *University of Washington, Seattle*

Associate Editors

Robert H. Bates   *Harvard University*
Peter Hall   *Harvard University*
Peter Lange   *Duke University*
Helen Milner   *Columbia University*
Frances Rosenbluth   *Yale University*
Susan Stokes   *University of Chicago*
Sidney Tarrow   *Cornell University*

Other Books in the Series

Stefano Bartolini, *The Political Mobilization of the European Left,
1860–1980: The Class Cleavage*
Mark Beissinger, *Nationalist Mobilization and the Collapse of the Soviet State*
Carles Boix, *Democracy and Redistribution*
Carles Boix, *Political Parties, Growth, and Equality: Conservative and Social
Democratic Economic Strategies in the World Economy*
Catherine Boone, *Merchant Capital and the Roots of State Power in Senegal,
1930–1985*
Catherine Boone, *Political Topographies of the African State: Territorial
Authority and Institutional Change*
Michael Bratton and Nicolas van de Walle, *Democratic Experiments in
Africa: Regime Transitions in Comparative Perspective*
Valerie Bunce, *Leaving Socialism and Leaving the State: The End of
Yugoslavia, the Soviet Union, and Czechoslovakia*
Ruth Berins Collier, *Paths toward Democracy: The Working Class and Elites
in Western Europe and South America*
Donatella della Porta, *Social Movements, Political Violence, and the State*
Gerald Easter, *Reconstructing the State: Personal Networks and Elite Identity*
Robert F. Franzese, *Macroeconomic Policies of Developed Democracies*

Continues after the Index

Votes and Violence

ELECTORAL COMPETITION AND ETHNIC RIOTS IN INDIA

STEVEN I. WILKINSON
Duke University

 **CAMBRIDGE** UNIVERSITY PRESS

CAMBRIDGE UNIVERSITY PRESS
Cambridge, New York, Melbourne, Madrid, Cape Town, Singapore, São Paulo

Cambridge University Press
The Edinburgh Building, Cambridge CB2 2RU, UK

Published in the United States of America by Cambridge University Press, New York

www.cambridge.org
Information on this title: www.cambridge.org/9780521829168

First published 2004

A catalogue record for this publication is available from the British Library

Library of Congress Cataloguing in Publication data

Wilkinson, Steven I., 1965–
    Votes and violence: electoral competition and ethnic riots in India / Steven I. Wilkinson.
      p. cm. – (Cambridge studies in comparative politics)
    Includes bibliographical references and index.
    ISBN 0-521-82916-X (hardback)
    1. Elections – India.   2. Political violence – India.   3. Ethnic conflict – India.
    I. Title. II. Series.

JQ292.W55   2004
303.6′2′08900954–dc22   2003068721

ISBN-13 978-0-521-82916-8 hardback
ISBN-10 0-521-82916-X hardback

Transferred to digital printing 2006

Contents

List of Figures		*page* viii
List of Tables		ix
Acknowledgments		xi
1	THE ELECTORAL INCENTIVES FOR ETHNIC VIOLENCE	1
2	EXPLAINING TOWN-LEVEL VARIATION IN HINDU-MUSLIM VIOLENCE	19
3	STATE CAPACITY EXPLANATIONS FOR HINDU-MUSLIM VIOLENCE	63
4	THE CONSOCIATIONAL EXPLANATION FOR HINDU-MUSLIM VIOLENCE	97
5	THE ELECTORAL INCENTIVES FOR HINDU-MUSLIM VIOLENCE	137
6	PARTY COMPETITION AND HINDU-MUSLIM VIOLENCE	172
7	THE ELECTORAL INCENTIVES FOR ETHNIC VIOLENCE IN COMPARATIVE PERSPECTIVE	204
8	DEMOCRACY AND ETHNIC VIOLENCE	236
Appendix A: Data Sources for Hindu-Muslim Riots		243
Appendix B: Data-Entering Protocol for Riot Database		255
Appendix C: Additional Results from Statistical Tables		263
References		267
Index		283

Figures

1.1 The relationship between party competition and a state's response to antiminority polarization and violence: Indian and non-Indian examples *page* 6

1.2 Hindu-Muslim riots since independence 12

1.3 State variation in deaths in Hindu-Muslim riots, 1977–1995 14

1.4 State variation in number of Hindu-Muslim riots, 1977–1995 15

2.1 The relationship between town- and state-level factors 58

2.2 Reported precipitating events and deaths during the February–April 2002 communal violence 60

5.1 The theoretical relationship between party competition and a state's response to antiminority polarization and violence 139

5.2 Predicted effect of party fractionalization on communal riots 152

5.3 Reported precipitating events and deaths during the February–April 2002 communal violence and patterns of party competition 159

6.1 The institutional origins of state-level differences in party competition 173

7.1 The relationship between party competition and a state's response to antiminority polarization and violence: Non-Indian examples 206

Tables

2.1	Electoral competition and occurrence of riots in 167 Uttar Pradesh towns, 1970–1995	*page* 43
2.2	Electoral competition and deaths in Hindu-Muslim violence in 167 Uttar Pradesh towns, 1970–1995	45
3.1	Police strength in the states	81
3.2	Declining judicial capacity	83
3.3	Frequency of police transfers in major states, 1973–1977	84
3.4	Police strength, judicial capacity, and riots in the 1990s	88
3.5	Arrests, prosecutions, and convictions after communal riots	89
3.6	State transfer rates and Hindu-Muslim riots, 1976–1985	92
3.7	Transfer frequency and Hindu-Muslim riots in Uttar Pradesh, 1988–1995	93
4.1	Scheduled Caste and Tribe representation in central government employment	125
4.2	India's changing consociational status and Hindu-Muslim violence	127
4.3	Minority representation and Hindu-Muslim violence in the states, 1975–1995	128
4.4	Congress, consociationalism, and the occurrence of Hindu-Muslim riots	133
5.1	Number of effective parties in major Indian states as of February 2002	143

5.2   Comparative educational levels among different
       religious groups in India   145
5.3   Electoral competition and communal riots
       in major Indian states, 1961–1995   151
5.4   Party competition and riot prevention,
       from February to April 2002   156
6.1   Do state-level differences in ethnic heterogeneity
       explain levels of party competition?   176
7.1   Election results and ethnic cleavages in Malaysian
       federal elections, 1964–1969   221
7.2   Selangor state election results, 1969   223

Acknowledgments

This study owes a great deal to my advisor at MIT, the late and much missed Myron Weiner, who along with Donald Horowitz and Stephen Van Evera urged me to test ideas I had developed on the basis of a study of Uttar Pradesh in a much wider comparative study.

I have been fortunate to have the opportunity to present large portions of the book to very smart members of two cross-disciplinary groups, whose constructive comments have helped me to identify areas where the argument or evidence needed more work. Members of the Laboratory in Comparative Ethnic Processes (LiCEP) have read several drafts of the main argument over several years, though they cannot be blamed, of course, for my inability or unwillingness to incorporate all their suggestions. I thank all the current and former members of this terrific group for their help: Arun Agrawal, Bob Bates, Kanchan Chandra, Christian Davenport, Jim Fearon, Karen Ferree, Elise Giuliano, Michael Hechter, Macartan Humphries, Stathis Kalyvas, Nelson Kasfir, Pauline Jones Luong, David Laitin, Ian Lustick, Dan Posner, Nicholas Sambanis, Smita Singh, Pieter van Houten, and Ashutosh Varshney. Several members of the group – Kanchan Chandra, Jim Fearon, Dan Posner, Nic Sambanis, and Elisabeth Wood – gave me so many additional detailed comments and suggestions that I should give them my special thanks. The second group that has read my work, the recently formed Network on South Asian Politics and Political Economy (Netsappe), commented on an earlier version of my main chapters at a conference at the University of Michigan in July 2002, and participants provided feedback that reflected both the theoretical and area expertise of the group. I thank all the members of Netsappe for giving me extremely detailed and insightful comments on the two chapters I presented. Special thanks must go to Yogendra Yadav for his comments on how I could revise some key portions of Chapters 2 and 5.

This book has been written at Duke, and while all of my colleagues here have helped in various ways I would like to single out a few for special thanks. My colleague Donald Horowitz first got me interested in the study of ethnic politics when I was a graduate student. Since then he has provided invaluable encouragement, advice, and, when needed, criticism of the theoretical arguments I make. I am grateful to him for his continuing mentorship. Special thanks must also go to Herbert Kitschelt, who helped me clarify my central argument about the relationship between party competition and violence at low levels of party competition. Were it not for our conversations together, the key diagrams in which I work out the relationship between party fractionalization and government response to antiminority violence would be one "branch" short. Herbert and John Aldrich also encouraged me to present several key chapters to the party politics course they coteach, from which I received additional valuable feedback. Others whose help went above and beyond the call of duty include John Transue, Scott de Marchi, and Meg McKean. Lastly, I should like to thank Mike Munger, not for his friendly nagging about whether I would ever get this book finished (though that too was appreciated, at least most of the time), but for his interest in my work and steady encouragement over the past five years.

In India, many people have helped me at various points in my research. In Delhi, Sunil and Anjali Kumar and their family have given me their friendship and encouragement – and often food and shelter as well – since my first visit to India in 1989. They make my trips to India seem like coming home. Others who provided hospitality and encouragement include Tejbir and Mala Singh in Delhi, Gyan and Jayati Chaturvedi in Agra, and S. K. Gupta in Varanasi. Many police officers and civil servants offered to share their expertise with me, and I would especially like to note the help I received from the late Ashok Priyadarshi, N. S. Saksena, and A. K. Dass.

Others who have helped along the way include Neil Carlson, who was a huge help in solving data management and aggregation issues, Charles Franklin, who offered advice on the statistical model to use, and David Cline and Carrie Young, whose work on the regional database was invaluable. Paul Brass, whose own work on ethnic conflict is central to the field, read and commented on approximately half the manuscript. I am sure that we still do not agree, but I thank him for taking the time to offer his incisive and constructive comments. Devesh Kapur also deserves thanks for his

Acknowledgments

continuing willingness to pick up the phone when I want to try out a new idea, and then tell me how my argument could be made better.

I would like to thank my editor at Cambridge University Press, Lew Bateman, for his help and encouragement throughout the process of getting this book published, and also Margaret Levi, for agreeing to include the book in the comparative politics series. I would also like to thank Brian MacDonald, my production editor at Cambridge, and Joe Grant, who checked the accuracy of my references and gave much help besides.

Lastly, on a personal note, I would like to thank my parents, Maurice and Janette Wilkinson for their patience and encouragement over the years. My wife Elizabeth has provided so much love, support, and encouragement over the past decade and a half that I can truly say that I would have produced very little without her. To her, and to our sons Alex and Nicholas, I offer my profound thanks.

Parts of Chapter 4 were originally published as "India, Consociational Theory and Ethnic Violence," *Asian Survey* 40, no. 5 (October 2000), pp. 767–91.

1

The Electoral Incentives for Ethnic Violence

In the 1960s Richard Nixon, reflecting on race riots in America, tried to define the difference between riots and other types of violent conflict. "Riots," he said, "are spontaneous. Wars require advance planning."[1] My argument in this book, by contrast, is that ethnic riots, far from being relatively spontaneous eruptions of anger, are often planned by politicians for a clear electoral purpose. They are best thought of as a solution to the problem of how to change the salience of ethnic issues and identities among the electorate in order to build a winning political coalition. Unpleasant as this finding may be, political competition can lead to peace as well as violence, and I identify the broad electoral conditions under which politicians will prevent ethnic polarization and ethnic violence rather than incite it. I demonstrate, using systematic data on Hindu-Muslim riots in India, that electoral incentives at two levels – the local constituency level and the level of government that controls the police – interact to determine both where and when ethnic violence against minorities will occur, and, more important, whether the state will choose to intervene to stop it.

Pointing out that there is a relationship between political competition and ethnic violence is not in itself new. Ethnic violence has often been portrayed as the outcome of a rational, if deplorable, strategy used by political elites to win and hold power. Bates, for example, argued two decades ago that in Africa, "electoral competition arouses ethnic conflict."[2]

---

[1] Richard M. Nixon, "The War in Our Cities," address before the National Association of Manufacturers, New York City, December 8, 1967, quoted in James J. Kilpatrick, *Evening Star* (Washington, D.C.), December 26, 1967, p. A13.

[2] Robert H. Bates, "Modernization, Ethnic Competition and the Rationality of Politics in Contemporary Africa," in Donald Rothchild and Victor Olorunsola, eds., *State versus Ethnic Claims: African Policy Dilemmas* (Boulder: Westview Press, 1983), p. 161.

1

And many scholars have since blamed the upsurge of ethnic violence in Eastern Europe in the 1990s on the strategies of ex-Communist politicians like Milošević who used ethnic nationalism to distract attention from their own past sins and their countries' present economic and social problems.[3] The organization Human Rights Watch even concluded, on the basis of a worldwide survey of ethnic violence in the 1990s, that ethnic riots and pogroms are *usually* caused by political elites who "play on existing communal tensions to entrench [their] own power or advance a political agenda."[4]

There are, however, at least three reasons why I find most "instrumental" political explanations for violence to be unsatisfying. First, because scholars who study ethnic violence generally look at political elites who *have* incited ethnic violence, they offer us little insight into why some politicians seem to do exactly the opposite and use their political capital and control of the state to prevent ethnic conflict. Why, for example, did President Houphouet-Boigny of Côte d'Ivoire respond to attacks on traders from the Mauritanian minority in Abidjan in 1981 by sending police to protect Mauritanians and then going on national radio to praise Ivoirians who had guarded the traders' property while they were under police protection?[5] Why more recently in India was Chief Minister Narendra Modi of Gujarat so weak in responding to large-scale anti-Muslim violence in his state, whereas other chief ministers such as Chandrababu Naidu in Andhra Pradesh or Digvijay Singh in Madhya Pradesh were successful in preventing riots in their states?[6] Second, many political explanations for ethnic violence fail to account for

---

[3] Claus Offe, "Strong Causes, Weak Cures: Some Preliminary Notes on the Intransigence of Ethnic Politics," *East European Constitutional Review* 1, no. 1 (1992), pp. 21–23; Tom Gallagher, *Romania after Ceausescu: The Politics of Intolerance* (Edinburgh: Edinburgh University Press, 1995), pp. 3–5. For an examination of the role of elites in preventing compromise and exacerbating the security dilemma, see Stuart Kaufman, "The Irresistible Force and the Imperceptible Object: The Yugoslav Breakup and Western Policy," *Security Studies* 4, no. 2 (1994–95), p. 282.

[4] Human Rights Watch, *Slaughter among Neighbors: The Political Origins of Communal Violence* (New Haven: Yale University Press, 1995), pp. 2, 7, 65–66 (emphasis added).

[5] *FBIS* (West Africa), April 21–22, 1980, p. T4; *Tanzanian Daily News*, March 12, 1981; *West Africa*, September 30, 1985, p. 2064; *Le Monde*, September 6, 1985; *Economist Information Unit Country Report #1: Côte d'Ivoire 1992* (London: Economist Information Unit, 1992), p. 12.

[6] Steven I. Wilkinson, "Putting Gujarat in Perspective," *Economic and Political Weekly* (Mumbai), April 27, 2002, pp. 1579–83. For details of the Gujarat government response to the riots, see "'We Have No Orders to Save You': State Participation and Complicity in Communal Violence in Gujarat," *Human Rights Watch* 14, no. 3 (C) (2002).

2

the variation in patterns of violence within states. In part because elite theories of ethnic violence focus on the strategies and actions of national-level political leaders such as Franjo Tuđman and Slobodan Milošević in former Yugoslavia or Daniel Arap Moi in Kenya, they cannot explain why, within a state, violence breaks out in some towns and regions but not in many others. Why, for example, when the 1969 riots in Malaysia were allegedly about national-level political issues, did riots break out in Kuala Lumpur and elsewhere in Selangor state but not in the states of Penang, Johore, and Kedah?[7] Why in India did riots over the "national" issue of the Babri Masjid–Ram Janambhoomi site in 1989–92 take place in some towns and states but not in others? Third, the role of political incentives in fomenting violence is generally "proven" from the simple fact that ethnic violence has broken out and that some politician gained from the outbreak; seldom are political incentives independently shown to exist and to be responsible for the riots.

My aim in this book is to understand why Hindu-Muslim violence takes place in contemporary India, which necessarily involves addressing three general problems in the instrumentalist literature on ethnic violence.[8] First, I want to account for interstate and town-level variation in ethnic violence in India: why do apparently similar towns and states have such different levels of violence? Second, when dealing with the role of the political incentives for ethnic violence, I want to understand the conditions under which the politicians who control the police and army have an incentive both to foment and to prevent ethnic violence. Third, I want to demonstrate that the political incentives I identify as important actually work in the way I suggest, by tracing through individual cases where politicians fomented or restrained violence.

---

[7] William Crego Parker, "Cultures in Stress: The Malaysian Crisis of 1969 and Its Cultural Roots" (Ph.D. dissertation, MIT, 1979), 1:183.

[8] I treat Hindus and Muslims as "ethnic groups" in the sense that Weber defines them, as having a "subjective belief in their common descent because of similarities of physical type or of customs or both, or because of memories of colonization and migration." Max Weber, *Economy and Society: An Outline of Interpretive Sociology*, vol. 1, ed. Guenther Roth and Claus Wittich (Berkeley: University of California Press, 1978), p. 389. For others who integrate a discussion of Hindu-Muslim violence into their general theories of ethnic conflict, see Donald L. Horowitz, *Ethnic Groups in Conflict* (Berkeley: University of California Press, 1985), pp. 50–51; John Breuilly, *Nationalism and the State* (Chicago: University of Chicago Press, 1994), pp. 206–15; Ashish Nandy et al., *Creating a Nationality: The Ramjanmabhumi Movement and Fear of the Self* (Delhi: Oxford University Press, 1995), p. vi.

3

The Electoral Incentives for Ethnic Violence

My central argument is that town-level electoral incentives account for where Hindu-Muslim violence breaks out and that state-level electoral incentives account for where and when state governments use their police forces to prevent riots. We can show that these town- and state-level electoral incentives remain important even when we control for socioeconomic factors, local patterns of ethnic diversity, and towns' and states' previous levels of Hindu-Muslim conflict.

At the local level I begin with the constructivist insight that individuals have many ethnic and nonethnic identities with which they might identify politically.[9] The challenge for politicians is to try to ensure that the identity that favors their party is the one that is most salient in the minds of a majority of voters – or a plurality of voters in a single-member district system – in the run-up to an election. I suggest that parties that represent elites within ethnic groups will often – especially in the most competitive seats – use polarizing antiminority events in an effort to encourage members of their wider ethnic category to identify with their party and the "majority" identity rather than a party that is identified with economic redistribution or some ideological agenda. These antiminority events, such as provoking a dispute over an Orange Lodge procession route through a Catholic neighborhood in Ireland, or carrying out a controversial march around a disputed Hindu temple or Muslim mosque site in India, are designed to spark a minority countermobilization (preferably a violent countermobilization that can be portrayed as threatening to the majority) that will polarize the majority ethnic group behind the political party that has the strongest antiminority identity.[10] When mobilized ethnic groups confront each other, each convinced that the other is threatening, ethnic violence is the probable outcome.

Local electoral incentives are very important in predicting where violence will break out, though as I discuss in Chapter 2 they are not the only local-level factor that precipitates or constrains ethnic riots. Ultimately, however, there is a much more important question than that of

---

[9] For a survey of how "constructivist" research has affected the study of ethnic conflict, see the special issue of the American Political Science Association's comparative politics newsletter devoted to "Cumulative Findings in the Study of Ethnic Politics," *APSA – CP* Newsletter 12, no. 1 (2001), pp. 7–22.

[10] An important enabling condition here is the presence of some preexisting antiminority sentiment among members of the ethnic majority.

the local incentives for violence: the response of the level of government that controls the police or army. In virtually all the empirical cases I have examined, whether violence is bloody or ends quickly depends not on the local factors that caused violence to break out but primarily on the will and capacity of the government that controls the forces of law and order.

Abundant comparative evidence shows that large-scale ethnic rioting does not take place where a state's army or police force is ordered to stop it using all means necessary. The massacres of Chinese in Indonesia in the 1960s, for instance, could not have taken place without the Indonesian army's approval: "In most regions," reports Robert Cribb, "responsibility for the killings was shared between army units and civilian vigilante gangs. In some cases the army took direct part in the killings; often, however, they simply supplied weapons, rudimentary training and strong encouragement to the civilian gangs who carried out the bulk of the killings."[11] Antiminority riots in Jacksonian America were also facilitated by the reluctance of local militias and sheriffs to intervene to protect unpopular minorities.[12] And recent ethnic massacres in Bosnia, Rwanda, and Burundi were likewise possible only because the local police forces and armies refused to intervene against or even directly participated in the violence.[13] Finally, the worst partition massacres in India in 1946–47 took place in those provinces – Bengal, Punjab, and Bihar – in which the elected local governments, each controlled by the majority ethnic group, made it plain at various times that they would not intervene against "their" community to protect the ethnic minority from attack. In Bihar, for example, after anti-Muslim riots broke out in October 1946 the province's Hindu premier refused to allow British troops to fire on Hindu rioters, ignored Congress leaders' complicity in the riots, held no official inquiry, and made only a few token arrests of those who had participated in anti-Muslim pogroms that killed 7,000 to 8,000 people.[14]

---

[11] Robert Cribb, "Problems in the Historiography of the Killings in Indonesia," in Cribb, ed., *The Indonesian Killings, 1965–66: Studies from Java and Bali* (Melbourne: Centre for South East Asian Studies, Monash University, 1990), p. 3.

[12] Michael Feldberg, *The Turbulent Era: Riot and Disorder in Jacksonian America* (New York: Oxford University Press, 1980), pp. 28, 111.

[13] See, e.g., René Lemarchand, *Burundi: Ethnic Conflict and Genocide* (New York: Woodrow Wilson Center Press/Cambridge University Press, 1996), pp. 96–100.

[14] Vinita Damodaran, *Broken Promises: Popular Protest, Indian Nationalism and the Congress Party in Bihar, 1935–1946* (Delhi: Oxford University Press, 1992), pp. 354–56.

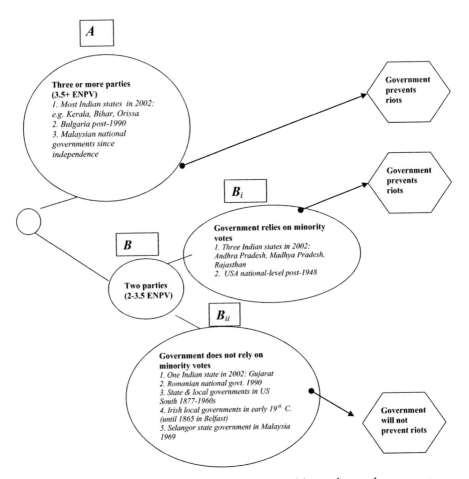

Figure 1.1 The relationship between party competition and a state's response to antiminority polarization and violence: Indian and non-Indian examples (ENVP = effective number of parties)

If the response of the state is the prime factor in determining whether ethnic violence breaks out, then what determines whether the state will protect minorities? My central argument is that democratic states protect minorities when it is in their governments' electoral interest to do so (see Figure 1.1). Specifically, politicians in government will increase the supply of protection to minorities when either of two conditions applies: when minorities are an important part of their party's current support base, or the support base of one of their coalition partners in a coalition government; or when the overall electoral system in a state is so competitive – in terms of the effective number of parties – that there is therefore a high probability that the governing party will have to negotiate or form coalitions with minority supported parties in the future, despite its own preferences.[15] The necessity to engage in what Horowitz calls "vote-pooling" in order to win elections and maintain coalitions is what forces politicians to moderate their demands and offer protection to minorities. "The prospect of vote pooling with profit," as he points out, "is the key to making parties moderate and producing coalition with compromise in severely divided societies."[16] In India, vote pooling moderates even the behavior of nationalist parties that have no minority support, as long as these parties are forced to form coalitions with parties that *do* rely on minority votes. On the other hand, politicians in government will restrict the supply of security to minorities if they have no minority support and the overall levels of party competition in a state are so low that the likelihood of having to seek the support of minority-supported parties in the future is very low.

In addition to these three competitive situations, Figure 1.1, lists the Indian states in each category (as of February 2002). Most Indian states today fall into category *A*, where the presence of high levels of party competition (3.5–8 effective parties, using the effective number of parties or ENPV measure) forces politicians to provide security to minorities because to do otherwise would be to destroy present-day coalitions as well as future coalitional possibilities.[17] A handful of Indian states falls into category *B*, with bipolar party competition (which amounts to 2–3.5 effective parties using

---

[15] The formula for the effective number of parties is $ENPV = 1/\Sigma v_i^2$, where v_i is the *vote share* of the *i*th party. This widely used measure weights parties with a higher vote share more heavily than those parties with a very low vote share, thus providing a better measure of the "real" level of party competition than if we were to simply count the total number of parties competing in a state.

[16] Donald L. Horowitz, *A Democratic South Africa: Constitutional Engineering in a Divided Society* (Berkeley: University of California Press, 1991), pp. 177–83 (quotation from p. 177).

[17] The effective number of parties (votes) or ENPV is a measure that places higher weight on parties with high vote shares than parties with very low vote shares, thus providing a much better measure of the "true" level of party competition than if we were simply to count the total number of parties competing in a state election. For example if we were simply to count the total number of parties competing in the Gujarat and Madhya Pradesh state elections of 1998 (17 parties and 41 parties, respectively), we would have a misleading impression of the true level of party competition in these states, because both states in 1998 were in fact two horse races between the BJP and the Congress, with the BJP and Congress obtaining 93.4% of the total votes between them in Gujarat and 80% in Madhya Pradesh. The effective number of votes measure (ENPV) of 2.97 parties for Gujarat and 3.09 parties

7

the ENPV measure). In 2002 there were four large Indian states with such bipolar patterns of party competition: Gujarat, Madhya Pradesh, Andhra Pradesh, and Rajasthan. Three of these states – Andhra Pradesh, Madhya Pradesh, and Rajasthan – fall into subcategory B_i, in which the party in power in the state relied heavily on a multiethnic supportbase that includes substantial or overwhelming Muslim support. Only in Gujarat in 2002 did we have the worst-case scenario (subcategory B_{ii}) where there were both lowlevels of party competition in the state (2.97 effective parties) and a government in power, the Bharatiya Janata Party (BJP), that did not have any minority support base and therefore had no incentive to protect Muslims. The reaction of state governments to violence in 2002 is predicted almost perfectly by their degrees of party competition and minority support, as I discuss in Chapter 5.

The basic electoral incentives model presented here can easily be extended to account for patterns of government riot-prevention in other multiethnic democracies as well (see Chapter 7).[18] In looking at patterns of state riot prevention in the U.S. South, for example, the key explanatory factor that explains greater federal government willingness to intervene to protect African Americans after World War II was the fact that black voters who had emigrated from the South between 1910 and 1950 became a vital constituency for the Democratic Party in several important swing states in the north, such as Michigan and Illinois. This shift (from category B_{ii} to category B_i in Figure 1.1) prompted northern Democratic leaders finally to intervene in the South to protect the civil rights of African Americans.[19]

---

for Madhya Pradesh represents this true level of competition much better than counting the total number of parties.

[18] Although the argument I develop in this book applies to democratic governments, in principle there is no reason why it could not also be extended to explain the conditions under which authoritarian governments will prevent antiminority violence. Authoritarian regimes need not be concerned about voters, but they still have to be concerned about constituencies that can offer financial, political, and military support. If an ethnic minority is well placed to offer such support to an authoritarian regime, then we would expect the regime to protect the minority even if it is very unpopular with the majority of the population. In Indonesia, for example, the Chinese minority did well under Suharto because it offered financial support, but the Chinese have done less well in a democracy.

[19] In India the day-to-day responsibility for law and order rests with the states, not with local or federal governments. Therefore explaining where and when antiminority violence breaks out and whether it is suppressed by the state in India is explicable by looking at electoral incentives at two levels. In cases where, as in the United States, local, county, state, and national authorities all have shared authority over local law enforcement, then

To give another example: in Ireland in the 19th century the high levels of Protestant-Catholic violence in Belfast in the early 1860s compared with that in other cities in Ireland can be explained by the fact that the police force in Belfast, unlike elsewhere in the country, was locally controlled by a Protestant-majority town council that did not rely on Catholic votes and therefore had no electoral incentive to intervene to protect Catholics from Protestants (situation B_{ii}). Only once the control of local policing was taken away from the Belfast council in 1865 and transferred to a national administration that was determined to prevent Protestant-Catholic violence do we see a significant increase in the state's degree of riot prevention.

Testing the Electoral Incentives Explanation

One general problem in testing theories of ethnic violence is that in most cases we lack systematic data on ethnic riots or their likely economic, social and political causes.[20] There is, for example, no equivalent for intranational ethnic violence of the massive "Correlates of War" project in international relations, which collects data on all international violence from 1816 to 1980.[21] In the past decade several scholars have tried to collect detailed data on ethnic violence in the former Soviet Union, where Western security interests, and hence foundation research funds, are substantial.[22] But political scientists have not yet matched the efforts of their colleagues in history in collecting basic information about each country's internal pattern

---

the model outlined here can simply be extended to incorporate electoral incentives and power asymmetries across different levels of governments.

[20] The United States is the obvious exception to this general statement. I have been able to identify only one study on ethnic violence in the developing world that collects systematic intranational data: Remi Anifowose, *Violence and Politics in Nigeria: The Tiv and Yoruba Experience* (New York: Nok Publishers, 1982).

[21] For a review of the research the Correlates of War project inspired, see John A. Vasquez, "The Steps to War: Towards a Scientific Explanation of Correlates of War Findings," *World Politics* 40, no. 1 (1988), pp. 109–45.

[22] Marc Beissinger at the University of Wisconsin has collected information on all reported "nationalist mobilization" and violence in the Former Soviet Union from 1987 to 1991. See Beissinger, "How Nationalisms Spread: Eastern Europe Adrift the Tides and Cycles of Nationalist Contention," *Social Research* 63, no. 1 (1996), pp. 97–146. Ian Bremmer and Ray Taras provide a "Chronology of Ethnic Unrest in the USSR, 1985–92," in their edited volume *Nations and Politics in the Soviet Successor States* (Cambridge: Cambridge University Press, 1993), pp. 539–49.

of ethnic riots before putting forward theories to explain why they occur in one place and not another.[23]

A few pioneering collaborative projects have collected aggregate statistics on the largest incidents of ethnic violence reported by the Western media.[24] But for my purposes, these surveys underreport small and nondeadly ethnic riots, which account for the majority of incidents in most countries. In India, for example, press data suggest that most Hindu-Muslim riots lead to no deaths and 80% of those riots in which deaths do occur are much smaller in size (1–9 deaths) than would typically prompt a report in the international news media. Moreover, the aggregate data provided by such studies as the Minorities at Risk project, though good for interstate comparisons, do not provide the detailed town-by-town information on violence that would allow us to test many of the leading microtheories of ethnic conflict.

In this book I test my electoral explanation argument for ethnic riots using state- and town-level data on Hindu-Muslim riots in India over the past five decades.[25] To address the lack of good data on town- and state-level ethnic violence in India, I utilize a new dataset on Hindu-Muslim riots in India, jointly collected by myself and Ashutosh Varshney, now at the University of Michigan. The 2,000 riots in the database cover the years 1950–95. When combined with a separate database I collected independently

---

[23] For historical research in which systematic data collection on riots plays a major role in theory testing, see Manfred Gailus, "Food Riots in Germany in the Late 1840s," *Past and Present* 145 (1994), pp. 157–93; James W. Tong, *Disorder under Heaven: Collective Violence in the Ming Dynasty* (Stanford: Stanford University Press, 1991); John Bohstedt, "Gender, Household and Community Politics: Women in English Riots, 1790–1810," *Past and Present* 120 (1988), pp. 88–122; Frank Neal, *Sectarian Violence: The Liverpool Experience, 1819–1914* (Manchester: Manchester University Press, 1988).

[24] Notably the Minorities at Risk Project at the University of Maryland, which covers c. 300 ethnic groups. See Ted Robert Gurr and Barbara Harff, *Ethnic Conflict in World Politics* (Boulder: Westview Press, 1994). For details, see the project's web site at <http://www.bsos.umd.edu/cidcm/mar/indmus.htm>.

[25] Donald L. Horowitz defines a "deadly ethnic riot," as "an intense, sudden, though not necessarily wholly unplanned, lethal attack by civilian members of one ethnic group on civilian members of another ethnic group, the victims chosen because of their group membership." Horowitz, *The Deadly Ethnic Riot* (Berkeley: University of California Press, 2001), p. 1. I define "Hindu-Muslim riots" in essentially the same way in this book, dropping only the "lethal" requirement in Horowitz's definition of "deadly riots." Hindu-Muslim riots often lead to deaths and injuries, but sometimes they do not. For alternative definitions, see Susan Olzak, *The Dynamics of Ethnic Competition and Conflict* (Stanford: Stanford University Press, 1992), pp. 233–34; Richard D. Lambert, "Hindu-Muslim Riots" (Ph.D. dissertation, University of Pennsylvania, 1951), p. 15.

for the years 1900–49, the dataset represents the most comprehensive existing source on Hindu-Muslim violence (for full details, together with a protocol explaining how events were coded, see Appendixes A and B). Collecting these data on Hindu-Muslim riots involved reading through every single issue of India's newspaper of record from 1950 to 1995, as well as (for my 1900–49 data) hundreds of reports in other newspapers, official government reports, and archives in India, England, and the United States. Because the resulting data are town-level as well as state-level, and extend back more than a century (unlike Government of India aggregate figures on communal violence, which have only been published since 1954), they allow me to test theories of Hindu-Muslim violence much more completely than has been done before, which should increase confidence in my conclusions.[26]

In addition to this effort to gather material on Hindu-Muslim riots, I also spent several years gathering town- and state-level data in India and from Indian government documents with which to operationalize and test the main theories of ethnic violence. For example, to test institutional decay theories, which argue that a decline in the state's bureaucratic and coercive capacity leads to ethnic violence, I gathered data on politically motivated transfer rates, the changing ethnic and caste balance of the police and administration, and statistics on corruption. To test economic theories that focus on town-level Hindu-Muslim economic competition, I combined census data on employment with case studies, surveys, and government directories on particular handicrafts to develop a dummy variable that indicates whether, according to the theory, any particular town is likely to suffer from communal violence.[27] And to test ecological theories that argue that the Hindu-Muslim population balance or presence of Hindu refugees causes riots, I used a mix of census data, poverty data, and World Bank data that I collected for all major Indian states.

---

[26] For examples of the way in which post-1954 government data are used by scholars, see Paul Brass, *The Politics of India since Independence* (Cambridge: Cambridge University Press, 1990), p. 199; Atul Kohli, *Democracy and Discontent: India's Growing Crisis of Governability* (Cambridge: Cambridge University Press, 1990), p. 7; Lloyd I. Rudolph and Suzanne Hoeber Rudolph, *In Pursuit of Lakshmi: The Political Economy of the Indian State* (Chicago: University of Chicago Press, 1987), pp. 226–27.

[27] The main all-India survey I use is S. Vijayagopalan, *Economic Status of Handicraft Artisans* (New Delhi: National Council for Applied Economic Research, 1993). The Uttar Pradesh government also publishes directories that allow us to establish religious breakdowns for wholesalers and self-employed artisans. See, e.g., *Uttar Pradesha Vyapar Protsahan Pradhikaran* (Udhyog Nirdeshalaya: Kanpur, 1994).

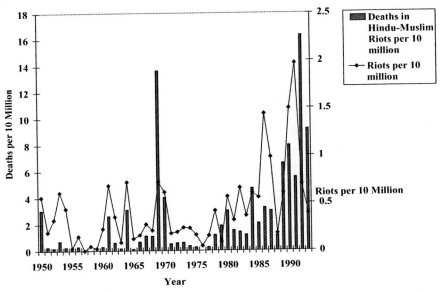

Figure 1.2 Hindu-Muslim riots since independence (data from Varshney and Wilkinson)

The Importance of Understanding Hindu-Muslim Violence

For those concerned about the welfare of the world's most populous democracy, understanding the causes of Hindu-Muslim riots is of more than just theoretical importance. Hindu-Muslim riots threaten the stability of the Indian state, its economic development, and the country's delicate international relations with its Muslim neighbors, especially its nuclear-armed rival Pakistan. Since the 1950s, as we can see in Figure 1.2, the number and gravity of Hindu-Muslim riots in India has grown to alarming proportions, reaching a dangerous peak in 1992–93, when nationwide riots broke out after the destruction by Hindu militants of the Babri mosque in the northern Indian town of Ayodhya. Since 1992 there has also been one further major outbreak of mass rioting, in the western state of Gujarat in 2002, in which an estimated 850 to 2,000 people were murdered.[28]

By some measures the numbers involved may not seem large. The approximately 10,000 deaths and 30,000 injuries that have occurred in reported Hindu-Muslim riots since 1950 are, after all, only a fraction of the

---

[28] "We Have No Orders to Save You," p. 4.

60,000 people who die on India's chaotic, congested roads each year, and the annual rate of deaths from Hindu-Muslim riots is much lower than that of the number of women murdered in so-called "dowry deaths" (3,000–4,000).[29] India's per-capita death rate from Hindu-Muslim riots is also low when compared with that in some of the world's other well-known ethnic conflicts. For example, deaths in Northern Ireland since 1969 run at 50 times the per-capita rate in India due to Hindu-Muslim violence.[30]

But the importance of the Hindu-Muslim divide lies in more than just the number of people who have died in riots since independence. The divide is also important because the Hindu-Muslim cleavage has split the Indian state apart once already and has the potential to do so again. An estimated 200,000 people were murdered and 13 million forced to migrate from their homes in 1946–48 when India was partitioned into Muslim and Hindu majority states.[31] Because Hindus and Muslims live side by side throughout the length and breadth of India, this cleavage poses a potentially much more serious threat to the country than separatist conflicts in the North and Northeast, which have so far claimed a greater number of lives.[32] This is especially so because Hindu-Muslim violence affects some states at some times so much more than others. As I show in Figures 1.3 and 1.4, which report data on Hindu-Muslim riots after the 1977 emergency, states such as Gujarat and Maharashtra have had, even allowing for population, considerably higher average monthly levels of riots and deaths over the past three decades.[33]

Hindu-Muslim riots also have damaging, though often ignored, effects on India's economic development, and these effects again are concentrated

---

[29] In 1989, for example, when the Ayodhya agitation was nearing its height, 521 people died in communal riots compared to 3,894 women who were murdered over dowry. Annexure no. 117, *Rajya Sabha Debates*, Appendix 155, August 7–September 7, 1990, pp. 558–60. This official rate of dowry deaths is of course widely recognized to be a gross underestimate.

[30] According to 1995 Royal Ulster Constabulary (RUC) figures, 3,462 people have died in the Northern Ireland conflict out a population of c. 1.5 million. Mervyn T. Love, *Peace Building through Reconciliation in Northern Ireland* (Avebury: Aldershot, 1995), p. 38.

[31] My estimate of deaths comes from Penderel Moon, *Divide and Quit* (London: Chatto and Windus, 1961), p. 269. Moon gives a clear explanation of how he arrived at this figure. Scholarly and journalistic estimates that claim a million or more deaths are common but unsubstantiated. Keller for instance quotes a figure of "up to 1 million" dead in communal rioting. Stephen L. Keller, *Uprooting and Social Change: The Role of Refugees in Development* (Delhi: Manohar Book Service, 1975), p. 17.

[32] Horowitz, *Ethnic Groups in Conflict*, p. 37.

[33] Interestingly, as we can see from Figures 1.3 and 1.4, riots seem to be much more evenly spread than casualties across states. We will try to explain in subsequent chapters why, even though riots break out across India, they only seem to lead to large numbers of deaths in some states.

13

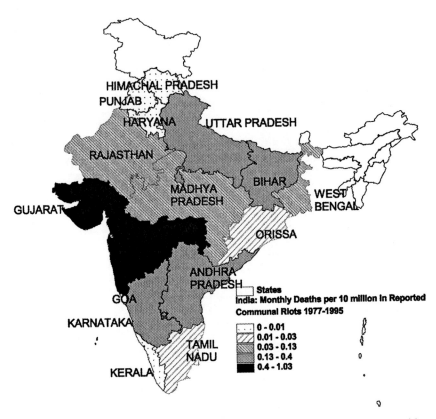

Figure 1.3 State variation in deaths in Hindu-Muslim riots, 1977–1995: Monthly average per 10 million inhabitants (based on data collected by Varshney and Wilkinson from *Times of India* reports)

in certain states.[34] The Hindu-Muslim riots of January 1993, for example, cost the city of Mumbai (Bombay) alone an estimated Rs. 9,000 crores ($3.6 billion) in lost production, sales, tax revenues, property losses, and exports and reportedly forced one industry, synthetic textiles, to at least temporarily abandon Mumbai altogether.[35] Industries in which Muslims account for a disproportionately large share of the work force, such as leather, jewelry,

[34] "Mosque Demolition: Consequences for Reform," *Economic Times* (Bombay), December 10, 1992.

[35] The Mumbai-based Noorani family, the owner of Zodiac clothing, temporarily fled the city and has since directed its new investments outside Maharashtra, mainly in Bangalore. Many Indian statistics are given in units of a *crore* (ten million) or a *lakh* (hundred thousand). The figure on total losses is from the business consultancy Tata Services, reported in Ashgar

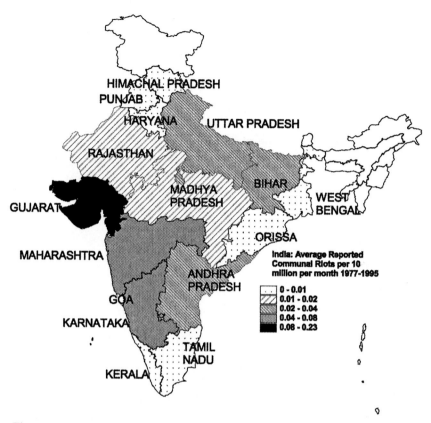

Figure 1.4 State variation in the number of Hindu-Muslim riots, 1977–1995: Monthly average per 10 million inhabitants (based on data collected by Varshney and Wilkinson from *Times of India* reports)

bakeries, and textiles, were particularly hard hit.[36] In Mumbai's ready-made garment industry, for instance, where Muslims from the northern states of Uttar Pradesh and Bihar are employed in hand and machine embroidery, the 1993 migration of Muslims back to their towns and villages cost manufacturers more than $3 million a day in lost production.[37] The Muslim exodus from Mumbai, by drying up remittances, further impoverished the economies in the migrants' home districts in Uttar Pradesh, Bihar, and Bengal.

Ali Engineer, "Bombay Riots: Second Phase," *Economic and Political Weekly*, March 20–27, 1993, pp. 505–8.

[36] For details, see Raju Kane and Teesta Setalvad's report in *Business India*, January 18–31, 1993, pp. 54–66.

[37] *Times of India*, January 25, 1993.

15

Hindu-Muslim riots also endanger India's international security and the security of Hindus living outside India. Every Hindu-Muslim riot increases tensions between Pakistan and India, South Asia's two nuclear powers.[38] Since the 1950s large anti-Muslim riots in India have often sparked tit-for-tat violence against Hindu minorities in Pakistan and Bangladesh. In December 1992 and January 1993, for example, anti-Muslim riots in India were swiftly followed by serious anti-Hindu riots in Karachi, Lahore, and Dhaka. The mass migration of South Asians to other countries and the spread of global news media have also increased the likelihood that riots in India will lead to violence against Hindus far from India's borders. The 1992 Hindu-Muslim riots had repercussions as far away as Dubai, Thailand, and Britain (where Muslim mobs in Bradford and other northern English cities attacked Hindu temples).[39]

Plan of the Book

I begin in Chapter 2 by examining the town-level causes of Hindu-Muslim riots and the broader question of intrastate variation in ethnic violence. Using systematic town-level data on riots and socioeconomic variables from India's most populous state, Uttar Pradesh, I show that the probability of whether a town will have a Hindu-Muslim riot is highly related to its level of electoral competition, even once we hold factors such as a town's demographic balance or its past record of Hindu-Muslim violence constant. Towns with a close electoral race are considerably more likely to have a Hindu-Muslim riot than towns with uncompetitive races. I also address the important question of whether historical and geographical variation in Hindu-Muslim violence is best explained using town- or state-level factors. Ashutosh Varshney, for instance, has made a good case for the primacy of town-level factors, which he argues can constrain the actions of state-level officials when it comes to riot control.[40] Although, of course, both play a role, I show that state-level patterns of law enforcement dominate

---

[38] Seymour M. Hersh, "On the Nuclear Edge," *New Yorker*, March 29, 1993, pp. 56–73; Devin T. Hagerty, "Nuclear Deterrence in South Asia: The 1990 Indo-Pakistani Crisis," *International Security* 20, no. 3 (1995–96), pp. 79–114.

[39] *Times of India*, December 8 and 9, 1992; *Hindustan Times*, December 11, 1992. "Damned by Faith," *Newsline* (Lahore), January 1993, pp. 114A–118. For information on the Bangladesh violence, see *Hindustan Times*, December 12, 1992.

[40] Ashutosh Varshney, *Ethnic Conflict and Civic Life: Hindus and Muslims in India* (New Haven: Yale University Press, 2002), p. 10. My own view, however, developed in more detail in Chapter 2, is that state-level incentives in India are clearly dominant over local factors.

local factors: state law enforcement can prevent violence even in so-called riot-prone towns and facilitate it even in towns with no previous history of riots.

If the law-and-order policies of India's state governments are more important than local-level factors in determining where Hindu-Muslim violence takes place, the key question is obviously, What explains these state-level policies? In Chapters 3 and 4 I examine and test two of the major explanations that are usually provided to explain why some states have lower levels of ethnic violence than others: state capacity and governance arguments, and consociational arguments.[41] I find that neither differences in state capacity nor in the degree of consociational powersharing can explain the variation we observe in states' levels of Hindu-Muslim violence or in their performance in preventing riots.

Chapter 5 tests the main argument of the book, by examining the importance of state-level electoral incentives in explaining Hindu-Muslim violence. I show that from 1961 to 1995, higher levels of party competition in the 15 major Indian states are statistically associated with lower levels of Hindu-Muslim violence. I also provide qualitative evidence to show that politicians do act in the way in which my model predicts and that the level of political competition for Muslim voters does have a direct effect on whether a riot breaks out. An additional question this chapter examines is why Muslims should increasingly be the pivotal voters in Indian state politics? Why has increased political competition not placed Hindu nationalist voters, rather than Muslim voters, in the pivotal position in state politics? I argue that Muslims are especially desirable voters for Hindu politicians to court because of the relatively large size of their community and the relatively few economic and employment demands they make compared with middle- and lower-caste blocs of Hindu voters.

If, as I argue in Chapter 5, the degree of party competition is crucial in explaining the level of Hindu-Muslim violence in various Indian states, then it raises the question, What explains states' different levels of party competition? I address this question in Chapter 6 through three case studies, tracing the history of Hindu-Muslim conflicts and party politics in the states of Tamil Nadu, Bihar, and Kerala. I describe how, in large part because

[41] For the former, see Atul Kohli, *Democracy and Discontent: India's Growing Crisis of Governability* (Cambridge: Cambridge University Press, 1990); for the latter, see Arend Lijphart, "The Puzzle of Indian Democracy: A Consociational Interpretation," *American Political Science Review* 90, no. 2 (1996), pp. 258–68.

17

of institutional incentives for "backward-caste" mobilization provided by the colonial state, intra-Hindu party political competition emerged much earlier (1920s–1930s) in the southern states of Tamil Nadu and Kerala than in northern India. I show that strong postindependence intra-Hindu competition for the Muslim vote led to governments in Kerala and Tamil Nadu that were serious about preventing and stopping Hindu-Muslim riots. The growing strength of similar lower- and middle-caste parties in northern India since the late 1980s, I predict, although it led to a short-term increase in violence, will eventually lead to a similar decline in Hindu-Muslim violence in the North.

In Chapter 7, I demonstrate that the electoral incentives we see at work in India also help account for the pattern of ethnic violence in other countries. I select one case from each of the three great waves of democratization identified by Samuel Huntington, during which multiethnic societies moved from uncompetitive party systems to competitive systems in a relatively short space of time: the "first wave," from 1828 to 1926, when the franchise was extended to 50% or more of adult males in many countries in Europe, the Americas, Australia, and New Zealand; the "second wave," after World War II, when former colonies and many formerly authoritarian countries in Latin America became democratic; and the "third wave," which began with the Portuguese Revolution of 1974 and continued with democratic liberalization in Eastern Europe, the former Soviet Union, and Africa. In each of these three cases I examine (19th-century Ireland, postindependence Malaysia, and postcommunist Romania), I argue that the pattern of ethnic violence in these countries as well as in other states such as the United States has been consistent with my general explanation: ethnic riots took place where political competition was fiercest, and the state's reaction to this violence was determined by its own support base and the overall degree of party competition in the state.

The broader question this book inevitably raises is whether democratic competition inflames or reduces ethnic violence? Does the fact that electoral incentives often lead to ethnic violence mean that I agree with John Stuart Mill and Thomas Jefferson, both of whom at various times argued that free institutions are next to impossible in multiethnic states? No. In Chapter 8 I argue that, although electoral competition can foment violence, there are many ways in which political competition as well as cleavage structures can also be altered so that politicians have incentives to be moderate toward minorities.

18

2

Explaining Town-Level Variation in Hindu-Muslim Violence

Most explanations for Hindu-Muslim violence focus on the importance of town-level socioeconomic factors similar to those identified in the broader comparative literature on ethnic riots.[1] The town-level explanations focus on such factors as the relative size of a town's minority and majority populations, a town's total population, the divisive effects caused by the presence of refugees from previous ethnic conflicts in a town, or the degree of Hindu-Muslim economic competition in an ethnically divided labor market.[2] In the past few years, several major studies of communal violence in India have also highlighted the importance of such variables as a town's level of interethnic "civic engagement" or the presence or absence of "institutionalized riot systems" to explain why some towns are violent while others are not.[3]

This book is focused, in contrast, squarely on the state level and on political incentives. While town-level factors need to be taken into account, I argue that it is even more important to understand why India's states sometimes use force to prevent riots and at other times allow or even seem to encourage violence. Force matters because studies of riots have found that rioters are generally unwilling, whatever the strength of the town-level

---

[1] Data collected by myself and Ashutosh Varshney found that 93% of deaths from 1950 to 1995 took place in towns. This figure probably exaggerates the urban-rural discrepancy somewhat because riots in villages in rural areas are less likely to be reported.

[2] For a review of these theories in the context of the U.S. literature on race riots, see Manus I. Midlarsky, "Analyzing Diffusion and Contagion Effects: The Urban Disorders of the 1960s," *American Political Science Review* 72, no. 3 (1978), p. 996, and Susan Olzak, *The Dynamics of Ethnic Competition and Conflict* (Stanford: Stanford University Press, 1992).

[3] Ashutosh Varshney, *Ethnic Conflict and Civil Strife: Hindus and Muslims in India* (New Haven: Yale University Press, 2002); Paul R. Brass, *Theft of an Idol: Text and Context in the Study of Collective Violence* (Princeton: Princeton University Press, 1997).

factors promoting violence, to confront armed and determined police or soldiers who are prepared to use deadly force to stop them.[4] And states matter, because it is India's state governments, rather than the country's national, municipal, or district governments, that control the local police and paramilitary forces and decide how much force to use to prevent or stop riots at the local level. Under the Indian constitution, central forces may only legally intervene to stop a riot if asked to do so by the local state officials or by the state government itself. This is the case even if a serious Hindu-Muslim riot breaks out only a few miles from an Indian army base, as it did for example at Ranchi-Hatia, in Bihar, in August 1967.

Despite my focus on the states and on what determines the state-level response to the threat of communal riots, it is nonetheless still important to test the many influential theories about the significance of such factors as the ethnic division of labor or the local ethnic balance in causing violence. Especially in those states where the state government is weak in ordering its officials to prevent violence or is openly biased, local economic, social, and political factors will, I acknowledge, often be important in determining the location and scale of ethnic riots – in explaining why, as one journalist put it, Bombay burned while Bhiwandi did not?[5] So in this chapter I address the causes of this town-level variation.

The Importance of Local Electoral Incentives

My main argument in this chapter is that local electoral incentives explain much of the variation in when and where polarizing events and communal riots will break out, even when we control for towns' previous levels of violence and their socioeconomic attributes. The idea that there is a connection between political competition and ethnic violence is not of course new, and in the previous chapter I discussed some of the broader comparative studies that focus on political incentives to foment ethnic conflict. In India, too, there has been no shortage of scholars and politicians who have highlighted the role that electoral competition plays in precipitating communal violence. G. Ram Reddy, for example, reports that large Hindu-Muslim riots broke out in the state capital of Andhra Pradesh during

---

[4] As Horowitz's recent study of several hundred riots throughout the world confirms, "Force seems generally to deter. As police hesitation reduces inhibition in a crowd, early, determined police action can avert what might have been a very serious riot." Donald L. Horowitz, *The Deadly Ethnic Riot* (Berkeley: University of California Press, 2001), pp. 363–64.

[5] Rahul Singh, "Lessons from Bhiwandi," *Indian Express*, July 18, 1993, p. 8.

the major municipal, state, and national elections held during the 1980s.[6] Christophe Jaffrelot's work on Madhya Pradesh has also examined the link between electoral competition and riots.[7] Individual politicians frequently blame their rivals for inciting violence; Prime Minister Indira Gandhi, for example, in a debate on large-scale riots in Gujarat in 1970, taunted the Jana Sangh leader (and later prime minister) Atal Bihari Vajpayee by asking him whether it was "a coincidence that when people who belong to the RSS [Rashtriya Swayamsewak Sangh] or the Jan Sangh go somewhere, soon afterwards there is a riot close to that place?"[8]

But none of these individual attempts to connect electoral polarization with ethnic violence amounts to a general testable theory that might have some predictive power about the specific conditions under which politicians have an incentive to foment violence in some constituencies and not others. In this chapter, therefore, I first build a general explanation for when and where specific electoral incentives will lead to violence and then test this explanation while controlling for the main alternative explanations identified in other town-level analyses of violence. My claim is not that elections and electoral competition explain all town-level variation in communal violence. Given the complexity of the town-level precipitants of violence, putting forward a unicausal explanation of when violence breaks out would be unrealistic. But I think that close electoral competition is, once we control for previous conflict and socioeconomic factors, the major precipitant of communal riots in contemporary India.

An Electoral Incentives Model of Ethnic Riot Occurrence

A central problem facing individual politicians is how they can ensure that voters will identify themselves with a politician's party and the group he or she claims to represent, at least on polling day, rather than with other ethnic or nonethnic groups, parties, and interests. The choice of *which* identity politicians choose to invoke in an election is complex and depends on the interplay of many different factors: the extent to which existing ethnic

---

[6] G. Ram Reddy, "The Politics of Accommodation: Caste, Class and Dominance in Andhra Pradesh," in Francine Frankel and M. S. A. Rao, eds., *Dominance and State Power in Modern India: Decline of a Social Order*, vol. 1 (Delhi: Oxford University Press, 1989), pp. 265–321.

[7] Christophe Jaffrelot, *The Hindu Nationalist Movement in India* (New York: Columbia University Press, 1996), pp. 513–14.

[8] *Lok Sabha Debates, 10th Session, 4th Series Vol. XLI, No. 58, May 14th 1970* (New Delhi: Lok Sabha Secretariat), p. 323.

identities are sustained by social, religious, and economic institutions; the number of votes needed to win an election under any particular electoral system (we would not expect politicians to emphasize identities that would, even if successful in attracting their target group, result in the support of too small a percentage of the electorate to win the election);[9] the degree of ethnic heterogeneity within a constituency; political alliances with other ethnic parties; the strength of the party's internal discipline; and the number and ethnic heterogeneity of other seats in which the party is competing.[10]

Once politicians have decided which ethnic or nonethnic identity to invoke, they face the challenge of how to make this identity the most politically salient identity among their target voters. One approach is obviously to highlight the range of programmatic (policy) or clientelistic benefits (i.e., direct transfers to specific voters) the party will deliver to the ethnic group once it wins the election: government jobs; subsidies to areas and economic sectors in which their target group is concentrated; and religious and cultural protections.[11] But, in situations where a party is dominated by a segment of an ethnic group that enjoys a disproportionate share of wealth, power, and government employment, promises to share the wealth with others (whether through policy shifts or clientelistic transfers) will be viewed with skepticism by the have-nots, and with horror by those haves who already support the party. In Uttar Pradesh, for example, promises of the upper-caste Bharatiya Janata Party (BJP) in 1995 to introduce affirmative action benefits for "backward" Hindu castes was met with skepticism

---

[9] For example, in India, upper-caste politicians who once formed an overwhelming majority of the electorate have been forced to change their group appeals as the electorate has expanded from c. 2% of the adult population in the 1920s to 14% after 1935 to 100% of the adult population after 1950. See Harold Gould's study of the town of Faizabad, which traces the changes in political appeals from the preindependence period, when only a few thousand upper castes could vote, to the postindependence mass electorate. Harold A. Gould, *Grass Roots Politics in India: A Century of Political Evolution in Faizabad District* (New Delhi: Oxford & IBH, 1994), p. 52.

[10] For example, while it might be beneficial for a politician to highlight a subethnic cleavage such as "Presbyterian" in a by-election for a Presbyterian-dominated seat in Northern Ireland, this gain has to be set against the fact that the overall number of safe Presbyterian seats is small, and that the politician's party may need to forge alliances with Methodists and Episcopalians in many other seats at the next election in order to defeat Catholic candidates. For a general discussion of the ways in which politicians make such calculations, see George Tsebelis, *Nested Games: Rational Choice in Comparative Politics* (Berkeley: University of California Press, 1990).

[11] For the distinction between programmatic and clientelist appeals, see Herbert Kitschelt, "Linkages between Citizens and Politicians in Democratic Polities," *Comparative Political Studies* 33, nos. 6–7 (2000), pp. 845–79.

from backwards, who wondered about its sincerity, and succeeded in infuriating the BJP's own upper-caste supporters, who forced the party to quietly withdraw its proposals.

In this situation, I argue that the most effective method for elite-dominated ethnic parties to mobilize those target voters who are at risk of voting for the main rival parties will be to use ethnic wedge issues to increase – albeit in the short term – the salience of ethnic issues that will favor their party. In India, both upper castes and Muslims live disproportionately in urban areas in most states. In Uttar Pradesh, for example, 17% of the total state population is Muslim but Muslims account for 31% (1991 census) of the state's urban population. Although no precise census figures are available for upper castes, it is generally agreed that upper castes are also concentrated in urban areas, a fact reflected in the last caste census in 1931. Because these two groups frequently vote cohesively, they often constitute the two main voting blocs in bipolar urban races, with the pivotal political position between upper-caste- and Muslim-supported parties in towns occupied by middle- and lower-caste voters. The challenge for upper-caste politicians and parties in urban areas, therefore, is how to win over these pivotal Hindu voters.

They meet this challenge by highlighting the threat posed by Muslims. Upper-caste-dominated parties can highlight anti-Muslim wedge issues – for example, Muslims' alleged slaughter of cows, the renaming of a town with a Muslim origin name with an "authentic Indian" (i.e., Hindu) name,[12] taking a Hindu procession route through a Muslim neighborhood, or disputing the status of a plot of land claimed or occupied by Muslims. These wedge issues allow these parties to potentially rally a large proportion of Hindus (82% of the Indian population) to their side, while entailing no economic cost for the party's existing upper-caste supporters. In Indian terms, the upper castes are fighting *Mandal* – the name of a commission that in 1980 recommended large-scale affirmative action programs for the backward castes – with *Mandir* (a Hindu temple).[13]

The particular form of antiminority mobilization used depends on both the identity politicians wish to make salient and the fact that the Indian state,

---

[12] The BJP proposed in 1990 and 2001 that Ahmedabad be renamed "Karnavati." *Hindu*, June 11, 2001. Similar proposals have been made to rename Allahabad "Prayag."

[13] The incentives for Muslim candidates to polarize the vote exist theoretically but not often in practice because Muslims are 40% or more of the population in only 11 of the 219 largest cities in the country, and constitute a majority in only 6. R. Ramachandran, *Urbanization and Urban Systems in India* (Delhi: Oxford University Press, 1992), p. 177.

like other states, institutionally privileges some forms of mobilization – and, in particular, "traditional" religious ceremonies and processions – over others.[14] A favorite strategy of Hindu party leaders who calculate that they will gain electorally from polarization around a Hindu identity is to organize unusually large religious processions that take new routes through minority neighborhoods, to hoist the national flag over a disputed site, or to sponsor processions to celebrate national anniversaries. These tactics make it very difficult for the local administration to ban the event, for who could possibly object to the performance of a religious obligation, the raising of the national flag, or the celebration of a national day?[15] But the organizers, once permission has been granted, can easily introduce symbols and speech into these events that is likely to provoke the other community.[16]

If members of the other ethnic group gather to watch the event and defend their neighborhood or community symbols, this countermobilization can then be portrayed as an illegitimate provocation by the minorities on the part of the organizers. Defensive countermobilization by minorities also greatly increases the probability of ethnic violence because, when crowds face each other, the power of individuals to influence their group's actions – whether that individual is a political organizer who wants to incite violence deliberately or a nervous youth intimidated by members of the other community – becomes magnified enormously. If one demonstrator throws a stone, it is interpreted as "the crowd" throwing stones: if one Muslim or Catholic or Jew fires a shot, it is interpreted as "the Muslims" or "the Catholics" or "the Jews" shooting. The instant this kind of violent

[14] The principle that government should be "neutral" toward religions and allow, to the maximum extent possible, each religion to carry out processions and ceremonies began to be introduced in the 1830s, and became a cornerstone of post 1857-government policy, despite the conflict and political mobilization around religious identities it has caused. For an examination of this policy shift and how it was related to 19th-century riots, see C. A. Bayly, *Ruler, Townsmen and Bazaars: North Indian Society in the Age of British Expansion, 1770–1870* (Cambridge: Cambridge University Press, 1988), pp. 335–38, and Katherine Prior, "Making History: The State's Intervention in Urban Religious Disputes in the North-Western Provinces in the Early Nineteenth Century," *Modern Asian Studies* 27, no. 1 (1993), pp. 200–2.

[15] Administrations in such circumstances must always tread a fine line between preventive action sufficient to prevent riots and preventive action that is so heavy-handed (mass arrests, beating of religious figures, etc.) that it begins to alienate large swaths of the majority community.

[16] For a fine analysis of processions as a form of mobilization, see Christophe Jaffrelot, "The Politics of Processions and Hindu-Muslim Riots," in Amrita Basu and Atul Kohli, eds., *Community Conflicts and the State in India* (Delhi: Oxford University Press, 1998), pp. 58–92.

action occurs, a crowd member's identity becomes completely and involuntarily subsumed to that of his ethnic group. As James Rule points out, "The behavior of many, perhaps most individuals in the crowds may not have changed, yet the social construction of their actions may move them from the non-rioter category into that of rioters."[17]

The minority countermobilization or ethnic violence that results from this kind of electoral mobilization will not, of course, be sufficient to scare all the Hindu swing voters into rallying behind the most pro-Hindu party. Many voters, after all, will have firm political allegiances to particular ideological or ethnic political parties. And some voters will have a greater degree of bias toward minorities than others. But to win an election it is not necessary to appeal to every voter but only to pivotal swing voters, especially those undecided voters who are uninformed, unlikely to vote (unless scared into doing so), and most likely for whatever reason to fear the consequences of not taking a strong defensive posture toward members of the other ethnic group.[18] In the southern United States, for example, James Glaser interviewed campaign managers who had a clear sense that ethnic wedge issues would appeal more to some groups among the white electorate than others. For example, one campaign manager told him that rural white voters were normally Democratic but that racial issues could swing them to the Republicans.[19]

Organizing processions and other types of mobilization designed to highlight ethnic cleavages requires scarce resources: time, effort, and money. Therefore we should not expect divisive ethnic mobilization to take place at all times or in every seat in which ethnic parties compete. First, it seems likely that polarizing events will occur disproportionately before elections as politicians try use inflammatory issues to solidify their own ethnic community's support or to intimidate their ethnic opponents.[20] In Kenya, for example, Daniel Arap Moi was accused of fomenting intertribal

---

[17] See James B. Rule, *Theories of Civil Violence* (Berkeley: University of California Press, 1988), p. 47.

[18] William H. Riker, *The Strategy of Rhetoric: Campaigning for the American Constitution* (New Haven: Yale University Press, 1996), pp. 50–51.

[19] James M. Glaser, *Race, Campaign Politics and the Realignment in the South* (New Haven: Yale University Press, 1996), p. 69.

[20] If, on the other hand, democratic politics are not well institutionalized within a country (in the first election after a period of authoritarian rule, for instance) we would expect to see a different pattern of ethnic violence, as losers challenge the legitimacy of the electoral process itself. This happened in the Congo, for example, where more than 2,000 died in ethnic violence following the 1993 election. *Agence France Presse*, January 13, 1995.

violence in order to bolster his KANU party's chances of winning in the 1992 election. In Côte d'Ivoire, during the months before the October 1994 presidential election, the government was also accused of fomenting ethnic violence in which 35 people died.[21] Second, it seems likely that an ethnic party that expects, based on previous electoral results, to win handily or to lose massively a local electoral contest has less of an incentive to foment violence in that seat than in seats where the race is close. Instead, the rational strategy is for a party to direct its mobilizing efforts to those close seats in which its efforts will pay the greatest electoral dividends. A great deal of research in American and European politics, for example, has confirmed the relationship between the closeness of an election and politicians' efforts at mobilization. Munger and Cox, for example, found that "Closeness clearly stimulates House expenditures and House expenditures do boost turnout." The incentives for ethnic polarization and ethnic riots follow the same general logic: the incentives are greatest in those seats where electoral races are closest.[22]

Alternative Explanations for Town-Level Riot Variation

The Economic Division of Labor Hypothesis

Ethnic violence is often portrayed as the outcome of economic competition and material interest. Conflict among Tajiks, Uzbeks, and Kyrgyz in Kyrgyzstan, according to some, is a simple struggle for jobs and land, with each group using ethnic claims to assert its right to these resources.[23]

---

[21] *New African*, May 1992, pp. 17–18.

[22] Gary W. Cox and Michael C. Munger, "Closeness, Expenditures, and Turnout in the 1982 U.S. House Elections," *American Political Science Review* 83, no. 1 (1989), pp. 217–32. See also Charles J. Pattie, Ronald J. Johnston, and Edward A. Fieldhouse, "Winning the Local Vote: The Effectiveness of Constituency Campaign Spending in Great Britain, 1983–1992," *American Political Science Review* 89, no. 4 (1995), pp. 969–83. For a comprehensive review of the literature, which includes an assessment of the effects of different electoral systems on levels of elite mobilization, see Gary W. Cox, "Electoral Rules and the Calculus of Mobilization," paper presented at the Shambaugh Comparative Legislative Research Conference, Iowa City, Iowa, April 16–19, 1998 (available at <http://gcox.ucsd.edu/iomob4.htm>). One caveat to this general proposition would be that in any state some sites may be so symbolically important that they may attract political mobilization campaigns even if there is no close electoral race within the town itself. Examples would include capital cities, historic battlefields, or centers of religious pilgrimage.

[23] Annette Bohr and Simon Crisp, "Kyrgyzstan and the Kyrgyz," in Graham Smith, ed., *The Nationalities Question in the Post-Soviet States*, 2nd ed. (New York: Longman, 1996), p. 396.

Race riots in the United States have often been explained in the same way. Spilerman, for example, in his article examining the 1960s riots, found that towns in which the blacks were moving into "white" occupations in large numbers had more riots than those where their employment opportunities were more restricted. He argued that riots took place because whites resented and felt threatened by minority progress.[24] The Hutu massacres of Tutsis in Rwanda in 1994 and before have also been seen as motivated by an acute shortage of arable land in one of Africa's most overpopulated states.[25]

Two main economic explanations are applied specifically to explain Hindu-Muslim riots. The first, most recently identified with the 1992–93 riots in Bombay and Calcutta and the 2002 riots in Ahmedabad, sees communal violence as a strategy used by slumlords and real-estate developers to displace people from valuable land, which can then be developed or sold for a high price.[26] This theory is extremely difficult to test systematically, as we would need good town-level data on such variables as land prices and ownership over time, data that I have found impossible to obtain. The second theory, and by far the leading economic explanation for Hindu-Muslim riots, sees riots instead as the result of growing competition in ethnically divided labor markets.[27] P. R. Rajgopal, for example, argues that the 1984 riot in the western Indian textile town of Bhiwandi, in which 109 people

---

[24] S. Spilerman, "Structural Characteristics of Cities and the Severity of Racial Disorders," *American Sociological Review* 41 (1976), pp. 771–93.

[25] Anver Versi, "Rwanda's Killing Fields," *New African*, June 1994, pp. 11–13; Russell Hardin, *One for All: The Logic of Group Conflict* (Princeton: Princeton University Press, 1995), pp. 171–72.

[26] See "The Burning of Bombay," *Sunday*, January 24–30, 1993, pp. 28–37; Dilip Thakore, "Paying for Socialism," *Sunday*, January 24–30, 1993, pp. 54–55; and Suranjan Das, "The 1992 Calcutta Riot in Historical Continuum: A Relapse into 'Communal Fury'?" *Modern Asian Studies* 34, no. 2 (2000), p. 301.

[27] Ashgar Ali Engineer, "The Causes of Communal Riots in the Post-Partition Period in India," in Engineer, ed., *Communal Riots in Post-Independence India* (Hyderabad: Sangam Books, 1984), pp. 33–41; Amiya Kumar Bagchi, "Predatory Commercialization and Communalism in India," in S. Gopal, ed., *Anatomy of a Confrontation* (New Delhi: Penguin, 1990), pp. 193–218; Moin Shakir, *Islam in Indian Politics* (New Delhi: Ajanta Publications, 1983), p. 47; Zenab Banu, *Politics of Communalism* (Bombay: Popular Prakashan, 1989), pp. 82–83; Dildar Khan, "Meerut Riots: An Analysis," in Pramod Kumar, ed., *Towards Understanding Communalism* (Chandigarh: Center for Research in Rural and Industrial Development, 1992), p. 465. Although the thesis is most often linked to recent economic changes, it dates to at least 1886, to when the British viceroy Lord Dufferin described the Delhi riots of that year as a product principally of Hindus' jealousy of Muslims' efforts to improve their economic and social conditions. Ikram Malik, *Hindu-Muslim Riots in the British Punjab, 1849–1900: An Analysis* (Lahore: Jamal Mahmud Press, 1984), pp. 9–10.

were killed and 100 injured, was an organized attempt by Hindu cloth merchants to burn and loot the properties of their new Muslim competitors.[28] Dildar Khan similarly claims that in the town of Meerut, the Hindu Rastogi, Bania, and Marwari castes that control the wholesale cloth trade have started riots to destroy Muslim loom owners who want to move into this business.[29] Riots in the towns of Jabalpur, Kanpur, and Moradabad have also been depicted as organized attempts to drive out new Muslim competitors in, respectively, the *bidi* (cheap cigarette) and brasswares businesses.[30]

Two different types of evidence are used to "prove" arguments that competition in ethnically divided labor markets "causes" communal violence. First, scholars try to show that riots take place disproportionately in towns that are centers for small-scale craft production, where economic competition is said to be especially fierce.[31] The term "small-scale" refers to the system of production in small units and should not give the misleading impression that these industries are unimportant. In 1990 the production of eight major handicrafts including jewelry, weaving, and wood carving accounted for 70% of India's export earnings.[32] Many of the most important crafts – brasswares, silk weaving, the famous *chikan* embroidery of Lucknow, cotton rug weaving, brocade, and wood carving – have work forces that are overwhelmingly (70–95%) Muslim at the national level and often exclusively Muslim at the local level.[33] Although Varanasi *district* has a mixed work force, for example, virtually all the silk weavers within the *city* of Varanasi are Muslim, while Hindu weavers live in nearby villages.[34] In some large centers of handicraft production such as Moradabad, a north Indian

---

[28] P. R. Rajgopal, *Communal Violence in India* (New Delhi: Uppal Publishing House/Centre for Policy Research, 1987), p. 81. For descriptions of the riots, see *Times of India*, May 19–31, 1984.

[29] Khan, "Meerut Riots: An Analysis," p. 465.

[30] Shakir, *Islam in Indian Politics*, p. 47; Ashgar Ali Engineer, "Communal Violence in Kanpur," *Economic and Political Weekly*, February 26, 1994, pp. 473–74.

[31] Engineer, "The Causes of Communal Riots," p. 36.

[32] S. Vijayagopalan, *Economic Status of Handicraft Artisans* (New Delhi: National Council for Applied Economic Research, 1993), p. 9.

[33] A 1991 survey gives the following ethnic breakdown of minority workers in various crafts: art metalware (76% Muslim); embroidery (87.5%); cotton rugs (67%); *zari* (gold thread/brocade) and *zari* goods (89%); and wooden wares (72%). Ibid. For similar figures on Muslim Chikan workers, see *Eighth Annual Report of the Minorities Commission (1986)* (New Delhi: Controller of Publications, 1989), p. 189.

[34] Nita Kumar, *The Artisans of Banaras: Popular Culture and Identity, 1880–1986* (New Delhi: Orient Longman, 1995), p. 51.

28

city famous for its brasswares, more than half the city's Muslim population works in the handicraft sector.[35]

Muslim artisans are generally impoverished, work in crowded and unsafe conditions, and are often highly indebted to the Hindu merchants (known as *mahajans or kothidaars*) who supply them with raw materials such as silk, brass, or wood, which the artisans then sell back as finished goods.[36] In Moradabad, for example, 300 *mahajans*, almost all of whom are Hindus, control the brass industry. The workers in Moradabad are almost all Muslims, and according to one study in the early 1990s, 37% of Muslim households in the city owe half a year's income to the moneylenders and *mahajans*. Some Muslim artisans have built up these debts paying for one-time expenses such as equipment, medical treatment, or marriages. Others need loans to cover the period between completion of the brass work and payment from the *mahajan*, which is often a month or more if the goods are being exported.[37]

Studies of communal violence claim that the stability of this ethnic division of labor has come under increasing pressure in the past few decades as Muslim craftsmen have begun to start their own wholesaling businesses. In the town of Mau, for example, a major handloom center in eastern Uttar Pradesh, Muslim *grihasthas* (subcontractors) began in the late 1970s to compete with the Hindu middlemen who controlled the business. Muslims in Varanasi, of whom there were only a handful in the wholesale silk trade thirty years ago, are now reported to account for one merchant in five. If Varanasi and Mau are at all typical, there seem to be two main reasons why Muslims have been able to compete effectively against established Hindu merchants. First, because the new Muslim entrepreneurs are themselves skilled craftsmen, they do not have to employ extra staff (as do the Hindu merchants) to deal with their contract craftsmen and perform quality checks on the goods they buy. Second, research conducted by Nita Kumar in Varanasi suggests that, because it is easier for craftsmen to complain about arbitrary deductions by the wholesaler when they are

---

[35] Kishwar Shabbir Khan, *Brassware Industry of Moradabad and Its Muslim Artisans* (Aligarh: Interdisciplinary Centre of Development Studies, Aligarh Muslim University, 1991), pp. 49, 187.

[36] For an older survey of handicraft production that describes regional specializations and the middlemen-artisan relationships, see Radhakamal Mukerjee, "Organization of Cottage Industries and Handicrafts," in Radhakamal Mukerjee and H. L. Dey, *Economic Problems of Modern India*, vol. 2 (London: Macmillan, 1941), pp. 3–27.

[37] Khan, *Brassware Industry of Moradabad*, pp. 133, 212.

both of the same religion, some Muslim craftsmen prefer to work for their coreligionists.[38]

The second type of evidence used to support arguments about the importance of economic motivations in such violence is information about the distribution of casualties and property losses due to such violence. There is broad agreement that Muslims suffer disproportionately as a result of Hindu-Muslim riots.[39] Hard numbers are difficult to obtain, but of 526 Hindu-Muslim incidents that occurred from 1985 to 1987 in 10 major states, Muslims (12% of the population) accounted for 60% of the 443 deaths, 45% of the 2,667 injuries, and 73% of the property damage.[40] Given that Muslims are, as a community, much poorer than Hindus the relative effect of communal riots on Muslims' economic life is even greater than these percentages suggest. Although the Indian government's policy is not to publish income and wealth data cross-tabulated by religion, leaked statistics from India's National Sample Survey reveal that, while almost half (47%) of urban Hindus work in the organized sector of the economy, the figure for Muslims is only 29%. The majority of urban Muslims (53%, compared with 36% of Hindus) are in the "self-employed" category, which includes craftsmen and craftswomen, bicycle rickshaw drivers, other daily-wage workers such as porters, and small shopkeepers. These self-employed workers are the most vulnerable to both temporary work stoppages and the looting that accompanies riots.[41] The fact that Muslims suffer disproportionate losses in riots and that Muslim businessmen are more often the victims of looting has convinced many scholars and activists that riots are nothing more than a particularly brutal method of protecting Hindu merchants' market share.

Despite the disparate impact of riots on Hindus and Muslims, however, little hard evidence suggests that Hindu merchants and financial interests are fomenting anti-Muslim riots for economic gain; in addition, there are

---

[38] Conversation with Nita Kumar, Delhi, September 1995, and Kumar, *The Artisans of Banaras*, pp. 42–44.

[39] Even the Hindu nationalist leader Atal Bihari Vajpayee agreed that Muslims suffer most of the casualties in riots in a debate in 1970, although in his view this served the community right for starting the riots in the first place. "Vajpayee's Thesis on Riots Evoke Vehement Protest," *Times of India* (Bombay), May 15, 1970.

[40] *Ninth Annual Report of the Minorities' Commission, 1-4-1986 to 31-3-1987* (New Delhi: Controller of Publications, 1988); *Tenth Annual Report of the Minorities' Commission (for the period 1-4-1987 to 31-3-1986* (New Delhi: Controller of Publications, 1989).

[41] Abusaleh Shariff, "Socio-Economic and Demographic Differentials between Hindus and Muslims in India," *Economic and Political Weekly*, November 18, 1995, pp. 2947–53.

three counterarguments to challenge the economic competition hypothesis. First, if town-level economic explanations were correct, we would surely see at least a few cases in which, in the very small number of towns in which Muslims are economically dominant, Muslims start riots against their Hindu competitors.[42] But there is no evidence that Muslims ever start or profit from violence in such towns, for example, as Udaipur in Rajasthan.[43] Second, the economic thesis seems to confuse cause with effect. The fact that economically motivated violence against Muslims occurs *after a riot breaks out* does not necessarily prove that this is why the violence broke out in the first place.[44] Third, some journalists and scholars have argued that an ethnically divided labor market might actually promote economic interdependence and peace between Hindus and Muslims rather than economic competition. In Varanasi, for example, journalists reported that a Hindu-Muslim riot was imminent in the city as thousands of Muslims gathered to pray at the disputed Gyanvapi mosque in the center of the city, and 50,000 Hindus gathered at the nearby Kashi Vishvanath temple. A riot did not break out, however, because the local Hindu traders association, the Kashi Vyapar Mandal, reportedly defused the tension.

One columnist explained why Hindu traders, a group that was solidly behind the BJP and the movement to build a temple at Ayodhya, should have acted in this way:

The issue is not whether these erstwhile supporters of the BJP have suddenly turned secular, but that they have found it necessary to maintain peaceful co-existence. If Varanasi goes the Ayodhya way, the traders would be worst hit as lawlessness and killings would drive away thousands of tourists who flock to this temple city and also kill a flourishing business in carpets and saris that caters to both the home and export markets. Since both Hindus and Muslims are equally dependent on this commerce, it is plain that economic interests have prevailed over political or communal prejudices.[45]

[42] A. R. Saiyed gives examples of target choice that is inexplicable from the perspective of the economic-competition theory in "Changing Urban Ethos: Reflections on Hindu-Muslim Riots," in A. R. Saiyed, *Religion and Ethnicity among Muslims* (Jaipur: Rawat, 1995), pp. 326–27. The issue of target selection is explored in detail by Donald Horowitz in his *Ethnic Groups in Conflict* (Berkeley: University of California Press, 1985), pp. 108–13, 131–35.

[43] See Banu's study of Udaipur, *Politics of Communalism*, pp. 82–83.

[44] A point made by Saiyed, "Changing Urban Ethos: Some Reflections on Hindu-Muslim Riots," in K. S. Shukla, ed., *Collective Violence: Genesis and Response* (New Delhi: Indian Institute of Public Administration, 1985), pp. 97–119, at p. 102.

[45] Vivek Bharati, "Lessons of Varanasi: Pitting Economy against Hindutva," *Times of India*, January 6, 1993. The economic interdependence argument has also been used to explain why Moradabad remained peaceful in December 1992 and why Malegaon was peaceful

The Demographic Balance–Security Dilemma Hypothesis

Research on urban violence in the United States has extensively explored the relationship between the local ethnic balance and the likelihood of ethnic violence. Spilerman, for example, found that the number of race riots in the 1960s was positively related to the size of a city's black population. In a society where racial tension is high, he argued, a larger number of minorities creates more opportunities for contact and, therefore, for conflict between the majority and minority communities. The larger the total population of an oppressed group, the greater the probability that, once an incident occurs, there will be a critical mass of people with a low threshold for participating in violence.[46]

Within India "ethnic balance" explanations for town-level variations in Hindu-Muslim violence are ubiquitous.[47] One version of this theory – more often heard in conversation than in academic studies – postulates a simple positive and linear relationship between the number of Muslims in a town and the likelihood of violence. According to one police officer I interviewed, for example, the postpartition decline in violence in the town of Bareilly in western Uttar Pradesh was in part the result of the emigration of a large number of the town's Muslims to Pakistan in 1947: fewer Muslims, especially from particular castes alleged to be prone to violence, meant fewer riots.[48] Towns such as Moradabad are also sometimes described as "dangerous" simply because of their high proportion of Muslims.[49]

The particular variation of the "ethnic balance" argument that is most common, however, predicts not a linear but a curvilinear relationship between a town's Muslim population and its level of Hindu-Muslim violence.

prior to 1963. "Against All Odds," *India Today*, March 31, 1994, pp. 179–81; July 31, 1983, pp. 38–39.

[46] Seymour Spilerman, "The Causes of Racial Disturbances: Tests of an Explanation," *American Sociological Review* 36 (1971), pp. 427–42.

[47] See Richard D. Lambert, "Hindu-Muslim Riots" (Ph.D. dissertation, University of Pennsylvania, 1951), p. 25; Shakir, *Islam in Indian Politics*, p. 47. See also S. K. Ghosh, *Riots: Prevention and Control* (Calcutta: Eastern Law House, 1972), pp. 52–53; N. C. Saxena, "The Nature and Origin of Communal Riots," in Ashgar Ali Engineer, ed., *Communal Riots in Post-Independence India* (Hyderabad: Sangam Books, 1984), pp. 51–67.

[48] N. S. Saksena, IP, told me that "The ones who fight are the Lodhas, Ahirs, Jats and Thakurs, and among the Muslims not the Saiyyids, but the Pathans, Mirzas and also the Qureshis. There was a huge exodus of the Muslims from Bareilly in the 1940s. . . . many of those who left were from these 'fighting cock' groups. Those who are left are Ansaris and Julahas." interview, Bareilly, Uttar Pradesh, August 30, 1995.

[49] I met a Hindu sub inspector in 1995 who quite plainly told me that Moradabad was a dangerous town because it had lots of Muslims.

32

Riots, the argument goes, occur most often as the population of Hindus and Muslims approaches parity, but then their frequency declines as one community or the other establishes overwhelming numerical dominance.[50] In 1951 Richard Lambert, in one of the first serious social-scientific studies of Hindu-Muslim violence, noted that "Urban riots occurred generally in localities where the communities were more balanced in numbers."[51] More recently, Moin Shakir has argued that Hindu-Muslim riots occur where Muslims are "numerous enough to be reckoned with, yet not sufficient to be overwhelming," while P. R. Rajgopal claims that "As a general proposition, communal riots occur in places where neither of the communities has a preponderance in number."[52]

The Embittered Refugee Hypothesis

Those who flee ethnic persecution in one state are likely to harbor a grudge against members of the group that committed aggression against them if they encounter them in their new home.[53] The 50,000 Tutsis who fled Rwanda for Burundi from 1959 to 1965, for example, were reported to have embittered ethnic relations between Burundi's own Hutus and Tutsis. René Lemarchand, for example, argues that anti-Hutu violence in Ntega and Marangara provinces in 1988 – in which 15,000 people were killed – was in large part the result of the settlement in these provinces of many of these Tutsi refugees, whose "strong anti-Hutu sentiments are almost universally recognized by local inhabitants."[54] More recently analysts of the Bosnian civil war have argued that refugee flows were often the catalyst for violence directed against members of local minority populations.

The mass migration of 7.5 million Hindu and Sikh refugees from Pakistan to India in the wake of the partition of the country in 1947 is alleged to have had a similar negative effect on Hindu-Muslim relations in

[50] Roger Jeffery and Patricia M. Jeffery encountered similar arguments in their study of communal violence in Bijnor, "The Bijnor Riots, October 1990: Collapse of a Mythical Special Relationship?" *Economic and Political Weekly*, March 5, 1994, p. 551.

[51] Lambert, "Hindu-Muslim Riots," p. 25.

[52] Rajgopal, *Communal Violence in India*, p. 19; Shakir, *Islam in Indian Politics*, p. 47. See also Ghosh, *Riots*, pp. 52–53; Saxena, "The Nature and Origin of Communal Riots," pp. 51–67.

[53] For the political effects of large-scale refugee flows, see Cheryl Bernard, "Politics and the Refugee Experience," *Political Science Quarterly* 101, no. 4 (1986), pp. 617–36.

[54] René Lemarchand, *Burundi: Ethnic Conflict and Genocide* (New York: Woodrow Wilson Center Press/Cambridge University Press, 1996), pp. 60–61.

northern and western India.[55] From 1947 to 1950 there was a succession of urban riots in India, as Hindu and Sikh refugees took out their anger on local Muslims whom they held responsible for their hardships.[56] The most detailed postpartition surveys of the effects of refugees on communal relations were carried out in Uttar Pradesh, the destination for more than 490,000 refugees from Pakistan between 1947 and 1951 (5.07% of the state's 1951 population). Only 11% of these refugees settled in rural areas of Uttar Pradesh; most migrants flocked instead toward resort towns they had visited before partition, such as Mussoorie and Dehra Dun, or to major trading centers, such as Meerut (10% refugee by 1951), Saharanpur (21%), and Agra (10%). Social distance surveys done in some of these towns in the 1950s and 1960s found that recent refugees from Pakistan had much worse relations with the local Muslims than longtime Hindu residents. A study of Dehra Dun, for example, where the population was 25% refugee in 1951, found that "Not a single Muslim had any positive liking for the Hindu and Sikh refugees as a community. The latter shared their maximum hostility."[57]

In the 1980s scholars noticed that some of the largest communal riots had taken place in towns such as Saharanpur, Moradabad, and Aligarh in Uttar Pradesh and Godhra in Gujarat, where substantial numbers of Hindu refugees and their families had settled. Several scholars argued that this was not coincidental and proposed that "If in . . . an [urban] area, there is a sprinkling of the post-partition migrants from Pakistan then the area is positively combustible, in the communal sense."[58] There is, however, some difference of opinion over the precise mechanism through which Hindu refugees and their descendants are supposed to have an effect in making an area more combustible. For some, the focus on refugees reflects little more than the stereotype that people from Punjab and Sind are pushy and aggressive. Others point to the fact that refugees are very often traders with economic incentives for anti-Muslim violence; they therefore see the

[55] These refugee numbers are estimates provided by Stephen L. Keller, *Uprooting and Social Change: The Role of Refugees in Development* (Delhi: Manohar Book Service, 1975), p. 17.

[56] For examples of these "refugee riots," see reports on the Delhi riot of September 1947, in which perhaps 2,000 Muslims died, the Godhra riot of March 1948, and the Allahabad riot of January 1948. *Times*, September 25, 1947; *Pioneer* (Lucknow), January 20 and April 6, 1948.

[57] Raghuraj Gupta, *Hindu-Muslim Relations* (Lucknow: Ethnographic and Folk Culture Society, U.P., 1976), p. 171.

[58] Shakir, *Islam in Indian Politics*, p. 47; Ghosh, *Riots*, p. 52.

"refugee theory" as a variant of the general economic competition theory of violence.[59]

Probably the most common explanation is simply that refugee participation in violence is the result of higher levels of antipathy toward Muslims on the part of Hindu and Sikh refugees who hold Muslims responsible for their past hardship and emigration, and a higher level of refugee support for Hindu nationalist political parties, which are in turn often blamed for provoking communal riots.[60] The high degree of refugee support for the Hindu right is related to events immediately preceding and following partition. As their position became increasingly insecure in the years before 1947, many members of the Hindu minority in West Punjab, Sind, and the North West Frontier Province (areas that became part of Pakistan) joined the Rashtriya Swayamsewak Sangh (RSS), a militant Hindu nationalist organization that offered some form of collective protection. In Punjab, for example, the RSS's membership grew from 14,000 in late 1945 to 46,000 in December 1946, and to 59,200 by June 1947.[61] After partition, the RSS took a leading role in providing aid for refugees who had fled to India, thus increasing its support among refugees, who continue to support the RSS and BJP in large numbers. Several studies in the 1950s and 1960s confirmed the disproportionate support given by refugees to the Hindu right, and the prominent BJP leaders L. K. Advani (the current Indian home minister) and M. L. Khurana (former Delhi chief minister) are both refugees from Pakistan.[62]

The Violence-Begets-Violence Hypothesis

A widespread belief among those who study communal riots is that violence leads to more violence. Even if an initial riot has been deliberately fomented

---

[59] On this point, see Engineer on the 1980–81 riots between the Sindhis and Ghanchi Muslims of Godhra, and Banu on the 1965–66 riots in Udaipur. *On Developing Theory of Communal Riots* (Bombay: Institute of Islamic Studies, 1984), p. 25; Zenab Banu, "Reality of Communal Riot: Class Conflict between the Haves of Hindus and Muslims," *Indian Journal of Political Science* 41, no. 1 (1980), pp. 100–14.

[60] Jeffery and Jeffery, "The Bijnor Riots, October 1990," p. 553.

[61] Governor's Reports, Punjab (IOR) L/PJ/249, L/PJ/250.

[62] L. K. Advani was RSS secretary in Karachi before leaving for India in 1947. R. N. Saksena and Geeta Puri both found high levels of refugee support for the RSS and Jana Sangh in separate studies carried out in Dehra Dun, Rishikesh, and Delhi. Saksena, *Refugees: A Study in Changing Attitudes* (London: Asia Publishing House, 1961), p. 21; Geeta Puri, *The Jana Sangh* (Delhi: Sterling, 1978).

for political or material ends, violence is widely believed to create new fears, hatreds, and motives for revenge that cannot be easily erased. Stanley Tambiah, for example, tells us that "intermittent ethnic riots form a series, with antecedent riots influencing the unfolding of subsequent ones."[63] Chaim Kaufmann doubts whether it is in "anyone's power to resolve ethnic hatreds once there has been large-scale violence, especially murders of civilians."[64] In India, government officials and scholars alike continually use categories such as "riot-prone" and "communally sensitive" to denote towns where violence has occurred and is most likely to break out again.

One way in which violence in the past might influence the likelihood for violence in the present is by creating the urge for revenge on the part of the victims. The most common explanation for the way in which the past level of violence influences the present, however, focuses on the way in which communities assess their security and the threat posed by others. Barry Posen, for instance, argues that, in a situation where the armed forces that usually prevent violence are weak, and settlement patterns place groups in close proximity, ethnic groups assess the threat posed by others by looking to history: "[H]ow did other groups behave the last time they were unconstrained? Is there a record of offensive military activity by the other?" If violence has occurred in the past, he argues, then the likelihood of groups perceiving their security at risk and therefore initiating ethnic violence is high.[65] István Deák makes a similar case for Yugoslavia, arguing that "If Serbs and Croats kill each other today, it is mainly because they fear a repetition of the massive killing of the last World War."[66] In India, as in the former Yugoslavia, many argue that once severe communal riots have afflicted a town or state, the need for revenge and the fear of what will happen if one does not make a "defensive" attack upon members of the other community increase to the point where violence becomes self-perpetuating. Accidents of the sort that happen every day can, in this environment, be the spark for cataclysmic violence: the driver of a truck that killed a Muslim

---

63 Stanley Tambiah, *Leveling Crowds: Ethnonationalist Conflicts and Collective Violence in South Asia* (Berkeley: University of California Press, 1996), p. 214.

64 Chaim Kaufmann, "Possible and Impossible Solutions to Ethnic Civil Wars," *International Security* 20, no. 4 (1996), p. 173.

65 Barry Posen, "The Security Dilemma and Ethnic Conflict," *Survival* 35, no. 1 (1993), pp. 30–31, 38.

66 István Deák, "The One and the Many," review of Aleksa Djilas's *The Contested Country: Yugoslav Unity and Communist Revolution, 1919–1953* (Cambridge, Mass.: Harvard University Press, 1991), *New Republic*, October 7, 1991, pp. 29–36.

youth sparked off a large riot in Jaipur in 1969; and in the most famous incident of all, a pig that wandered into a Muslim festival in Moradabad in 1980 was believed by Muslims to have been deliberately released by the Hindus, sparking off riots in which 112 people died.[67]

Testing the Theories

One problem with assessing the value of these various town-level explanations for violence is that scholars of ethnic violence have tended to develop their theories and "prove" their hypotheses by looking at an unrepresentative sample of the places where violence *has* taken place, rather than at a large sample of all towns. The study of Hindu-Muslim violence is no exception. The tendency in India to develop explanations on the basis of those cases where Hindu-Muslim riots *have* occurred has led to scholars inferring, wrongly, that virtually every socioeconomic characteristic shared by riot-affected cities such as Moradabad, Meerut, Aligarh, and Ahmadabad must be a cause of violence. Cities that share the same socioeconomic characteristics as these violent cities but that have been generally peaceful, such as Bareilly, Allahabad, and Jaunpur, have been largely ignored.[68] A second problem is the absence of good data on riots and their likely causes, which has made it difficult to say conclusively which factors are associated with high levels of Hindu-Muslim violence and which are not.

To test the main town-level theories, I use a specially collected dataset that contains data on violence, socioeconomic, and political variables for all towns with more than 20,000 inhabitants in India's most populous state, Uttar Pradesh, over the course of three decades. I gathered data from newspapers, social surveys, the Indian census, and electoral returns for every major town and city in the state ($N = 167$) from 1951 to 1991 in the case of census data and from 1970 to 1995 in the case of electoral data. The resulting town-level dataset has 47,642 monthly observations from 1970 to 1995, although because of missing data the number of observations on many variables drops to around 40,000.

I selected the state of Uttar Pradesh for several reasons. First, the state is diverse and populous (2001 population 166 million), with substantial variation in levels of the town-level factors most often associated with Hindu-Muslim violence. Second, a large number of former bureaucrats, police

---

[67] *Times of India,* June 15, 1969; August 21, 1980.

[68] See Steven I. Wilkinson, "U.P.'s 'Riot-Prone' Towns," *Seminar* 432 (1995), pp. 27–34.

officers, politicians, and academics have written on this state, making a much wider range of information on local-level factors and individual riots available than we could hope to find in less well studied states such as Orissa or Rajasthan. Third, Uttar Pradesh has had a unified state administration with virtually the same boundaries since the early nineteenth century. This improves the availability and quality of historical data on violence and its purported causes compared with data available from the many other Indian states that have had frequent boundary changes or inconsistent data collection procedures.[69]

The source for my data on state level ethnic violence is a dataset on Hindu-Muslim riots from 1950 to 1995, collected by Varshney and Wilkinson (see Appendixes A and B). Details were collected on every riot reported during this period in the *Times of India* (Bombay), India's newspaper of record. Data include injuries, deaths, and duration of each event. A total of 138 reported riots took place in these towns in Uttar Pradesh over this 25-year period, in which 1,151 people were killed and 2,345 injured. In this study I use these data to construct the following two indicators of Hindu-Muslim violence: *RIOTS*, the monthly number of Hindu-Muslim riots in each state; and *KILLED*, the deaths per month in Hindu-Muslim riots. To test for the effect of previous violence on communal conflict, I also calculate the cumulative total of deaths in previous 60 or 120 months, to create the variable *RIOT5YR* or *RIOT10YR*.

These riot data are, of course, an imperfect way of measuring the total number of *polarizing events*.[70] Although an electoral incentives theory predicts that close electoral competition will provide incentives for politicians to organize events such as processions and disputes over sacred sites, which in turn will often, but not always, lead to Hindu-Muslim riots, the dataset lacks town-level information on the precipitating events that

---

[69] None of these three reasons makes Uttar Pradesh unrepresentative in terms of the factors believed to lead to communal violence. The present day state of Uttar Pradesh shares virtually the same boundaries as the colonial provinces of Agra and Oudh, annexed by the British in 1801 and 1856. These provinces were administered as two separate units until 1902 (although after 1877 the same lieutenant governor headed both governments), when they were joined together as the "United Provinces of Agra and Oudh." After independence in 1947, the small Princely States of Rampur, Banaras, and Garhwal were added to the United Provinces to form the new state of Uttar Pradesh, Hindi for "Northern State." In 2000, as this book was being written, the western hill districts of Uttar Pradesh, accounting for 5% of the state's population, were carved out to form the new state of Uttaranchal.

[70] See Appendix A for a detailed discussion of data quality issues.

do not lead to riots. Precisely because the majority of potentially precipitating events do not lead to violence, they are generally not reported in newspapers and other sources from which these data on violence were generated. It might be possible to create a complete dataset on precipitating events from police, press and secondary sources. For example, each local police station in India keeps a festival register with records of exactly which festivals and processions are allowed, any restrictions that apply, and whether the procession takes place.[71] In the case of religious processions, these notebooks specify the route to be taken, whether music is allowed, and matters such as the allowable height of religious symbols to be carried in the procession.[72] This register could be combined with other police and local press reports about all local processions, demonstrations, and protests to provide an accurate picture of the total number of "precipitating events" that take place in a town. The creation of such a dataset would, however, involve huge problems, both in terms of the sheer labor involved and in securing government approval to examine local police records.

In addition to the problem of lack of information on precipitating events, the dataset used here covers only Hindu-Muslim riots rather than all forms of ethnic and nonethnic collective violence, so we cannot address the fascinating question of how different types of violence vary together and

---

[71] Interview with an officer, Indian Administrative Service (IAS), December 15, 1994.

[72] The height of objects carried in a procession may appear trivial but there have been cases where *tazias* (symbolic tombs) carried in a Muslim procession sparked violence when some processionists demanded that branches be taken off a Hindu-owned tree or that some other obstacle be removed to allow the procession to pass without lowering the *tazia*. This happened, for instance, at Hazaribagh in Bihar in April 1935, when Muslim processionists claimed that Hindu banners along their route would contaminate the *tazias*. Police officers in such cases sometimes tried to avoid conflict by digging the road deeper so that the *tazia* would not have to be shortened and would still not hit the tree. A former senior police officer, M. K. Sinha, has a good description in his memoirs of a riot averted in this way at Siwan, Bihar, in the 1930s. M. K. Sinha, *In Father's Footsteps: A Policeman's Odyssey* (Patna: Vanity Books, 1981), p. 196. It hardly needs emphasizing that the height of the tazia or the placement of obstacles along the route is not always independent of their potential to cause conflict. In the 1920s several electricity companies in Uttar Pradesh's newly electrified towns had to spend large sums of money taking electricity wires down before *tazia* processions, and then putting them up again after the festivals had finished. This process imposed heavy and unsustainable costs on the fledgling private electricity companies, which appealed to the government for help. "Instructions Regulating the Height of Electric Wires So as Not to Interfere with the Passage of Tazias at the Time of Muharram," UPSA, GAD, file no. 361/1929.

whether, for example, the same factors that lead to a reduction in Hindu-Muslim violence might lead to an increase in caste violence.[73]

Testing the Economic Competition Hypothesis

Testing the religious division of labor or economic-conflict argument has proved especially difficult, because of a lack of data on occupational and income distributions by religion. The type of town-level yearly data on the ethnic division of labor used by Susan Olzak, for example, in her study of racial violence in the United States is simply not available for India, even at the state level.[74] This lack of data reflects a conscious decision taken by the Indian government in 1949 not to cross-tabulate economic and ethnic data because it was felt that such tables had heightened communal and caste sensitivities during the colonial period.[75] What I have done to address this lack of data in this study, at least partly, is to combine two different sources to help identify whether towns possess industries generally associated with increasing Hindu-Muslim economic competition. First, I used the town directories compiled by the census of India in 1971 and 1981 to establish which industries were important in any particular towns. Then I combine this information with case studies, monographs, and economic surveys that have been carried out to identify those industries in which there is an ethnically divided labor force and in which Hindu-Muslim economic competition is most intense. This allows me to create a new dichotomous measure of whether an industry associated with high levels of Hindu-Muslim economic competition is important in any particular town.[76] Towns in which these industries are present would, if an economic theory of ethnic violence were correct, have higher levels of ethnic violence than towns in which they are not.

---

[73] I am however gathering data on this issue, the preliminary results of which are reported in "Ethnic Mobilization and Ethnic Violence in Post-Independence India," paper presented at the panel on "Operationalizing Ethnicity and Ethnic Conflict," APSA annual convention, Atlanta, September 2–4, 1999.

[74] Olzak, *The Dynamics of Ethnic Competition and Conflict*.

[75] *Times of India*, December 5, 1949.

[76] The main all-India survey I use to identify industries prone to Hindu-Muslim economic competition is S. Vijayagopalan, *Economic Status of Handicraft Artisans* (New Delhi: National Council for Applied Economic Research, 1993). The UP government also publishes directories that allow us to establish religious breakdowns for wholesalers and self-employed artisans. See, e.g., *Uttara Pradesha Vyapar Protsahan Pradhikaran* (Kanpur: Udhyog Nirdeshalaya, 1994).

Explaining Town-Level Variation

Measures of Town-Level Electoral Competition

In the absence of any town-level opinion poll data on the intensity of political competition at the local level, I use the previous state and national election results as my primary indicator of the degree of electoral competition in individual towns. My assumption is that politicians calculate which seats are most competitive based on the previous election results and concentrate their polarizing efforts in these seats. Unfortunately systematic data on municipal elections are not readily available, even though press reports and case studies give us good reasons to think that the relationship between electoral competition and violence also exists in municipal politics.[77]

I have collected data for the following variables: *VSMARGIN*, the percentage margin of victory in a town's Vidhan Sabha (state assembly) constituency in the previous state election; *LS MARGIN*, the margin of victory in a town's Lok Sabha (parliamentary) constituency in the previous national election; and *VS CLOSE/LS CLOSE*, races where the previous election in the VS or LS was won with less than a 5% margin. To test whether riots happen more frequently during election campaigns I use the dummy variable *ELECALL6*, which measures whether there is a state or national election in the next six months.

To measure the main socioeconomic hypotheses, I rely primarily on census data. My main measure of a town's population is *CTYPOP*, interpolated from data reported in the decadal census. To test for a direct linear relationship between a town's Muslim percentage and its level of riots and deaths, I use the variable *MUSLIMPCT*, the Muslim percentage in each town interpolated on the basis of the decadal census of India. To test for a curvilinear relationship between a town's Muslim population percentage and its level of riots and deaths, with riots becoming more frequent the closer the Hindu-Muslim percentages are to 50–50, I also ran the regression using *MUSLIMPCTCURVE*, the Muslim percentage defined as the square of (50% − x%), where x is the town's Muslim percentage. We would expect that as *MUSLIMPCTCURVE* goes down, the level of riots should go up.

To test for the thesis that refugee percentages affect a town's level of violence, I use the variable *REFUGEEPCT*, a measure of the proportion

---

[77] See, e.g., Ashgar Ali Engineer's reports on the July 1992 Ahmedabad riots in, "Communal Riots in Ahmedabad," *Economic and Political Weekly*, August 1–8, 1992, pp. 1641–43, and press reports on riots in Jalgaon, *Times of India*, January 12, 1972.

of refugees in any particular town. To calculate this I use the "displaced persons" figures for the urban portion of each district reported in each of the 56 separate district census handbooks for Uttar Pradesh for the 1951 census. A displaced person was defined as "any person who has entered India having left or being compelled to leave his home in Western Pakistan on or after the 1st March 1947, or his home in Eastern Pakistan on or after the 15th October 1946, on account of civil disturbances or on account of the setting up of the two Dominions of India and Pakistan."[78]

Statistical Model

To analyze these data, I ran several multivariate regressions using a negative binomial model. One advantage of the negative binomial model is that it uses more information about the underlying distribution of my event count data: a large number of towns with no riots and a few riot-affected towns, compared with a model that uses a normal distribution. Another advantage is that, unlike in the case of ordinary least squares (OLS) regression analyses, the negative binomial model does not generate implausible negative predictions of events such as riots. Although the Poisson model is often used for event count data, several of the key assumptions of the Poisson model do not hold when looking at Hindu-Muslim riot data: more than one riot can occur in each month; the probability of a riot occurring is not constant within each month; and the probability of a riot is likely not independent of other riots.[79]

In Table 2.1, I present the regression results. The electoral competition variables I highlight in this chapter clearly do matter, even while controlling for previous violence, variables that reflect alternative hypotheses, and socioeconomic factors specific to each town. I find that proximity to an election sharply increases the likelihood of a riot. In terms of substantive effects, if an election is six months or less away the predicted number of riots in any town per month more than doubles, increasing from .0011 to .0024 riots. The closeness of the previous Vidhan Sabha election also seems to be positively related to the likelihood of a riot taking place before

[78] *Census of India, 1951 District Census Handbook Uttar Pradesh* (Allahabad, 1954–55), p. xi.

[79] J. Scott Long, *Regression Models for Categorical and Limited Dependent Variables* (Thousand Oaks, Calif.: Sage, 1997), pp. 217–63.

Table 2.1. *Electoral Competition and Occurrence of Riots in 167 Uttar Pradesh Towns, 1970–1995*

	Hindu-Muslim Riots			
	(1)	(2)	(3)	(4)
Town population (100,000s)	0.151**	0.148**	0.236**	0.231**
	(0.022)	(0.024)	(0.022)	(0.022)
Industries associated with	0.535	0.504	0.533	0.553
Hindu-Muslim economic competition	(0.282)	(0.301)	(0.295)	(0.298)
Muslim percentage	−1.144	−0.598	−1.019	−0.920
	(1.127)	(1.141)	(1.134)	(1.146)
Muslim percentage (curvilinear)	−10.232*	−7.208	−9.171*	−9.388*
	(4.040)	(4.124)	(4.091)	(4.112)
Percentage of refugees from	−6.846	59.770	76.360	77.469
Pakistan	(36.287)	(74.817)	(71.457)	(73.938)
Riots in previous 5 years	0.409**	0.476**		
	(0.030)	(0.035)		
Upcoming national or state	0.777**	0.716**	0.812**	0.812**
elections (6 months)	(0.212)	(0.219)	(0.213)	(0.214)
Less than 5% margin in previous	0.259	−0.166	−0.417	−0.273
national election	(0.282)	(0.339)	(0.329)	(0.332)
Less than 5% margin in previous	0.489*	1.295**	1.088**	
state election	(0.232)	(0.320)	(0.303)	
Closeness of previous Lok Sabha		−0.699	−1.702	−1.545
constituency race		(1.039)	(1.052)	(1.066)
Closeness of previous Vidhan		4.322**	3.391**	2.546
Sabha constituency race		(1.117)	(1.114)	(1.347)
Riots in previous 10 years			0.323**	0.296**
			(0.028)	(0.027)
Less than 10% margin in previous				0.466
state election				(0.300)
Constant	−6.523**	−7.407**	−6.735**	−6.579**
	(0.607)	(0.704)	(0.679)	(0.719)
Observations	46,494	34,974	34,974	34,974
Number of towns	162	158	158	158

Notes: Standard errors in parentheses. * significant at 5%; ** significant at 1%.

the next election, with the variable *VS CLOSE* statistically significant across all models at the 95% confidence level. Having a close race in the previous state legislative election has a clear substantive effect: holding all other variables constant having a margin of 5% or less in the previous election leads to a predicted 0.003 riots per month, compared with 0.0009 riots in a town with wider election margins in the previous race.

Turning now to the socioeconomic factors most often regarded as precipitants of riots – the presence of industries often associated with Hindu-Muslim economic competition, the linear hypothesis about a town's Muslim percentage, and the percentage of refugees from Pakistan living in a town – we can see in Table 2.1 that these are not statistically significant in explaining the occurrence of riots. Many towns in India have a large number of refugees from Pakistan and industries with a sharp ethnic division of labor, and it appears as if scholars have wrongly inferred that these factors cause riots purely because they are so prevalent. On the other hand two socioeconomic factors do increase the likelihood of riots: as a town's Hindu-Muslim balance approaches 50–50, its level of violence goes up; and as a town's population goes up, so does the likelihood of having a Hindu-Muslim riot. The finding about the significance of population is not unexpected, because virtually every comparative study of ethnic and nonethnic violence (such as U.S. race riots) finds that the level of violence increases with a town's population. The finding that ethnic parity is related to violence also seems to fit well with the general political competition model outlined here: if we assume relatively cohesive Muslim and Hindu voting patterns, the incentives to polarize will increase as the relative sizes of the community approach parity and it becomes more important to win over the small group of swing voters.

The level of previous violence in a town is clearly associated with a higher incidence of riots, with the 5-year cumulative total of riots being highly significant in every model in explaining both the occurrence of riots and the rate of casualties. The measure of the 10-year cumulative total of riots, which I have run on several models, is also significant, although its coefficient is approximately half that of the 5-year lag, suggesting that the effects of violence do diminish through time. Going from a town with no riots in the previous 10 years to a town with a history of 15 riots while holding all other factors constant at their mean would result in a large predicted increase in riots per month, from 0.0012 to 0.1613.

Moving from the occurrence of riots to the level of deaths in Hindu-Muslim violence (Table 2.2), we see that electoral competition variables and several of the socioeconomic variables are also, not surprisingly, associated with higher levels of deaths due to communal violence. In terms of substantive effects, the predicted number of deaths per month in a

Table 2.2. *Electoral Competition and Deaths in Hindu-Muslim Violence in 167 Uttar Pradesh Towns, 1970–1995*

	Deaths in Hindu-Muslim Riots			
	(1)	(2)	(3)	(4)
Town population (100,000s)	0.197**	0.191**	0.336**	0.329**
	(0.011)	(0.011)	(0.010)	(0.010)
Industries associated with	0.061	−0.202	−0.156	−0.056
Hindu-Muslim economic	(0.111)	(0.121)	(0.116)	(0.115)
competition				
Muslim percentage	−1.726**	−1.299*	−2.268**	−2.316**
	(0.509)	(0.531)	(0.537)	(0.547)
Muslim percentage (curvilinear)	−22.458**	−18.361**	−22.467**	−23.509**
	(2.077)	(2.131)	(2.171)	(2.200)
Percentage of refugees from	48.773**	105.480**	125.473**	123.517**
Pakistan	(11.571)	(32.002)	(30.183)	(30.825)
Riots in previous 5 years	0.634**	0.725**		
	(0.014)	(0.017)		
Upcoming national or state	1.233**	1.335**	1.288**	1.249**
elections (6 months)	(0.085)	(0.090)	(0.084)	(0.083)
Less than 5% margin in previous	1.198**	0.604**	0.229	0.553**
national election	(0.093)	(0.127)	(0.119)	(0.116)
Less than 5% margin in previous	0.452**	1.629**	1.587**	
state election	(0.090)	(0.130)	(0.119)	
Closeness of previous Lok Sabha		−0.762	−2.403**	−2.144**
constituency race		(0.441)	(0.440)	(0.446)
Closeness of previous Vidhan		6.256**	5.630**	3.609**
Sabha constituency race		(0.409)	(0.390)	(0.477)
Riots in previous 10 years			0.440**	0.402**
			(0.013)	(0.012)
Less than 10% margin in previous				0.511**
state election				(0.117)
Constant	−4.369**	−5.529**	−4.437**	−3.947**
	(0.265)	(0.304)	(0.295)	(0.305)
Observations	46,494	34,974	34,974	34,974
Number of towns	162	158	158	158

Notes: Standard errors in parentheses. * significant at 5%; ** significant at 1%.

town goes up by around 75% if there was a close race in the previous election (0.03 to 0.014 per month). The percentage of refugees in a town and its Muslim percentage and Hindu-Muslim balance are positively associated with a higher level of deaths. Proximity to an election also increases the predicted number of deaths in riots by around 75%, and the closeness of previous state assembly races are also positively associated with deaths in Hindu-Muslim rioting.

The statistical finding that the presence of industries associated with Hindu-Muslim economic competition is not associated with the *occurrence* of ethnic violence supports a point made many times in case studies, qualitative research, and riot investigations: that economic motivations may come into play once violence has begun but that they do not seem to be important in explaining the initiation of violence. If we look at the sequence of violence and looting, not just during ethnic violence in India but around the world, it is striking how many reports describe how looting only occurs once it is obvious that the costs of seizing the property of the minority community are low and that there is little risk of the police intervening. In Bosnia, for example, a Muslim woman, Vahida Kartal, told a reporter in 1994 how "At the beginning, the Serbs said they would not force us out and simply ordered us to hand over our weapons," but that after a few months it became clear that the Bosnian Serb police would not intervene to protect Muslims. Once this became apparent to local Serbs, Kartal described how "In the middle of the day, an armed Serb would come and take the television, or a refrigerator, or whatever he chose that had some value."[80]

In India Justice Dayal investigated the Ranchi riots of 1967 and concluded that economic rivalries between Muslims and Hindus had not sparked the violence, "though this feeling could have been exploited once the disturbances started."[81] A similar picture emerges from other detailed riot inquiries. The 1931 Kanpur riot report found that Hindu and Muslim mobs on the first day of the riot were concerned purely with inflicting physical harm on members of the opposite community. It was only on the second day, after the weak police response to the first day's killings, that large-scale looting began.[82] Similarly in the Bombay riots that followed the destruction of the Ayodhya mosque, the bulk of the economically motivated attacks on Muslim businesses and slums and lumber yards that were prime targets for property development only took place in January 1993, *after* the Maharashtra state police had already shown, by its actions in the December

---

[80] "How Serbs Drove Out Their Muslim Neighbors," *New York Times*, August 30, 1994.

[81] Quoted in Rajgopal, *Communal Violence in India*, p. 99.

[82] East India (Cawnpore Riots), *Report of the Commission of Inquiry and Resolution of the Government of the United Provinces* (London: HMSO, 1931), pp. 18–31.

1992 violence, that it was unwilling to intervene to protect Muslim lives and property.[83]

Qualitative Evidence on the Relationship between Electoral Competition and Violence

Qualitative research on other towns and states in India supports the statistical finding that increases in electoral competition are associated with a rise in the likelihood of communal riots, even if we control for previous levels of Hindu-Muslim violence. Reports on the riots that broke out in the Maharashtra town of Nasik, for example, describe how politicians from the Shiv Sena Party tried to solidify Hindu support against the Muslim-supported Congress (I) in advance of the 1986 elections by taking processions through Muslim-dominated areas of the town, shouting political slogans as they passed through the Hamid Chowk. Muslims stoned the processions as they went by, sparking several days of violence between Hindus, Muslims, and the police in which 8 people were killed and 65 injured. A former Congress member of the Legislative Assembly (MLA) Shantaram Bapur explained at the time that the riots took place because the Sena "wants to create terror, divide the people, and show themselves as protectors of Hindus."[84]

Perhaps it is a sign of how many politicians feel themselves to be immune from the law that many are quite open about the relationship between communal violence and an improvement in their electoral prospects. In January 1986, for instance, riots broke out in Aurangabad (Maharashtra) following processions and protests organized by the Shiv Sena, which was trying to break the electoral hold of the Congress in the city. The riots helped the Sena defeat the Congress (I) in the subsequent elections, and the Shiv Sena chief in the city, Chandrakant Khaire, had no doubt about the connection. He claimed that the riots were critical in building support for the Sena in the city and that "ever since the first stir our party has received tremendous sympathy from the Hindus." In 1993 Neeraj Chaturvedi, an MLA from a constituency in the major industrial town of Kanpur, was similarly frank when he told a journalist that Hindu-Muslim riots sparked

---

[83] *Damning Verdict: Reprinting of the Justice B. N. Srikrishna Commission Appointed for Inquiry into the Riots at Mumbai during December 1992–January 1993 and the March 12, 1993 Bomb Blasts* (Mumbai: Sabrang, n.d.).

[84] "Maharashtra: Communal Cauldron," *India Today*, June 15, 1986, p. 65; *Times of India*, May 11, 12, 13, 17, 20, 1986.

by a procession of his BJP supporters would polarize Hindu voters in his favor.[85]

One fruitful way to trace the connection between electoral competition and subsequent efforts by politicians to polarize a community is to examine what happens when an institutional reform changes uncompetitive seats into competitive seats in which Hindus are a majority of the electorate. Do Hindu politicians respond quickly as an electoral theory would predict by trying to polarize the electorate along Hindu-Muslim lines? The evidence from the few cases where such transformations have been studied in detail suggests that they do. In the state of Andhra Pradesh, Ratna Naidu has described how electoral boundary changes in the city of Hyderabad in 1976 led to a new, highly competitive political situation, which in turn led directly to an increase in communal mobilization efforts that sparked off Hindu-Muslim riots during election campaigns in 1983, 1984, and 1985.[86] Prior to 1976 the state assembly constituencies that included Hyderabad's old city had a solid majority of Muslim voters, and the Muslim Majlis Party represented the seats. Hyderabad was free of riots. But the 1976 boundary changes created two new constituencies, Karwan and Chandrayangutta, in which Hindus and Muslims were for the first time almost equal in numbers.

Hindu and Muslim political parties responded to this newly competitive political environment by organizing religious events that would provoke the other community and unify their own. In the late 1970s, Naidu describes how Hindu politicians began to combine the small local processions devoted to the god Ganesh into several new, large processions that converged at Charminar in the heart of the old city. And after 1981 the Hindu Bonalu festival procession route was changed so that it followed the new Ganesh route. The previous Ganesh and Bonalu processions had traveled through Hindu areas, but these new processions deliberately went through Muslim areas on the way to Charminar, where they were then addressed by Hindu politicians. These processions were not only larger but also much noisier than in the past, and processionists were supplied with drums and loudspeakers calculated to offend the local Muslims, especially those in the

---

[85] Chandrakant Khaire, quoted in *India Today*, June 15, 1988, p. 50. R. K. Srivastava, "Sectional Politics in an Urban Constituency: Generalganj (Kanpur)," *Economic and Political Weekly*, January 13–20, 1996, pp. 111–20.

[86] See Ratna Naidu, *Old Cities, New Predicaments: A Study of Hyderabad* (New Delhi: Sage, 1990), pp. 117–43. The description of Hyderabad politics I provide here draws from Naidu's excellent study.

48

mosques that abutted the new route. The very first Bonalu procession that used the new route sparked off a major Hindu-Muslim riot in 1981, as it passed through the Muslim Golconda neighborhood; 30 died and 90 were injured.[87]

Responding in kind to this Hindu mobilization, the main Muslim political party began its own new *pankha* religious festival after Hindu politicians reorganized the Ganesh festival in 1978. The *pankha* festival takes place three days before the Ganesh festival and travels through several Hindu bazaar areas during a winding route to and from a Muslim shrine in the old city. This procession, like the Ganesh festival, is then addressed by political rather than religious leaders once it reaches its terminus. In 1983 the *pankha* procession sparked off a serious riot when some processionists allegedly desecrated a Ganesh idol in the Moazamjahi market.[88]

Electoral Effects of Town-Level Mobilization

Polarizing the electorate through communal processions and other events likely to divide people and increase the salience of religious identities is a highly effective electoral strategy. In Uttar Pradesh I have examined several interelection periods to learn more about the constituencies where riots take place. Most of the constituencies that experienced riots were ones in which the upper-caste BJP was competing with a Muslim-supported backward-caste party for political power. Between the 1989 state elections and 1991 state elections, for instance, a total of 33 riots in which 295 people died took place in Uttar Pradesh. Of this total, 19 riots and 188 deaths from 1989 to 1991 took place in the small proportion of urban constituencies (18% of all constituencies) in which the BJP had been one of the top two finishers in the 1989 elections: these constituencies accounted for 57% of the total number of riots and 67% of the total number of deaths.

Press accounts of these electorally motivated riots describe how in every case, the precipitating event for violence was an organized Hindu nationalist attempt to disrupt an anti-Muslim procession, to hold an anti-Muslim public meeting, or to raise the fears that Muslims were just about to turn upon Hindus. In Agra for example a major riot took place in December 1990

---

[87] Ibid., pp. 120–33.

[88] These 1983 riots led to 45 deaths and 150 injuries. The police detained Mr. A. Narendra, a BJP state assembly member under the under National Security Act as well as three members of the main Muslim party. The police also closed down the Urdu daily, *Munsif*, for 15 days. *Times of India*, September 10–28, 1983.

because Muslims objected to a Hindu nationalist attempt to take a procession carrying the ashes of "Hindu martyrs" through Muslim neighborhoods of Tajganj and Loha Mandi.[89] In Saharanpur in March, violence broke out when members of a Hindu procession deliberately shouted provocative slogans in front of a mosque.[90] In Ganjdundwara the riot followed a speech by the firebrand BJP member of Parliament Ms. Uma Bharati.[91] In Aligarh in December violence was triggered by published reports in the Hindi newspaper *Aaj* (Today), later found to be false, that Muslim doctors in the Jawaharlal Nehru Medical College Hospital had murdered dozens of Hindu patients.[92]

This polarization paid off for the BJP on polling day. Riot-affected towns saw a jump in their BJP vote far larger than that in towns not affected by violence. Towns affected by Hindu-Muslim riots saw their BJP vote go up by an average of 24%, from 19% to 43%, while the average town saw its BJP vote go up only 7%, from 29% to 36%. The vote was also more polarized in riot-affected towns than in towns in general, with the two major parties in riot-hit towns securing a combined average 69% share of the vote compared with 64% in the average town. In terms of electoral outcomes, the effect of this BJP boost was dramatic. The BJP defeated incumbents from the middle-caste, Muslim-supported Janata Dal in all but two of the riot-affected towns, and in eight towns its share of the vote rose to around 50%. Although no polling data are available for these towns, it seems likely based on what we know about the ethnic support base of each party that many Hindu voters, alarmed by the riots, switched their votes from the Janata Dal Party to the Hindu nationalist BJP in order to keep out the Muslim-supported parties.

The hypothesis that Hindu-Muslim violence improved the BJP's electoral performance in the 1990s (as it improved the Congress Party's performance in some states in earlier decades) is also supported by Christophe Jaffrelot's research on riots and state elections in Madhya Pradesh in the 1990s.[93] Muslims in Madhya Pradesh, although only 5% of the total population, are highly concentrated in towns and are electorally important (more

[89] *Times of India*, April 1, 1991.

[90] *Times of India*, December 15, 1990.

[91] *Times of India*, December 6, 1990.

[92] The official death toll in these Aligarh riots was 37 though the unofficial total was over 65. *Times of India*, December 11, 1990.

[93] Jaffrelot, *The Hindu Nationalist Movement in India*, pp. 513–14.

than 20% of the population) in 12 key urban constituencies. The state had always elected a handful of Muslim MLAs from these seats. The state's capital, Bhopal, is the former capital of a Muslim-ruled princely state and the Bhopal North constituency (40–45% Muslim), in the heart of the old city, had before 1993 always been held by a Muslim MLA.

In December 1992 riots broke out in urban areas throughout Madhya Pradesh. The riot in Bhopal was especially bad, with 107 deaths (mainly Muslims), 400 injured, and 2,500 arrests.[94] These riots, which Jaffrelot found were instigated by Hindu nationalist organizations, and against which the BJP state government took no firm action, had the same dramatic impact on the electoral results in the 1993 assembly elections that we saw in Uttar Pradesh.[95] Hindus in the 12 urban constituencies where Muslims were electorally significant voted solidly for the Hindu parties with the best chance of keeping the Muslim-supported parties and candidates out. The BJP won in 8 of the 12 seats. Jaffrelot found that Scheduled Caste Hindus, who live in close proximity to the Muslim neighborhoods, and were therefore most worried about the prospects of Hindu-Muslim violence, shifted their votes to the BJP.[96] In the 1993 elections, for the first time in Madhya Pradesh's history, not one Muslim was elected to the state assembly.

The effects of Hindu-Muslim polarization due to the riots were most dramatic in the Bhopal North constituency. In 1989 the constituency's Muslim independent candidate Arif Aqueel had been able to fend off a BJP challenge because the Congress candidate, who received 8% of the votes, split the Hindu vote. But in 1993, in the aftermath of the riot, the BJP candidate Ram Sharma won with more than 50% of the votes on a very heavy turnout (76% compared with 62% in 1989), handily defeating Aqueel's 43%. The victorious Sharma unhesitatingly credited his victory to the riots, telling Jaffrelot that Hindu women in particular had been frightened by the riots into switching their votes to the BJP.[97]

---

[94] Anil Sharma, "Riots Shatter Peace in Bhopal," *Times of India*, December 17, 1992, p. 12.

[95] Jaffrelot tells us that "The BJP state government in Madhya Pradesh showed little urgency in containing the rioting or caring for the victims, while rioters from the Bajrang Dal became almost accustomed to receiving government protection." Jaffrelot, *The Hindu Nationalist Movement in India*, p. 462.

[96] Ibid., pp. 447–48.

[97] Ibid., pp. 513–14.

Alternative Hypotheses Not Tested: Institutional Riot Mechanisms and Civic Engagement

In this chapter I have not tested town-level hypotheses that have been advanced in two important recent studies, one by Paul Brass, who highlights the importance of what he calls "institutionalized riot systems," and the other by Ashutosh Varshney, who focuses on the importance of civic engagement at the town level in preventing violence. I have not systematically tested these theories largely because of the difficulty I have had in collecting time-series data for them across a sufficiently large number of towns in Uttar Pradesh. However, because these studies are important and influential, and my book will undoubtedly be compared with them, I want to at least deal with some of their central arguments here.

In *Theft of an Idol*, Paul Brass argues that one important factor that explains Hindu-Muslim violence (a category that he himself skillfully deconstructs) is the existence of town-level "institutionalized riot systems," by which he means "a network of actors, groups, and connections involving persons from different social categories whose effect . . . is to keep a town or city in a permanent state of awareness of Hindu-Muslim relationships."[98] Riot specialists – agents provocateurs – specialize in inflaming emotions and identifying individual events as part of a wider "Hindu-Muslim conflict," and at times they deliberately incite violence.[99] Brass's general approach, as well as his acknowledgment of the role of state-level political actors, is certainly compatible with the state-level arguments I make in this and subsequent chapters. Brass in fact explicitly highlights, as I do, the complicity of the state in failing to prevent violence.[100]

The problem with empirically testing his arguments about the role of "institutionalized riot systems" at the town level, however, is that to do so we would need to be able to verify independently the existence of such systems through time and across different cities, in addition to controlling for all the other town-level factors likely to restrain or to lead to violence. Establishing the presence of such riot systems therefore seems a formidable task, even if we could assemble a large group of scholars and devote years of fieldwork to the task: the difficulty in testing this hypotheses is perhaps suggested by the fact that even Brass at times in his book seems to demonstrate that institutionalized riot systems exist more by inferring their existence from

[98] Brass, *The Theft of an Idol*, p. 284.
[99] Ibid., pp. 258–59.
[100] Ibid., pp. 286–88.

whether a riot has occurred or not, rather than independently proving that such systems are present on a year-by-year basis.

Ashutosh Varshney has put forward the idea that the presence of high or low levels of interreligious interaction, what he terms "civic engagement," can explain why some towns experience riots and others do not. The central insight here has a distinguished history: in social psychology, Gordon Allport's "contact hypothesis" long ago recognized the importance of particular kinds of majority-minority social interactions (those promoting contact as equals and directed toward superordinate goals) in reducing intergroup prejudice and conflict.[101] Clifford Manshardt's study on Hindu-Muslim violence in India in 1936 argued that organized as well as informal civic interaction could prevent communal tensions and violence, because "the strain between the groups is lessened as the common contacts multiply."[102] Manshardt reported the views of contemporaries such as Jayakar who advocated U.S. style civic engagement as a way of dealing with the communal problem.

In America, citizens of all classes meet together to discuss common sanitary problems, to lay plans for making the city beautiful, and for improving the general level of life. The secret of the success of these organizations is that they deal with common problems, and through dealing with common problems other problems are made common. Common interests are created where they do not exist. . . . Planting trees, providing open spaces, and the like are not very controversial problems, but the friendships gained through these activities are a powerful solvent of matters of controversy. If we could carry out activities of this kind in India, it would be a very splendid thing. . . . Communal harmony will not come until a man realizes that his own interests are the interests of his brother.[103]

Varshney's study is nevertheless new and important because he systematically builds a theory about how such interactions – especially through the work of interethnic civic associations – work to reduce violence, and then assesses the significance of civic engagement by looking at three pairs of cities, with one violent and one peaceful city in each pair, and controlling each pair for key factors that might lead to violence: Aligarh and Calicut, Ahmedabad and Surat, and Hyderabad and Lucknow. On the basis of case studies, historical research, and interviews in these cities, he argues that,

---

[101] Gordon W. Allport, *The Nature of Prejudice* (1954; reprint, Boston: Addison Wesley, 1997), especially chap. 16 on "The Effect of Contact."

[102] Clifford Manshardt, *The Hindu-Muslim Problem in India* (London: G. Allen & Unwin, 1936), p. 37.

[103] Ibid., pp. 124–25.

in urban areas, daily contacts in intercommunal associations exercise an important effect in reducing communal violence. He finds that:

> In peaceful cities... an institutionalized peace system exists. When organizations such as trade unions, associations of businessmen, traders, teachers, doctors, lawyers, and at least some cadre-based political parties (different from the ones that have an interest in communal polarization) are communally integrated, countervailing forces are created. Associations that would suffer losses from a communal split fight for their turf, making not only their members aware of the dangers of communal violence, but also the public at large. Local administrations are far more effective in such circumstances. Civic organizations, for all practical purposes, become the eyes and ears of the administration.... In the end, polarizing politicians either don't succeed or eventually stop trying to divide communities by provoking and fomenting communal violence.[104]

The main problem we face in testing whether a social capital or contact hypothesis theory of violence actually works is that there are few good statistics on "social capital" that tell us about town-by-town differences in social interaction, social distance, and the presence of town-level *mohalla* committees. Good research on interreligious attitudes and social distance was done in the 1950s, when Gardner Murphy coordinated a Unesco-sponsored study of social tensions in India. But this and similar studies covered only a few towns: Aligarh, Lucknow, Bombay, Dehra Dun, and Calcutta.[105] When I traveled to Uttar Pradesh I hoped to find such data to use in a large-N study, but my interviews with the UP officials whose job it is to register local associations convinced me that government figures on associational life are deeply flawed.[106] To test the civic engagement thesis fully in this chapter would therefore require detailed surveys on social interaction and associational life through time at the town level for a large number of UP towns – while also controlling for socioeconomic factors and the likely precipitants of violence – and such data do not exist.

While I cannot therefore test the civic engagement thesis here, there are several reasons, while applauding any effort to bring members of different communities together for interreligious interaction, that I think we ought to be skeptical about claims that intercommunal interaction or interethnic associations are sufficient in themselves to prevent large-scale ethnic riots.

---

[104] Varshney, *Ethnic Conflict and Civic Life*, p. 10.
[105] Gardner Murphy, *In the Minds of Men: The Study of Human Behavior and Social Tensions in India* (New York: Basic Books, 1953); Gupta, *Hindu-Muslim Relations*.
[106] Interviews with Mr. Dixit of UP Societies Registration and Mrs. N. S. Kumar, Chair of Nari Sewa Samiti, Lucknow, August 1995.

First, the fact that many societies with rich traditions of interethnic associational life have experienced very high levels of ethnic violence suggests that associational life may be more the result than the cause of communal peace and that, in any event, it is insufficient in itself to prevent violence. The classic case is pre-civil-war Yugoslavia, a society with high levels of residential integration, interethnic friendship and intermarriage, and multiethnic associational life. None of these factors prevented a brutal civil war and mass violence in the early 1990s. More recently the vibrant Muslim-Christian associational life in Nigerian towns such as Kano and Kaduna (2002) has not been sufficient to prevent ethnic violence in these towns.[107] And while Varshney argues that the interethnic associations he looks at in some Indian towns have constrained the strategic behavior of politicians who want to foment violence, even during partition, it seems that an interethnic political party and local associations were not sufficient to prevent mass violence in 1947 in Pakistani and Indian Punjab, where the same arguments about associational density, civic engagement, and economic interdependence could surely have been made.[108]

The Punjab after all was, before independence, the home of India's most successful, genuinely multiethnic party, the Punjab Unionist Party. The party's leader, Khizr Tiwana, saw the party's pursuit of a multiethnic Punjabi identity as a direct outgrowth of the everyday social interaction between Hindus, Muslims, and Sikhs in the state, arguing that "There are Hindu and Sikh Tiwanas who are my relatives. I go to their weddings and other ceremonies. How could I possibly regard them as coming from another nation."[109] And at the local level we can point to successful multiethnic unions, for example among the drivers for Lahore's major form

[107] A reporter who interviewed people in Kaduna after November 2002 riots in which 200 people were killed reported that "Even now most families are made up of those who believe in Jesus and those who follow Muhammad – not to mention all those who worship the trees and rocks like generations of animists before them. Christians recall being invited to Muslim weddings. A devout Muslim recalls kneeling down and praying with his Christian cousins." See "Piety and Politics Sunder a Riot-Torn City," *New York Times*, February 22, 2003, p. A4.

[108] Varshney, *Ethnic Conflict and Civic Life*, p. 10. One additional indicator of the interethnic nature of associational life in the Punjab would be the strength of the multiethnic Unionist Party, which won provincial elections in 1937 and 1946.

[109] Roderick MacFarquhar, foreword, in Ian Talbot, *Khizr Tiwana: The Punjab Unionist Party and the Partition of India* (Karachi: Oxford University Press, 2002), p. xii. For a general the success of the Unionist party in appealing to both Hindus and Muslims in the 1920s and 1930s, see Talbot, *Khizr Tiwana*, and David Gilmartin, *Empire and Islam: Punjab and the Making of Pakistan* (Berkeley: University of California Press, 1988), pp. 108–44.

of public transport, the horse-drawn *tongas* in the decade before independence. Yet desirable as all these developments were, they were not sufficient to prevent violence once some political leaders determined to provoke it in 1947.[110]

Second, as a methodological issue it is very difficult to separate out the effects of interethnic contact and associational life from the influence of all the other socioeconomic and political factors likely to predispose a town to peace or violence. Varshney properly qualifies his claims at various points in the book by stressing that the relationship between civic engagement and riots is "probabilistic, not lawlike."[111] But without good time-series information on all the likely factors that might reasonably influence a town's level of violence – including data on attempts by organizations and individuals to precipitate violence as well as preventive measures by the state – it will be difficult to determine just how much of a probable contribution interethnic associations make to peace.[112] Inferring that interethnic associations are successful from a town's overall low level of violence might be misleading for several reasons: logically the most successful peace committees – if success is judged in terms of how much they reduce violence – might actually be in the most violent cities. In South Africa, for example, many observers felt that the most effective interethnic community peace committees were, paradoxically, in the most violent areas of Kwa-Zulu Natal.[113] Another difficulty is that the same police officials and district magistrates who have been most active in promoting interreligious associations in India, such as Suresh Khopre in Bhiwandi and the late Ashok Priyadarshi in Lucknow, are also those who have the best reputation for strictly enforcing law and order and using force early against riots.

---

[110] Som Anand, *Lahore: Portrait of a Lost City* (Lahore: Vanguard Books, 1998), pp. 34–35. For another account of prepartition social life in Punjab, see Prakash Tandon's *Punjabi Century, 1857–1947* (Berekeley: University of California Press, 1968).

[111] Varshney, *Ethnic Conflict and Civic Life*, p. 11.

[112] An additional difficulty is establishing exactly which level or threshold of civic engagement is necessary to lead to peace, something that methodologically needs to be assessed independently from knowing whether violence has or has not broken out: for example, we need to understand why a level of 60% of Hindus and Muslims visiting each other in Aligarh should be too low to preserve peace, whereas 84% of Hindus and Muslims visiting each other in Calicut should lead to a good outcome there. Ibid., p. 127.

[113] Centre for Policy Studies, *Crying Peace Where There Is None? The Functioning and Future of Local Peace Committees of the National Peace Accord*, Research Report no. 31 (Transition Series) (Johannesburg, 1993).

In addition, nongovernmental (NGO) and local officials, forever in search of grants or promotions, are tempted to overplay the significance of their local initiatives in preventing violence. Journalists and editors, hungry for good news to counteract the bad, are also only too willing to run stories on the latest bureaucratic or NGO "quick fix" for ethnic violence. The head of one of Uttar Pradesh's main women's organizations expressed her skepticism to me about NGO claims that they could, in addition to reducing poverty, alleviating malnutrition, and empowering women, alleviate ethnic conflicts as well. With a wry smile she remarked to me "The grants go to those who write the best proposals, not to those who do the best work."[114]

A third issue is that the contact hypothesis, which forms the intellectual basis for many of our assumptions about the benefits of interethnic interaction, may very well be invalid because it too easily assumes that the proven effects of intergroup contact at the individual level easily translate into the same phenomenon at the group level. Several important studies have found that social institutions that bring members of different groups together to work for common goals may have only limited effects. Cook, for instance carried out research on black-white relations in the United States and found that, while black-white cooperation did reduce prejudice toward other participants in the activity, levels of prejudice toward the other ethnic group as a whole were barely affected.[115] R. M. Williams's study of race relations in four American cities in the 1960s went further and found that, while individual intergroup contacts were negatively correlated with ethnic prejudice, high levels of intergroup contact at the city-level were actually *positively correlated* with ethnic prejudice.[116]

Which Level of Analysis: Town or State?

This chapter has explored the contribution of various town-level factors, especially the role of electoral incentives, in accounting for where and when

---

[114] Interview with Mrs. N. S. Kumar, Chair of UP Nari Sewa Samiti, Lucknow, August 22, 1995.

[115] S. W. Cook, "Interpersonal and Attitudinal Outcomes in Cooperating Interracial Groups," *Journal of Research and Development in Education* 12 (1978), pp. 97–113. For a general discussion of the "Contact Hypothesis," see Rupert Brown, *Prejudice: Its Social Psychology* (Oxford: Blackwell, 1995), pp. 235–70.

[116] R. M. Williams, *Strangers next Door: Ethnic Relations in American Communities* (Englewood Cliffs, N.J.: Prentice-Hall, 1964). For a systematic review of the problem of aggregating individual outcomes from contact to ethnic groups, see H. D. Forbes, *Ethnic Conflict: Commerce, Culture and the Contact Hypothesis* (New Haven: Yale University Press, 1997).

	State Government Determined to Prevent Riots	State Government Not Determined to Prevent Riots
Local Precipitants of Violence Present (e.g. high electoral competition, previous violence, low levels of civic engagement)	**Second Lowest Level of Violence** More riots break out but they are quickly contained by the state.	**Highest Level of Violence** More riots break out, and these are prolonged and bloody because they are unrestrained by either the state or local community
Local Precipitants of Violence Absent (e.g. low levels of electoral competition, no previous violence, high levels of civic engagement)	**Lowest Level of Violence** Fewer riots break out and those that do are contained by the state.	**Second Highest Level of Violence** Fewer riots break out but they continue because they are not contained by the state.

Figure 2.1   The relationship between town- and state-level factors

communal violence breaks out. But the following chapters make a case for the importance of *state-level factors*, especially the level of political competition in a state, in explaining patterns of violence. I differ then with Varshney when he says that "the relationship between state-level and city-level statistics clearly establish the city as the unit of analysis for a study of the causes of communal violence. India's Hindu-Muslim violence is city-specific. State (and national) politics provide the context within which the local mechanisms linked with violence are activated."[117]

This seems to me to place too much emphasis on town-level factors. My view, depicted in Figure 2.1, is that while local precipitants are important, state-level politics does much more than simply provide the context for local mechanisms to work. Because states control the police and the local deployment of force, state-level politics in fact largely determines whether violence will break out, even in the most riot-prone towns – those with "bad" levels of previous violence, civic engagement, or whichever other factor is associated with communal violence.

[117] Varshney, *Ethnic Conflict and Civic Life*, p. 106.

58

To understand the crucial role of state-level factors, consider the all-India pattern of Hindu-Muslim riots in the two months following the murder of 58 Hindu nationalists and their family members on a train in Godhra in Gujarat on February 27, 2002. This event precipitated attempts to foment violence and Hindu nationalist mobilizations across the country, including polarizing events in a large number of towns that have historically experienced large numbers of riots. Communal demonstrations, strikes, processions, or attacks of the type that usually precipitate violence were reported in 2002 in more than a dozen of the 25 most "riot-prone" towns that Varshney identifies in his book: Ahmedabad, Aligarh, Aurangabad, Bhiwandi-Thane, Bhopal, Bombay, Calcutta, Hyderabad, Indore, Jaipur, Jalgaon, Surat, Vadodara, and Varanasi.[118]

If town-level factors such as high or low civic engagement, the ethnic division of labor, and the previous level of violence were truly the most important variables in explaining where riots break out (whether directly, or indirectly by constraining or not constraining the behavior of politicians toward minorities), we would surely have expected the riots that followed the Godhra violence to be primarily, or at least disproportionately, located in these "riot-prone" towns, regardless of state. If a state-level explanation is correct, on the other hand, we would expect there to be substantial state-level variation in the pattern of riots, with violence being controlled even in the "bad towns" in those states determined to keep order and violence breaking out even in the "good towns" in those states that were not prepared to use full force to prevent riots.

The pattern of polarizing events and riots from February to April 2002 seems to show clearly that the state-level explanation can better account for riot occurrence. In Figure 2.2 I have mapped all the reported events from February 27 to April 30, 2002, of the kind that normally precipitate communal riots in India, such as religiously polarizing processions, Bajrang Dal and Vishwa Hindu Parishad violent demonstrations and strikes, and individual acts of violence such as stabbings and stone throwing against members of the other religious community. This map is striking for two reasons. First, we can see that there were attempts to precipitate violence throughout India during the period from February to April 2002. Second, we can see that these nationwide attempts only led to deaths on a large scale in Gujarat. All the most-riot-prone towns outside the state of Gujarat avoided large-scale deadly riots because the state governments in Madhya

---

[118] See ibid., table 4.1, pp. 104–5, for a list of riot-prone cities.

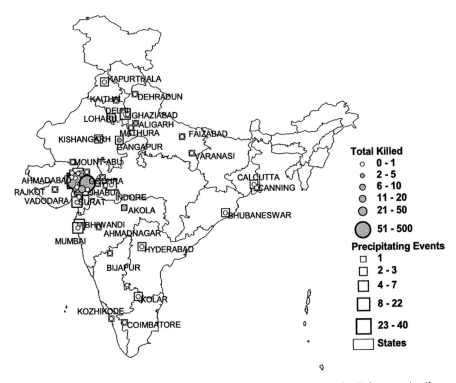

Figure 2.2 Reported precipitating events and deaths during the February–April 2002 communal violence (data collected by Wilkinson based on *Indian Express* reports)

Pradesh, Rajasthan, Andhra Pradesh, West Bengal, and elsewhere were prepared to use the full strength of their police forces to prevent riots and to call on the services of central forces promptly where necessary.[119]

In Madhya Pradesh, for example, attempts to provoke large-scale violence in the two most riot-prone cities in that state – Indore and Bhopal, both of which have experienced numerous communal riots in the past – were effectively stopped by curfews, mass arrests of militants, deployment of the central Rapid Action Force, and the imposition of the National Security

[119] As I discuss in Chapter 5, those casualties which did take place outside Gujarat were largely the result of police firing to break up riots and prevent attacks, rather than – as in Gujarat – the result of members of one community attacking another.

Act.[120] In Rajasthan, mass deployments of state police forces and the police force's orders to fire on rioters if necessary prevented serious incidents in Jaipur (one of the 28 most riot-prone cities in India, and the site of serious violence in 1989, 1990, and 1992), Gangapur, and elsewhere from erupting into mass violence.[121] In Andhra Pradesh, where the capital Hyderabad is one the 5 most riot-prone cities in India, it was a similar story: despite a large-scale stone-throwing incident on March and later strikes and isolated attacks, the state government's arrests and the speedy deployment of police prevented large-scale riots from taking place.[122] In West Bengal, although Calcutta is one of the most "riot-prone" cities in India, with a total of 67 riots and thousands of deaths reported since 1920, the West Bengal state government forces prevented riots by arrests, police deployment, and a willingness to use force – deadly if necessary – to break up unauthorized demonstrations by Vishwa Hindu Parishad (VHP) militants on March 10.[123]

In Gujarat, on the other hand, even some towns with no recent history of large-scale riots experienced violence. Once the Gujarat state government had shown that it was not prepared to stop the riots, both by its inaction as well as its actions – such as delays in calling in central forces, failing to make preventive arrests, and transferring officials who were determined to use force and arrests to prevent violence – then riots broke out in rural areas as well as in towns such as Bodeli and Akola where there had been no reported violence for at least 50 years.[124] To be sure, the violence in Gujarat was worst in the most riot-prone towns, especially in Ahmedabad, Vadodara, and Godhra. But it was also bad in towns such as Modasa and Akola, where there had been no reported violence for decades.

This state-specific pattern of violence is only explicable once we acknowledge that the response of the state government forces is the main factor in determining whether large-scale ethnic violence breaks out and

---

[120] "Over 200 Arrested in Indore Violence," *Indian Express*, March 12, 2002. Indore has had reported communal riots in 1927 (5 killed, 20 injured), 1969 (10 killed, 208 injured), 1970, 1973, 1975, 1989 (23 killed, 75 injured), and 1990 (11 killed). Bhopal has had riots in 1946, 1953, 1954, 1970, 1987 and most recently in 1992, when 107 were killed and 400 injured.

[121] "Police Firing in Rajasthan, Two Killed," *Indian Express*, March 26, 2002.

[122] "Andhra Police on High Alert," *Indian Express*, February 28, 2002.

[123] See "Cops Take No Chances, Bengal Put on Red Alert," *Indian Express*, March 12, 2002, and "1 Killed in Firing on West Bengal VHP Activists," *Indian Express*, March 11, 2002.

[124] For the delay in bringing in the army and carrying out other preventive measures in Gujarat, see "Police to Decide on Army Use: Modi," *Indian Express*, March 2, 2002; "Full 18 Hours after Godhra: Gujarat Police Has an Action-Not-Taken Report," *Indian Express*, March 6, 200; and "Dial M for Modi, Murder?" *Indian Express*, March 24, 2002.

continues. In the following chapters I assess the various explanations that have been put forward to explain why this will is sometimes present and at other times not. First I show that the "capacity" of state governments – in terms of institutional quality – has been wrongly identified as a critical factor in riot control. Then I consider in Chapters 4 and 5 whether consociational factors or levels of electoral competition can explain this variation.

3

State Capacity Explanations for Hindu-Muslim Violence

The State is held at ransom by bootleggers, smugglers and all such anti-social people. Many politicians are their close associates. A very considerable section of the police are on the pay-roll of these people. If those people want a disturbance to occur, a disturbance will occur. The State does not have the power to stop it.

Amal Datta, MP, 1986[1]

Social scientists often argue that we can explain variation in mass violence by focusing on the strength or weakness of state institutions. Neil Smelser's research on England, Mexico, and the United States in the 18th and 19th centuries, for example, finds that periods in which police corruption was rife, training and equipment were poor, and local political interference high were invariably accompanied by large increases in riots.[2] James Tong's study of violence in Ming China found that riots occurred most often in peripheral areas where the effectiveness of the Chinese state was weakest.[3] More recently, studies of collective mobilization and violence in places as diverse as Los Angeles, the former Soviet Union, and the former state of Yugoslavia have identified state capacity, and the impact it has on individuals' decision about whether to participate in violence, as a crucial factor in

---

[1] Amal Datta, an MP from West Bengal, speaking during a parliamentary debate on riots in Gujarat. *Lok Sabha Debates*, July 22, 1986, p. 314.

[2] Neil J. Smelser, *Theory of Collective Behavior* (London: Routledge and Kegan Paul, 1962), chap. 8, pp. 231–34, 261–68.

[3] Tong argued that riots were concentrated in the periphery because there the "likelihood of surviving hardship is minimal but the likelihood of surviving as an outlaw is maximal." James W. Tong, *Disorder under Heaven: Collective Violence in the Ming Dynasty* (Stanford: Stanford University Press, 1991), p. 93.

determining where and when violence takes place.[4] DiPasquale and Glaeser, for example, draw on standard economic price theory to explain the 1992 Los Angeles riots, concluding that rioting was greatest in those places where the financial gains were highest, and the state's capacity to punish individual rioters weakest.[5]

This chapter examines whether, as many analysts seem to think, differences in state capacity can also account for the historical and state-level variation in Hindu-Muslim violence. Many Indian politicians and journalists link different state responses to riots and therefore the overall levels of Hindu-Muslim violence in India's states to what they see as the growing politicization, corruption, and institutional weakness of Indian state governments. The roots of this state weakness, it is widely agreed, lie in politicians' efforts in the postindependence period, especially during the premiership of Indira Gandhi, to use (and misuse) their control of the state bureaucracy and police to build political support and to deny it to their rivals.[6] Many observers believe that the police have now been so cowed by political interference and so debilitated by a lack of resources and frequent punitive transfers that local administrations are now incapable of taking independent action to prevent riots and, even worse, are unable to prevent riots even if ordered to do so by politicians.

My central argument in this chapter is that, despite these arguments, state weakness does not account for these state-level differences in the level of Hindu-Muslim violence. That is not to say that I disagree with scholars who argue that most Indian states have become weaker since the 1960s, using indicators that measure politicization, corruption, and fiscal instability. But I argue that Indian states' loss of autonomy and capacity, undesirable though

---

[4] Ibid.; Denise DiPasquale and Edward L. Glaeser, *The L. A. Riot and the Economics of Urban Unrest*, NBER Working Paper no. W5456, February 1996; Valerie Bunce, "From State Socialism to State Disintegration: A Comparison of the Soviet Union, Yugoslavia and Czechoslovakia," paper presented at the conference on "Democracy, Markets and Civil Societies in Post-1989 East Central Europe," Harvard University, May 17–19, 1996; Mark R. Beissinger, "Nationalist Violence and the State: Political Authority and Contentious Repertoires in the Former USSR," *Comparative Politics* 30, no. 4 (1998), pp. 401–22.

[5] DiPasquale and Glaeser, *The L. A. Riot and the Economics of Urban Unrest*.

[6] See, e.g., Atul Kohli, *Democracy and Discontent: India's Growing Crisis of Governability* (Cambridge: Cambridge University Press, 1990); James Manor, "Party Decay and Political Crisis in India," *Washington Quarterly* 4, no. 3 (1981), pp. 25–40; Myron Weiner, "The Indian Paradox: Violent Social Conflict and Democratic Politics," in Ashutosh Varshney, ed., *The Indian Paradox: Essays in Indian Politics* (New Delhi: Sage, 1989), pp. 21–38; Arend Lijphart, "The Puzzle of Indian Democracy: A Consociational Interpretation," *American Political Science Review* 90, no. 2 (1996), pp. 258–68.

it is, has simply been too widespread across Indian states to account for the large degree of historical and state-level variation in levels of ethnic violence. Even the weakest state governments, like Bihar and Uttar Pradesh, still seem to possess the minimal state capacity necessary to prevent Hindu-Muslim riots if this is made a priority by their political leaders. The fact that we see sharp differences in levels of communal violence from one elected regime to another suggests that the problem is not so much state capacity – most states still seem to possess at least the limited capacity they need to prevent Hindu-Muslim riots – as the instructions given by politicians to state officials telling them whether to protect or not to protect minorities.[7]

This chapter is divided into four parts. In the first section, to provide some necessary background, I briefly describe the structure of the local law-and-order machinery in India. Then I outline the main arguments that link levels of Hindu-Muslim violence to either state autonomy or state capacity. Next, I show that by most indicators there *has* been a reduction in both the autonomy and capacity of most Indian state administrations over the past few decades. In the final section, however, I argue that when we examine the relationship between specific indicators of state weakness – such as politically motivated transfers, judicial backlogs, and political interference – these indicators do not seem to account for the variation in ethnic violence.

The Structure of Local Law Enforcement in India

The basic unit of Indian administration is the district, of which there were 593 in 2001: the smallest states and territories contain as few as 1 or 2 districts; midsize states have several dozen districts, while the 166 million people in India's most populous state, Uttar Pradesh, are spread across 70 districts. Under the Indian Constitution, law and order are the responsibility of India's 28 elected state governments, which pass orders down through their police and civil service hierarchies to the key district-level officials in charge of law enforcement: the district magistrate (DM, also known as the "collector") and the superintendent of police (SP) or, in the

---

[7] Some level of state capacity is clearly necessary to prevent riots, so my argument is not that state capacity is unimportant as such, only that it has not yet deteriorated in India to the point where states cannot prevent violence. We know this because even the weakest states – such as Bihar – can successfully prevent large-scale violence when ordered to do so by politicians.

most populous or important districts, to the senior superintendent of police (SSP). By law the positions of DM and SP or SSP must be filled, respectively, by members of two elite all-India services: the Indian Administrative Service (IAS) and the Indian Police Service (IPS).[8] While the SP or SSP is directly in charge of the local police force, the DM has broader responsibility for law and order in a district and, in some states, has supervisory authority over the SP. This system of joint control has at times created tensions between the police and civil service at the local level, made worse by interservice friction over the superior prestige, pay, and promotion opportunities of IAS officers compared with those of the police.[9]

Under the SP there are assistant superintendents (ASP), deputy superintendents (DSP), subinspectors (known as station house officers, or SHOs, because they are in charge of local police stations), and other ranks all the way down to head constables and constables, who constitute 85% of the force. All ranks below ASP are staffed by officers recruited wholly within the state, through a statewide examination in the case of the DSPs and SHOs, and at the discretion of local SPs in the case of constables. The number of police in any one town or district is set by the state government, and the per-capita deployment of police can vary widely, according to the political importance of the town, its perceived sensitivity, its physical area, and the particular state in which it is located. Small states and sensitive border states are heavily policed: states in the Northeast generally have more than 3 policemen per 1,000 inhabitants, while Punjab averaged 2.8 per 1,000 in the early 1990s. Large, populous states usually have less than half this number of policemen: the number of policemen in the major states in the

---

[8] The states also reserve a small proportion of the places in each state's IPS and IAS cadre for promotees from the state services. As these promotees do not join the IAS and IPS until late in their career, they occupy relatively junior positions.

[9] See *Fifth Report of the National Police Commission* (New Delhi: Government of India, 1980), p. 40. India staffs its elite civil service and police positions (the Indian Administrative Service, Indian Foreign Service, Indian Income-Tax Service, etc.) through a single national examination. Those candidates who receive the highest rank in this annual exam, run by the Union Public Service Commission, can choose whichever service they wish. They invariably choose one of the hundred or so positions in the IAS, which has higher pay, better conditions, and superior promotion prospects to the IPS. In 1980, for instance, the highest-ranked candidate to select the IPS stood 124th in the national order of merit. Until the rules were changed to prohibit multiple retakes in the late 1980s, many IPS officers spent their police probationary period resitting the UPSC exams in an effort to switch to the IAS. *Sixth Report of the National Police Commission* (New Delhi: Government of India, 1981), pp. 5–6.

early 1990s ranged between 0.9 police officers per 1,000 in Bihar and 1.6 per 1,000 in Maharashtra.

To prevent riots, the police rely on information from local police officers, informants, members of the public, and the "Special Branch," specially trained plain-clothes officers who collect intelligence on likely threats to public order. This information is written up each week by the SP in a confidential report, copies of which are sent to the DM, to the SP's own superior in the police (a deputy inspector general, responsible for several districts), and to the State Intelligence Department. The district magistrate, who has his own sources as well as relying on the police for crime reports, forwards important information to each state's Home Ministry every two weeks in "the FDO" (Fortnightly Demi-Official Report).[10] To provide some institutional memory about likely sources of trouble, each police station maintains a register of local criminals and "known bad characters," as well as a "Festival Register" that lays down in minute detail procession routes and customs, the maximum dimensions of religious objects allowed to be taken out in the processions, the boundaries of religious sites, and other information necessary to regulate activities that are likely to lead to violence.[11]

If, on the basis of all these sources, the DM believes that a communal riot is imminent, he has the power under section 144 of the Code of Criminal Procedure to control entry to the town, make preventive arrests, and ban processions and other activities he thinks are likely to lead to violence. If violence actually breaks out, the DM and SP can also concentrate the district police force wherever they wish, deploying forces according to a preexisting riot plan, which specifies "the number and location of police pickets and patrols, the equipment to be carried by them, measures for rounding up of bad characters and communal elements and to mobilize the support of respectables, control over fire-arms, measures for the enforcement of curfew, etc."[12] In addition to each district's regular police force, the SP can also call upon a reserve "armed police" unit of perhaps 50 to 100 men, ready to be moved at short notice.[13] If the combined civil and district armed

[10] M. Zaheer and Jagdeo Gupta, *The Organization of the Government of Uttar Pradesh: A Study of State Administration* (Delhi: S. Chand, 1970), pp. 724–25.

[11] Interview with an IAS officer, December 15, 1994.

[12] *Annexure V: Measures Taken by the District Administration to Deal with the Communal Problem in Delhi*, in *Report of the One-Man Commission of Inquiry into the Sadar Bazar Disturbances, 1974* (New Delhi: Government of India Press, 1975) pp. 206–7.

[13] Many of the "civilian" police are in fact armed. The main difference is that the armed police are stationed in barracks and trained as a military-style strike force.

police forces are not adequate to prevent a riot, the DM and SP can then call in each state's paramilitary forces, based in barracks at various strategic points throughout the state. If any of these forces are unavailable or, in the opinion of the DM, insufficient to stop a Hindu-Muslim riot, the DM can as a last resort call in the army. The army, though its officers uniformly detest riot duty, cannot legally refuse a request from a DM to intervene to "aid the civil power."

All policemen and bureaucrats, whether they are from the state or all-India services, are supposed to obey the law first and their political masters second. But, in practice, government officers enjoy very different levels of protection from political retaliation. Members of the state police force and civil services can be punished for disobeying politicians with very little oversight. Only IAS and IPS officers, as members of one of the central services, enjoy substantial protection from state government retaliation. Although under the operational control of the state, they cannot be dismissed from the service by a state government without the permission of the union government in New Delhi.

This does not however mean that IAS and IPS officers are immune to political influence. The state governments have the power to transfer IAS and IPS officers for a wide variety of reasons, and using these transfers punitively can be an effective way of bending most officers, though certainly not all of them, to politicians' will. First, frequent transfers play havoc with an officer's professional and family life, especially when an officer has children and the transfer occurs during the school year. Second, not all jobs are equally desirable. Politicians can transfer officers who refuse to do their bidding to especially difficult or undesirable jobs, to posts that offer no opportunities for making money (for those officers for whom this is known to be a goal), or to a post that is clearly incommensurate with an officer's rank. As well as using their power to transfer, state politicians can also punish officers by suspending them, denying them promotions to good positions in the state government, or writing such negative annual reports that officers who wish to "escape" the state and transfer to a position in the central government will find it difficult to do so.[14]

---

[14] *Commission on Centre-State Relations Report Part 1* (Nasik: Government of India Press, 1988), p. 226. The commission appealed (sec. 8.10.4, p. 226) for the states to stop these tactics and recommended that the central governments refer state suspensions to the Union Public Service Commission to let it determine if the officer was really at fault.

State Autonomy, State Capacity, and Hindu-Muslim Violence

Samuel Huntington, in his classic *Political Order in Changing Societies*, argued that "violence, rioting and other forms of political instability are more likely to occur in political systems without strong parties than in systems with them."[15] Taking their cue from Huntington, Atul Kohli, James Manor, and several other scholars have argued that the decrease in state autonomy and India's rise in Hindu-Muslim violence is linked to the institutional and electoral decline of what had once been the country's "premier conflict-managing institution," the Congress Party.[16] Because Congress and India's other political parties are institutionally weak, they have misused their state administrations to raise money illegally, pay off political supporters and hurt the opposition, and insulate themselves and their supporters from prosecution and investigation.

Atul Kohli's book *Democracy and Discontent* shows how Congress Party in-fighting in the 1960s severely weakened the party's organizational strength and the capacity of party leaders in the states to control their followers.[17] After Indira Gandhi's faction of Congress won a crushing electoral victory over the opposition in 1971, she replaced many of the established Congress Party leaders in the states with politicians personally loyal to her.[18] These politicians, with no local organization or power base, then used the state administrations as an instrument of personal patronage and control. In Bihar, for example, Kohli describes how Chief Minister Jagannath Mishra and his associates interfered with arrests, prosecutions, police and civil service recruitment, and policies toward mobs and criminal gangs in an effort to protect his political allies and increase his support. Those state officials who went along with this illegal political interference were rewarded with promotions and prize postings; those who resisted were given punitive transfers, demotions, and suspensions.

---

[15] Samuel P. Huntington, *Political Order in Changing Societies* (New Haven: Yale University Press, 1968), p. 409.

[16] Manor, "Party Decay and Political Crisis in India," pp. 25–40; Weiner, "The Indian Paradox: Violent Social Conflict and Democratic Politics," pp. 21–38; Lijphart, "The Puzzle of Indian Democracy: A Consociational Interpretation," pp. 258–68.

[17] Kohli, *Democracy and Discontent*.

[18] State parties, convinced of Mrs. Gandhi's vote-winning power, competed to see who could offer the center the most influence. After the March 1972 elections in Bihar, for example, the state Congress Party asked her to nominate the state's chief minister rather than select its own. By the mid-1970s, the all-important decisions over who would be Congress candidates in state and national elections were made in New Delhi, rather than in the states.

Although Kohli's book focuses on the Congress Party, it is clear that the same arguments about political interference and state autonomy could also be made about other political parties. State governments of every political stripe – the United Front governments in the 1960s, the Janata Party coalitions in the late 1970s, the Bharatiya Janata Party state governments in the 1990s, and the Communist governments in Kerala and West Bengal, to name but a few – have all been accused of illegally using their state administrations to reward their political friends and punish their political enemies.

Political interference with state autonomy is alleged to increase the number of Hindu-Muslim riots in several different ways. First, politicians' actions in forcing the police to drop investigations or prosecutions against their political allies is thought to reduce sharply the deterrent effect of police arrests and prosecutions on potential rioters, as well as the police force's own morale and willingness to follow the law. Second, although there is wide agreement in the literature on riots that early preventive measures by the police are crucial, the process of politicization encourages the exact opposite: the police are so worried about political retribution that they delay taking strong preventive measures – especially against groups perceived to enjoy the protection of the state governments – until they have clear political approval for their actions, a process that can take days.

Analytically distinct from state autonomy – though, of course, political interference can affect autonomy – is the question of state capacity. Many observers think that, even if a state government gives clear orders to prevent riots, state administrations now simply lack the administrative capacity to do so. In part due to politicization, there is said to have been such a fundamental decline in the police force and civil service – in terms of organization, cohesion, manpower, and equipment – that they can no longer perform their main functions. As Kohli puts it, "what started out as a strategy to enhance political control has unanticipated and unfortunate consequences: When leaders now need to call on the police arm of the state, that arm is relatively limp."[19]

Several specific aspects of state capacity are linked to poor state performance in preventing riots. First, many state governments have become financially weaker since the 1960s, which affects the amount of money states have to raise, train, and equip their police forces and special

[19] Kohli, *Democracy and Discontent*, p. 217.

70

riot-control forces. A lack of money for training and ammunition results in police who are ill-trained and ill-equipped to prevent violence, and low pay makes police and civil service more susceptible to bribery and hence less autonomous from society. Second, the police and judicial system in many states are understaffed and overloaded, which reduces the perceived risk rioters face of arrest, prosecution, and conviction. In the early 1970s, for example, the central government responded to a wave of riots by passing permissive legislation allowing states to establish special courts to try riot cases in the belief that better prosecution rates would reduce violence.[20] Third, the main way in which politicians bend police officers and officials to their will – through punitive transfers – is thought to have an independent negative effect on riot preparedness, because frequent transfers reduce officers' knowledge about their districts, their potential trouble spots, and the best way to prevent a riot. As one officer I interviewed put it, "each district has its own dynamics, its own flare points, and all this takes time to understand . . . sometimes the most elementary measures will work to defuse tensions. . . . But this requires a detailed knowledge and it takes six to eight months to know the districts. Now I think the average [tenure in a district] is down to weeks."[21] The National Police Commission echoed this complaint in the early 1980s, when it pointed out that "In one recent riot, everyone from the SHO onward in the police and the magistracy were new to the city and had little local knowledge."[22]

The Decline of State Autonomy and State Capacity

Although arguments about the effects of what is variously termed "state weakness," "governance," or "state capacity" are used to explain a wide variety of phenomena, from economic growth to levels of violence, they are unfortunately difficult to test because independent data on state capacity

---

[20] "Special Courts to Try Riot Cases," *Times of India*, April 22, 1972.

[21] Interview with a retired IPS officer, New Delhi, August 8, 1995. Several officers I interviewed also mentioned the fact that prior to the 1970s, outgoing district magistrates and superintendents of police used to prepare "Charge Notes" to introduce their successors to the district and its problems. These notes included detailed information on who had started riots in the past and who was likely to do so in the future. "Now, of course, nobody writes them," one officer said, "as they don"t know who's going to be reading them next and they're only in the post for such a short space of time." Interview with serving IAS officer, New Delhi, July 23, 1995.

[22] Government of India, National Police Commission, *Sixth Report of the National Police Commission*, sec. 47.12.

are hard to obtain.[23] The central problem is that the quality of data on state weakness is negatively affected by the very weakness it tries to measure: the more corrupt or criminalized a state, the worse its measures of corruption and criminality will be. For example, if the Indian Central Bureau of Investigation (CBI) wants to file a corruption case against Indian state officials or politicians, it needs the permission of the state government. As the head of the anticorruption bureau has pointed out, "if [a case] involves the chief minister or other highly politically connected persons, such consent will not be forthcoming." As a result, the most corrupt Indian states might actually record fewer cases of corruption than less corrupt states because their governments are less willing to give permission for the CBI to prosecute.[24]

Organizations such as the World Bank have tried to address the problem of poor data on state capacity by gathering cross-national indicators on such factors as the pay differentials of government servants and the vertical imbalance of federal spending, which measures subnational expenditure minus the share of subnational revenue. The bank argues that these indicators have been found to be highly correlated with poor institutional performance in the comparative literature on "governance" that has developed over the past decade.[25]

---

[23] In part because of the poor quality of the data, the existence of state weakness and its relationship to Hindu-Muslim riots are all too often inferred from the mere occurrence of violence – "a riot happened, therefore the state must have been too weak to prevent it" – rather than state weakness being independently shown to exist and then to have an effect upon violence.

[24] N.Vittal, Central Vigilance Commissioner, "Towards Effective Governance," lecture at IIC, New Delhi, June 16, 2000, available at <http://cvc.nic.in/vscvc/cvcspeeches/jun2k2.html>. Another good example of this endogeneity issue is the problem with crime data in India; such data depend at the local level on citizens' ability to register criminal cases, which will then be accurately recorded by the police. To file a criminal case in India it is necessary to record a First Information Report at the local police station. It is well documented that policemen often demand bribes to record cases, a fact that obviously depresses crime figures. In addition, because policemen receive promotions based on how few crimes take place, and because the likelihood of punishment for nonrecording of crimes is low, police officials also have an incentive to underreport crimes to advance their career. The late N. S. Saksena, IP, conducted the most complete study of this problem when he was in charge of crime records in Uttar Pradesh in the 1960s, and he shared his research with me during several interviews in Bareilly in the mid-1990s.

[25] General indicators of state Weakness identified by the World Bank and other international organizations: "Public Sector Board, Poverty Reduction and Economic Management Network," September 2000; "Reforming Public Institutions and Strengthening Governance," World Bank, September 2000, pp. 175–76.

The problem with using such general indicators of state capacity to look at state variation in communal violence, however, is that in many cases we have no good theoretical reason for believing that factors such as pay differentials ought to have any relationship to ethnic violence. In this chapter, therefore, rather than rely on the type of general state capacity indicators favored in the literature on governance and development, I focus instead on two distinct aspects of state weakness that have been linked specifically to the occurrence of ethnic violence: state autonomy, defined as the ability of the police and local administration to take independent action to prevent Hindu-Muslim riots in accordance with established rules, procedures, and the law, and state capacity, as measured by each state's financial strength, its police strength and judicial capacity, and its rate of turnover among senior officers in charge of law and order in the districts.

The Decline of State Institutional Autonomy

There is no doubt that the autonomy of police officers to enforce the law independently has declined over the past few decades. A wide variety of sources – press reports, independent inquiries, and books by politicians and serving and retired officers – all make it clear that politicians now frequently interfere with local law-and-order decisions, arrests, and prosecutions. To acknowledge this it is not necessary to subscribe to the idea, sometimes put forward by retired policemen and civil servants, that there was ever a "golden age" in which politicians simply stood back and let the professionals enforce the law and prevent riots without fear or favor. There were in fact complaints about political interference in day-to-day policing decisions – including politicians bypassing police and civil service hierarchies and giving direct orders to officials – dating as far back as the introduction of self-government in the mid-1930s.[26] As early as 1939, for example, the governor of the United Provinces (Uttar Pradesh) complained

[26] I certainly do not mean to imply here that only democratic systems have problems, and that India would have been better off with the pre-1935 authoritarian system. There is at least some evidence to suggest that some officials in the British colonial administration deliberately adopted a hands-off approach to controlling violence in order to discredit the independence movement. The massive Kanpur riots of 1931, for instance, which took place during the Congress civil disobedience campaign, were made much worse by police reluctance to intervene quickly with deadly force, the result (Congress argued) of a deliberate strategy to discredit its political movement. Richard D. Lambert, "Hindu-Muslim Riots" (Ph.D. dissertation, University of Pennsylvania, 1951), p. 106, especially n. 56.

that Congress ministers were transferring police officers and other officials not because of their lack of professional competence but because they had refused to be pressured by local legislators, and by 1947 the senior-most police official in the state was forced to resign after complaining about Congress politicians bypassing his authority and giving direct orders to local policemen.[27] In several states during partition there were also more specific allegations that Congress and Muslim League politicians were interfering in measures to control riots.[28]

Independence, however, accelerated the process of generalized political interference in local law-and-order decisions (as the bureaucrats saw it) or increased accountability and democracy (as politicians tended to see the issue). A high proportion of the cadre of senior officers who had grown used to substantial bureaucratic autonomy, and who were therefore most inclined and best able to resist pressure from politicians, took early retirement at Partition or left to serve in Pakistan, their places being filled by less experienced officers.[29] Even more important than this factor, however, was that politicians, seeing themselves as the ultimate representatives of the

---

[27] Sir Harry Haig, Governor of UP, to All Ministers, May 1, 1939, United Provinces Governors Reports 1939, IOR L/PJ/5/276. The former UP home secretary Rajeshwar Dayal describes how the British inspector general of police, Sir Philip Measures, was forced out shortly before independence by Congress Home Minister Rafi Ahmed Kidwai, in his memoir *A Life of Our Times* (Delhi: Orient Longman, 1998), pp. 80–81.

[28] The classic case of Muslim League interference with local riot control measures came during the August 1946 "Day of Action" riots in Calcutta, before which the league government transferred Hindu police officers who might have controlled Muslim League mobs. Richard Lambert, one of the few people to gain access to the riot inquiry, reports that as a result, "On the first day of rioting police efforts to stop rioting were half-hearted. Their participation in looting and non-interference in rioting is evident from almost all the testimony before the Spens Committee." Lambert, "Hindu-Muslim Riots," pp. 177–78. "Similar events are reported from Congress states such as Bihar and Uttar Pradesh during the partition years. In August 1947, for example, the UP governor (Sir Francis Wylie) wrote to the viceroy (Lord Mountbatten) complaining that the police were unable to press charges against Hindus accused of murdering Muslims because "the Police Station Officer is either afraid to run in bad hats under these sections or, when he does so, finds his efforts to get convictions stultified by the interference of small local Congressmen." He supported this claim with tables that showed that, while riots and other violent crimes had all increased since 1945 by 56–105%, the number of preventive detentions had gone down by 13–30%. Wylie to Mountbatten, August 2, 1947, United Provinces Governor's Reports January–August 1947, IOR L/PJ/5/276.

[29] In Uttar Pradesh, for instance, the inspector general of police, 7 of the 8 deputy inspector generals, 30 of the 56 superintendents of police, and 40% of the assistant superintendents left the state in 1947–48 for Britain or Pakistan. *Report of the Uttar Pradesh Police Commission, 1960–61* (Allahabad: Superintendent of Printing and Stationery, UP, 1962), p. 3.

people, were determined to force the police force and local administration to do their bidding regardless of the law, regulations, or protestations of their officials.

The sentiment of the times is quite well captured in the memoirs of a police officer from Madhya Pradesh, K. D. Sharma, who describes how a local district Congress committee president tried to pressure him through a public address after Sharma refused to drop criminal cases against allies of Arjun Singh, later a senior Congress politician and at the time a member of the Legislative Assembly: "It is we who elect the MLAs. The MLAs then elect the Chief Minister. Therefore the Chief Minister and the Ministers . . . are our servants. And the government servants are servants of our servants whether it is the Collector or the S. P. . . . Hence the servants of our servants can never be our masters!"[30] The memoirs of Sharma and other officials who served in a number of states in the two decades immediately after independence provide vivid examples of politicians who gave punishment postings to officials who investigated or charged their political allies, refused to lodge false cases against political rivals, or refused their requests to transfer junior police officers or civil servants to positions where they would be of most use to the politicians. Sharma for instance was transferred from his district in Madhya Pradesh and had his promotion blocked for defying Arjun Singh in 1960, while V. Vaikunth in Madras (now Tamil Nadu) describes how he was punitively transferred to the North East Frontier Agency in the mid-1960s by Madras's ruling Congress Party politicians after he refused to file a false criminal case against opposition Dravida Munnetra Kazhigam (DMK) workers.[31]

These individual accounts cannot be dismissed as unrepresentative because they are backed up by the findings of every independent inquiry into state policing that was carried out in the 1950s and early 1960s – in West Bengal (1960–61), Uttar Pradesh (1959), Kerala (1959), Punjab (1961–62), and Delhi (1961–62). All these inquiries established that political interference had increased dramatically since independence. In the North, for instance, the Punjab Police Commission (1961–62) criticized what it described as the postindependence trend for "members of political parties, particularly of the ruling party, whether in the legislature or outside, to

[30] K. D. Sharma, *Trials, Tribulations and Triumphs of the Police-Men* (Noida: Trishul Publications, 1991), p. 91.

[31] Ibid., pp. 90–92; V. Vaikunth, *An Eye to Indian Policing: Challenge and Response* (Madras: EastWest, 2000), p. 44.

interfere in the working of the force for unlawful ends."[32] In the South, the Kerala Police Reorganization Committee found in 1959 that "The result of partisan interference is often reflected in lawless enforcement of laws, inferior service, and in general decline of police prestige followed by irresponsible criticism and consequent widening of the cleavage between the police and the public affecting the confidence of the public in the integrity and objectives of the police force."[33]

Although the commission reports and memoirs paint a grim picture of the situation in the late 1950s and early 1960s, things became still worse after the mid-1960s. In contrast to the 1947–67 period – where we can point to several examples where senior Congress politicians such as Vallabhai Patel, D. P. Mishra in Madhya Pradesh, Kamaraj in Madras, and Charan Singh in Uttar Pradesh tried to rein in the tendency of local Congress politicians to interfere with day-to-day law-and-order decisions or otherwise undermine officials – senior politicians in the late 1960s began publicly to sanction and encourage political interference in the police and civil service.[34] In 1969, most famously, the president of the All Indian Congress Committee, Jagjivan Ram, made a speech in which he argued that "the so-called neutral administrative machinery is a hindrance, not a help" and that the philosophy of a neutral administration was "hardly relevant to Indian conditions." Other senior Congress leaders, including the prime minister, Mrs. Gandhi, swiftly echoed his remarks about the need for what was later termed a "committed bureaucracy."[35] The ability of the services by the late 1960s to resist this political pressure had simultaneously been weakened by two decades of steadily declining salaries and conditions, and by the fact that most of the officers who had been trained under a more bureaucratically autonomous system had now left the service or were near retirement. In 1971 the second Uttar Pradesh Police Commission complained that recent political interference had resulted in a "warped enforcement of law" and a

---

[32] Unpublished extracts from the *Report of the Punjab Police Commission, 1961–62* , pp. 18–19 (in possession of author).

[33] Cited in ibid., p. 20.

[34] B. Krishna, *Sardar Vallabhai Patel: India's Iron Man* (New Delhi: Indus, 1995), pp. 476–77, 482. Even K. D. Sharma, in the midst of his general condemnation of politicians, has good things to say about Mishra's support of the police in Madhya Pradesh.

[35] David Potter, *India's Political Administrators: From ICS to IAS* (Delhi: Oxford University Press, 1996), p. 155. The term "committed bureaucracy" is associated especially with Mrs. Gandhi's secretary in the prime minister's office, P. N. Haksar.

"general decline in the police in its integrity."[36] One sign of how bad things had become was that the UP Commission recommended that, in future, relations between the police and politicians be governed by the principle that the "request from the politician should be within the law."[37]

The destruction of the Congress state party machines by Indira Gandhi and her appointment of her own nominees as chief ministers helped to remove whatever constraints were left on political interference with state administrations in the 1970s and early 1980s. Her appointed chief ministers such as Kamlapathi Tripathi (Uttar Pradesh, 1971–73) and Arjun Singh (Madhya Pradesh, 1980–84) used their control of the state to build up political support through patronage and interference with law enforcement. Arjun Singh, for instance, reportedly bought off the internal party opposition from Congress MLAs loyal to the Sethi and Shukla factions by allowing each MLA the right to make four major transfers of civil servants and several minor ones.[38] In Uttar Pradesh, Kamlapathi Tripathi built his own political machine by transferring large numbers of officials at the request of local businessmen and other constituents who wanted to have a "troublesome" police officer or civil servant removed and a more amenable officer transferred in. A third of Tripathi's cabinet was reported to be corrupt, but he refused to take any action against his subordinates. The formal chain of administrative command was ignored by Tripathi, who allowed his relatives to phone up district officials and give them direct orders.[39]

These examples are again not exceptional but representative of wider trends. The Government of India's Shah Commission, set up in the aftermath of the 1975–77 emergency, uncovered evidence that throughout India, many officers had obeyed orders from Congress politicians that they knew to be improper and illegal, including "forging of records, fabrication of ground of detention, ante-dating of detention orders, and callous disregard of the rights of detainees."[40] The Indian Police Commission, set up at the same time, also confirmed that the problem of political interference

---

[36] "Political Pressure on U.P. Police," *Times of India*, June 6, 1972. *Report of the U.P. Police Commission*, August 31, 1971, Office of the Secretary of the UP Police Commission, Lucknow. (Original English typed copy seen by author in Uttar Pradesh.)

[37] *Report of the U.P. Police Commission*, August 31, 1971, Office of the Secretary of the UP Police Commission, Lucknow, no. 235 p. 657.

[38] Sharma, *Trials, Tribulations and Triumphs of the Police-Men*, p. 221.

[39] *Times of India*, June 26, 1973.

[40] Potter, *India's Political Administrators*, p. 157, quoting the Shah Commission Interim Report II (1978), p. 142.

had reached alarming proportions in most Indian states. The commission identified several cases in which corrupt or politically connected junior officers had their more honest seniors transferred, and one case in which a state's inspector general (the most senior police officer) was demoted to an insignificant post when he refused to make large numbers of politically motivated transfers.[41]

The non-Congress parties that began to form state governments with greater frequency after 1967 were no less likely to misuse the state administrations than the Congress. In some ways they were perhaps more likely since they felt the need to reshape administrations in which Congress allies in the administration were already entrenched. Politicians frequently now conduct mass transfers of officials after they take office, when they install loyal officials or those known to be pliable to the most politically important positions and try to sideline officials thought to be hostile to the regime or not pliable enough. Political competition and the regular alternation of parties has, by lessening politicians' focus on the long-term strength of state institutions and increasing their need to staff the service with reliable officers in the short term, increased the instability in the administration.

In the 1980s and 1990s, the political interference with daily law-and-order decisions has remained high across Indian states. Politicians frequently transfer officials for disobeying their (almost always verbal) illegal orders. For example, a police inspector in Bihar was removed from his post in 1986 for continuing to investigate a government minister's complicity in a massacre even after he had been warned off.[42] And a police official in Uttar Pradesh complained in the early 1980s that he could not arrest people guilty of murder because "Anyone who touches them is transferred."[43]

One thing that made the quality of political interference even worse in the 1980s and 1990s is that politicians were increasingly either in league with criminals or were criminals themselves. In the late 1960s it was acknowledged that some politicians used local criminals to help them win and hold power. But by the 1970s, some criminals had decided to cut out the middleman and enter politics directly. By the early 1980s the head of the Bihar police was complaining that around half a dozen members of the state legislature had criminal records, a figure that in retrospect seems to

[41] *Second Report of the National Police Commission* (New Delhi, 1979), p. 23. The state in question was Madhya Pradesh.

[42] "Transfer Tremors," *India Today*, July 15, 1986, p. 63.

[43] *India Today*, September 30, 1983, pp. 31–32.

mark a golden era of probity for the Bihar Vidhan Sabha.[44] In August 1997 the Election Commission of India, as part of its campaign to disbar candidates with a criminal record from running for office – at present they are allowed to stand as long as their appeals continue, which can be a decade or more – released data showing that 40 sitting members of the 525 strong National Parliament and around 700 of the 4,072 members in the various State Assemblies had a criminal record.[45] The former president of India, Dr. K. R. Narayanan, felt compelled to make an embarrassing public appeal to political parties not to nominate criminals for public office.[46]

The Decline of State Capacity

Press reports, books and articles, and official inquiries, as well as my interviews with officials who have served in the police and civil service, make it clear that there has also been an observable decline in state capacity over the past few decades in terms of all three factors linked in the literature to riot performance: fiscal weakness, police strength and judicial capacity, and frequent transfers of the officers in charge of law and order.

India's state governments have, since the 1960s, become progressively less able to support the costs of state government, including the police. State salaries are sometimes paid late, and in many states there is little money to pay for maintenance, equipment, and such necessary if low-profile expenses as training and housing for low-level government employees. In the early 1960s the states were able to raise 66% of the costs of government from their own state fees and taxes, but by the late 1990s this percentage had dropped to 55%, and most states were running large deficits.[47] Several states are now officially close to bankruptcy, and in June 2001 the state of Kerala publicly announced that it had exhausted the supply of government and international organizations prepared to lend it money.

---

[44] *India Today*, October 31, 1981.

[45] "Discussion Document," National Commission to Review the Workings of the Constitution, New Delhi, September 2000, p. 17.

[46] "Speech on the 50th Anniversary of the Election Commission of India," *Times of India*, January 18, 2001.

[47] Amaresh Bagchi, "Fiscal Management: The Federal Dimension of Developing Countries," in Parthasarathi Shome, ed., *Fiscal Policy, Public Policy and Governance*, Symposium to commemorate the 20th Anniversary of the National Institute of Public Finance and Policy, December 5–6, 1996 (New Delhi: Centax, 1997), p. 282.

One problem is structural: under the Indian Constitution most of the lucrative taxes are collected by the central government, which hampers the states' ability to plan using their own resources. The other problem is clearly political: the Reserve Bank of India has found that deficits have grown so large because of two policies that stem directly from politicians' spending in order to win political support: a massive increase in the number of state employees; and large subsidies provided to the state transport corporations, higher educational institutions, and state electricity boards (SEBs), which provide services at well below their real cost.[48] Farmers, for example, pay an average of Rs. 0.25 per kilowatt hour for electricity, even though the average cost to the SEBs, excluding their capital costs, is Rs. 2.81 per kilowatt hour. As a result of these subsidies, covering the SEB deficits accounted for 10% of total Indian state plan expenditures in 1992–93, a percentage that rose to 30% of all state plan expenditure by 1999–2000.[49]

Despite the fiscal crises in the states the overall numbers of police officers in the major states have remained more or less constant, as we can see from Table 3.1. The notable exceptions to this have been those states which have experienced major uprisings, such as Punjab, where the force increased by almost 50% as a result of the expansion of the police to meet the militancy during the 1980s and early 1990s. But in most major states the total number of police per 1,000 did not increase or decrease dramatically. In qualitative terms though this relative stability in terms of police numbers may mask a decline over time. One issue is that an increasing proportion of police officers are now diverted away from general law-and-order duties to guard politicians' ever increasing demands for bodyguards, to guard government buildings, as well as to man the ever expanding police bureaucracy. Another issue is that state governments have not made heavy investments in the equipment and technology and housing for the police forces.

The postindependence nadir for the police forces was in the 1970s. In May 1979 years of police unhappiness over pay, conditions, and political interference culminated in a massive wave of police strikes throughout India – in Punjab, Haryana, Chandigarh, Himachal Pradesh, Andhra Pradesh, Bihar, Delhi, Gujarat, Kerala, Maharashtra, Orissa, Tamil Nadu,

---

[48] *Reserve Bank of India Bulletin*, February 1998 (Supplement: Finances of State Governments, 1997–98).

[49] Montek S. Ahluwalia, "State Level Performance under Economic Reforms in India," Stanford CREDR Working Paper, March 2001.

Table 3.1. *Police Strength in the States*

State	Police per 1,000 Inhabitants			Change in Force	
				1970s to	1980s to
	1970s	1980s	1990s	1980s	1990s
Andhra Pradesh	0.89	0.91	0.99	1%	9%
Arunachal Pradesh	2.08	3.12	4.37	50%	40%
Assam	1.67	1.88	1.91	13%	2%
Bihar	0.90	0.91	0.88	1%	−4%
Delhi	4.00	4.27	4.71	7%	10%
Goa	2.22	2.37	2.11	7%	−11%
Gujarat	1.54	1.54	1.44	0%	−6%
Haryana	1.39	1.46	1.59	4%	10%
Himachal Pradesh	1.83	1.96	2.15	7%	10%
Jammu and Kashmir	2.71	3.48	3.70	28%	7%
Karnataka	0.99	1.08	1.10	9%	2%
Kerala	0.89	1.01	1.21	13%	20%
Maharashtra	1.49	1.62	1.63	9%	1%
Meghalaya	3.42	3.91	3.85	14%	−2%
Mizoram	4.06	4.82	6.62	19%	37%
Manipur	5.26	5.67	5.94	8%	5%
Madhya Pradesh	1.21	1.41	1.30	16%	−8%
Nagaland	12.05	14.07	12.88	17%	−8%
Orissa	1.04	1.08	1.01	4%	−6%
Punjab	1.73	1.87	2.77	8%	49%
Rajasthan	1.34	1.24	1.16	−7%	−7%
Sikkim	4.91	5.66	6.17	15%	9%
Tamil Nadu	0.97	1.05	1.15	8%	10%
Tripura	2.96	3.20	3.45	8%	8%
Uttar Pradesh	1.06	1.19	1.10	12%	−8%
West Bengal	1.35	1.22	1.09	−9%	−11%

and Rajasthan. Only after these strikes did chief ministers decide to take some steps to improve pay and conditions. Things have improved since the late 1970s, but by common consent the underlying problems of a lack of investment in training, equipment, and infrastructure still remain.

The decline in the speed and effectiveness of the judicial system has been much more serious, according to most government and independent inquiries. In the preindependence period the courts were expected to prosecute and convict criminal cases within four months of their being filed, but since the mid-1950s the court system has become increasingly clogged.[50] In the early 1950s the realization that the courts were building up arrears of cases prompted the central government to launch an enquiry headed by the then attorney general, M. C. Setalvad, who recommended such steps as an end to political interference with judicial appointments, the prompt appointment of judges to vacancies (politicians had often delayed appointments for months or years), new appointments and courts, and an increase in financial resources to turn the situation around.[51]

Unfortunately none of these recommendations has been fully implemented, and as a result in the decades since the delays and backlogs in the judicial system have become worse: Table 3.2 shows statistics I collected on the rise in the high courts' backlog between 1976 and 1996. In all cases the rise in pending cases has far outstripped India's circa 55% rate of population growth between these years. By 1996 no major state was able to clear a majority of its cases within a year, and in some states, such as West Bengal and Uttar Pradesh, only a tiny minority of cases was heard within a year. In five major states – Punjab and Haryana, West Bengal, Uttar Pradesh, and Gujarat – more than 10% of the cases pending in the high courts in 1996 were more than 10 years old, and in West Bengal 34% of all pending cases were more than 10 years old.

As political interference and state regime changes have increased in recent years, so has the number of transfers. The timing of transfers – coming immediately after changes in government, with officers frequently being told at short notice or outside office hours – makes it obvious that they have little to do with their stated purpose of "tuning up" the administration. In fact, politicians' need to create punishment posts to which to transfer officers punitively without breaking service seniority rules has led to the deliberate creation of permanent positions that have a high nominal rank but no real power, such as the police deputy inspector general ranks of "DIG Housing," and "DIG Fire Fighting," and various "Director, Vigilance" posts in State Corporations.[52]

---

[50] Law Commission of India, *Seventy-Seventh Report on Delay and Arrears in Trial Courts* (November 1978), p. 3.

[51] Law Commission of India, M. C. Setalvad, Chairman, *Fourteenth Report (Reform of Judicial Administration)* (Government of India, Ministry of Law, n.d.), pp. 65–69.

[52] As Dharam Vir, the former head of the National Police Commission, put it, "Instead of one D.G.[director general], even small states like Haryana and Tripura and such like have four, sometimes five D.G.s. As new Governments came in the old D.G. was shifted and another person of their liking was brought in. The salary and other perks could not be touched,

Table 3.2. *Declining Judicial Capacity*

| | Total Pending Cases | | | Increase, 1976 to 1996 | Cases Pending in 1966 | |
| | | | | | Less Than 1 Year | More Than 10 Years |
	1976	1986	1996			
Jammu and Kashmir	3,846	35,945	96,414	2,407%	24%	4%
Orissa	5,964	37,854	66,820	1,020%	41%	3%
Andhra Pradesh	14,390	86,137	135,621	842%	31%	0%
Kerala	24,427	120,890	217,823	792%	39%	0%
Gujarat	12,289	52,623	91,953	648%	29%	12%
Tamil Nadu	42,078	187,250	310,640	638%	41%	4%
Uttar Pradesh	120,022	288,060	865,455	621%	13%	20%
Delhi	22,908	77,191	153,537	570%	17%	21%
Assam	6,190	17,880	33,018	433%	42%	0%
Rajasthan	20,254	48,921	97,768	383%	31%	5%
Maharashtra	50,099	133,245	234,058	367%	21%	8%
Himachal Pradesh	4,415	8,820	17,166	289%	41%	0%
Punjab	43,542	53,568	161,562	271%	25%	11%
Karnataka	43,130	66,741	150,965	250%	24%	1%
West Bengal	76,866	156,447	264,312	244%	10%	34%
Bihar	30,832	56,904	93,310	203%	35%	7%
Madhya Pradesh	42,723	53,888	86,142	102%	27%	3%

Sources: 79th Report on Delay and Arrears in High Courts and Other Appellate Courts (Law Commission of India, May 10, 1979), appendix 7, p. 98–99; *124th Report on the High Court Arrears: A Fresh Look* (Law Commission of India, 1990). Data for Patna, Rajasthan, are for December 31, 1985, for Allahabad and Kerala for June 30, 1986, and for Bombay, Andhra Pradesh, Delhi, Punjab and Haryana, Gujarat, Orissa, Jammu and Kashmir, and Sikkim for June 30, 1987; *Annual Report, 1997–1998, Ministry of Law, Justice and Company Affairs* (Government of India, 2001), Annexure X, "Age-Wise Pendency of Cases in High Courts (As on 31-12-1996)," p. 57.

In the 1970s the Police Commission collected data on the turnover of senior officers in the major states (Table 3.3) and found that the average duration in the job for superintendents of police, the main officials in charge of the police in a district, had dropped dramatically since independence – when

but they created new positions such as D.G. (Fire fighting), D.G. (Housing), funny names were given for the Director General and now we have as many D.G.s as used to be I.G.s before and there is no coordination because everybody can be shifted without any notice by the powers that be." *National Police Commission: Its Relevance Today*, papers and discussions at seminar organized by Nehru Centre and Hindustani Andolan, April 19, 1997 (Mumbai: Nehru Centre, 1997), p. 11.

Table 3.3. *Frequency of Police Transfers in Major States, 1973–1977*

Rank	Average Duration in Post	Comments
Inspector general	1 year 8 months	In one state 6 inspectors were changed, and in three states 5. were changed.
Superintendent of police	1 year 7 months	In one state duration is as low as 11 months.
Subinspector	1 year 2 months	In one state duration is as low as 7 months, and in three others it was 10 months.

Source: Second Report of the National Police Commission (New Delhi: Government of India, 1979), p. 24.

three-year postings were frequent – to less than a year and seven months. The commission came across one unlucky police officer who broke down in front of them while describing how he had been transferred 96 times in 28 years.[53] Despite the sorry situation in the mid-1970s, a central government investigation into police effectiveness headed by former home secretary K. Padmanabaiah in 2000 found that things have got considerably worse since then across India's states. Padmanabaiah reports that "Interference and transfers right from SHO (station house officer) level onwards has reached such a level that the average tenure of an SP and DM is about four months."[54]

Frequent transfers of officials from district to district have reduced both the incentives for an individual officer to work hard to understand a district and deal with its problems as well as to reduce the "institutional memory" within each local administration. Officials have little incentive to get to know a district and take decisions that will only bear fruit in the medium to long term when they might be transferred at any moment.[55] And frequent transfers even remove the institutional memory in local administration by

[53] *Second Report of the National Police Commission* (New Delhi: Government of India, 1979), p. 24.
[54] "Transfers Undermine Police Control: Panel," *Times of India*, August 31, 2000.
[55] After the Congress Party dissolved nine state assemblies in 1980, for example, it was reported that 2,000 bureaucrats were incapable of making decisions because "Each one of us goes to the office with the apprehension that he will be transferred by the evening." *India Today*, April 1–15, 1980, p. 21.

leaving senior police officials unfamiliar with local troublemakers, militants, criminals, and potential trouble spots within their districts.

Are Growing State Weakness and Hindu-Muslim Violence Related?

Scholars are undoubtedly correct when they argue that most Indian states have become weaker since the 1960s, using indicators that measure politicization, corruption, and fiscal instability. But this institutional weakness is so widespread across India that it cannot explain state-level and temporal variation in Hindu-Muslim violence. Even those states with the very weakest state governments, such as Bihar and Uttar Pradesh, seem still to possess the basic state capacity to prevent violence when and if officials are given clear directions to do so by their political leadership. The fact that we see sharp differences in levels of communal violence from one elected regime to the other suggests that the problem is not so much state capacity – most states still seem to possess at least the limited capacity they need to prevent Hindu-Muslim riots – as the instructions given by politicians to state officials to protect or not to protect minorities.

Even in the very weakest Indian states, in which institutional decay and political interference is acknowledged to be worst, the number of Hindu-Muslim riots is not consistently high or low, as we might expect it to be if state strength were the most important factor in explaining ethnic riots. Instead, the number of Hindu-Muslim riots seems to vary dramatically depending on the orders given by the political party in power.[56] Independent commissions in low-violence states such as Tamil Nadu and Kerala complain about police interference just as much as those in the North or West.[57] Political interference in Tamil Nadu became so widespread under the AIADMK (All India AnnaDravida Munnetra Kazhagam) government of M. G. Ramachandran in the early 1980s, that seven IAS and IPS officers took the unprecedented step of retiring en masse from the services. One of

---

[56] Even if we make the argument that state capacity would not necessarily lead to consistently high or low levels of communal violence – because there would still be local variation in the precipitants of violence – my argument that state capacity is not the crucial factor in explaining variation is still valid, because in many states the level of communal violence drops as low as zero under some regimes. This indicates that states do have the capacity to prevent violence.

[57] See extracts from 1971 Tamil Nadu police commission in "Political Interference and Misuse of Police," in S. K. Ghosh and K. F. Rustamji, eds., *Encyclopaedia of Police in India*, vol. 2, sec. A (New Delhi: Ashish, 1994), pp. 855–80.

the officers, K. J. M. Shetty, protested that his political masters had transferred him every two or three months.[58] Yet Tamil Nadu has performed
very well in preventing violence in the 1990s.

Even Bihar, which is generally agreed to have the weakest state administration in India, has been able to prevent Hindu-Muslim violence
when its government has made this a priority. Administrators in Bihar –
especially after the murder of a district magistrate by politicians in 1995 –
may find their capacity for independent action limited, and political retribution has made many reluctant to take action against anyone they think
might be politically connected.[59] But the number of Hindu-Muslim riots in Bihar nonetheless fell sharply after Laloo Prasad Yadav took office
as chief minister in 1989. In 1992, when Hindu-Muslim riots broke out
throughout India after the destruction of the Ayodhya mosque, Bihar was
one of the few states to remain peaceful. Laloo Yadav, when asked to explain why Bihar had been so quiet despite its woeful record of past riots,
explained how his government had arrested returning militants from Uttar
Pradesh (the site of Ayodhya) before they could reach their towns and
villages, and how he had threatened all district magistrates and police station officers with the loss of their jobs if they allowed any riots to break
out in their towns. "The political will of the state government" he said,
"was clear."[60]

State Capacity

In terms of specific concrete indicators of state capacity, there also seems
to be no clear link between institutional capacity and levels of violence. In
terms of fiscal health, for example, the five states of Uttar Pradesh, Tamil
Nadu, West Bengal, Andhra Pradesh, and Kerala are in the worst financial
shape and accounted for 85.6% of the country's consolidated state revenue
deficits in 1997–98, the result of years of overspending.[61] Yet there seems
to be no clear correlation between a state's fiscal weakness and its level
of violence in the 1980s and 1990s. Among the high-deficit states Uttar

[58] *India Today*, October 16–31, 1980, pp. 36–37.

[59] For a classic survey of Bihar's problems, see the late Arvind N. Das's *The Republic of Bihar* (New Delhi: Penguin, 1992).

[60] Laloo Prasad Yadav, *Business India*, January 18–31, 1993, p. 44.

[61] *Reserve Bank of India Bulletin*, February 1998 (Supplement: Finances of State Governments: 1997–1998), p. 15.

Pradesh is a high-violence state, and Andhra and West Bengal are rated medium, however, Kerala and Tamil Nadu have some of the lowest levels of communal violence.

Nor does there seem to be a clear relationship between the strength of a state's police force, its judicial capacity, and its level of violence. In Table 3.4 I present some data on police strength, judicial capacity, and state levels of violence from the 1990s. This table shows that some of the states with the lowest levels of police per 1,000 and most overloaded judicial systems also have some of the lowest levels of riots and deaths. The low levels of violence in the three states of Punjab, Himachal Pradesh, and Haryana can be explained by the fact that these three states now have hardly any Muslims, as a result of the partition massacres of 1947. The most notable remaining case is West Bengal, which has 1.1 police officers per 1,000 population, toward the low end for major states, as well as a sclerotic judicial system, the most backlogged in India, in which 34% of the pending cases in the high courts in 1996 were more than 10 years old. Yet despite this West Bengal in the 1990s has a low level of riots and deaths. At the other extreme, the high-violence states, we see that Maharashtra and Gujarat have high levels of violence despite their relatively high levels of police provision (1.6 and 1.4 per 1,000, respectively) and court systems that are overloaded at only an average level.[62] The lack of a clear relationship between indicators of police strength, judicial capacity, and violence is not simply a function of the fact that these data are from the 1990s: I have also collected the same data for the 1970s and 1980s, and the same lack of pattern persists.

I am certainly not claiming that the judicial system's ability to handle quickly the prosecution and conviction of those guilty of rioting has not declined since independence. In fact, some data I have been able to collect on prosecution and conviction rates over time (Table 3.5) suggest that there has been a measurable decline in the numbers convicted.[63] Although conviction rates in a few preindependence cases seem to have been around 25%, the most complete data I have been able to find – for the whole state of the United Provinces for 1927 – suggest that fewer that 10% of those arrested

---

[62] It might be argued that backlogs in the courts are even a deterrent, since arrest usually means a substantial term of imprisonment while under trial, even if one is ultimately released or found innocent.

[63] I say "suggests" because systematic data on whether rioters today face a greater risk of arrest, prosecution, and conviction is impossible to obtain, because we never know exactly what proportion of the total number of rioters are arrested and prosecuted.

Table 3.4. *Police Strength, Judicial Capacity, and Riots in the 1990s*

	Police per 1,000	Armed Police per 1,000	Riots per 10 Million	Killed per 10 Million	Total Pending Cases in the High Courts	Cases Pending	
						1 Year or Less	10 Years or More
Himachal Pradesh	2.1	0.6	0.000	0.000	17,166	41%	0%
Punjab	2.8	0.5	0.000	0.000	161,562	25%	11%
Kerala	1.2	0.2	0.014	0.023	217,823	39%	0%
Haryana	1.6	0.2	0.016	0.031	161,562	25%	11%
Tamil Nadu	1.2	0.1	0.014	0.033	310,640	41%	4%
Orissa	1.0	0.2	0.025	0.067	66,820	41%	3%
West Bengal	1.1	0.3	0.019	0.107	264,312	10%	34%
Rajasthan	1.2	0.2	0.018	0.143	97,768	31%	5%
Bihar	0.9	0.2	0.031	0.162	93,310	35%	7%
Madhya Pradesh	1.3	0.4	0.016	0.286	86,142	27%	3%
Andhra Pradesh	1.0	0.1	0.020	0.331	135,621	31%	0%
Uttar Pradesh	1.1	0.2	0.049	0.524	865,455	13%	20%
Karnataka	1.1	0.2	0.107	0.547	150,965	24%	1%
Maharashtra	1.6	0.2	0.040	1.337	234,058	21%	8%
Gujarat	1.4	0.3	0.231	1.780	91,953	29%	12%

Sources: Police per 1,000 calculated from census data and annual reports of *Crime in India*, 1990–95; *Annual Report, 1997–1998, Ministry of Law, Justice and Company Affairs* (Government of India, 2001), Annexure X, "Age-Wise Pendency of Cases in High Courts (As on 31-12-1996)," p. 57. Riot data for 1990–95 from Varshney and Wilkinson dataset.

Table 3.5. *Arrests, Prosecutions, and Convictions after Communal Riots*

Year: Riot	Court Cases	Convictions	Convictions to Cases Tried	Convictions to Cases Registered
1924: Khairuddinpur (UP)	26	4	15.4%	—
1924: Kandhla (UP)	39	10	25.6%	—
1924: Shahjahanpur (UP)	118	30	25.4%	—
1924: Lucknow (UP)	29	10	34.5%	—
1927: UP (whole state)	581	50	8.6%	—
1931: 4 villages near Kanpur	—	—		—
1957: Hospet (KA)	47	25	53.2%	—
1964: Rourkela (BI)				
Jainpur village	27	4	14.8%	—
1967: (Gorakhpur dt., UP)	25	16	64.0%	—
1970: "Place A"	6	3	50.0%	27.3%
1970: "Place B"	35	8	22.9%	4.9%
1967: "Place C"	15	5	33.3%	13.2%
1980: Moradabad (UP)	125	6	4.8%	1.5%
1983: Hyderabad (AP)	146		2.0%	0%
1984: Bhiwandi (MA)				
Dabgarwad	185	4	2.2%	0.7%
1985: (Ahmedabad)	63	0	0%	—
1984: Kalyan (MA)	63	0	0%	0.0%
1989: Bhagalpur (BI)	251	29	11.6%	3.5%
1985: Ahmedabad (GU)	63	0	0%	—
1992–93: Bombay (MA)	42	8	19.1%	0.4%

Sources: UPSA GAD, file no. 438/1927 (figures for those convicted for 1927 riots are as of January 1928); "Ujagar and others v. Emperor," *AIR* 1933 Allahabad, pp. 834–35; *AIR* February 1961 Mysore 57 (V 48 C13) "P. Abdul Sattar and Others v. State"; "Manilal Sahu and others v. State" 1969 *Cri.L. J.* 990 (vol. 75 C. N. 274) *AIR* 1969 Orissa 176 (v 56 c59); *AIR* Supreme Court 2246 Sherey & Others v. State of UP, Respondent/also in 1991 *CRI.L. J.* 3289 Sherey & Others v. State of UP; *Sixth Report of the National Police Commission* (New Delhi Government of India, 1981); P. R. Rajgopal, *Communal Violence in India* (New Delhi: Uppal Publishing House, 1987), pp. 75–93; *Sixth Annual Report of the Minorities Commission* (from 1-4-1983 to 31-3-1984), pp. 313–26; 1991 1(SCC) "Dilaver Hussain v. State of Gujarat"; 1995 *Cri.L. J.* 2355 (Bombay High Court) Babu Hamidkhan Mestry, Appelant v. State of Maharashtra; RS Appendix 159 (1991) p. 246; *EPW*, February 10, 1990, pp. 305–7; *Hindustan Times*, May 27, 2000; Supreme Court Cases (1991) 1 "Dilaver Hussain and others versus State of Gujarat and Another"; *Hindu*, May 12, 1998; "The Committee for the Protection of Democratic Rights v. The Chief Minister of the State of Maharashtra," JT 1996 (10) S.C. 538.

for rioting in the preindependence period were convicted. Partly this low conviction rate is because proving that individuals are guilty of the crime of rioting, rather than simply present in an area during a riot, has always been difficult, especially given laws of evidence that place less weight on the evidence of "hostile" groups in such cases.[64] The conviction rates in the colonial era probably overestimate the effectiveness of the state, because we know that many of those convicted in large riots in the colonial period were later prematurely released in order to "restore harmony" between the communities or (after 1936) at the instance of elected provincial governments.[65]

Since independence these low prosecution rates have declined further. The ways the data are sometimes presented sometimes makes it seem as if the state has become more effective since independence, because convictions as a percentage of cases brought to trial look quite high. But this ignores the fact that most people who have been arrested and have cases registered against them are now not brought to trial, which is a sharp departure from in the colonial period, when the norm was for arrested rioters to come up for trial and sentencing within a year of the offense. The percentage of convictions to those arrested seems to be 1% or less in the majority of the postindependence cases (the exception is a 1964 riot in a village in Gorakhpur district) for which we have data.

But despite the drop in prosecution and conviction rates – to say nothing of the massive increase in the length of time it takes for cases to come up for trial – it seems unlikely that the prosecution and conviction rates explain much of the cross-state and historical variation in Hindu-Muslim violence. As Table 3.5 shows, and as a recent multicountry study by Horowitz confirms, prosecution and arrest rates for communal violence throughout the world have always been relatively low, and therefore it is doubtful if calculations about the marginal likelihood of prosecution affect the individual rioter very much.[66] The primary means by which governments prevent riots is not by prosecuting the guilty after the fact but by taking prompt preventive action and by being prepared to use force to break up riots once they have broken out.

If we try to assess independently the degree of state weakness in a state, we find that those periods of the greatest institutional weakness do not, as

---

[64] See *Babu Hamidkhan Mestry v. State of Maharashtra*, Bom C.R. (1995) 1, pp. 340–42, where the defendant was acquitted of participating in the Thane riots of 1986 on appeal because the prosecution could not satisfy the Supreme Court's 1965 requirement that multiple impartial witnesses testify as to his guilt.

[65] Suranjan Das, *Communal Riots in Bengal, 1905–1947* (Delhi: Oxford University Press, 1993), pp. 260–61, nn. 10 and 29.

[66] Donald L. Horowitz, *The Deadly Ethnic Riot* (Berkeley: University of California Press, 2001), pp. 364–66.

an institutional theory would predict, coincide with the years of greatest communal violence. In Uttar Pradesh, for example, I found wide agreement in my interviews with politicians and members of the UP police and civil services that the institutional nadir of the state's law-and-order forces was during the 1970s.[67] The Pradeshik Armed Constabulary (PAC), the state's main antiriot force, had been founded during World War II as an elite military-trained strike force, with pay considerably above that of the rest of the UP police and a generous daily allowance. But in the 1960s the PAC was progressively starved of money and equipment. The daily allowance, set at 5 Rs. in 1942, was not raised until 1971.[68] The force became something of a dumping ground for officers who were thought to be incompetent or regarded as too honest or inflexible for their own good. According to one well-informed source, by the 1970s the police did not even have ammunition for firing range practice, with the result than when the time came for their firing tests only two in five men could pass. The superior officers chose to pass the men anyway because they did not want to be blamed for the deterioration in the service.[69]

In early 1973 several PAC units refused to obey orders to perform guard duty when Mrs. Gandhi visited the state, and then in June the force as a whole mutinied over pay and conditions. Armed units in Lucknow set fire to the university and rampaged throughout the surrounding area.[70] The mutiny was only put down after 100 PAC men had been killed in gun battles with the Indian army. For the following three years, the force was basically unfit for duty while internal investigations into the mutiny continued and ringleaders were prosecuted. Meanwhile, the effectiveness of the rest of the state's police force was simultaneously weakened because it had seen the government give the PAC improved pay and conditions only after the force mutinied. After 1973 the civilian police in Uttar Pradesh therefore launched a series of police strikes and agitations over poor pay and conditions, which eventually culminating in a statewide police strike in 1979.

If an institutional strength theory of ethnic violence is correct, then the mid-1970s ought to have been one of the most violent periods in UP history. The costs associated with ethnic mobilization were, after all, dramatically

---

[67] Interviews with ex-PAC officers and UP police officers, New Delhi and Bareilly, July and August 1995.

[68] Interview, with ex-DIG PAC, New Delhi, July 24, 1995.

[69] Interview with ex-PAC officer, Delhi, August 1995.

[70] *India Today*, June 16–30, 1979.

Table 3.6. *State Transfer Rates and Hindu-Muslim Riots, 1976–1985*

	Proportion of IAS Officers in Posts for Less Than 1 Year (average)	Average Riots per 10 Million per Month	Average Killed per 10 Million per Month
West Bengal	41.33	0.006	0.025
Maharashtra	49.89	0.011	0.014
Gujarat	50.83	0.130	0.450
Kerala	51.56	0.013	0.000
Madhya Pradesh	54	0.075	0.352
Tamil Nadu	54	0.014	0.024
Himachal Pradesh	54.11	0.000	0.000
Karnataka	56	0.030	0.047
Bihar	56.22	0.019	0.237
Uttar Pradesh	58.33	0.031	0.218
Rajasthan	60.22	0.002	0.000
Andhra Pradesh	60.33	0.041	0.240
Haryana	63.11	0.000	0.000

Source: Riot data collected by Wilkinson and Varshney; transfer data from David Potter, "IAS Mobility Patterns," *Indian Journal of Public Administration* 33, no. 4 (1987), pp. 845–56.

lowered by the presence of an ineffective police force and indecisive state leadership. Yet there were virtually no Hindu-Muslim riots in Uttar Pradesh during these years. In 1973 there were two small riots, in which two people were killed, and 1974–75 was also exceptionally quiet – one small riot took place in which no deaths occurred. In 1979, the year in which the police general strike took place, there was only one reported Hindu-Muslim riot in Uttar Pradesh.

The lack of a connection between indicators of state strength and the prevalence of riots is also evident if we look at transfer rates (Table 3.6), which many argue are positively correlated with Hindu-Muslim violence. At the aggregate level, if we compare some systematic data on transfers collected by David Potter for the period 1976–85 with some systematic riot data for the same period, we find that transfer levels were actually slightly *higher* in the low-violence states of Kerala and Tamil Nadu than they were in the most violent states in India, Gujarat and Maharashtra.[71]

[71] David Potter, "IAS Mobility Patterns," *Indian Journal of Public Administration* 33, no. 4 (1987), pp. 845–56.

Table 3.7. *Transfer Frequency and Hindu-Muslim Riots in Uttar Pradesh, 1988–1995*

Year: Ministry	Transfers per Month	Riots per Month	Deaths per Month
1988–89: Congress (N. D. Tiwari)	36.8	0.5	5.2
1989–91: Samajwadi Party (M. S. Yadav)	42.9	1.8	16.4
1991–92: BJP (K. Singh)	28.9	0.3	1.8
1992–93: President's Rule (Congress)	45.8	0.6	16.8
1994–95: SP-BSP (M. S. Yadav)	45.2	0.4	0.6
1995: BSP-BJP (Mayawati)	47.0	0.1	0.0
AVERAGE	41.1	0.6	6.8

Sources: India Today, November 15, 1992, pp. 67–68; July 31, 1995: *Pioneer*, December 17, 1995; *Frontline*, August 27, 1993.

A finer-grained study I conducted that compared transfer rates and violence across several administrations in Uttar Pradesh in the 1990s found the same lack of a relationship between transfer frequency and violence. In Uttar Pradesh, as we can see in Table 3.7, the 1991–92 regime of Kalyan Singh, the 1994–95 regime of Mulayam Singh Yadav, and the 1995 government of Ms. Mayawati were all highly successful in controlling the level of Hindu-Muslim violence in Uttar Pradesh. Especially remarkable is the success of the 1994–95 coalition governments led by Mulayam Singh Yadav and Ms. Mayawati, because these regimes were excoriated in the Indian press for their institutional weakness, corruption, and lawlessness. Under the Yadav regime, 33 of the ruling Samajwadi Party's MLAs (one-quarter of its members) had criminal records, as did 13 MLAs from its coalition partner, the Bahujan Samaj Party (BSP). The BSP's Uma Kant Yadav, the honorable member for Jaunpur, was the prime suspect in an astonishing 44 cases, including several for murder and abduction.[72]

In institutional terms these UP governments had the wrong politicians and took all the "wrong" actions. They transferred unprecedentedly large numbers of senior bureaucrats and police officers in a short period of time (814 and 329, respectively), many of them allegedly because of their caste. The Mayawati-led BJP-BSP coalition for example, transferred 57 IAS officers and 108 IPS officers in only 18 days and replaced 60% of them with officers from Mayawati's own Scheduled Caste.[73] And yet these

---

[72] *Hindustan Times* (Lucknow), April 12, 1993.
[73] *India Today*, July 15, 1995, pp. 23–26.

two governments were both able to deliver on their promise of a state largely free from Hindu-Muslim violence.

The lack of a clear connection between transfer rates and riots should not be a surprise. The fact is that transfer rates alone tell us little about *why* officers are transferred. Transfers might indicate a regime that is prepared to allow antiminority violence: but they might also reflect a regime's determination to prevent Hindu-Muslim violence by taking punitive action against officials who fail to prevent riots. An example of the former type of transfers comes from Gujarat in 2002, where the director general of police reportedly complained that several senior police officials in Gujarat had been transferred out of their districts by the Modi government because they had prevented violence, suspended negligent police officers, and arrested riot instigators regardless of how connected they were to the ruling party.[74] For an example of the latter type of transfer we could point to the policy of the Mulayam Singh Yadav government in Uttar Pradesh in the 1990s, which publicly announced that it would automatically transfer the senior local officials in a district if they failed to bring a riot under control within 24 hours. As a result of this policy, which is also in force in Bihar and West Bengal, the DM and SSP of Aligarh, Mr. Gangadin Yadav and Mr. Bijendra Singh, were transferred after failing to control quickly a 1995 riot in the town, despite the fact that no one held they had acted in a biased manner toward the minorities.[75]

Conclusion

There is no doubt that Indian state administrations have often failed to prevent communal violence. We should not infer from this, however, that local administrations are too weak to prevent violence when given clear directions from their political masters. There is an important distinction to be made between state strength and capacity on the one hand and state performance on the other. Independent inquiries and newspaper investigations into the worst outbreaks of Hindu-Muslim violence have found that in almost all cases local police officers and magistrates had the forces available

---

[74] The transferred officials were the superintendent of police (SP) of Kutch, Vivek Srivastav, Bhavnagar SP Rahul Sharma, Banaskantha district SP Himanshu Bhatt, and DCP (Zone IV), Ahmedabad City, P. B. Godhia, "Modi Ties Hands of Cops Who Put Their Foot Down," *Indian Express* (New Delhi), March 26, 2002, p. 1.

[75] Ashgar Ali Engineer, "Aligarh Riots: Unplanned Outburst," *Economic and Political Weekly*, April 1, 1995, pp. 665–67.

to prevent violence (or could have quickly called them in) but that they failed to take preventive action, either because of direct orders from their political masters or because they feared retribution if they acted without first seeking political approval.[76]

After the 1969 Baroda riots, for example, the commission of inquiry found that the local magistrate's delay in calling in reinforcements was due to "what she may have thought to be the correct procedure, namely, to await orders from higher authorities."[77] After the 1969 Ahmedabad riots, the Reddy commission found that the delay in imposing the curfew (a delay during which 250 properties were damaged, 8 religious places attacked, 5 people murdered, and 4 injured) took place because "the Inspector General of Police before advising the Commissioner was not prepared to act on his own and was trying to seek the prior approval of the Government."[78] Independent investigations uncovered the same pattern of politically inspired delay in other riots such as those in Ranchi (1967), Bhagalpur (1989), and Bombay (1992–93).[79] During the serious riots in Bombay in January 1993, the police commissioner, S. K. Bapat, asked the government for permission to call in 40 army columns to control the rioting on the day violence broke out, January 6, 1993, but the government refused for four days before allowing 12 units into the city to perform limited duties.[80] Finally, the illegal destruction of the Babri Masjid in Ayodhya by Hindu militants took place in the presence of 19 companies of the UP Armed Constabulary. When one journalist at the scene asked a policeman why no one was taking any action, the policeman justified not enforcing the law on the grounds that "We had

---

[76] N. S. Saksena quotes a former head of the Central Reserve Police as saying that half of all communal riots take place because of oral orders from politicians. N. S. Saksena, *Communal Riots in India* (New Delhi: Trishul, 1990). A few officers, of course, *are* prepared to act independently to prevent violence regardless of the regime in power, and they demand formal written orders to do anything that might worsen a situation. But these officers are known to regimes and can be transferred out of positions where they might take actions contrary to the interests of those in power.

[77] N. S. Saksena, *Law and Order in India* (New Delhi: Abhinav, 1987), p. 269.

[78] *Report into the Communal Disturbances at Ahmedabad and Other Places in Gujarat on and after 18th September 1969*, Justice P. Jagmohan Reddy (Judge, Supreme Court of India) (Gandhinagar: Gujarat Government Press, 1971), pp. 124–26.

[79] *Report of the Commission of Inquiry on Communal Disturbances, Ranchi-Hatia (August 22–29, 1967)* (1968), pp. 108–9; *Damning Verdict: Reprinting of the Justice B. N. Srikrisna Commission Appointed for Inquiry into the Riots at Mumbai during December 1992–January 1993 and the March 12, 1993 Bomb Blasts* (Mumbai: Sabrang, n.d.), p. 221; Ashgar Ali Engineer, "The Bhagalpur Riots II," *Hindu*, June 23, 1995.

[80] *Damning Verdict: Reprinting of the Justice B. N. Srikrishna Commission*, p. 221.

no instructions."[81] In fact, leaks to the Indian press in 1992 suggested that the state government had gone further and had actually instructed the local police not to fire at the Hindu militants gathered to destroy the mosque.[82]

Political pressure explains why inflammatory acts such as processions through minority neighborhoods are allowed to take place in some states at some times and also why communal violence is often allowed to continue. The Indian criminal code and civil service and police regulations are quite clear that local officials possess the authority to ban processions and even (under section 129 of the Code of Criminal Procedure) to call in the army to disperse illegal crowds, but years of politicization and punishment transfers have made many officers reluctant to take any controversial steps before checking with their political masters, a fear that is well founded.[83] Officials hesitate to prevent violence until they have checked with the state government about whether the violence ought to be stopped and with how much force, preferably without taking measures that might involve action against government supporters.

Why do some states' politicians seem to have the will to prevent antiminority violence whereas others do not? One possibility that I explore in Chapter 5 involves the levels of electoral competition in some governments. Another possibility, explored in the next chapter, is that some states have a higher degree of consociational power sharing, which is associated with a lower level of violence.

---

[81] *Weekend Observer*, December 12, 1993, p. 4.

[82] *Indian Express*, December 20, 1992. Additional evidence to support the idea that the police inaction reflected state orders lies in the fact that the head of the UP police, Mr. Prakash Singh, who had been conscientious in protecting the mosque, was replaced by the BJP government in October 1992.

[83] For example, the superintendent of police (rural) in Ghaziabad, Mr. Rajesh Kumar Rai, was transferred to the Pradeshik Armed Constabulary (an assignment regarded as a punishment posting) in March 1992 by the BJP government after complaints against him by BJP workers in Hapur who were unhappy with his firm action in firing on Hindu nationalists about to attack Muslims during riots in the town in February 1992. *Times of India*, March 9, 1992.

4

The Consociational Explanation for Hindu-Muslim Violence

We have seen that "state capacity" explanations seem to tell us very little about which states successfully prevent Hindu-Muslim violence and which do not. This chapter now turns to one of the other main explanations for patterns of Hindu-Muslim violence: Arend Lijphart's "consociational" power-sharing theory. Lijphart argues in an important 1996 article that India has since independence been a de facto consociational state, by which he means a state with a political "grand coalition" that includes representatives of all the main ethnic groups, a minority veto over important legislation, and minority proportionality in government and employment.[1] Although India's Constitution does not require that minorities such as the Muslims and Sikhs will be included in government, he argues that the dominance of the Congress Party for most of the postindependence period nevertheless allowed these groups to gain effective representation and a veto over decisions harmful to their interests. India's consociational character, he claims, explains the country's relatively low level of ethnic violence, especially during the two decades immediately following independence, when Congress was dominant in Indian politics. Lijphart argues that the level of Hindu-Muslim violence in India has risen since the mid-1960s, however, as India has become "less firmly consociational," the dominant multiethnic Congress Party has lost power in many states, and Indian governments have become much less ethnically representative and respectful of minority rights.

My argument in this chapter is that Lijphart's explanation is wrong for two reasons: first, as I explore in the beginning of the chapter, he miscodes India as consociational from 1947 to 1966, when it was not, and codes

---

[1] Arend Lijphart, "The Puzzle of Indian Democracy: A Consociational Interpretation," *American Political Science Review* 90, no. 2 (1996), pp. 258–68.

India as "less firmly consociational" subsequently, at a time when, by most indicators, India was increasingly consociational. I show that from 1947 to 1966 both lower castes and the important Muslim minority were largely excluded from political power and government employment, and minority opinion was frequently overruled by the majority. Since 1967, however, and increasingly as Congress has lost power in many states in the 1980s and 1990s, India has if anything become more consociational. Growing political competition for lower-caste and minority votes has led to these groups' gaining an increasing share of political power, government employment, and spending.

Second, I show in the second half of the chapter that the Congress decline–consociational thesis cannot account for India's changing levels of communal violence. Lijphart's core argument about how consociational power sharing functions in India – through the dominance of the Congress Party, especially in the 1950s and 1960s – does not seem to stand up to statistical examination. Congress rule is positively related to violence in the Nehruvian period and negatively related to violence only for the 1980s and 1990s – in other words, in the years *after* the period identified by Lijphart as the one in which the party's conflict-managing role was greatest. This is not completely unexpected because Congress has always been a highly heterogeneous party that included communal politicians as well as staunch secularists in its period of greatest dominance.

India as a Test Case for Consociational Theory

The consociational model was first developed in the late 1960s by Arend Lijphart, to explain the puzzle of why Belgium, the Netherlands, and Switzerland were stable and democratic when their religious and ethnic diversity ought, according to many writers at the time, to have led to democratic instability and violence. The answer, he concluded in his 1977 book *Democracy in Plural Societies*, was that these countries had adopted four policies, which he collectively termed consociationalism: including minorities in a political "grand coalition," granting them cultural auton-omy, giving minorities a veto over important legislation, and making ethnic "proportionality . . . the principal standard of political representation, civil service appointments, and allocation of public funds."[2]

---

[2] Arend Lijphart, *Democracy in Plural Societies: A Comparative Exploration* (New Haven: Yale University Press, 1977), p. 25. Lijphart was particularly critical of Alvin Rabushka and

The Consociational Explanation

Since the late 1970s, consociational theory has developed from a *descrip-tion* of conflict-resolution as practiced in Western Europe into an influential set of *policy prescriptions* about how best to reduce ethnic conflict through-out the world. Lijphart and others have identified societies in which they think consociational policies have reduced ethnic conflict (e.g., Malaysia and Colombia, as well as Lebanon and Cyprus before their civil wars), and actively promoted consociationalism as the best policy option for the world's divided societies.[3] In 1985, for example, Lijphart argued that consociational power sharing was the most logical political solution for ethnically divided South Africa.[4] Lijphart's efforts to promote consociational power sharing have been highly successful, especially at convincing the many nongovern-mental organizations (NGOs) and research projects that were established in the 1990s to reduce ethnic conflict. The Carnegie Corporation, the Or-ganization for Security and Cooperation in Europe, and the International Institute for Democracy and Electoral Assistance have all funded projects that identify consociational policies as one of the best established ways to moderate ethnic conflict.[5] Many politicians in new democracies seem to agree that consociational policies are the best way to reduce ethnic vio-lence. In the former Soviet Union, for example, Tatars in the Crimea have argued that consociational policies will reduce conflict with Russians and Ukrainians, and in Moldova politicians agreed in 1994 that a consociational system offered the best chance of reducing ethnic tensions between ethnic Russians, Gagauz, and Moldovans.[6]

India has always been a key test case for both opponents and supporters of the model. Opponents such as Paul Brass argued in the late 1970s and early 1980s that India, because it lacked a *formal* consociational structure – with

Kenneth A. Shepsle, *Politics in Plural Societies: A Theory of Democratic Instability* (Columbus: Charles E. Merrill, 1972).

[3] Arend Lijphart, "Self-Determination versus Pre-Determination of Ethnic Minorities in Power-Sharing Systems," in Will Kymlicka, ed., *The Rights of Minority Cultures* (New York: Oxford University Press, 1995), p. 279, and Lijphart, "South African Democracy: Majori-tarian or Consociational?" *Democratization* 5, no. 4 (1998), pp. 144–50.

[4] Arend Lijphart, *Power-Sharing in South Africa*, Institute of International Studies Policy Papers in International Affairs no. 24 (Berkeley: University of California, 1985), p. 133.

[5] See, e.g., Timothy D. Sisk, *Power Sharing and International Mediation in Ethnic Conflicts* (Washington, D.C.: United States Institute of Peace and the Carnegie Commission of Pre-venting Deadly Conflict, 1996); Peter Harris and Ben Reilly, eds., *Democracy and Deep-Rooted Conflict: Options for Negotiators* (Stockholm: IDEA, 1998).

[6] Andrew Wilson, "The Post-Soviet States and the Nationalities Question," in Graham Smith, ed., *The Nationalities Question in the Post-Soviet States*, 2nd ed. (New York: Longman, 1996), pp. 23–45.

constitutionally guaranteed minority representation in the cabinet, for example – disproved the general argument that consociationalism is the best or only way to achieve a stable, peaceful democracy in a multiethnic society.[7] In the 1970s Lijphart's response to this criticism was simply to concede that India was an exception to his general theory.[8] By the mid-1980s, however, he had modified his view of the Indian case and argued that India was not exceptional because it possessed a few "striking consociational features."[9] After reexamining India in the 1990s, he then made an even bolder argument: that India is a de facto consociational state and, as such, an "impressive confirming case" for consociational theory and for his claim that consociational power sharing reduces ethnic violence.

Lijphart argues that India has managed to control ethnic conflict relatively well because it possesses all four consociational characteristics. For most of the period since independence in 1947, he says, India has been ruled by an ethnically inclusive "grand coalition" (the dominant Congress Party) that grants cultural autonomy to its religious and linguistic minorities; ensures minority "proportionality" in politics, education, and government employment; and gives minorities a veto over important social and religious legislation. Congress governments in New Delhi have, Lijphart says, "accorded shares of ministerships remarkably close to proportional, especially given the constraint of only about twenty positions usually available, to the Muslim minority of about 12% and even the much smaller Sikh minority (roughly 2%), as well as to the different linguistic groups, states, and regions of the country."[10]

These consociational policies explain not only India's relative stability, Lijphart argues, but also why ethnic violence was low after independence in 1947, and why it has risen since the mid-1960s. He says that India was most consociational under Jawaharlal Nehru, who led Congress and the nation from 1947 until his death in 1964. Since Nehru's death, however, and especially since Indira Gandhi became prime minister in 1966, politicians have increasingly threatened to abolish "crucial consociational rules put in place by power-sharing compromises: separate Muslim personal laws, minority

---

[7] Paul R. Brass, "Ethnic Conflict in Multiethnic Societies: The Consociational Solution and Its Critics," in *Ethnicity and Nationalism: Theory and Comparison* (London: Sage, 1991), pp. 333–48.

[8] For his original view of India as a "nonconsociational exception," see Lijphart, *Democracy in Plural Societies*, p. 225.

[9] Lijphart, *Power-Sharing in South Africa*, pp. 102–3.

[10] Lijphart, "The Puzzle of Indian Democracy: A Consociational Interpretation," pp. 259–62.

educational autonomy, and Kashmir's . . . autonomous status." "As Indian Democracy has become less firmly consociational," he argues, "inter-group tensions and violence have increased."[11] He points in particular to the rise in the number of incidents of Hindu-Muslim violence recorded by the Indian Home Ministry. When India was consociational, in the 1950s, the number of Hindu-Muslim incidents in a five-year period was only 339; but by the 1980s, the number of incidents in a five-year period had risen to 2,290, the number of people killed from 112 to 2,350, and the number injured from 2,229 to 17,791.[12]

Although the term "consociationalism" is seldom used in India, many Indians share Lijphart's belief that policies such as a minority veto or ethnic proportionality are effective in reducing a country's level of communal violence. In the 1980s one of the Indian government's main justifications for the decision not to reform Muslim personal law was that overruling the minority veto on this issue would intensify religious violence. On the issue of proportionality, a large number of Indian politicians and journalists and even a few police officers have argued explicitly that a more representative police force and civil service would reduce the country's level of ethnic violence. After large and bloody riots in Gujarat in 1969, for example, the journalist and author Khushwant Singh wrote that the best way to stop communal violence was to ensure that each state's police force contained 15–20% minorities. In 1983, the Gopal Singh Committee on minorities recommended that minority representation be sharply increased in order to increase Muslim confidence in the police and reduce riots.[13] And in the late 1980s, in the aftermath of serious riots in the town of Meerut in which the police allegedly massacred dozens of Muslim youths, Muslim political leader Syed Shahabuddin urged the Home Ministry to prevent riots by increasing Muslim representation in the police force to their proportion in the general population (12%), placing minority policemen in all riot-prone districts, and establishing a special antiriot force with at least 50%

---

[11] As Lijphart's use of the term "less firmly consociational" indicates, he has over the years altered the way in which he measures consociationalism from a dichotomous variable (that is or is not present) to one that is continuous (a state is more or less consociational). Supporters of Lijphart might argue that I ought to judge the effectiveness of the model as it was presented in the mid-1970s rather than the 1990s. My own view is that it is fairer to judge Lijphart on what he regards as the "new and improved" version of consociational theory, especially in reassessing his 1996 article on India.

[12] Lijphart, "The Puzzle of Indian Democracy: A Consociational Interpretation," pp. 259, 263–65.

[13] *Muslim India* 2, no. 18 (June 1984), p. 261.

of its personnel drawn from the Muslim, Christian, Scheduled Caste, and Scheduled Tribe communities.[14]

When Was India Consociational?

Although India *was* in many respects a consociational state before independence, from 1947 to 1966 it was, contra Lijphart, a nonconsociational state, closer to what scholars have termed a "ranked" or a "control" society in which one ethnic group clearly dominates the others.[15] Lijphart miscodes India as consociational from 1947 to 1966 for two reasons. First, he pays too much attention to the actions of the federal government in New Delhi and not enough to those of the state governments, which under the Indian constitution have the primary responsibility for such important issues as law and order, the protection of linguistic minorities, and police recruitment. Second, in part because of his focus on New Delhi, Lijphart infers that India is consociational from reading the Indian Constitution and looking at government *policies* rather than by examining central and state government *actions*. The problem with this is that from 1947 to 1966 there was a substantial gap between Nehru and his successor Lal Bahadur Shastri's promises on minority rights and the actual performance of Congress state governments. Nehru himself was well aware of the problem, and in his public speeches and his letters to chief ministers he often referred to the problem of antiminority bias in the party and in the states. Addressing the All-Indian Congress Committee in May 1958, for example, he said that although "the Congress stood for a secular society, the workers were slipping away from the principles of secularism and becoming more and more communal minded."[16]

Within three years of independence India's central government and most Indian states abolished rules that guaranteed Muslim, Sikh, and Christian proportionality in politics and employment, and they also reneged on

---

[14] Shahabuddin's "Note to the Home Ministry on Measures to Contain Communalism," *Muslim India* 7, no. 79 (July 1989), pp. 317–18, quoted in Omar Khalidi, *Indian Muslims since Independence* (New Delhi: Vikas, 1995), p. 38. See also "IUML: Memorandum of 5 June 1987 to the President of India," *Muslim India* 5, no. 55 (July 1987), p. 296.

[15] The terms are from Horowitz, *Ethnic Groups in Conflict* (Berkeley: University of California Press, 1985), pp. 24–36, and Ian Lustick, "Stability in Deeply Divided Societies: Consociationalism and Control," *World Politics* 31, no. 3 (1979), pp. 325–44.

[16] Partha S. Ghosh, *Cooperation and Conflict in South Asia* (New Delhi: Manohar, 1989), p. 38. See also reports of Nehru's efforts to improve the position of Urdu in Uttar Pradesh in the mid-1950s in "Uttar Pradesh Newsletter," Lucknow, July 22, *Times of India*, July 25, 1953.

preindependence promises to Muslims to promote the Hindustani lingua franca in both Hindi *and* the Urdu style used predominantly (though not exclusively) by Muslims. State governments also restricted Muslims' rights to slaughter cows for food and religious purposes. Although almost every Indian cabinet has had its minority representatives, these men and women were kept well away from positions of real power. Meanwhile, the principle of minority "proportionality" was ignored, minorities' separate political representation was abolished, and Hindu majorities in most Indian states ran roughshod over the minority veto. The overall situation from 1947 to 1966, far from being consociational power sharing, was in fact not that different from the majority-dominated state that existed in Northern Ireland from 1921 to 1972, which Lijphart has criticized for its neglect of Catholic interests.[17] The largest apparent exceptions to this dismantling of proportionality, the benefits extended to the Scheduled Castes and Scheduled Tribes, do not in fact invalidate the general view that India was nonconsociational. This is because, although the Scheduled Castes and Tribes were guaranteed proportional representation in government employment, their political influence within Congress was weak and their actual representation in senior positions was only a tenth of their allotted quota.

Since the late 1960s, however, far from becoming "less firmly consociational," as Lijphart claims, India has in fact become more consociational. This is in large part due to the rise of political parties representing backward- and lower-caste Indians, which have sought to enlist members of religious minorities as part of broad lower-caste coalitions. Due to the electoral success of these coalitions, and the fact that Congress and more recently the BJP have had to match the policies of these parties in order to stay in power, there has been a massive expansion in the number of state and central government programs designed to achieve ethnic proportionality in political representation, government employment, and spending.

India from 1919 to 1947: A Consociational State

As at least two scholars have already noticed, India was in many respects a consociational state during its preindependence period of "responsible

---

[17] Lijphart, "Self-Determination versus Pre-Determination of Ethnic Minorities in Power-Sharing Systems," p. 277.

government."[18] Central and provincial governments observed the consociational principles of minority proportionality in politics and employment; guaranteed cultural autonomy for minorities; and gave the Muslims, India's most important religious minority, an effective veto over important constitutional reforms.

The principle of proportionality was introduced into Indian government through the 1909 Morley-Minto constitutional reforms, which guaranteed Muslims political representation through separate constituencies in which only Muslims could vote. The principle of proportionality then became firmly entrenched through the 1916 Lucknow Pact.[19] At Lucknow, Congress politicians agreed to the Muslim League's demand that, as the reward for league participation in the campaign for greater Indian autonomy, both parties would press the central government to guarantee separate electorates for Muslims and minority overrepresentation in future provincial assemblies. The British accepted the proposals, partly because of their own interest in dividing the opposition, and in 1919 granted disproportionate Muslim representation in newly created assemblies in six Hindu-majority provinces, and Hindu and Sikh overrepresentation in three Muslim-majority provinces. The Lucknow principle of minority overrepresentation was then applied to a host of new municipal councils, district boards, and provincial and central legislatures established in the wake of the 1919 constitutional reforms.[20]

In Bombay, for example, the 20% Muslim minority was guaranteed 33% of the seats in the provincial assembly; in the Central Provinces the 4% Muslim minority was given 15% of the seats, while in Muslim-majority

---

[18] Lustick, "Stability in Deeply Divided Societies: Consociationalism versus Control," pp. 325–44; Ian Talbot, "Back to the Future? The Punjab Unionist Model of Consociational Democracy for Contemporary India and Pakistan," *International Journal of Punjab Studies* 3, no. 1 (1996).

[19] Some elected bodies reserved minority seats before 1916, as in the case of the Amritsar, Multan, and Ambala municipalities, which also had separate electorates for Sikhs, Hindus, and Muslims. But the practice of separate and proportional representation only became widespread after the Lucknow Pact. B. B. Misra, *The Administrative History of India, 1834–1947* (New Delhi: Oxford University Press, 1970), pp. 608–9.

[20] The system used in the UP District Boards Act of 1922 was typical of how the principle of minority "weightage" was applied. Where Muslims were 1% of the population they received 10% of the seats; where they were 1–5% of the population they received 15% of the seats; where they were 5–15% of the population 25% of the seats; and where they were 15–30% of the population they received 30% of the seats. In those districts where Muslims were more than 30% they received the same percentage of seats as their share in the population. Wylie to Wavell, March 9, 1947, IOR L/PJ/5/276.

Punjab the Sikh and Hindu minorities (43% of the province's population) got 49% of the seats.[21] The few princely states that established legislative assemblies in the 1920s and 1930s, such as Travancore, Cochin, and Mysore, followed the example of British India and introduced reserved seats, though not separate electorates, for their own religious and caste minorities. The state of Mysore, for example, reserved seats for Muslims, lower-caste Hindus, and Christians and established additional nominated seats that could be used to represent small communities unable to secure representation through the ballot box.[22] By 1947 Christians, Sikhs, Europeans, Scheduled Castes, Marathi speakers (in Bombay), and in some provinces and princely states "depressed" Hindu castes and Tribal peoples were guaranteed a share of the seats in local legislatures.[23]

Before 1947 the central and provincial governments also observed the principle of ethnic proportionality in government employment. In 1925 the Indian government accepted minority requests to reserve a proportionate share of the jobs for them in the all-India civil service. Muslims, 23.8% of India's preindependence population, were guaranteed a minimum 25% share of central government jobs, with other communities such as Sikhs, Christians, and Anglo-Indians allotted a further 8.3% to 14%, depending on the category of the job.[24] Elected provincial governments were in turn allowed to set their own ethnic quotas, and almost all provinces chose to guarantee local religious minorities – Muslims in northern and southern India, Hindus in Bengal, Hindus and Sikhs in Punjab, and Hindus in the new province of Sind – at least a proportional share of government jobs. Several states also established reservations to ensure that caste and linguistic minorities such as backward castes in Mysore and Madras, Telegu and Malayali speakers in Madras, and Bengali speakers in Bihar were guaranteed

---

[21] *East India (Progress and Condition) Statement Exhibiting the Moral and Material Progress and Condition of India, during the Year 1926–27* (HMSO, 1928), pp. 15–16.

[22] Dirk Kooiman, *Communities and Electorates: A Comparative Discussion of Communalism in Colonial India* (Amsterdam: VU University Press, 1995) p. 58; M. Shama Rao Bahadur, *Modern Mysore* (Bangalore: Higginbothams, 1936), pp. 320–21, 427; and M. J. Koshy, *Constitutionalism in Travancore and Cochin* (Trivandrum: Kerala Historical Society, 1971), p. 154.

[23] For details of these provincial quotas, see table H in Judith Brown, *Modern India: The Origins of an Asian Democracy* (Oxford: Oxford University Press, 1985), p. 281.

[24] This 1925 policy is laid out in the 1934 Home Department Resolution on "Reservation of Posts for Minorities and Backward Classes: Government of India," reprinted in Maurice Gwyer and A. Appadorai, eds., *Speeches and Documents on the Indian Constitution*, vol. 1, *1921–1947* (Bombay: Ernest Benn, 1957), pp. 116–19.

a proportionate share of government jobs. By 1947, helped by these reservations, religious and some caste and linguistic minorities were proportionally
represented, and often overrepresented, in national and provincial government employment. In Madras, for example, reservations introduced in the
1920s led to a steady decline in the share of the Brahmins (3% of the population) in the civil service and a steady rise in the representation of the more
populous backward-caste and Scheduled Caste Hindus.[25] In Bihar, meanwhile, Muslims (10.1% of the population) and Bengali speakers (c. 5%) had
17.8% and 28.5%, respectively, of the senior police positions.[26]

The consociational principles of cultural autonomy and the minority
veto were also observed in preindependence India. Although Indians were
subject to the same civil and criminal codes, Muslims, Hindus, and Sikhs
each administered their own personal laws, and the state guaranteed minority cultural rights such as Muslims' rights to slaughter cows for food and
religious festivals. The Urdu language spoken and written by most literate
northern and central Indian Muslims (and by many Hindus) enjoyed equal
status with Hindi as an official language in the central government and
provincial administration, and it remained dominant in many government
departments, especially the police and the courts, until the end of colonial
rule.[27] As late as July 1947, for example, 9 out of every 10 cases filed by
policemen in the northern range districts of the United Provinces were

---

[25] The share of Brahmins in junior civil service positions, which had been more than 50% at
the beginning of the century, declined sharply after reservations were introduced, to 45%
in 1935 and 28% in 1947. *Report of the Backward Classes Commission Tamil Nadu*, vol. 1, *1970*
(Madras: Government of Tamil Nadu, 1974), pp. 89–90; S. Saraswathi, *Minorities in Madras
State* (Delhi: Impex, 1974), pp. 224–25.

[26] *Bihar Legislative Assembly Debates Official Report*, III, 1–6, 1, March 5,1938, pp. 220–22.

[27] Some explanation of the relationship between Hindi and Urdu might be helpful at this point.
Hindi and Urdu can be thought of as two different styles of the north Indian vernacular,
Hindustani, which was spoken by 42% of the population in 1951. Hindi draws more of its
vocabulary from Sanskrit and is usually written in the Nagari script, while Urdu draws its
vocabulary more from Persian and Arabic and is usually written in a slightly modified version
of the Arabic script. Both Hindi and Urdu can be written in both scripts. During Mughal and
British rule many literate Hindus, especially those who worked in government service, freely
used many words of Arabic and Persian origin, reflecting the Muslim dominance of the
bureaucracy as well as the syncretic culture of much of India. In the late 19th and early 20th
centuries, however, many Hindu politicians and cultural organizations promoted a version
of Hindustani, Hindi, that was written in the Nagari script and that drew almost exclusively
on Sanskrit vocabulary, avoiding "foreign," though often more widely understood, Persian
and Arabic words.

still written in Urdu.[28] Senior national Congress leaders such as Nehru and Gandhi, conscious of Muslim sensitivity over the issue of language, made a point of supporting the most inclusive version of the north Indian lingua franca – Hindustani, written in both the Urdu (Arabic) and Nagari (Sanskrit) scripts – as the future national language. This policy, confirmed in the Congress Party's 1934 constitution, was a clear rejection of the Hindu right's demand for Sanskritized Hindi, in the Nagari script, as the only national language.[29]

The Muslims, India's most important minority, also had a veto over important constitutional reforms at the center. The importance attached to the principle that Muslim agreement was necessary for a constitutional settlement ultimately led to the partition of India when the Muslim League leader's demands for power sharing, including the right of Muslim-majority provinces to secede in the future if they were unhappy with their position in the new federal system, were rejected by Congress. At the provincial level, minorities did not have a legislative veto, but both the 1919 and 1935 constitutional reforms gave governors the "special responsibility for safeguarding the legitimate interests of the minorities," and governors had the power to veto bills or even dissolve provincial assemblies if minorities complained of abuse by the majority.[30]

Finally, the colonial government provided two institutional incentives to ensure the formation of ethnically inclusive "grand coalitions." First, as we have noted, a large percentage of the seats in local and provincial assemblies was reserved for minorities. The hope was that this would make it difficult for parties from the majority community to form governments without substantial minority representation.[31] Second, the 1919 and 1935 constitutional reforms gave the governors a good deal of leeway over which party to invite to form the government after provincial elections. Governors did not necessarily have to pick the party with the largest number of seats, as

---

[28] Of 3,267 cases filed in the northern range in July 1947, 2,889 (88%) were in Urdu, 39 (1%) in English, and 339 (10%) in Hindi. U.P.S.A. Home Police, box 373, file 640/46, "Police Reorganisation Committee."

[29] "Resolutions of the All-India Hindu Mahasabha," *Indian Annual Register, 1938* (Calcutta: Annual Register Office, 1939), 2:339.

[30] *Government of India Act, 1935. Draft of Instrument of Instructions Which It Is Proposed to Recommend His Majesty to Issue to the Governors of Indian Provinces, House of Commons Accounts and Papers, 5 Session, 3 November 1936–22 October 1937*, vol. 20, 1936–37, p. 4.

[31] Of course, another aspect of this policy to bolster minority representation was that (in theory) it made a united front against British rule much less likely.

was the practice in Britain. Instead, they were advised to select those leaders and parties most likely to form ethnically inclusive administrations.[32] The most famous case in which a governor actually passed over the largest party in order to form a more ethnically inclusive administration was in Punjab following the 1946 elections. Although the Muslim League was the largest single party after the elections, Sir Bertrand Glancy instead asked a coalition of Hindu and Sikh parties to join with the few Muslims who had been reelected on the Unionist Party ticket to form a provincial government under Khizar Hyat Tiwana.[33]

India from 1947 to 1966: A Nonconsociational State

From 1947 to 1966, despite several central government initiatives and Nehru's sincere efforts to include minorities in Congress governments at all levels, India was closer to a ranked than a consociational state. In the first few years after independence, the central government and the states abolished the consociational policies that had been in force before 1947. The general feeling among most Congress politicians was that consociational policies were divisive and had led to partition. This feeling, combined with antipathy toward the Muslims over partition, led to the rapid dismantling of minority proportionality in politics and government employment, the non-fulfillment of previous Congress pledges to protect minority languages, and the overruling of the minority veto when minorities such as the Muslims and Sikhs protested over their treatment at the hands of the majority.

The End of Ethnic Proportionality

As far as political representation was concerned, provincial governments began to dismantle consociational protections for important minorities as soon as it became clear in mid-1947 that independence and partition were imminent and that it was no longer necessary to compromise with Muslims at the provincial level in order to further a national political settlement. In April 1947, for example, the Congress rank and file in the United Provinces forced their leaders to go back on a compromise with Muslim League leaders over the *gaon hukumat* (village government) bill, which the Muslim

---

[32] *Government of India Act*, p. 3. These 1936 instructions to the governors were based on instructions first issued in 1919.

[33] Ian Stephens, *Pakistan* (London: Ernest Benn, 1967), pp. 138–40.

League opposed because it introduced joint electorates at the village level.[34] In November, eleven weeks after independence, the UP minister for local self-government introduced two bills that eliminated separate electorates for district boards and town councils. These were also quickly passed by the Assembly over the objections of the Muslim League members.[35] Outside the United Provinces, other states also dismantled separate electorates for local government elections in 1947–48, deliberately preempting the Constituent Assembly's discussions on minority representation in New Delhi. In West Bengal, for example, the new Congress government announced in September 1947 that it would unilaterally introduce joint electorates for the provincial assembly and Calcutta Corporation in November, despite Muslim objections.[36] The process of abolishing minority representation was complete by May 1949, when the central Constituent Assembly, recognizing that the issue had already been effectively decided by state governments, voted to abolish separate electorates and end guaranteed representation for India's religious minorities in national elections.

Minority proportionality in government employment for religious minorities was also abolished within a few years of independence. In the central government the abolition of job reservations for Muslims, Sikhs, and Christians in 1949 reflected Nehru's belief that employment reservations were divisive and resulted in declining standards in government service.[37] Nehru not only supported the abolition of proportionality for religious groups but also wanted the Assembly to go further and abolish the remaining reservations for the Anglo-Indians, Scheduled Castes, and Scheduled Tribes; however, despite his wishes, these reservations were instead "temporarily" extended for 10 years.[38] In the 1950s, when members of the backward castes

---

[34] This Congress-League compromise would have introduced a "family head" electoral system that avoided choosing either joint or separate electorates. *Pioneer*, April 12, 16, 1947.

[35] *Pioneer*, November 7, 1947.

[36] *Pioneer*, September 28, November 8, 1947.

[37] In 1955, for example, Nehru stated that "It is a most undesirable custom to give statutory protection to minorities. It is sometimes right that you should do that to give encouragement, for example, to backward classes, but it is not good in the long run." Speech in Lok Sabha, December 21, 1955; Sarvepalli Gopal, *Jawaharlal Nehru: An Anthology* (Delhi: Oxford University Press, 1983), pp. 521–23.

[38] *Constituent Assembly Debates*, May 26, 1949, p. 331. The Scheduled Caste and Tribe quotas have been renewed by parliament every 10 years since they were introduced. Only the Anglo-Indian reservations proved to be temporary (they ended in 1960), largely because the community was small (and hence electorally unimportant) as well as unpopular because of its support of the British and the privileges the community had received under British rule.

pressed the central government for job reservations, Nehru's home minister rejected their requests by arguing that the caste system was "the greatest hindrance in the way of our progress toward an egalitarian society, and the recognition of specified castes as backward may serve to maintain and perpetuate the existing distinctions on the basis of caste."[39] Nehru himself was even more forceful: "I am grieved," he wrote to the state chief ministers, "to learn how far this business of reservation has gone based on communal or caste considerations. This way lies not only folly, but disaster."[40] He and his cabinet insisted that future eligibility for government assistance had to be based on economic backwardness rather than membership in particular ethnic groups.[41]

In India's states, job reservations were also dismantled in the late 1940s, although the process there reflected less of a Nehruvian desire to reduce the focus on ethnicity than the wish of Hindu majorities to reward their own supporters with jobs (the UP premier recruited the first 1,000 armed policemen from his home region of Kumaon and Garhwal in the summer of 1947) and discriminate against groups that they felt were disloyal or had been unduly favored by the colonial government.[42] As with political reservations, as soon as it became clear that partition was imminent and that broader compromise with the Muslim League was no longer necessary, Congress governments had no compelling political reason to preserve job reservations for religious minorities. These reservations were in any event highly unpopular among Hindus and had been the target of several campaigns by the militant Hindu Mahasabha, which accused the Congress of discriminating against Hindus and publicly urged the Congress governments to dismiss Muslims from the cabinet and administration.[43]

---

[39] Quoted in Marc Galanter, *Competing Equalities: Law and the Backward Classes in India*, 2nd ed. (Delhi: Oxford University Press, 1991), p. 173.

[40] Letter to Chief Ministers, June 27, 1961, in G. Parthasarathi, ed., *Jawaharlal Nehru: Letters to Chief Ministers, 1947–1964*, vol. 5, *1958–1964* (New Delhi: Oxford University Press, 1989), pp. 446–59.

[41] Ibid., and also Galanter, *Competing Equalities*, p. 176. Former cabinet minister N. V. Gadgil reports that Nehru agreed to reinstate proportional Muslim representation in central and state government employment as part of his March 1950 pact with Liaquat Ali Khan of Pakistan. But according to Gadgil, this section of the pact had to be dropped because of deep opposition from within the Indian cabinet. N. V. Gadgil, *Government from Inside* (Meerut: Meenakshi Prakashan, 1968), p. 48.

[42] Wylie to Mountbatten, June 9, 1947, UP Governor's Reports 1947 (IOR) L/PJ/5/276.

[43] Statement of Mahant Digvijaynath, *Pioneer*, October 20, 1947.

In May 1947 the Muslim League government in Sind, which was to become part of Pakistan in August 1947, transferred Hindu employees from some key positions and announced that the proportion of Hindus in government service would be reduced from more than 50% to 30%, their proportion in the population. Congress governments immediately came under intense pressure from their own membership and the Hindu Mahasabha to take "retaliatory measures."[44] There is firm evidence that the Congress national leader, Sardar Patel, was also urging at least one state government to stop employing Muslims entirely until their share dropped to their level in the population.[45] In response to this pressure, Congress governments in the United Provinces, Bihar, and the Central Provinces announced in June 1947 that they would reduce Muslim representation in government service to the Muslim share in the population and end minority reservations completely for higher government appointments.[46]

Given that Muslims were already overrepresented in government employment, this new policy meant in effect that no Muslims would be hired in these states for the foreseeable future. Choudhry Khaliquzzaman, the prominent Muslim League leader, complained to Nehru as early as the autumn of 1947 that the recruiters for 8,000 new police posts in the United Provinces had been told not to take any Muslims.[47] The widespread feeling among Hindus that Muslims were disloyal or might emigrate to Pakistan further reduced the chances of any Muslims being employed in key posts or being recruited to the police. When UP police minister (and future Congress prime minister) Lal Bahadur Shastri announced in October 1947 that he was forming an "absolutely loyal" investigative force to combat anti-state activities, there was no need for him to spell out what "absolutely loyal" meant in terms of ethnic composition.[48] One senior Indian police officer who served in the United Provinces during partition described to me in an interview how "Verbal instructions were given in 1947 by the state government, led by Mr. Pant, not to recruit Muslims in the police. Some of this was resentment at partition, but there was also the feeling that if you

---

[44] *Pioneer*, May 21, 1947.

[45] Vallabhai Patel to Premier G. B. Pant, May 15, 1947, reprinted in B. R. Nanda, ed., *Selected Works of Govind Ballabh Pant*, vol. 11 (Delhi: Oxford University Press, 1998), pp. 489–90.

[46] *Pioneer*, May 21, June 1, 7, 1947.

[47] Choudhry Khaliquzzaman, *Pathway to Pakistan* (Lahore: Longmans Green, 1961), p. 410.

[48] *Pioneer*, October 30, 1947. The paper also reported that Muslim officials were being transferred out of the major cities.

employ them, they'll leave to go to Pakistan, because at this time some police people, without giving notice, would just pack up and go overnight."[49] A decade after independence the general perception that Muslims were not welcome in state employment was so widespread that in 1959 and again in 1961 Prime Minister Nehru felt obliged to write to the state chief ministers urging them to be more open to recruiting Muslims.[50]

The end of job reservations, discrimination in recruitment and employment, and the emigration of large numbers of minority employees to Pakistan sharply reduced Muslim representation in the police and administration. In the United Provinces, renamed Uttar Pradesh in 1950, internal government files reveal that the proportion of Muslims among the senior police force and civil service officers dropped from 40% in 1947 to 7% in 1958.[51] In Bihar, Muslim representation in senior posts dropped from around a third in 1947 to a little more than 5% of the 9,773 posts in 1960, an indication that virtually no Muslims had been recruited in the preceding decade.[52] In Delhi, only 3 Muslim policemen were recruited to the 2,058 strong force in the five years following partition, a period during which the number of Muslims in the force dropped from 1,470 to 56.[53] The fact that many Muslims who went on to successful careers in Pakistan left India several years after partition suggests that worries over continuing discrimination in India (as well as the attraction of good career prospects in Pakistan, where there was an acute shortage of trained civil servants) accelerated the decline in the number of Muslims in administration.[54] In the central government, as in the states, the number of Muslims also declined precipitously, due to the emigration of a large number of officers to Pakistan, and the emigration or impoverishment of many people from the Muslim middle and upper classes, which in the past had provided recruits for midlevel and senior government positions.[55]

[49] Interview with A. K. Dass, IP, Lucknow, August 25, 1995.

[50] Parthasarathi, *Jawaharlal Nehru*, pp. 233–46, 427–32, 446–59.

[51] "Inquiry Made by the Government of India about the Employment of Members of the Minority Communities," Uttar Pradesh State Archives, Lucknow, file 49H/1958.

[52] Sharif al-Mujahid, *Indian Secularism: A Case Study of the Muslim Minority* (Karachi: University of Karachi Press, 1970), p. 153.

[53] Ibid., chap. 7, "Representation in Services," pp. 149–59

[54] See the entries in *Biographical Encyclopedia of Pakistan, 1960–61* (Lahore: International Publishers, 1961).

[55] See Mushirul Hasan, *Legacy of a Divided Nation: India's Muslims since Independence* (London: Hurst, 1997).

The most significant exception to the general dismantling of ethnic proportionality in government employment after 1947 appears to be the treatment of the ex-untouchable Scheduled Castes (15% of India's population
in the decades after independence) and the Scheduled Tribes (7.5%). The
Indian Constitution explicitly exempts both these groups from the general
constitutional ban on preferential treatment toward any ethnic group, although it leaves the precise level of the benefits they may receive up to the
central and state governments. The central government, and most of the
states, set the Scheduled Castes and Scheduled Tribe quotas at their share
in the population.[56] The exception is apparent rather than real, however,
because these quotas were, during the 1950s and 1960s, almost totally ineffective. By the time Nehru died in 1964, Scheduled Castes and Tribes
combined accounted for only 1.54% of the most senior class I positions
and 2.99% of the class II jobs in central government employment, far short
of their combined 22.5% reservation for national government positions.
The government commission appointed to supervise protections for these
castes complained in 1965 that, despite 15 years of job reservations, "the
rise in the percentage of representation of these communities is insignificant."[57] Commissions set up to examine ethnic quotas in the states found a
similar picture. In Bihar, for example, Scheduled Castes, despite their 15%
state quota, held only 2.3% of class I jobs and 2.7% of class II jobs by 1972,
while Scheduled Tribes, despite their 10% quota, held only 2% of class I
posts and 1.1% of class II posts.[58]

There is, however, one genuine exception to the thesis in this chapter that India was not consociational from 1947 to 1966: the situation in
the three southern states of Madras, Mysore (renamed Karnataka in 1973),
and Kerala. The implementation of large-scale reservations for backward
castes in these states since the 1920s and the subsequent development of
strong backward-caste political parties made it politically impossible for

---

[56] The quotas for the Scheduled Castes and Tribes have remained at the 15% and 7.5%
population levels of these two groups in the 1961 census of India, although as of 1991 the
two groups' share of the population had risen to 16.48% and 8.08%.

[57] *Fourteenth Report of the Commissioner for Scheduled Tribes and Castes* (Delhi: Government of
India, 1964–65), p. 148.

[58] Sachchidananda, "Reservation and After: The Case of Bihar," in V. A. Pai Panandikar,
ed., *The Politics of Backwardness: Reservation Policy in India* (New Delhi: Konark, 1997),
pp. 161–82. A 1976 study in West Bengal found similarly low levels of Scheduled Caste
and Scheduled Tribe representation. Mohit Bhattacharya, "Reservation Policy: The West
Bengal Scene," in ibid., pp. 185–86.

Congress to abolish reservations in the south after independence.[59] When the Madras High Court ruled in July 1950 that reservations were unconstitutional, backward-class politicians in the South organized large protests in major cities and ensured that a constitutional amendment was passed in 1951 that allowed the system to continue.[60] Southern Muslims and Christians benefited because many of their reservations were retained along with those of the more politically powerful backward castes. In Tamil Nadu, for example, Tamil-speaking *labbai* Muslims and Scheduled Caste Christians were proportionally represented in the state civil service after 1947 because they were counted as backward castes and Scheduled Castes for the purpose of reservations.[61] In Mysore (Karnataka), Muslims did better still, and in 1951–52 were recruited to 10.6% of the open government positions even though they accounted for only 6.3% of the population.[62] It should be emphasized, however, that developments in these three southern states were not typical and policies in the South differed substantially from the policies adopted in the North, West, and East.[63]

The Loss of Cultural Autonomy

As well as the loss of proportionality in political representation and government employment, Hindu majorities in New Delhi and in the states also took measures against minority languages and the Muslim minority's right to slaughter cows in the years after 1947. The official language policy of the central government after 1947, as Lijphart and many Indian historians rightly point out, continued to be generally moderate, although the September 1949 decision to make Hindi in the Nagari script the only national language was opposed by almost all Muslim politicians. Once several

---

[59] See Chapter 6.
[60] P. Radhakrishnan, "Backward Class Movements in Tamil Nadu," in M. N. Srinivas, *Caste: Its Twentieth Century Avatar* (New Delhi: Viking 1996), pp. 121–22.
[61] For statistics, see *Report of the Backward Classes Commission Tamil Nadu*, vol. 2, *1970* (Madras: Government of Tamil Nadu, 1975), p. 41; *Report of the Backward Classes Commission Tamil Nadu*, vol. 1, *1970*, pp. 90–91.
[62] *Mysore Legislative Assembly Debates*, August 7, 1953.
[63] The South, as well as being more consociational from 1947 to 1966, also had (and has today) a lower level of Hindu-Muslim violence. This fact might be used to argue that consociationalism does after all lead to lower levels of violence. However, this argument ignores the statistical findings later in this chapter that consociational indicators are unrelated to violence as well as the fact that, as I explore in Chapters 5 and 6, the evidence suggests that electoral rather than consociational mechanisms are responsible for low levels of violence in the more peaceful states.

large linguistic states were created in the 1950s, not as Lijphart suggests with Nehru's support but in fact over his strong opposition, Nehru took several steps to protect the rights of speakers of Urdu and other minority languages and hold the Hindi chauvinists in check.[64] Although Hindi was declared to be India's national language, articles 345 and 347 of the Constitution permitted the president of India and the various state legislatures to recognize other languages in which to transact state business. The central government's Kher Commission on Official Languages also recommended in 1957 that government officers should use Urdu words interchangeably with Hindi words, providing that these words were generally recognized.[65] Nehru also tried to help Urdu speakers in the states. In 1958, for instance, he asked the UP government to declare Urdu an official language in large parts of the state and to make sure that Urdu speakers were not at a disadvantage when applying for government jobs.

The problem with these central government initiatives, however, was that India's states, not the national Congress government, possessed the constitutional power to implement language policy. And India's states, despite making specific commitments (in conferences in 1958 and 1961) to protect the rights of their linguistic and religious minorities, have had a generally poor record on protecting the rights of linguistic minorities.[66] In northern India, no sooner had independence been achieved in August 1947 than the trickle of local councils that had begun to introduce Hindi-only policies targeted at Muslims over the summer turned into a flood: in October 1947 Bareilly gave its employees six months to learn Hindi or be dismissed, while in November Jhansi gave its employees only two months

---

[64] For Nehru's initial opposition to linguistic states, see *Constituent Assembly of India (Legislative) Debates*, November 27, 1947, pp. 792–93. The only linguistic state Nehru was prepared to consider in 1947 was Andhra Pradesh. In December 1955, Nehru again voiced his unease about linguistic states to the Lok Sabha: "The question of language has somehow come to be associated with the question of states' reorganization. I repeat that I attach the greatest importance to language but I refuse to associate it necessarily with a state. In our country there are bound to be states where a single language is predominant. But there are also bound to be areas where there are two languages. In such instances, we should encourage both of them." Sarvepalli Gopal, *Jawaharlal Nehru*, pp. 521–23. The powerful Congress leader Sardar Patel, who died in 1950, was also firmly opposed to linguistic states. See B. Krishna, *Sardar Vallabhai Patel: India's Iron Man* (New Delhi: Indus, 1995), p. 482.

[65] Donald E. Smith, *India as a Secular State* (Princeton: Princeton University Press, 1963), p. 401.

[66] The chief ministers' commitments to linguistic minorities are reprinted in *Facilities Provided for Linguistic Minorities in Uttar Pradesh* (October 1, 1966), published by Bhasha Vibhag, Uttar Pradesh Sarkar.

to master the language.[67] In autumn 1947 the provincial UP and Central Provinces governments, in actions publicly denounced as divisive by Gandhi, decided that Hindi in the Nagari script would henceforth be the only acceptable language for government business.[68] Bihar followed suit with its own Hindi-only laws in 1950 and 1955.

The yearly reports of the Commission for Linguistic Minorities, a central watchdog body set up to monitor compliance with constitutional and legal protections, provide a comprehensive picture of efforts by state governments to understate the size of their minorities, deny them educational facilities in their own languages, and fail to provide copies of government publications and civil service examinations in minority languages. In Uttar Pradesh, despite Nehru's pleas on behalf of Urdu speakers, the state government told the Linguistic Minorities' Commission in 1964–65 that it would not open more Urdu high schools because it was simply "not inclined to provide secondary education through the mother tongue of linguistic minorities."[69] The commission uncovered similar evidence of discrimination against Bengali, Urdu, and Oriya speakers in Bihar, Telugu and Kannada speakers in Tamil Nadu, Punjabi speakers in Haryana, and Hindi speakers in Tamil Nadu. In Bihar (c. 10% Urdu-speaking) the government refused to print pamphlets describing linguistic protections for minorities, print common forms in Urdu, or implement its own official policy (agreed at the 1961 chief ministers' conference) to let Urdu be an additional language for entrance exams for the state civil service.[70]

Another attack on minorities' cultural autonomy came over the divisive issue of their right to slaughter cows for food and (in the case of Muslims) for religious sacrifices. Because of the extensive political conflict over the issue before 1947 – when Muslims' right to slaughter cows was portrayed by the Muslim League as a bellwether of Congress governments' concern for Muslim issues – Nehru and Gandhi were anxious not to abolish cow slaughter without Muslim agreement. Neither Nehru nor Gandhi could

---

[67] *Pioneer*, October 6, November 5, 1947.

[68] *Pioneer*, October 15, 16, 1947.

[69] *Second Report of the Commissioner for Linguistic Minorities* (Ministry of Home Affairs, 1960); *Report of the Commissioner for Seventh Linguistic Minorities* (Ministry of Home Affairs, 1965), p. 205. For Nehru's attempt to intervene to help Urdu speakers, see Sarvepalli Gopal, *Jawaharlal Nehru: A Biography*, vol. 3 (Cambridge, Mass.: Harvard University Press, 1984), pp. 27–28.

[70] *Twelfth Report of the Commissioner for Linguistic Minorities in India, July 1969–June 1970* (Ministry for Home Affairs, 1971), pp. 16–19; *Twenty Fifth Report of the Deputy Commissioner for Linguistic Minorities in India, 1984–85* (Ministry for Home Affairs, 1986), p. 289.

prevent Congress politicians in the Constituent Assembly from inserting a clause in the Indian Constitution making the protection of the cow one of the fundamental goals of the Indian state.[71] But when Congress opponents of cow slaughter tried to turn "directive principle" into law, Nehru was resolute. In April 1955 he threatened to resign if a bill to ban cow slaughter was passed by the Lok Sabha, thereby ensuring its defeat by 95 votes to 12.[72]

As in the case of Urdu, however, Nehru's efforts in Parliament to preserve Muslims' right to slaughter cows were largely irrelevant because policy was made and implemented in the states. The attorney general had determined in 1954 that cow slaughter was the "exclusive sphere of the State Legislature[s]."[73] And in India's states, in a process that will by now be familiar, Hindu majorities began unilaterally to declare cow slaughter illegal as soon as broader political compromise with the Muslim League was off the agenda in mid-1947. In the United Provinces, for instance, a succession of Congress-controlled local and district boards in the state – Kannauj, Chandausi, Hapur, and Roorkee – banned cow slaughter outright in July 1947. By the end of 1947, Hindu majorities in such important districts as Allahabad, Varanasi, Ghaziabad, Jhansi, Meerut, Mirzapur, and Mathura had all banned cow slaughter, the votes sometimes provoking mass walkouts by the elected Muslim members. In Varanasi, for example, the municipal board voted 12 to 5 to ban cow slaughter in September 1947, prompting all five Muslim members to walk out in protest.[74]

From 1947 to 1957 many major states – Rajasthan, Bihar, Madhya Pradesh, Mysore, Uttar Pradesh, and Bombay – simply ignored Nehru's

---

[71] Sarvepalli Gopal, *Jawaharlal Nehru: A Biography*, vol. 2, *1947–1956* (Cambridge, Mass.: Harvard University Press, 1979), p. 78. The directive principle in question asks the central government to prevent "slaughter of cows, calves and other milch and draught cattle" (Article 48).

[72] See Smith, *India as a Secular State*, pp. 483–89, and Nehru's letters of February 23, 1955, and April 4, 1955, in G. Parthasarathi, ed., *Jawaharlal Nehru Letters to Chief Ministers, 1947–1964*, vol. 4, *1954–1957* (New Delhi: Oxford University Press, 1988), pp. 130–40, 141–48.

[73] Statement of Attorney General, Shri M. C. Setalvad, on May 1, 1954. This judgment failed however to head off the supporters of the 1955 vote in the Lok Sabha, who moved the bill under constitutional provisions allowing the center to overrule states in cases of "economic necessity." *Lok Sabha Debates*, March 16, 1979.

[74] "Resolutions Passed by District Boards Regarding Stoppage of Cow Slaughter," U.P.S.A. Local Self Government Department, box 395, file 771(A) 1947; *Pioneer*, September 22, November 5, 1947. Other towns, such as Nawabganj, Unnao, Lucknow, Agra, Bareilly, and Fatehpur Sikri, banned cow slaughter in January and February 1948. *Pioneer*, January 7, 21, 24, 25, 26, February 9, 12, 1948.

wishes and unilaterally restricted or banned cow slaughter.[75] In several of these states abolition followed the recommendations of statewide committees that included a few Muslim members to give the appearance of minority consultation. Better evidence of the true state of Muslim opinion on the issue is provided by the number of prosecutions of Muslims who disobeyed the new laws (in Mysore alone 51 people were imprisoned and 361 fined from 1948 to 1950);[76] by local opinion polls (Raghuraj Gupta's survey of Muslims in Dehra Dun in the 1950s and 1960s found that 70% of Muslim men opposed the ban); and by court records, which show that a large number of Muslims filed legal suits claiming that these state bans were unconstitutional infringements of either their right to freedom of religion or, in the case of those in the tanning and beef trade, their constitutional right to livelihood.[77]

Overruling the Minority Veto

The nationalist interpretation of the abolition of proportionality and minority protections after independence is that India's minorities finally realized that it was better to join the national mainstream than to continue to demand special rights that divided them from other Indians. One account, for example, describes how "after the partition of the country on communal lines, the minorities themselves gave notice for an amendment to the effect

---

[75] For examples, see the Mysore Animal Protection Act 1948, the Orissa Livestock Control of Movement and Transactions Order of 1947, the C.P. & Berar Cattle, Sheep and Goats (Slaughter and Movement) Control Act of 1947, the Bihar Preservation and Improvement of Animals Act of 1956, the M.P. Animal Preservation Act of 1956, and the Bombay Animal Preservation Act of 1954. These state bills made it illegal to kill cattle under a certain age, usually 10–16 years. For a comprehensive list of state-level restrictions passed in 1947–48, see *Constituent Assembly of India (Legislative) Debates*, August 11, 1948, pp. 142–43. For other cases, see *Pioneer*, May 31, 1948; Smith, *India as a Secular State*, pp. 483–89; and Nehru's letters of February 23, 1955, and April 4, 1955, in Parthasarathi, *Jawaharlal Nehru Letters to Chief Ministers 1947–1964*, vol. 4, *1954–1957*, pp. 130–40, 141–48.

[76] *Mysore Legislative Assembly Debates Official Report*, vol. 1, *15 March to 4th April 1950*, pp. 841–42.

[77] *M. H. Qureshi v. State of Bihar, 1958*, SCJ 1958, p. 992. These legal appeals were largely unsuccessful: the supreme court held in *M. H. Qureshi v. State of Bihar* (1958) that Muslim religious laws did not *require* cow slaughter at festivals, but only allowed it as one option along with goat and camel slaughter; and that the ban on cow slaughter did not interfere with Muslim's livelihood, because certain bulls, buffaloes, and bullocks could still be killed. This decision did not satisfy Muslims, who argued that, even though the Koran did not require cow slaughter, banning it was still discriminatory against poor Muslims, who could not afford to sacrifice the more expensive camels or goats.

that in view of the conditions having vastly changed, since the Advisory Committee made their recommendations in 1947 [the committee's interim recommendation in mid-1947 had been to abolish separate electorates but keep reserved seats for Muslims], it was appropriate that the reservations for minorities should be done away with."[78]

There is, however, abundant evidence that minority politicians generally opposed the abolition of consociational policies by the central and state governments after 1947. Sikh politicians, for example, demanded in November 1948 that Sikhs (2% of India's population and 30% of East Punjab's population) receive 5% of seats in the national Parliament and services, a minimum of two cabinet positions, and 50% reservation in the Punjab legislature and services, among other measures.[79] The Sikh leader Tara Singh complained that the proposed abolition of job quotas and political reservations for his community was "an attack on the Sikhs' very existence."[80] The minority veto over these issues was, however, ignored by Congress majorities in the state and central legislatures. When Muslim legislators in Uttar Pradesh complained that the imposition of Hindi in the province in October 1947 broke Congress's official policy and past promises, Hindu politicians told them that after partition, all pledges to the minorities had been canceled. When the Muslim League members walked out of the assembly in protest after losing the vote, Congress legislators jeered them with cries of "Don't come back; go to Pakistan."[81] When Gorakhpur's municipal council took a whole series of anti-Muslim actions at one tumultuous meeting in August 1947 – banning cow slaughter, the sale of beef, and the official use of Urdu – the Muslim council members protested while a crowd of 500 Hindus celebrated outside.[82]

[78] Kamlesh Kumar Wadhwa, *Minority Safeguards in India* (New Delhi: Thomson, 1975), p. 65. For a similar view, see Pratap Kumar Ghosh, *The Constitution of India: How It Has Been Framed* (Calcutta: World Press, 1966).

[79] Nehru's letter to Chief Ministers, December 6, 1948, in G. Parthasarathi, ed., *Jawaharlal Nehru Letters to Chief Ministers, 1947–1964*, vol. 1, *1947–1949* (New Delhi: Oxford University Press, 1985), pp. 230–45.

[80] Letter to Chief Ministers, December 6, 1948, in ibid., pp. 47–49.

[81] The November 4 vote on the Hindi-only policy passed 105 to 23. All those who voted against were from the Muslim League. *Pioneer*, November 5, 1947. For details of a similar divisive vote in Madras, over the abolition of separate Muslim electorates for seats in municipal government, see Debate on the Madras City Municipal (Second Amendment) Bill, 1947, February 13, 1947. *Madras Legislative Assembly Debates, 30 January–14th February 1947*, p. 621.

[82] *Pioneer*, September 1, 1947.

A good example of how the minority veto was overruled despite a veneer of consultation even at the national level is the case of the abolition of separate electorates and reserved minority seats by the Constituent Assembly in May 1949. Although Congress subsequently claimed that this measure was undertaken with the full support of the minorities, eyewitness accounts suggest a different story. The majority of Muslim politicians in 1949, just as in 1947, wanted to preserve both separate constituencies and reserved seats. But most members of the main Muslim party, the Muslim League, had by May 1949 either left for Pakistan or were boycotting the Constituent Assembly.[83] Muhammad Ismail, one of the few Muslim League politicians who was actually present for the debate on abolition, expressed amazement that the Advisory Committee could claim that the minorities were in favor of the measure. "The Muslim League," he pointed out, " ... has more than once within this year not only expressed a definite view in favour of reservation of seats, but has also urged the retention of separate electorates. ... Now if the majority community or the party in power wants to do away with any of these safeguards, that is one thing. But I submit that it is not fair to place the responsibility for doing away with such safeguards on the shoulders of the minority."[84]

The few Congress Muslim representatives in the assembly also wanted to keep reserved seats for Muslims, although they like the rest of their party were committed to abolish separate electorates. But when the vote for abolition came up on May 26, the Congress Muslim leader Maulana Azad ordered his fellow Muslim legislators not to speak out against the measure. In the event, the senior Congress Party politician behind the amendment, Sardar Vallabhai Patel, could only persuade a single Muslim MP, Begum Aizaz Rasul, to propose the measure ending both separate electorates *and* reserved seats. The attempt by Patel to give the abolition the appearance of a consociational-style agreement between Congress and the minorities did not go altogether smoothly:

The representatives of the Nationalist Muslims sat silent. ... Begum Aizaz Rasul, afraid of being severely attacked by the Nationalist Muslims, could not summon up courage to speak. There was no one to propose that the Muslims did not want reservation, and the fate of the most important issue – joint electorates without

---

[83] According to Tajamul Hussain, MP, there were 34 Muslim members of the Assembly (32 from former British India and 2 from the states), of whom only 15 were present on the day of the vote. Hussain identified 9 of these 15 as favoring abolition. *Constituent Assembly Debates*, vol. 8, no. 8, May 25, 1949, p. 337.

[84] The same point was made by Syed Muhammad Saadulla, ibid., pp. 277–78, 304.

reservations – hung in the balance.... [But after prompting by Patel and Munshi] somehow she summoned up courage and walked up to the lectern. She pleaded in a very hesitant manner for the abolition of reservations for Muslims left in India: they were an integral part of the nation, she said, and should play their part in the general electorate.

No sooner had she resumed her seat than Sardar, who perhaps was aware of Azad's instructions, said: "I am very glad that the Muslims are unanimously in favour of joint electorates without reservation. We will now adjourn.[85]

Far from being the unanimous request of India's Muslims, or indeed of other minorities such as the Sikhs, the new electoral system was opposed by the overwhelming majority of minority politicians in 1949.[86] In the late 1950s and early 1960s, Theodore Wright's interviews with dozens of Muslim legislators confirmed the strength of their support for reserved seats for Muslims.[87] The abolition only passed in 1949 because the Hindu majority wanted it, Muslim League MPs had largely left the Assembly, and Congress Muslims were afraid to oppose openly a measure that was supported by Nehru, whose support they needed to protect their community from even more extreme policies being advocated by militant Hindus in Congress such as UP's Purushottam Das Tandon.[88]

Many Muslim legislators, tired of exercising "voice" to no effect, decided simply to stop participating in a constitutional process they saw as stripping minorities of their rights. When ethnic proportionality was abandoned in the United Provinces in 1947, Hafiz Muhammad Ibrahim, a leading nationalist Muslim and the Congress minister for communications and public works, resigned from the government in protest.[89] In August 1949 the most senior Congress Muslim politician, Maulana Azad, resigned from the

---

[85] K. M. Munshi, *Indian Constitutional Documents*, vol. 1, *Pilgrimage to Freedom (1902–1950)* (Bombay: Bharatiya Vidhya Bhavan, 1967), pp. 207–8. The journalist and editor Durga Das confirms Munshi's version of events in *India from Curzon to Nehru and After* (New York: John Day, 1970), pp. 272–73.

[86] See the demands of the Sikh-dominated Minorities Committee of the East Punjab Legislature. Letter to Chief Ministers, December 6, 1948, in Parthasarathi, *Jawaharlal Nehru Letters to Chief Ministers, 1947–1964*, vol. 1, *1947–1949*, pp. 230–45.

[87] Theodore P. Wright, "The Effectiveness of Muslim Representation in India," in Donald E. Smith, ed., *South Asian Politics and Religion* (Princeton: Princeton University Press, 1966), pp. 102–37.

[88] Nehru, welcomed the decision of the minorities' committee, claiming that it would "get [us] out of the vicious circle in which we have been for the last several decades." Letter to Chief Ministers, June 3, 1949, in Parthasarathi, *Jawaharlal Nehru Letters to Chief Ministers, 1947–1964*, vol. 1, *1947–1949*, pp. 354–67.

[89] *Pioneer*, June 14, 1947.

central government committee in charge of drafting the language clauses of the constitution after he realized that most members would not accept an official role for either Urdu or the widely understood "Hindustani" variant of the northern Indian vernacular. He complained that "from one end to another narrow-mindedness reigned supreme."[90] In September 1949 the prominent Muslim League member Z. H. Lari followed suit and resigned from the Constituent Assembly "to express resentment at the decision taken by that body to replace Hindustani by Hindi as the 'lingua franca' of India and to adopt the Devanagiri script to the entire exclusion of the Urdu script."[91]

Were Congress Governments Grand Coalitions?

The ethnic "grand coalitions" within Congress and the various governments were neither as widespread nor as significant as Lijphart imagines. They were not as widespread because a 1957 internal investigation into the party's treatment of minorities found that "In spite of a general directive by the Congress Working Committee that minorities should get proportionate and in any case at least 15 per cent of nominations for the Parliament and State Assemblies, many states did not carry out this directive. The same position holds in respect of District Boards, Municipalities, Corporations and other local bodies."[92] They were not as significant because, even when minorities *were* given ministerial appointments, they were kept well away from the most important and sensitive posts. From 1947 to 1964, for example, no Muslim was appointed to the key central cabinet portfolios of Home Affairs, Foreign Affairs, or Defense. Muslims were appointed to less important central ministries such as Science and Cultural Affairs, or to Education, which under the Constitution was primarily a state subject.[93] An instructive example of the way in which minorities were kept away from power is the case of Rafi Ahmed Kidwai, the Muslim home minister in the

---

90 Smith, *India as a Secular State*, p. 399, and B. Shiva Rao et al., *The Framing of India's Constitution: A Study* (New Delhi: Indian Institute of Public Administration, 1968), pp. 784–92.

91 *Times of India*, September 17, 1949.

92 Humayun Kabir, *Minorities in a Democracy* (Calcutta: K. L. Mukhopadhyay, 1968), pp. 40–43.

93 Calculated from yearly lists of Indian Cabinet members in A. B. Kohli, *Councils of Ministers in India, 1947–1982* (New Delhi: Gitanjali Publishing, 1983), and Omar Khalidi, "Muslims in Indian Political Process: Group Goals and Alternative Strategies," *Economic and Political Weekly*, January 2–9, 1993, pp. 43–54.

United Provinces from 1946 to 1947. Kidwai was forced to resign his state-level position shortly before independence because many Hindu politicians argued that a Muslim home minister was a security risk.[94] Nehru then avoided Kidwai's public humiliation by elevating him to the unimportant central government portfolio of communications. But Kidwai was told not to interfere in UP politics, and his family complains to this day that his career was stunted due to "the policy of keeping Muslim ministers at a distance from the main state policies."[95]

India since the Mid-1960s: Increasingly Consociational

Since the mid-1960s and the deaths of Nehru and his immediate successor as prime minister Lal Bahadur Shastri (1964–66), Indian politics has become much more competitive. This is due to both the institutional decay of the Congress Party as well as the rise of new parties, especially those representing regional ethnic minorities and middle- and lower-caste Hindus. The effect of this increasingly intense competition has been to make swing votes, especially minority votes, much more valuable. Politicians now gain and hold power by offering Muslims, the Scheduled Castes, and the "Other Backward Castes" a growing array of job reservations, linguistic protections, special economic programs, and reserved seats in state legislatures. By 1990 backward-caste and Scheduled Caste and Tribe communities were guaranteed from 50% to 68% of state jobs in states in the South, while in the North reservations ranged from 27.5% (Haryana) to 35% (Uttar Pradesh).[96] The biggest beneficiaries of these programs in the past two decades have been the backward castes and the Scheduled Castes, but Muslims have also benefited.

To get round the constitutional ban on religiously based job reservations, state governments simply follow the longtime practice in Kerala and Karnataka and list specific Muslim, Sikh, or Christian castes as backward castes.[97] Before the 1994 state elections, for example, the chief ministers of

---

[94] For the Hindu campaign against Kidwai, see the remarks of Pandit Gopi Nath Kunzru, vice president of the UP Hindu Sabha, reported in *Pioneer*, May 24, 1947.

[95] Anwar Jamal Kidwai, "An Unsung Hero of the Freedom Struggle: Rafi Ahmed Kidwai," *Islam and the Modern Age* 24, no. 2 (1993), p. 102.

[96] For the different levels of backward-caste quotas in each state, see Mihir Desai, "The Need for Reservations: A Reply to Shourie and Others," *Lokayan Bulletin* 8, nos. 4–5 (1990), pp. 9–33.

[97] See *Muslim India* 1, no. 10 (October 1983), p. 466, and 13, no. 145 (January 1995), p. 17, for details of which Muslim castes are included in state lists.)

Andhra Pradesh, Bihar, Karnataka, and Assam each promised "backward" Muslims substantial quotas (10–27%) in government employment if they were reelected.[98] Even the army and paramilitary forces, which have long opposed ethnic preferences as a threat to their operational efficiency, have had to compromise. The Assam Rifles, the Border Security Force, and the Central Reserve Police Force were all forced to implement reservations for the Scheduled Castes and Scheduled Tribes in the early 1980s. And in 1990 and 1994, responding to decades' old complaints about the ethnic bias of India's Hindu-dominated paramilitary forces, New Delhi created two new units – the Rashtriya Rifles and the Rapid Action Force (RAF) – with de facto quotas for Muslims and other minorities in each platoon and company. By 1996 the 13,180 strong RAF comprised 17.21% religious minorities, 13.64% Scheduled Castes, and 4.76% Scheduled Tribes.[99]

India, as a result of politicians' desire to woo newly mobilized minority and lower-caste voters, has in fact become much more ethnically "proportional" in the 1980s and 1990s than ever it was under Nehru. The increase not just due to the larger number of groups now eligible for affirmative action programs but also to better enforcement. In the mid-1970s, for example, Congress politicians began to worry that they were losing the support of the Scheduled Caste and Schedule Tribe "vote banks," as their leaders expressed increasing unhappiness with the few tangible rewards they had received from Congress rule. So, for the first time, Congress politicians were obliged to enforce the job reservations that had been in place since the 1950s. New rules were introduced to tackle the widespread practice of not filling such vacancies because there were "no qualified candidates." Rules were introduced so that every seventh or eighth new recruit now had to be a Scheduled Caste or Tribe. Not surprisingly, the share of such recruits in central and state government employment shot up during the late 1970s and the 1980s. In the central government, as we can see in Table 4.1, the share of Scheduled Castes and Tribes in the two most senior categories of central government employment rose from 1.54% and 2.99% in 1963 to 10.75% and 13.65% in 1989.[100] Developments in the states followed

---

[98] "Minority Matters," *India Today*, November 30, 1994, pp. 42–43.

[99] Government of India, Press Information Bureau, Booklet on Minorities. Downloaded on February 22, 1999, from the Government of India's web site at <http://www.nic.in/India-Image/PIB/bminor.html>. *Muslim India* 160 (April 1996), p. 180.

[100] The army, navy, and air force are still exempted from these Scheduled Caste and Tribe quotas. Judging by recruitment data, the proportion of these officers in the Indian armed forces is less than 1%, the proportion of other ranks around 5%. The quotas have, since

Table 4.1. *Scheduled Caste (SC) and Scheduled Tribe (ST) Representation in Central Government Employment*

	1963		1989	
	Total Employees	Percentage of SC & ST employees	Total Employees	Percentage of SC & ST employees
Group I	18,176	1.54	61,176	10.75
Group II	29,482	2.99	86,018	13.65
Class III	1,007,415	8.90	2,224,212	19.37
Class IV	1,063,525	20.69	1,092,175	26.87

Source: Report of the Commissioner for Scheduled Caste and Scheduled Tribes for the Year, 1962–63 (Twelfth Report, Part One) (Delhi: Controller of Publications, 1964), and *Formulation, Implementation and Monitoring of Reservation Policy*, Committee on the Welfare of Scheduled Castes and Scheduled Tribes (1993–94), Tenth Lok Sabha, 24th Report (New Delhi: Lok Sabha Secretariat, 1993).

the same pattern. In the state of Bihar, for example, where the Scheduled Castes have had a 14% quota since the 1950s, their actual representation in class I and class II government positions rose from 2.3% and 2.7% in 1972 to 14.77% and 18.24%, respectively, by 1990.[101]

Politicians' emphasis on proportionality in government employment and on enforcing existing job reservations has been accompanied by a new emphasis on the proportional allocation of government resources. In the early 1980s, central and state governments sharply increased the budget allocations for programs targeted at Scheduled Castes, Scheduled Tribes, and backward castes. To avoid expenditure being diverted away from these groups, as had often happened in the 1950s and 1960s, governments established new "Special Component Plans" that made it easy to determine, at a glance, exactly how much money was going to each group. The proportion of government expenditure explicitly set aside for the Scheduled Castes and Tribes rose as a result from 0.96% in 1970 to 7.77% in 1990.[102] Although New Delhi has, so far at least, resisted extending the principle of financial proportionality to religious minorities, it began checks in 1983 to

the early 1980s, also been applied to the 400,000-strong paramilitary forces. *Committee on the Welfare of Scheduled Castes and Scheduled Tribes (1985–1986) Eighth Lok Sabha, Sixth Report* (Delhi: Ministry of Home Affairs, 1986).

[101] Sachchidananda, "Reservation and After: The Case of Bihar," pp. 161–82.

[102] These statistics exclude general government spending on infrastructure and development projects, for which no ethnic breakdowns are available. Giridhar Gomango, *Constitutional Provisions for the Scheduled Castes and the Scheduled Tribes* (Bombay: Himalaya Publishing, 1992), pp. 14–15.

ensure that Muslims and other minorities were receiving their "fair share" of jobs and economic programs.

The increased importance of minority votes has also persuaded politicians to start taking minority cultural rights more seriously. In the 1980s and 1990s, for example, governments in Bihar and Uttar Pradesh reversed some of the laws their states had passed from 1947 to 1950 and, despite sometimes angry protests from Hindus, reestablished Urdu as a second official state language. Mulayam Singh Yadav, chief minister of Uttar Pradesh, ordered that all government office signs be in Urdu as well as Hindi.[103] In Bihar, Chief Minister Jagannath Misra gave Muslim religious school certificates the same official status as those from state schools.[104] Nepali speakers in West Bengal, Tamil and Kannada speakers in Kerala, and Urdu, Malayalam, Telegu, and Kannada speakers in Andhra have also been given official recognition by their state governments. Perhaps most significant, the attempt to reform the Muslim Personal Law code in the 1980s – which Lijphart interprets as a "weakening" of consociationalism – resulted in a significant strengthening of the constitutional position of Muslim personal law.

Consociationalism, Congress Decline, and Communal Violence

Does India's pattern of communal violence increase as the presence of consociational indicators declines, as consociational theory predicts? At the national level, the level at which Lijphart provides most of his data, it does not. Once we recode India's consociational character and realize that India was consociational from 1919 to 1947, nonconsociational from 1947 to 1966, and increasingly consociational since the 1960s, we can see (Table 4.2) that consociationalism seems, if anything, to have been accompanied by *higher* national levels of Hindu-Muslim violence.

In support of the consociational theory we could, of course, still argue that there is a relationship between the Congress Party, consociational policies, and India's level of communal violence but that this relationship is difficult to spot if we aggregate information from all India's states as we have done in Table 4.2. If we measured the consociational character and strength of the Congress in each of India's states individually, one could

---

[103] For details on the recognition of Urdu in Bihar, see *Muslim India* 2, no. 21 (September 1984), pp. 433; 7, no. 82 (October 1989), p. 458; *India Today*, July 16–30, 1980, pp. 27–28.
[104] *India Today*, August 31, 1983, pp. 24–25.

Table 4.2. *India's Changing Consociational Status and Hindu-Muslim Violence*

	"Responsible Government" (1919–47)	Nehruvian Era (1947–66)	Post-Nehru (1967–95)
Yearly average of deaths in Hindu-Muslim riots (per 10 million)	3.5	0.7	3.3
Level of violence	High	Low	High
Status	Consociational	Nonconsociational "ranked" state	Increasingly consociational

Sources: Wilkinson 1919–50 data and Varshney & Wilkinson 1950–95 data. To avoid skewing the data, I exclude the Hindu-Muslim partition riots that took place from 1946–47 when calculating the average deaths in the preindependence period.

argue, we would then be able to see that these factors are indeed related to lower levels of violence.

To test this state-level hypothesis at least partially, I decided to gather some statistical data to see if some of the key factors identified by Lijphart are associated with higher or lower levels of violence in the way his model would predict. In particular I wanted to examine whether the key mechanism through which he claims consociationalism works in India – Congress rule – is negatively related to Hindu-Muslim violence, especially in the period from 1947 to the mid-1960s when Lijphart argues that consociational power sharing was at its peak. I also provided a very imperfect test, at least for the past two decades, to see whether minority proportionality in Indian state governments and police forces seems to be related to state levels of Hindu-Muslim violence. Data on whether Congress or non-Congress governments were in power in a state in any particular month were obtained from *India Decides*, a well-known reference book on Indian elections. I compiled data on the ethnic proportionality of state cabinets using a name analysis of Indian state cabinets, which are reported in the Lok Sabha's *Journal of Parliamentary Information*. Unfortunately these data are only available for a relatively narrow period, from 1974–75 onward. Data on the ethnic proportionality of the state police forces are also available for several years in the 1980s and 1990s, largely through the efforts of the various minorities commissions set up by the central government.

Even just looking at the descriptive statistics presented in Table 4.3 – which represent average levels of minority proportionality and Hindu-Muslim violence in state governments from 1975 to 1995 – we can see

Table 4.3. *Minority Representation and Hindu-Muslim Violence in the States, 1975–1995*

	State Muslim	Average Riots per Month	Average Killed per Month	Cabinet Over- or Under-representation of Muslims	Police Over- or Under-representation of Muslims	Combined Under-representation
Andhra Pradesh	9%	0.15	1.27	−4%	1%	−3%
Bihar	14%	0.19	2.86	−5%	−12%	−17%
Gujarat	9%	0.80	3.69	−4%	−3%	−7%
Haryana	4%	0.01	0.02	−1%	−3%	−5%
Himachal Pradesh	2%	0.00	0.00	−2%	−1%	−2%
Karnataka	11%	0.22	0.94	0%	−3%	−3%
Kerala	22%	0.03	0.02	−10%	−13%	−23%
Madhya Pradesh	5%	0.09	0.73	−1%	0%	−2%
Maharashtra	10%	0.54	4.61	−4%	−6%	−10%
Rajasthan	8%	0.07	0.29	−4%	−3%	−7%
Tamil Nadu	5%	0.06	0.13	−1%	0%	−1%
Uttar Pradesh	17%	0.49	4.28	−4%	−10%	−14%
West Bengal	23%	0.09	0.42	−15%	−16%	−32%

that proportionality is not a necessary condition in order to control violence. Some of the states with the lowest levels of Muslim proportionality in the administration and cabinets have done quite well in controlling their levels of communal violence. The two states that underrepresent Muslims the most in government and administration, West Bengal and Kerala, have levels of Hindu-Muslim violence that are considerably lower than states such as Andhra Pradesh and Madhya Pradesh that have done a much better job of representing Muslims in their cabinets and the state police forces. Kerala has fewer than half the number of Muslims in its police force that proportionality would require (10% compared with a Muslim population of 23%), but it has one of the lowest per-capita levels of riots and deaths of any major Indian state.[105]

---

[105] These police figures are in fact better than those for the state government as a whole. Muslims occupy only 2% of the most senior class I posts and 3% to 4% of Class II posts in the state government service. See U. Mohammed, "Educational Problems of the Muslim Minority in Kerala," in Ashgar Ali Engineer, *Kerala Muslims: A Historical Perspective* (New Delhi: Ajanta, 1995), p. 150. Muslim proportionality in Kerala's elite Indian Administrative

Additional evidence suggesting that proportionality may not be a necessary condition to control riots comes from the observation that the central government forces with the best record for impartiality and efficiency in stopping and preventing riots have exactly the same low proportion of Muslims as the state forces with the worst reputations. The central government's main antiriot force, for example, the 150,000-strong Central Reserve Police Force (CRPF), was only 5.5% Muslim in 1993.[106] Yet Muslims have frequently called on the CRPF to be stationed in towns because they do not trust forces such as the UP Armed Constabulary and the Bihar Special Police, which have an identically low proportion of Muslims.[107] Independent investigators who visited Aligarh after that city's riots in December 1990–January 1991 were told by local Muslims that they had absolute confidence in the CRPF and that without the CRPF they would have been killed.[108] The prominent Muslim politician Syed Shahabuddin demanded in December 1991 that the UP government withdraw the PAC from the riot-torn city of Varanasi and replace it with the CRPF.[109]

One way in which we can test the general relationship between Congress rule, ethnic proportionality, and the level of communal violence is through a multiple regression analysis, the results of which I present in Table 4.3. To test whether Congress rule is, as Lijphart's argument predicts, associated with lower levels of Hindu-Muslim riots, I used the measure *CONGRULE*, which codes for whether Congress or non-Congress governments were in

Service and Indian Police Service cadres is even worse than that in the state services: at 6% and 1%, respectively. *The Civil List of the Indian Police Service as of 1st January 1993* (New Delhi: Ministry of Home Affairs, 1993); *The Indian Administrative Service Civil List, 1995* (New Delhi: Ministry of Home Affairs, 1995).

[106] *National Commission for Minorities Second Annual Report* (FY 1994–1995) (New Delhi, 1997), sec. 7.97. The CRPF established a special 10-batallion rapid action force in the 1990s specifically to deal with the threat of communal riots and stationed it in highly sensitive cities throughout the country: Hyderabad, Ahmedabad, Allahabad, Bombay, Delhi, Aligarh, Thiruvanthapuram, Jamshedpur, Bhopal, and Meerut. Even this special antiriot force, though it was explicitly formed to be more ethnically representative, was only 6.9% Muslim in 1996. LSUQ, no. 982, dated March 7, 1996, by S. Gautam and R. Patidar, reported in *Muslim India* 14, no. 160 (April 1996), p. 180.

[107] See the Aligarh Muslim University Students' Union Statement of December 21, 1990, requesting the CRPF, Border Security Force, and army to be posted in Aligarh instead of the PAC. *Muslim India* 9, no. 101 (February 1991), p. 78.

[108] People's Union for Civil Liberties report on the December 1990 communal riots in Aligarh, reprinted in *Muslim India* 101 (May 1991), pp. 231–33.

[109] *Muslim India* 10, no. 109 (January 1992), p.32. See also the plea of the Muslim MP G. M. Banatwalla that the CRPF and BSF should be deployed in the town of Kalyan in preference to the Maharashtra armed police. Lok Sabha Debates, April 25, 1979, pp. 297–98.

129

power in a state in a particular month. Systematic data on other consociational indicators such as proportionality are much less easy to obtain, as the government of India does not make cross-tabulated data on ethnic minorities publicly available. For a very narrow sample of years we can get partial data on proportionality in the police (a few data points since 1982) and on minority representation in Indian state cabinets (since 1974–75), and I use these data, imperfect though they are, to get some sense of whether any relationship seems to exist in the past two decades. To test the hypothesis that the total Muslim representation in the cabinet is related to a state's level of violence, I calculate the number of Muslims in each state cabinet (*MUSLIM % IN CABINET*). By analyzing the names in each cabinet I have therefore been to been able to work out how many Muslims were in each ministry, both as full cabinet ministers and as members of the full Council of Ministers (which includes junior ministers and ministers of state).

For a partial measure of minority representation in the police I use the variable *MUSLIM % IN POLICE*. Data on ethnic proportionality in the Indian police are not widely available. But during the 1980s and 1990s the Indian Minorities Commissions and various retired and serving government officers made 2–3 yearly tables on state-by-state levels of Muslim representation available, which I have interpolated, so that we can at least get a very partial sense of whether Muslim representation in the police seems to affect a state's level of Hindu-Muslim riots and deaths.[110]

In addition to these indicators I also control for various other attributes that might plausibly affect the level of Hindu-Muslim violence. First, I control for each state's population size (logged), the figures for which I interpolate from the decadal censuses. Second, to control for the possibility that the level of violence in a state is merely the result of its level of ethnic diversity, I include controls that measure the linguistic and religious diversity of each state. I calculate *LANGFRAC*, my measure of state linguistic fractionalization, using Rae's index $(1 - \Sigma g_i^2)$, where g_i is the proportion of the population in linguistic group i.[111] I calculate *RELFRAC*, my measure of

---

[110] See, e.g., *Eighth Annual Report of the Minorities' Commission* (for the period 1-4-1985 to 31-3-1986) (New Delhi: Controller of Publications, 1989), pp. 108–9, table 11.17.2. Consolidated statement based on the data received from state directors general of police showing the number of minorities in police service as on March 31, 1995. *National Commission for Minorities Third Annual Report* (FY 1995–1996) pp. 143–46; V. N. Rai, "A Case for Representation of Minorities in the Police," *Towards Secular India* 1, no. 2 (1995), pp. 39–47.

[111] For a discussion of ethnic fractionalization indicators, see Peter C. Ordeshook and Olga V. Shvetsova, "Ethnic Heterogeneity, District Magnitude and the Number of Parties,"

religious fractionalization, using the same formula. To test for the effect of the interaction of ethnic and religious deversity I then interacted *RELFRAC*, and *LANGFRAC* to creat *ETHFRAC*, a measure of a state's overall ethnic diversity. The data I use are Government of India census data from 1961, 1971, 1981, and 1991 on the percentage of each religious group in a state (Hindus, Sikhs, Christians, Jains, Buddhists, Muslims, Others) as well as the percentage of each linguistic group that accounted for 1% or more of a state's population.[112] Unfortunately, it is not possible to get good state-level data on one of the most important ethnic identities in India, caste, because no nationwide caste census has been carried out since 1931.[113]

Within India, several explanations for violence focus on the percentage of the Muslim population in a state, with higher percentages thought to lead to more violence. So in several regressions I also controlled for the percentage of Muslims in each state, *MUSLIM%*, using data I obtained from the 1981 and 1991 Indian censuses.[114] To control for each state's level of urban poverty I use each state's urban Gini coefficient, calculated by the World Bank on the basis of data collected by the Indian National Sample Survey, *WBUGINI*. States that have an equal distribution of wealth (e.g., with around 20% of the population having 20% of the wealth, 50% having 50%, etc.) have a Gini coefficient of 0, whereas states with a highly unequal wealth distribution in which a few individuals have virtually all the wealth would have a Gini coefficient close to 1.

It is possible of course that previous levels of communal violence might in fact be the underlying cause of a state's current level of violence. This might be because previous violence creates animosities and cycles of revenge and retribution that lead to violence in the present. It might also be the case that

American Journal of Political Science 38, no. 1 (1994), pp. 100–23, and Gary Cox, *Making Votes Count: Strategic Coordination in the World's Electoral Systems* (Cambridge: Cambridge University Press, 1998).

[112] Sources for these data are: Government of India, *Census of India 1991, Paper 1 of 1995, Religion* (Delhi: Government of India: 1995), and Commissioner of Scheduled Castes and Tribes, *Report of the Commissioner for Scheduled Castes and Tribes, 1979–1980 and 1980–1981* (Delhi: Government of India, 1982).

[113] The census does collect data on the Scheduled Castes and Scheduled Tribes, because of the special constitutional provisions that apply to them, but does not for the remaining 60% of the Indian population who are members of the Hindu upper castes or so-called backward castes. A proposal prior to the 2001 census to reintroduce data on caste identity for non–Scheduled Castes and Tribes was defeated, partly because of worries that reintroducing questions on caste would permanently entrench casteism in Indian society.

[114] N. C. Saxena, "The Nature and Origin of Communal Riots," in Ashgar Ali Engineer, ed., *Communal Riots in Post-Independence India* (Hyderabad: Sangam Books, 1984), pp. 51–67.

previous violence leads to changes in other variables that might in turn have some relationship to violence. For example, previous violence might make a state's distribution of wealth more unequal or might make a state less diverse, either of which might make a state more likely to experience violence. To control for the effect of a state's previous level of violence, therefore, I use a monthly variable, calculated from the *Times of India* dataset I collected with Ashutosh Varshney, that measures the number of Hindu-Muslim riots that have taken place in each state in the previous five years, *RIOT5YR*. I also control for state-level characteristics, using fixed effects for each state.

The regression results are reported in Table 4.4. The first thing to note is that several key expectations of Lijphart's model are not borne out by the analysis. The results show that Congress rule, which is after all Lijphart's central mechanism through which consociationalism is supposed to work, does not have the expected negative relationship during the period of greatest Congress dominance in the 1950s and 1960s. Congress rule is positively related to the level of riots over the whole 1950–95 period and only becomes insignificant (column 2) or negatively related (column 3) to the level of riots once we introduce the variables that measure the Muslim percentage in the cabinet and the police, which restricts the observations to the years since 1974 and 1982, respectively. Only in the post-1982 period during which Lijphart sees a weakening of consociationalism does Congress rule in fact have the negative effect on riots that he asserted existed during the Nehru years.

Minority proportionality in state cabinets is also unrelated to a state's level of riots across all three regressions. A state's level of urbanization and its level of previous violence, as we might expect, does have an impact on a state's probability of violence. The size of the effect of previous violence is much less than we might think, however. For every extra riot a state has had in a previous five years, its number of expected riots in a month goes up by 0.02, making previous violence less important than factors such as whether a Congress or non-Congress government is in power.

There is a statistically significant and negative relationship between the level of minorities in the police and a state's level of Hindu-Muslim riots. Whether this indicates a causal relationship is questionable for several reasons however. First, the data on minority representation used in the regressions represent interpolations from only around 30 observations from the 1982–95 period, an extremely narrow and likely unrepresentative sample. As we explored earlier in the discussion of the 1919–47 period, we know that historically there have been periods when both minority representation

Table 4.4. *Congress, Consociationalism, and the Occurrence of Hindu-Muslim Riots*

	Riots		
	(1)	(2)	(3)
Congress rule	0.249	0.168	−1.535
	(0.109)**	(0.131)	(0.448)***
State population (log)	3.202	3.177	−49.541
	(1.043)***	(3.158)	(28.486)*
President's rule	−0.061	0.335	0.975
	(0.191)	(0.246)	(0.360)***
Literacy percentage	0.761	6.661	278.247
	(3.709)	(11.800)	(96.666)***
Urbanization percentage	−8.391	−27.023	−524.645
	(6.940)	(15.139)*	(187.283)***
Muslim percentage	−2.671	29.271	413.913
	(11.314)	(26.202)	(372.432)
Urban Gini coefficient	−0.038	−0.037	−0.170
	(0.020)*	(0.031)	(0.087)**
Religious fractionalization	−31.498	−88.306	133.512
	(6.692)***	(29.352)***	(405.221)
Linguistic fractionalization	−19.029	−106.824	
	(5.996)***	(43.830)**	
Ethnic fractionalization	74.354	338.257	−2,593.895
	(21.193)***	(128.387)***	(1,275.786)**
Riots in previous 10 years	0.009	0.005	0.076
	(0.002)***	(0.003)*	(0.021)***
Muslim percentage in cabinet		0.017	−0.039
		(0.016)	(0.026)
Muslim percentage in police			−2.563
			(0.658)***
Constant	−46.297	−27.674	936.636
	(16.262)***	(50.578)	(436.187)*
Observations	5,916	2,886	716
Number of states	14	14	11

Notes: Standard errors in parentheses. * significant at 10%; ** significant at 5%; *** significant at 1%. For state dummy coefficients, see Appendix C.

in the police and violence have been high: for example, in preindependence Bihar (33% Muslim) and Uttar Pradesh (50% Muslim). Second, there is the question of whether the Muslim percentage in the police is itself the cause of low levels of violence or whether both higher levels of Muslim representation in the police and low levels of communal violence might both be the outcome of some other factor, such as levels of political competition.

Conclusion

The lack of a relationship between the occurrence of Hindu-Muslim riots and minority proportionality in state government should not be surprising. There is a connection – which we examine in Chapters 5 and 6 – between minority representation and Hindu-Muslim riots but in no sense is this a direct relationship between the number of Muslims in a cabinet and a regime's attention to Muslim concerns. "Minority representation," as Donald Horowitz points out, can mean both "the tangible but narrow sense of ethnic office holding," as well as the "broader sense of incorporating the concerns and interests of a given ethnic or racial group in the calculations of politicians belonging to a variety of groups." Measures that achieve the first goal do not, he points out, necessarily achieve the second.[115] While one government with 12% Muslim representation and many Muslims in the police force may be genuinely attentive to and supported by Muslims, another may simply appoint Muslims to preserve a facade of inclusion. Governments with the worst records on minority rights often make the greatest efforts to include a large number of minorities as a deliberate effort to deflect criticism. After the May 1996 general elections, for example, India's short-lived BJP government demonstrated its "inclusiveness" by appointing a Muslim, Sikander Bakht, to an important cabinet position. But in a situation in which 97% of Indian Muslims had voted against the BJP, it is doubtful whether this move represented genuine "power sharing."[116] A government that already has substantial support from Muslims may in fact feel less need to have many Muslim senior ministers. N. T. Rama Rao in Andhra Pradesh got the lion's share of Muslim support in 1994 yet appointed only one Muslim to his 32-strong cabinet, to the Wakf Urdu and Minority Affairs portfolio.[117] To give another example, Mulayam Singh Yadav enjoys so much Muslim electoral support that his Hindu opponents once dubbed him "Maulana," a Muslim cleric. Yet in his first cabinet in Uttar Pradesh in 1990 not 1 of his 19 full cabinet members was a Muslim and only 4 of his 29 junior ministers.

Consociational power sharing's fundamental problem is its assumption that identities are fixed. This is at odds with one of the key findings of research into ethnic politics since the late 1960s, that ethnic identities

---

[115] Donald L. Horowitz, *A Democratic South Africa: Constitutional Engineering in a Divided Society* (Berkeley: University of California Press, 1991), p. 165.

[116] Yogendra Yadav, "Exit Poll: Who Voted for Whom," *India Today* 31 (May 1996), pp. 25–27.

[117] *Muslim India* 146 (February 1991), p. 57.

are multidimensional and oppositional. If we accept this finding, it follows that we ought to develop a healthy skepticism about consociational power-sharing proposals premised, like the 1998 Good Friday agreement in Northern Ireland, upon the continuing existence of solid ethnic groups. Does it really make sense to grant a linguistic or caste group's leaders a particular share of jobs and political power, or a minority veto over future constitutional reforms when it is likely that identities will change over time and that cleavages within a group will emerge that will lead to new conflicts over the distribution of scarce goods?

Arend Lijphart has rightly recognized the challenge that a constructivist understanding of ethnic identity poses for consociational approaches to moderating ethnic violence. He argues, though, that consociational solutions can avoid freezing ethnic identities by allowing groups to first self-identify themselves through a proportional representation electoral system.[118] But this solution seems to me to run into two problems. First, what happens when, as identities will inevitably change, we later need to increase or decrease sharply a group's allocation of political appointments, its share of government positions (including, presumably, its share in the police and army), or even its possession of a minority veto? The evidence from India and elsewhere suggests that such reallocation disputes will themselves often lead to violence, as already recognized and institutionally privileged groups resist new groups' efforts to seek a share of the pie. In 1998, for example, violent conflicts broke out in southern India as one privileged subcaste within the Scheduled Caste category, the Malas, refused demands from an even worse-off untouchable caste, the Madigas, that it be given a separate share within the Scheduled Caste quotas in education, spending, and government employment.

Second, we must surely have some concerns about the feasibility of recognizing and institutionalizing new ethnic identities ad infinitum as a means of solving ethnic conflicts. Nigeria has increased its number of states from 4 in 1963 to 37 today to try to break up larger ethnic groups and give smaller ones a proportionate share of political power. India now has 28 states (3 of which were created in 2000), and national and state governments now recognize the eligibility of more than 1,000 castes for state employment and educational benefits. Yet in both Nigeria and India numerous ethnic movements have been founded to demand yet more separate states and separate

---

[118] Lijphart, "Self-Determination versus Pre-Determination of Ethnic Minorities in Power-Sharing Systems," pp. 275–87.

shares of federal and state benefits and government jobs for particular ethnic groups. Surely at some point increasing the number of groups with pro-portional political representation, giving each group cultural autonomy, and providing each with a minority veto that allows them to block future changes will impose huge and unacceptable costs in terms of basic state capacities.

5

The Electoral Incentives for Hindu-Muslim Violence

Why do some political leaders in some Indian states impress upon their local officials that communal riots and anti-Muslim pogroms must be prevented at all costs? Why do governments in other states fail to protect their minorities or even incite violence against them? In previous chapters we showed that factors such as declining state capacity or India's changing level of consociational power sharing cannot explain the geographical or historical patterns in the effectiveness of states' response to the threat of communal violence. In this chapter, I argue that we can best explain state-level variation in levels of Hindu-Muslim violence if we understand the electoral incentives facing each state's government. I show that states with higher degrees of party fractionalization, in which minorities are therefore pivotal swing voters, have lower levels of violence than states with lower levels of party competition. This is because minorities in highly competitive party systems can extract promises of greater security from politicians in return for their votes.

The chapter is organized into three parts. First, I develop the theoretical argument about the importance of state-level electoral incentives and outline the conditions under which high levels of multiparty electoral competition will lead to higher levels of state protection for minorities. Second, using data from 1961 to 1995 for 14 major Indian states, I show that greater party fractionalization leads to a statistically significant reduction in states' levels of Hindu-Muslim riots. This is true even when we control for socio-economic variables, the particular party in power in a state, the previous level of ethnic violence in a state, and fixed effects for states. Third, I turn to qualitative evidence to determine if some of the mechanisms identified in the theoretical section of the chapter seem actually to be responsible for the observed state-level variation in riot prevention. Are politicians behaving

137

as we would expect in intensely competitive political situations, by offering security in return for the support of pivotal minority voters? How do the politicians in control of states act in situations where Hindus rather than Muslims are perceived to be the key marginal voters?

Electoral Competition and the Supply of State Protection for Minorities

What determines whether a local, state, or national government will order the police and army to prevent ethnic polarization and to stop ethnic violence against ethnic minorities? In democracies, governments will protect minorities when they rely on them directly for electoral support, or if party politics in a state is so competitive that there is a high probability that they will need to rely on minority votes or minority-supported parties in the future. We can think of three different types of party competition that will have different effects on a state's response to antiminority violence, which I have represented as A, B_i, and B_{ii} in Figure 5.1.[1]

My argument is that the best situation for minorities is situation A, where there are high levels of party fractionalization with three or more parties. In this situation, politicians will have a greater incentive to appeal to minority votes directly in order to win elections, especially in a first-past-the-post system such as India's where small shifts in votes can lead to large shifts in seats. If minorities are pivotal to electoral outcomes, politicians will increase the supply of security and prevent riots in order to attract their votes. Even if majority parties do not rely on minorities directly, a highly fractionalized party system will force ruling-party politicians to take actions that maximize their political options in the future, especially in terms of coalitions. In other words, ruling-party politicians must take care not to alienate minority voters who support parties that are likely to be future coalition partners, and this will also lead to ruling parties increasing the supply of security to minorities.[2]

---

[1] My theoretical arguments in this chapter – in particular the argument that low levels of electoral fractionalization can lead to high as well as low levels of violence depending on who is pivotal to the party in power – have benefited greatly from several conversations with Herbert Kitschelt.

[2] See Donald L. Horowitz, *A Democratic South Africa: Constitutional Engineering in a Divided Society* (Berkeley: University of California Press, 1991), pp. 177–85, for a general discussion of the value of majority and minority "vote pooling" in coalitions for increasing party moderation toward minorities.

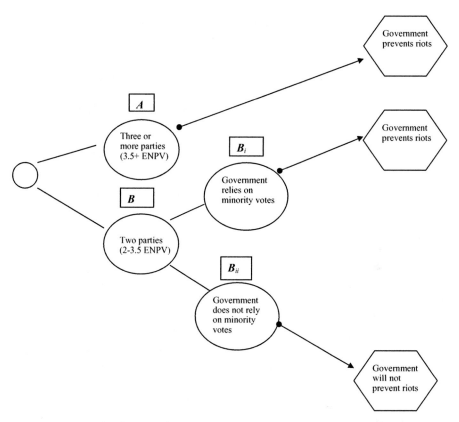

Figure 5.1 The theoretical relationship between party competition and a state's response to antiminority polarization and violence (ENVP = effective number of parties).

A more dangerous situation is when there are bipolar levels of party fractionalization in a state (i.e., less than 3.5 effective parties), represented by *B* in the chart, and one of these majority community parties effectively "owns" the antiminority issue while the other emphasizes some other cleavage, such as economic redistribution. In this case, we would expect the party that has the strongest antiminority identity to foment antiminority violence in order to attract swing voters away from its main competitor. Whether violence will actually result from this polarization, however, will depend on which party controls the state, the antiminority party or its competitor, and whether the party in power relies on minority votes. If the antiminority party with no minority support is in power (situation B_{ii}) we would expect it to allow antiminority mobilization and violence to occur, at least until such violence begins to result in such large economic and social costs that it begins to lose support from its own voters in the majority community. In situation B_i, however, where the party that "owns" the issue of economic redistribution and relies on minority support is in power, we would expect a different outcome. The party in power, worried that it would lose support from antiminority polarization, has every incentive to prevent violence that threatens its support base. As long as the state has sufficient institutional capacity to prevent violence and the party in power has control over the various police forces in a state, we can expect it to act firmly to prevent riots in this case, and to stop them quickly once they break out.

Why Should Minorities Benefit from High Levels of Party Fractionalization?

There are of course several enabling conditions to this model of the effects of party competition on the prevention of antiminority violence. First, I assume the existence of multiple issue dimensions in politics rather than simply the existence of a single majority-minority polarization. Second, I assume that minorities will be willing to "bid low" in terms of what they demand from majority parties across most issues in order to maximize their security. Third, I assume that the majority community does not regard increasing the minority's security as fundamentally threatening its own dominant position in the state and its own security.

These three conditions are necessary to help us understand why minorities should be the beneficiaries of greater levels of electoral competition and become pivotal voters in a state, rather than extremists from the majority community. We can think of some cases, for instance, where intense competition and high levels of party fractionalization has given more leverage to extremist voters and antiminority parties than to moderates dedicated to improving majority-minority relations. In Israel, for example, the moderate Mapai Party was in a pivotal coalition-forming position in the Knesset (the Israeli parliament) from 1949 until 1977. But then increased electoral competition in the Knesset elections of 1977, 1981, and 1988 put more conservative voters and their parties (Agudat Yisrael, Shas, and Degel Ha'Thora) in the pivotal position. These conservative voters and their parties used their pivotal position to draw Israeli politics away from majority compromise with the minorities rather than toward it.[3]

---

[3] Abraham Diskin, *Elections and Voters in Israel* (New York: Praeger, 1991), pp. 180–84.

First, where social, ideological, economic, and intraethnic cleavages among the majority community are highly salient, we would expect a greater willingness to reach out to minority voters. These cleavages are certainly not carved in stone and, as we will explore in the next chapter, they can and do change over time in response to state policies and incentives as well as individual actions.[4] In societies where such intragroup cleavages are strong, politicians from the ethnic majority will often prefer to seek minority support rather than the support of segments of their own ethnic group with which they may be in competition for scarce economic and political goods. In the United States, for example, the growth of economic divisions between white industrialists in the North and planters in the South from the 1920s to the 1950s created political incentives (when combined with the migration of blacks to the North) on the part of white northern politicians to appeal to minorities.[5]

The second factor that determines the degree to which parties will compete for minority support is the number of votes minorities can deliver and the cost to majority parties of the demands minority voters and politicians make, relative to the demands made by other groups within the majority community.[6] The number and intensity of the demands minority politicians and voters make will depend on factors such as whether antiminority violence has occurred in the past, whether a minority has a substantial educated mobilized middle class that relies on state employment (e.g., Anglo-Indians in India in the 1940s and 1950s or Sri-Lankan Tamils in the 1970s and 1980s), or whether the minority controls a large section of the economy (e.g., Chinese in Indonesia or Asians and whites in 1960s East Africa).

---

[4] For a discussion of the "hierarchy of cleavages," see Seymour Martin Lipset and Stein Rokkan, "Cleavage Structures, Party Systems, and Voter Alignments: An Introduction," in Lipset and Rokkan, eds., *Party Systems and Voter Alignments: Cross-National Perspectives* (New York: Free Press, 1967), p. 6. For an example, see David Laitin's *Hegemony and Culture: Politics and Religious Change among the Yoruba* (Chicago: University of Chicago Press, 1986), who shows how colonial policies privileged "ancestral city" identities in Yorubaland in Nigeria, a development that helps explain why Yorubaland has escaped the Muslim-Christian clashes that have occurred elsewhere in the country. In general a greater number of cross-cutting ethnic cleavages leads to an increase in party proliferation, but the relationship is certainly not a simple one, as we explore in Chapter 6: although most states in India are highly diverse, only some states have high levels of electoral fractionalization.

[5] Doug McAdam, *Political Process and the Development of Black Insurgency, 1930–1970* (Chicago: University of Chicago Press, 1982).

[6] The electoral system obviously makes a difference to how valuable small shifts in voter preferences will be: in India's plurality single-member system, small swings in votes can lead to dramatic swings in terms of seats.

141

Relatively poor and populous minorities that place a high value on one issue dimension that costs little for the majority to provide will be more attractive coalition partners than small wealthy, well-educated minorities with many demands that are costly, such as physical protection, government employment for educated members of groups, or the maintenance of a privileged economic status.[7]

Third, security for minorities will be inexpensive to provide as long as the measures taken do not seem to threaten the majority's own sense of physical security. Under what conditions will the majority be threatened? Protection for minorities will be more costly for majorities to provide when the minority is in the demographic majority in some areas of the country (allowing polarizing claims that the minority is taking over to seem more credible) or if the party that minorities support has no majority leaders that can provide reassurance to members of the majority population. Also, supplying greater security for minorities will be more politically costly in situations where minorities have substantial representation in the police, paramilitary forces, and army, because this representation can be used to convince people that supplying greater security is a prelude to minority domination of the majority. Lastly, once antiminority violence crosses a low or medium threshold and becomes widespread, the opposition party might be tempted to take an antiminority stance as well in order to neutralize the threat to its support base.[8]

How Do Indian States Fit the Model?

Most states in India now have very high levels of party fractionalization, especially considering that India has a single-member, district-plurality voting

---

[7] A similar argument, though put in formal language, has been made in the American politics literature by James M. Enelow and Melvin J. Hinich, "Non-Spatial Candidate Characteristics and Electoral Competition," *Journal of Politics* 44, no. 1 (1982), pp. 115–30. Hinich and Enelow show how the greater intensity of minority preferences can influence majority policies much more than previous models of party competition would predict.

[8] We can think of several such cases where ethnic violence has so polarized majority-minority relations that it has become impossible for members of the majority community to hold their coalition together while simultaneously appealing to minority voters. This happened in the 1890s for white Progressives in the U.S. South, because of racist polarization against African Americans. It has also happened in Israel, where the strength of the Jewish-Arab cleavage within Israel was such that all the mainstream Jewish parties, even on the left, regarded the Arab-supported Communist Party and Arab Democratic Party for decades as politically untouchable.

Table 5.1. *Number of Effective Parties in Major Indian States as of February 2002*

State/Ruling Party[a]	Most Recent State Election	Effective Number of Parties	Vote Share of Two Largest Parties
Andhra Pradesh/TDP	1999	2.78	84.48
Himachal Pradesh/ –	1998	2.85	82.53
Gujarat/BJP	1998	2.97	79.66
Madhya Pradesh/Congress	1998	3.09	79.87
Rajasthan/Congress	1998	3.19	78.18
West Bengal/Left Front	2001	4.14	67.25
Karnataka/Congress	1999	4.19	61.53
Orissa/Biju JD & BJP	2000	4.26	63.18
Punjab/Akali Dal	1997	4.40	64.23
Tamil Nadu/AIADMK	2001	4.84	62.36
Uttar Pradesh/Under Central Rule	1996	4.99	54.32
Haryana/Indian National Lok Dal	2000	5.01	60.83
Maharashtra/Congress & NCP	1999	5.64	49.8
Kerala/UDF	2001	6.16	52.76
Bihar/RJD	2000	7.70	42.98

[a] TDP = Telegu Desam Party, JD = Janata Dal, AIADMK = All India Anna Dravida Munnetra Kazhagam, NCP = National Congress Party, UDF = United Democratic Front, RJD = Rashtriya Janata Dal.

Source: Calculated from Indian Election Commission Reports available at <www.eci.gov.in>. The calculation of effective number of parties excludes independents.

system, which is normally associated with convergence to a two-party system.[9] As of February 2002, as we can see in Table 5.1, there were only five major states where two parties shared 75% or more of the vote (fewer than 3.25 effective parties). In Rajasthan, Madhya Pradesh, Gujarat, and Himachal Pradesh elections are basically a straight fight between the Congress and the BJP, whereas in Andhra Pradesh a regional party, the Telegu Desam Party (TDP), competes with the Congress Party. In all the other major states, there are at least three major parties and often many more competing for power in each state, and the number of effective parties in each state ranges from 4.14 to 7.70.

All three of the necessary conditions for high levels of electoral competition to benefit minorities are also present in India: there are multiple issue

[9] Pradeep Chhibber and Ken Kollman, "Party Aggregation and the Number of Parties in India and the United States," *American Political Science Review* 92, no. 2 (1998).

dimensions in politics along such issues as economic redistribution rather than simply the existence of a single majority-minority cleavage; minorities place a very high value of security and are willing to "bid low" in terms of what they demand from majority parties across most issues in order to maximize their security; the majority community values other issues much more than the majority-minority cleavage and does not regard increasing the minority's security as threatening its own dominant position in the state and its own security.

First, in recent decades, there has been a dramatic growth of new Hindu-led parties that explicitly claim to represent the "oppressed," especially the middle and lower castes and minorities, groups that collectively represent a majority of the Indian population. Examples would include the Bahujan Samaj Party, which represents Scheduled Castes; the Samajwadi Party, which has a particular base among backward castes; and the Telegu Desam Party, which represents middle and lower castes in Andhra Pradesh. All these parties are keen to expand beyond their core social constituencies and include Muslims in a broader social and political coalition. The rise of these "pro-backward" parties – and hence the size of the overall "market" for Muslim votes – has therefore increased considerably over the past few decades.

Second, Muslim voters in India are in a good position to profit from this increasing state-level electoral competition over distributional issues because they demand less than most Hindu voting blocs. Muslims are a large proportion of the electorate (12% overall, but much more in some states and constituencies), they have intense preferences on one major issue (security), and they make fewer and less intense demands on other political issues than many of the main voting blocks within the majority Hindu electorate, even lower than those made by the middle and lower castes.[10] Muslims make fewer demands in part as a consequence of their community's relative economic backwardness. As we can see in Table 5.2, the Muslim community

[10] There have been several estimates over the years to determine how important the "Muslim vote" is in national politics. Rudolph and Rudolph, for example, identified 207 constituencies in the Lok Sabha where Muslims accounted for 10% or more of the vote. Lloyd I. Rudolph and Susanne Hoeber Rudolph, *In Pursuit of Lakshmi: The Political Economy of the Indian State* (Chicago: University of Chicago Press, 1987), pp. 194–95. There have been fewer attempts to do the same for state politics. Ashgar Ali Engineer and several others have estimated that Muslims in Uttar Pradesh, where they are 17% of the state population but 29% in urban areas, are of crucial electoral importance in around 60 of the 403 assembly seats. "Defeat of BJP Is Defeat of Communalism," *Secular Perspective*, March 1–15, 2002, downloaded on June 15, 2002, from <http://ecumene.org/IIS/csss71.htm>.

Table 5.2. *Comparative Educational Levels among Different Religious Groups in India (%)*

	Muslims	Hindus	Christians
Male illiteracy	42.4	25.3	18.8
Male graduates	2.3	7.9	8.1
Female illiteracy	59.5	45.2	22.7
Female graduates	0.8	4.5	5.5

Source: National Sample Survey 43rd Round, 1987–88, cited in *Times of India*, December 10, 1995.

has proportionately fewer educated or wealthy members whose demands have to be met than any other major ethnic group. A National Sample Survey in 1987–88, for instance, found that only 2.3% of Muslim men and 0.8% of women had university degrees, compared with 7.9% of Hindu men and 4.2% of Hindu women. Only 8.0% of Muslim men had completed secondary school, compared with 17.2% of Hindus. In landholdings, too, Muslims are on average much poorer than upper- and middle-caste Hindus, largely because of the effects of the post-Partition land reforms that hit Muslim landlords harder than Hindus.[11]

As a result of anti-Muslim riots in the past, we know that Muslims place a very high priority on one particular issue – that of physical protection or at least nonaggression from the state – compared with other issue dimensions that are more salient for Hindu voters. In a 1991 survey in Delhi, for example, 23% of Muslims named communal violence or the Ayodhya issue as the single most serious problem India's citizens faced compared with only 6.2% of Hindu upper castes, 1.5% of Hindu backward castes, and 7.9% of Hindu Scheduled Castes. Muslims were much less likely than Hindus to identify distributional issues such as price rises and unemployment as the key issues facing the country. Muslims and the minority Sikh community were also the most nervous about the long-term future of Indian democracy: 80.3% of Muslims and 67.2% of Sikhs said the future of democracy was not safe in India compared with 51.3% of upper-caste Hindus, 44.4% of Scheduled

---

[11] The most important reasons for Muslims' disadvantaged economic position today are the large-scale land reforms in the 1950s, which Hindus were better able to resist; the loss of minority reservations in government service; and the emigration of much of the commercial and political Muslim elite to Pakistan. For comprehensive data on Muslims' economic backwardness compared with that of Hindus, see Mushirul Hasan, *Legacy of a Divided Nation: Indian Muslims since Independence* (Delhi: Oxford University Press, 1997).

Caste Hindus, and 49.3% of the backward castes.[12] That Muslim voters value security so highly and that they have fewer educated, privileged members whose interests have to be satisfied than any other major ethnic group make Muslims a relatively inexpensive voting bloc. In contrast, middle- and upper-caste voters, groups well entrenched in the bureaucracy who are better educated and with larger landholdings, will be a much more "expensive" group of voters for a party to attract.

Third, these Muslim demands for security cannot be portrayed as threatening to the core interests of the majority for the following reasons. Muslims have a very low level of representation in the armed forces (less than 1%), so there is clearly no threat to Hindu control of the country there. Muslims are also a minority in almost all districts in the country, with the exception of the state of Jammu and Kashmir and a handful of districts in other states (such as Mallapuram in Kerala and Rampur in Uttar Pradesh), so it is difficult to claim that a greater supply of security will alter the political balance within the country as a whole or within states. Finally, because they are a minority in all but one state and in most constituencies, Muslims generally support Hindu-led parties, whose Hindu leaders can therefore reassure anxious members of the Hindu majority that moves to help Muslims are not threatening to Hindus.[13]

Testing for the Observable Implications of the Model

In the remainder of this chapter I test for the observable implications of my theoretical argument about the relationship between party competition and the prevention of violence. First, is there a statistical relationship between the quantitative indicator of the level of electoral competition, the effective number of parties in a state, and a state's level of Hindu-Muslim violence? Second, when we examine situations when antiminority mobilization is fomented across India, do we find that states in situations A, B_i, and B_{ii} act in the ways predicted by the model? Third, when we examine specific instances where riots did or did not break out can we find evidence that the politically strategic considerations outlined in the model are really the key mechanisms responsible in predicting where violence does or does not break out?

---

[12] "The Face of the Delhi Electorate in the Gallup Mirror," *Indian Institute of Public Opinion Monthly Public Opinion Surveys* 36, no. 809 (1991), pp. 10–16.

[13] The notable exception here is in the city of Hyderabad in Andhra Pradesh, where Muslims have supported a Muslim-led party, the MIM.

Party Competition and Riot Prevention

Because detailed state-level opinion poll data on minority support for parties is only available since the mid-1990s in India, it is impossible to test statistically my arguments about the effects of minority support on government actions at low levels of party competition (situations B_i and B_{ii}). However, I can test for my central argument that high levels of party competition lead to lower levels of antiminority violence and that bipolar party competition is generally associated with higher levels of violence. To carry out this test I have compiled a monthly dataset on Hindu-Muslim riots and socioeconomic and electoral variables for 14 major Indian states since 1961: Andhra Pradesh, Bihar, Gujarat, Haryana, Himachal Pradesh, Karnataka, Kerala, Orissa, Maharashtra, Madhya Pradesh, Rajasthan, Tamil Nadu, Uttar Pradesh, and West Bengal.[14] As of 1991, the most recent census for which data on religious identification are available, these states accounted for 95% of India's total population and 93% of its Muslim population. The Hindu-Muslim riot data I use here were collected jointly with Ashutosh Varshney in 1994–96. They are derived from daily newspaper reports (every issue of the *Times of India* published between 1950 and 1995) and include information on riot occurrence and deaths, in addition to many other factors. The data we collected are both more complete than publicly available government data on communal violence and more useful in statistical and other types of analysis, because, unlike government data, they are disaggregated by town, district, day, and month.[15] These Hindu-Muslim riot data are correlated at 0.64 with the post-1954 Government of India annual data on communal riots and at 0.7 with the post-1975 data on atrocities against Scheduled Castes and Tribes.

I use these riot data to create two variables that measure Hindu-Muslim violence: *RIOTS*, the monthly number of reported Hindu-Muslim riots in each state; and *KILLED*, the deaths per month in Hindu-Muslim riots in each state. To control for the possibility that past violence is driving both the level of electoral competition (by increasing polarization) as well as the level of present violence – due to revenge for past events, or perhaps because

---

[14] I select 1961 as a starting date because state reorganization was largely complete for major states by this date, and because the key demographic data for these new states is only easily available for 1961 onward. Assam is not included here because of decisions made during the collection of the riot data, which make the data for that state less reliable than for the others.

[15] For details of how the Varshney and Wilkinson data were collected, see Appendixes A and B.

past violence is evidence of the continuing existence in a state of what Paul Brass has termed "institutionalized riot networks" that foment violence – I also calculate the variable *PREVIOUS VIOLENCE*, which measures the number of casualties in each state in the previous 5 and 10 years.

To measure the degree of electoral competition in a state, I employ the most widely used indicator of electoral competitiveness, the effective number of parties (ENPV). The formula for this index is $ENPV = 1/\Sigma v_i^2$, where v_i is the *vote share* of the ith party. This measure weights parties with a higher vote share more heavily than those parties with a very low vote share, thus providing a better measure of the "real" level of party competition than if we were to simply count the total number of parties competing in a state. I use Butler, Lahiri, and Roy, *India Decides*, as the source for these Indian state election data.[16]

One reasonable objection to the use of ENPV as an indicator of party competition is that the best indicator of the competitiveness of a system might in reality be competition at the level of party factions (i.e., *below* the party level) or between competing blocs of parties with similar agendas and interests (i.e., *above* the party level).[17] Unfortunately I could obtain no reliable data on the shifting factional alignments that exist *within* the major Indian political parties, but I am able to carry out a test for the effects of alliance-competition at the level above the individual party. I do this by adjusting ENPV for the presence of preelection interparty alliances – if three parties were allied they would be counted as one party in calculating the index – to create the new variable *ADJENPV*. However because of the extreme instability of coalitions in Indian state politics, I believe that *ADJENPV* will be a less reliable indicator of party competition than the underlying number of parties.

[16] David Butler, Ashok Lahiri, and Prannoy Roy, *India Decides: Elections, 1952–1995* (New Delhi: Books and Things, 1995).

[17] Herbert Kitschelt et al., *Post-Communist Party Systems: Competition, Representation, and Inter-Party Cooperation* (Cambridge: Cambridge University Press, 1999), pp. 8–9. The "fit" between factions and parties in India, however, is probably better than in other countries where party control over campaigns and elections makes defection much more costly for the individual legislator and hence a voice through a party faction more likely. In the Indian political system it is relatively easy, even after the passage of several antidefection laws, for dissatisfied factions within parties to go off and form their own parties without having to resign their seats and fight for reelection. Local alignments are also often as important as national party support in winning an election, making defection less costly. Some parties in India are basically the vehicles of only a few politicians, as can be seen from the fact that registered parties are often named after their dominant personality (e.g., "Kerala Congress-Joseph," "ADMK-Janaki Ramachandran").

The Indian national government has the power to impose central rule on a state and suspend its state legislature if it believes that a state is not being governed in accordance with the Indian Constitution, or if no stable state government can be formed. Because this central rule results in a state's governor taking over the administration, it is sometimes called "governor's rule," though more often termed "president's rule," reflecting the fact that the imposition of central rule must be approved by the president of India. To control for these periods when each state was under central administration, I therefore use the dummy variable *PRESRULE* in my statistical analysis.[18]

To see if there are particular party effects on riot control over and above the level of party competition – as is often alleged by both supporters and detractors of Indian political parties – I also collected data on when the BJP, Communists, Congress, or "Others" (which includes the middle- and lower-caste and regional parties) were in power or in coalition in each state each month from 1961 to 1995. To do this, I relied on Butler, Lahiri, and Roy's volume *India Decides*, on published Election Commission of India (ECI) election returns, and on approximately 30 books or articles on state politics, which I list in Appendix A.[19] I code a party as ruling (e.g., the variables *CONGRULE, BJPRULE*) where it has a clear majority of the seats in a state's assembly (Vidhan Sabha). In cases where a party does not have a majority of the seats but it is participating in government, either as an official partner or in an arrangement where it supports the government from outside, I code it as participating in a coalition (e.g., *COMMCOAL, BJPCOAL*). In those cases where the Congress Party splits – as in Maharashtra in 1978 – I apply the same rule introduced by the 52nd Amendment and used by the Election Commission to determine whether MLAs have "defected" or split the party: the resulting coalition government is still coded as being "Congress" if it contains more than one-third of the previous Congress members.

In addition to these indicators of violence and political competition I control for the same socioeconomic variables I used in the regressions in Chapter 4: a state's total population, its linguistic and religious diversity

---

[18] Dates for these periods of "President's Rule" were obtained from Lok Sabha Secretariat, *President's Rule in the States and Union Territories* (New Delhi: Lok Sabha Secretariat, 1996).

[19] Butler et al., *India Decides: Elections, 1952–1995*. Most ECI reports are now available online at <www.eci.gov.in>. I am currently collecting data that will ultimately allow me to test for the effects of all major parties in the country, as well as the ethnic support base and ethnic appeals made by each party.

(*LANGFRAC* and *RELFRAC*),[20] its Muslim population, and a state's level of urban income inequality.[21] I also control for a state's literacy level, obtained from the Indian census. To analyze these data I use the same negative binomial model discussed in Chapter 2.[22]

Discussion of Regression Results

Table 5.3 reports the results when we examined the relationship between the effective number of parties and the number of riots in each state in each month from 1961 to 1995. The results in these regressions, and in others not displayed here, support the hypothesis that there is a negative relationship between the degree of electoral competition in a state and its level of communal riots. The number of Hindu-Muslim riots goes down as the effective number of parties goes up, with the coefficient for the effective number of parties significant at the 99% level across all models, including, most importantly, those regressions where I control for a state's previous level of violence, the parties in power or coalition in a state, and (through the use of dummy variables for each state) other important state-level effects.[23]

Several of the socioeconomic control variables were significant in almost all models. Urbanization rates and states' total population are both highly significant and positively related to the probability of riots, which is a finding consistent with virtually every other study ever done on urban violence. But two other variables seem to be related to violence in a surprising way: states with greater income inequality in urban areas (at least as measured by *WBUGINI*) actually seem to have lower levels of violence than those with a more equal income distribution. And states with higher levels of literacy

---

[20] For a discussion of ethnic fractionalization indicators, see Peter C. Ordeshook and Olga V. Shvetsova, "Ethnic Heterogeneity, District Magnitude and the Number of Parties," *American Journal of Political Science* 38, no. 1 (1994), pp. 100–23, and Gary Cox, *Making Votes Count: Strategic Coordination in the World's Electoral Systems* (Cambridge: Cambridge University Press, 1998).

[21] I calculate my measures of state linguistic and religious fractionalization, using Rae's index $(1 - \Sigma g_i^2)$, where g_i is the proportion of the population in linguistic or religious group i. For definitions of these variables and information on the data used to calculate them, see the discussion in the previous chapter.

[22] J. Scott Long, *Regression Models for Categorical and Limited Dependent Variables* (Thousand Oaks, Calif.: Sage, 1997), pp. 217–63.

[23] I also ran these regressions using the coalition-adjusted measure of party competition discussed earlier: this variable had the same negative direction as ENPV but was insignificant in explaining both riot levels and deaths.

Electoral Incentives

Table 5.3. *Electoral Competition and Communal Riots in Major Indian States, 1961–1995*

	Riots			
	(1)	(2)	(3)	(4)
Effective number of electoral parties	−0.217	−0.267	−0.258	−0.229
	(0.071)***	(0.074)***	(0.073)***	(0.076)***
State population (log)	0.819	2.044	2.225	1.371
	(0.117)***	(1.233)*	(1.244)*	(1.236)
State election within 6 months	0.376	0.432	0.410	0.418
	(0.139)***	(0.136)***	(0.137)***	(0.137)***
National election within 6 months	−0.367	−0.374	−0.351	−0.370
	(0.145)**	(0.142)***	(0.143)**	(0.143)***
President's rule	−0.077	−0.276	−0.322	−0.576
	(0.200)	(0.200)	(0.183)	(0.227)
Literacy percentage	4.828	10.216	9.825	10.691
	(1.092)***	(4.829)**	(4.847)**	(4.799)**
Urbanization percentage	−1.931	−23.110	−23.212	−19.576
	(1.523)	(8.590)***	(8.581)***	(8.635)**
Muslim percentage	10.439	24.344	24.153	18.437
	(1.808)***	(16.446)	(16.476)	(16.315)
Urban Gini coefficient (World Bank)	−0.034	−0.034	−0.033	−0.040
	(0.019)*	(0.020)*	(0.020)	(0.021)*
Religious fractionalization	−10.704	−48.662	−47.393	−49.269
	(2.598)***	(10.283)***	(10.344)***	(10.198)***
Linguistic fractionalization	−6.226	−23.210	−23.161	−23.910
	(2.392)***	(7.293)***	(7.305)***	(7.228)***
Interaction of Relfrac and Langfrac	26.641	77.518	76.273	79.913
	(8.564)***	(26.328)***	(26.403)***	(26.082)***
Communist rule	−1.303	−1.482	−1.576	−1.524
	(0.335)***	(0.457)***	(0.445)***	(0.447)***
Congress rule	0.364	0.043		−0.266
	(0.112)***	(0.115)		(0.156)*
Riots in previous 10 years	0.015	0.008	0.008	0.009
	(0.002)***	(0.002)***	(0.002)***	(0.002)***
Coalition dummy				−0.529
				(0.182)***
State dummies		Included	Included	Included
Constant	−14.742	−23.218	−26.345	−11.829
	(2.122)***	(19.297)	(19.469)	(19.428)
Observations	5472	5472	5472	5472
Number of states	14	14	14	14

Standard errors in parentheses. * significant at 10%; ** significant at 5%; *** significant at 1%. For state dummy coefficients, see Appendix C.

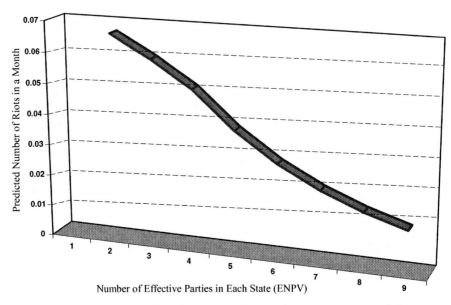

Figure 5.2 Predicted effect of state party fractionalization on communal riots

also seem to have higher levels of violence, despite predictions made by some that riots ought to decline as education rises. It is not the case, as we might think, that the effective number of parties is purely a function of a state's level of ethnic heterogeneity. The measure for party competition (ENPV) is not highly correlated with the measures of ethnic heterogeneity, and the effect of party competition remains robust even when we include measures of ethnic diversity. Interacting party competition variables with ethnic variables to look for their joint effect also had no discernible effect.

How much of a substantive effect does electoral competition have in explaining state levels of communal violence? We can see in Figure 5.2 that the predicted effect of moving from a state in which there were two effective parties to one in which there were eight parties, holding other factors at their mean, would be to reduce the expected number of riots in a state from 0.07 per month to .01 riots per month, a drop of more than 80%.[24] To give an example that is somewhat less abstract, the effect of moving from a state with Gujarat's level of party competition in 1995 (3.08 effective parties) to one with Kerala's level of party competition in that year (5.63 effective

[24] These marginal effects were all calculated using the stata7 command *mfx compute, at(x=value of interest mean)* following regression 3 in the table.

parties), while holding other factors constant at their mean, would have been to reduce the predicted number of riots in a state by half, from 0.05 to 0.025 riots in a month, or from 0.6 riots to 0.3 riots in a year.

Whether the BJP or the Congress had an overall majority in any particular state seems to have had no independent impact on the overall level of riot occurrence from 1961 to 1995.[25] In the case of BJP rule this may in part be a function of the fact that the BJP only began to win outright in state elections in the early 1990s, so there are very few observations, and that president's rule was imposed on four BJP-ruled states immediately after mass rioting broke out in December 1992, so the violence that some would argue resulted from BJP rule is classified under "president's rule" rather than "BJP rule." Congress rule was initially significant when I ran regressions (see column 1 in Table 5.3) but then became insignificant when I introduced dummy variables for states (in columns three and four in Table 5.3) and also when I ran the regression on only some decades from the time series. This makes sense for two reasons: first, Congress was in a dominant position for so many years in so many states that the variable CONGRULE is probably serving as a proxy for state- and time-specific factors; second, as we discussed in Chapter 4, despite Congress's official claims to always protect minorities, the party's status as the dominant catchall party for many years and its often weak party discipline has meant that at one time or another Congress politicians have both fomented and prevented communal violence for political advantage. Congress governments have failed, for example, to prevent some of India's worst riots (e.g., the Ahmedabad riots of 1969, the Moradabad riots of 1980, or the Meerut riots of 1987) and in some cases Congress ministers have reportedly instigated riots (Bihar ex-chief minister K. B. Sahay was allegedly involved in the 1967 Ranchi riots) and have blocked riot enforcement.[26] However, there does seem to be a clear party effect when we control for Communist rule. Communist rule is negatively related to the level of riots in a state in all versions of the model, no matter which other variables are included. The predicted effect of moving from a state where the Communists are not in power to one in which they have an overall majority, while holding other factors constant at their mean, would be to reduce the level of riots

[25] Only the coefficients for the regression in which the dummy variables for Congress rule were included are reported in Table 5.4.

[26] See, e.g., *Lok Sabha Debates*, May 14, 1970, p. 336, and October 7, 1982. p. 335, for details of alleged Congress interference with local riot prevention activities in Meerut and Jyoti Basu's allegations about Sahay's role in the 1967 Ranchi riots.

by three-quarters, from 0.51 riots per year to 0.12. One can speculate that this strong relationship is the result of two factors: a strong ideology of secularism, and (this would differentiate the party from Congress) a much greater degree of party discipline and ideological coherence over time.

Perhaps most interesting is that coalitions seem to have an independent effect in reducing the level of violence. When there is a coalition in a state, the predicted number of riots drops by more than half, from 0.56 riots per year to 0.33 riots. This effect applies even when coalitions include parties generally thought to foment violence, such as the BJP.

I also ran the same regressions I used on riots on the monthly level of deaths from communal riots in India's states from 1961 to 1995, rather than riot occurrence. The results were very similar to those for riots. The effective number of parties was again highly significant and negatively related to the level of deaths in a state: a rise in the number of effective parties from 2 to 8 in a state would lead, all other factors being equal, to a 50% reduction in the number of deaths. Moving from the number of effective parties in Gujarat in 1995 (3.08) to the number in Kerala (5.63) would have led to a predicted fall in the number of deaths of 25%. The dummy for Communist rule is again highly significant, with Communist rule associated with a reduction in deaths of almost 75% (from 0.92 to 0.24 per annum).

Party Competition, Minority Support, and State Riot Prevention

The fact that election surveys with detailed data on minority voting in state elections have only been collected since the mid-1990s makes it impossible to test systematically my hypothesis about the effects of minority support at low (bipolar) levels of party competition. However, it is possible to make use of the available exit survey data from the late 1990s together with party fractionalization data to provide at least a partial test of my arguments about the importance of levels of party·competition and minority support in explaining government response to riots. When we examine situations in which antiminority mobilization is fomented across India, do we find that states in situations A, B_i, and B_{ii} act in the ways predicted by the model?

To examine this issue, I look at state responses to attempts to foment violence throughout India during the Gujarat riots of February–April 2002. The Gujarat riots of 2002 have been extensively examined in the Indian press and by human rights organizations and academics. The BJP's "secular" Muslim-supported coalition partners in New Delhi were unwilling during this period to force the BJP to impose central rule on Gujarat, where the state government had allowed antiminority riots to continue for weeks after Hindu nationalists and family members were murdered at Godhra on February 27, 2002.

Many observers have argued that the Gujarat riots therefore symbolize the failure of coalitional politics in general to control communal extremism and communal violence in India.[27] I certainly acknowledge that the events in early 2002 showed that regional parties with minority support in their own states were unwilling to bring the central government down in order to protect minorities in Gujarat. However, this does not invalidate my general argument about the actions that politicians and parties will take in order to protect their own political futures in their own states. If we examine the state-level response to attempts to foment riots throughout India in 2002, we can see that state governments responded as predicted by my general model. States with high levels of party fractionalization prevented anti-Muslim mobilization even if the state government concerned (as in Orissa) included a Hindu nationalist party. In states with low levels of party competition, as predicted, the state response depended on whether the ruling coalition relied on Muslim votes. Where Muslims were an important support base for the ruling coalition, as in Madhya Pradesh (where exit polls from the most recent election suggest 97% of Muslims support the ruling party) or Maharashtra (99% Muslim support for the governing coalition), the state governments were highly effective in preventing violence. Where the governing party had no Muslim support, however, as in Gujarat, the government adopted a very weak and biased stance toward the riots.

In Table 5.4 I categorize the major Indian states in terms of whether they had low levels of party competition in which the governing party relies on minority votes (B_i) or does not rely on majority votes (B_{ii}) or in situations where there is high party competition in a state. Only in Gujarat did we have the most dangerous situation B_{ii}, where there was both a low level of party competition (2.97 effective parties, with Congress and BJP having obtained 80% of the vote between them in the previous election) and a party in power, the BJP, that did not rely on minority voters at all: election surveys estimated that the BJP got 0% of the minority vote in 1998. More-over, by 2002 the BJP, after a string of electoral reverses in by-elections and

---

[27] Syed Shahabuddin has long argued that the coalition allies have "compromised their secular ideology to join hands with the BJP and share power. Will they be willing to give up power if the BJP takes steps that are not to their liking? They may well look the other way." "Why Muslims fear the BJP," *Week*, April 12, 1998.

Table 5.4. *Party Competition and Riot Prevention, from February to April 2002*

State/Ruling Party[a]	State Coding	Effective Number of Parties	Vote Share of Two Largest Parties	Percentage of Muslim Voters Estimated to Support Governing Party	State Response to Riots
Andhra Pradesh/TDP	B_i	2.78	84.48	30%	Prevented
Himachal Pradesh/	B_i	2.85	82.53	NA	
Gujarat/BJP	B_{ii}	2.97	79.66	0%	Allowed
Madhya Pradesh/Congress	B_i	3.09	79.87	97%	Prevented
Rajasthan/Congress	B_i	3.19	78.18	92%	Prevented
West Bengal/Left Front	A	4.14	67.25	49%	Prevented
Karnataka/Congress	A	4.19	61.53	86%	Prevented
Orissa/Biju JD & BJP	A	4.26	63.18	16% (2% + 14%)	Prevented
Punjab/	A	4.40	64.23	NA	Prevented
Tamil Nadu/AIADMK	A	4.84	62.36	39%	Prevented
Uttar Pradesh/Under Central Rule	A	4.99	54.32	NA	Prevented
Haryana/Indian National Lok Dal	A	5.01	60.83	59%	Prevented
Maharashtra/Congress & NCP	A	5.64	49.8	99% (53% + 46%)	Prevented
Kerala/UDF	A	6.16	52.76	71%	Prevented
Bihar/RJD	A	7.70	42.98	61%	Prevented

[a] For acronyms, see Table 5.1.

Sources: CSDS and ORG-Marg opinion polls reported in *India Today* and *Frontline*. In all cases the most recent pre-2002 opinion poll is used as the most reliable indicator of the parties' support base, even if that was for the Lok Sabha national election in 1999. Sources: Madhya Pradesh: *Frontline*, November 19, 1999, pp. 46–48; Bihar: *Frontline*, March 31, 2000; Kerala: *India Today*, May 14, 2001, p. 26; Maharashtra: *Frontline*, November 19, 1999, pp. 44–45; Haryana: *Frontline*, April 14, 2000, pp. 52–53; Tamil Nadu: *India Today*, May 14, 2001, p. 21; Orissa: *Frontline*, April 14, 2000, pp. 52–53; Karnataka: *Frontline*, November 19, 1999, pp. 46–48; West Bengal: *India Today*, May 14, 2001, p. 23; Andhra Pradesh: *Frontline*, November 19, 1999.

important municipal elections over the preceding two years, was anxious to polarize the vote along majority-minority lines to bring Hindu voters back to the party in preparation for state elections that had to be held by mid-2003.

The result, as expected, was that the state performed very poorly in controlling the riots. According to press accounts and human rights investigations, the Narendra Modi regime facilitated the violence in many different ways: by transferring officials who had successfully prevented antiminority riots or who arrested Hindu militants involved in the violence; by delaying calling in the army until the worst of the violence was already over; by taking punitive action against people trying to register cases against the government's political allies; and by instructing state officials not to intervene in some cases to prevent the violence.[28] The link between government action and state response to riots was clear from the fact that the state BJP leaders met in late March, while the violence was still continuing, to discuss the possibility of calling early elections to benefit from the antiminority pro-Hindu wave the Godhra killings and subsequent riots had engendered.[29] As a result, Gujarat burned.

Outside Gujarat however, in states where there was relatively low competition but the party in power relied on Muslim votes or where party fractionalization was high, regardless of which party was in power, India's state governments performed very well in 2002 in preventing Hindu-Muslim violence from spreading as it had done in 1992–93.[30] This success came despite numerous attempts by Hindu nationalists – as well as a handful of attempts by Muslim militants – to foment violence in different states between February 27 and the end of April 2002. Figure 2.2 shows those cases where the press reported Hindu nationalist demonstrations, processions, bands, or attacks against minorities during this period, explicitly linked to the violence in Gujarat. As we discussed in Chapter 2, these are all events that one would have expected to lead in many cases to large-scale

---

[28] See "Modi Ties Hands of Cops Who Put Their Foot Down," *Indian Express* (New Delhi), March 26, 2002, p. 1; "Gujarat Pot Keeps Boiling as CM Looks the Other Way," *Indian Express*, March 29, 2002; *Indian Express*, March 28, 2002.

[29] See, for example, the reports in *Indian Express*, March 29, 2002, which describe political interference with law enforcement in Gujarat in March as well as BJP officials' discussions a few weeks after the riots began on whether to call early elections in the state to take advantage of the Hindu backlash.

[30] See Steven I. Wilkinson, "Putting Gujarat in Perspective," *Economic and Political Weekly* (Mumbai), April 27, 2002, pp. 1579–83.

violence, as they did in Gujarat. As we can see in Figure 2.2, very few of the precipitating events outside Gujarat led to significant numbers of deaths. The explanation for this lies in determined state law enforcement efforts, which themselves were the result of the electoral variables I have identified.

The map in Figure 5.3 shows data on precipitating events and deaths from February–April 2002 as well as data on the level of party competition in each state during this period. In states with low levels of party competition (75% of the vote or more split between 2 main parties) but in which the state governments relied on minority votes, we can see that the number of precipitating events that turned into large-scale riots was low. This was because the state governments in these states ordered their police forces to prevent violence in order to protect the multiethnic coalitions built around distributive issues on which they had won power.

In Andhra Pradesh (2.78 effective parties), Madhya Pradesh (3.09 effective parties), and Rajasthan (3.19 effective parties) the Congress governments of Ashok Gehlot (Rajasthan) and Digvijay Singh (Madhya Pradesh), determined to preserve their Hindu-Muslim coalitions before 2003 elections, put massive preventive measures into effect to prevent the violence from spreading into their states from adjacent Gujarat. In Madhya Pradesh the government rounded up thousands of militant Hindu nationalists, enforced curfews in dozens of districts, and ordered the police to take strong action against rioters. In Rajasthan too the police were under orders to prevent violence, and local police officers prevented riots from breaking out in Jaipur, Kishangarh, and Ajmer.[31] Chandrababu Naidu's TDP government in Andhra Pradesh was also absolutely determined to prevent violence: even though his party was in a national alliance with the BJP, it was well recognized that his party had been able to win 30% of the Muslim vote in 1999 because Naidu had always been able to prevent antiminority riots in the state and had paid special attention to Muslim voters in the capital, Hyderabad.[32] Naidu's police force arrested militants and was prepared to fire on militants to prevent them from starting a riot in Hyderabad in mid-March 2002.

---

[31] Though it is difficult to say for sure, it seems likely that early firm state action outside Gujarat – arrests, curfews, bands of movement – prevented some precipitating events from even occurring in the first place. For example, preventive measures stopped any precipitating events from taking place in towns such as Indore and Jhabua in Madhya Pradesh.

[32] *Frontline*, November 19, 1999. The Congress got an estimated 64% of the Muslim vote in Andhra Pradesh in the 1999 national elections.

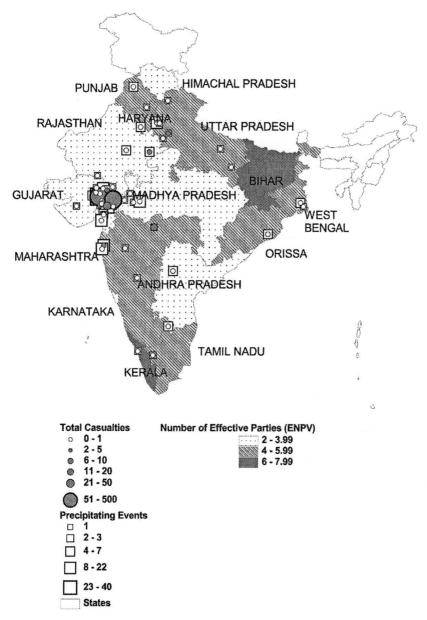

Figure 5.3   Reported precipitating events and deaths during the February–April 2002 communal violence and patterns of party competition (data on violence collected by Wilkinson based on *Indian Express* reports; data on levels of party competition calculated from Election Commission of India reports)

159

In states with high levels of party competition, governments were forced to take strong action to prevent riots in order to preserve their current coalitions or future political opportunities. This was true even when the governments included Hindu nationalist parties or parties formerly linked to communal movements, as in Orissa and Kerala. In Orissa the BJP–Biju Janata Dal (BJD) coalition government arrested 500 Vishwa Hindu Parishad (VHP) and Bajrang Dal activists to prevent violence during the March 1 strike called in the state.[33] In Bihar, with the highest level of party competition in India (with 7.7 effective parties), the ruling coalition repaid Muslims for their electoral support by massively deploying police in order to avert riots during Holi. Some states, such as West Bengal, benefited from having both an explicitly secular party in office and high levels of political competition (4.14 effective parties) that make the Muslims a crucial part of all the major parties' electoral arithmetic. The Communist Party (Marxist) or CPM took a firm line with attempts to cause trouble, and West Bengal police fired on *karsevaks* at Taldi in March when they refused to disperse, killing 1 and wounding 29.

The few apparent "exceptions" to the generalization that state governments outside Gujarat performed well in preventing violence in fact only go to prove the point. On closer investigation of these incidents – at Ajmer, Kishangarh and Gangapur (Rajasthan), Canning and Calcutta (West Bengal), Ahmadnagar (Maharashtra), and Bhubaneshwar (Orissa) – we find that the deaths that did occur were due largely to police action against rioters rather than the result of militants attacking minorities, as in Gujarat. One hundred percent of the casualties in Gangapur in Rajasthan, for example, were the result of police firing to break up an illegal Hindu militant attempt to block the route of a Muslim religious procession, killing 3 and injuring 15.[34]

How Electoral Competition Affects Riot Prevention

If we turn from the aggregate level to individual cases, can we also find evidence that the mechanisms outlined in this chapter are responsible for government action to allow or prevent actions likely to lead to riots? In this section I examine this question by looking at two cases from Uttar Pradesh in the 1990s where the UP government had to decide whether to

---

[33] "Partial Response in Orissa," *Hindu*, March 2, 2002.
[34] *Indian Express*, March 27, 2002.

prevent Hindu nationalist mobilizations that it knew were likely to lead to communal violence. In the first case, in Varanasi in 1991, the state government allowed the mobilization to continue, resulting in a riot in which 17 people were murdered. In the second case, at Mathura in 1995, the state government ultimately intervened to prevent the mobilization and averted communal violence. The difference between these two outcomes, I argue, can be explained when we look at three factors: the party in power: the BJP in 1991, a BJP-BSP coalition in 1995; the group of voters that the party in government saw as pivotal for its party's success in the next election (the BJP in 1991 wanted to attract Hindus, the BSP in 1995 wanted to attract Muslims); and the overall level of party competition in the state. Uttar Pradesh moved from a situation in 1991 in which the BJP felt that if it polarized the Hindu electorate it could win power unaided, to a more fluid system in the mid-1990s in which it was becoming clear no one group or party could form a government without the support of others. What happened in the town of Mathura in 1995 demonstrates the good effects of multipolar political competition in reducing violence, even in a situation where one of the two coalition partners in government, the BJP, was explicitly pro-Hindu and antiminority.

Varanasi, November 8–11, 1991

Although in retrospect it seems clear that a decisive shift toward multiparty competition took place in the political system in Uttar Pradesh in the early 1990s, this was not how it appeared to BJP leaders at the time. From 1989 to 1991 the party had launched a succession of demonstrations and processions around the Ayodhya mosque issue, and it won considerable sympathy from the state's Hindus when Mulayam Singh Yadav's police force fired at Hindu militants in Ayodhya in November 1989. In May 1991 the BJP won 34.5% of the vote in the state elections and a narrow majority (221 out of 425) in the UP Assembly. It appeared as if promoting Hindu issues was a sufficiently effective strategy so that the BJP would be able to avoid coalition politics in the future, and Kalyan Singh believed that the BJP, like the Congress Party it had replaced, could thrive as the dominant party in a system in which its opponents split the anti-incumbent vote.

The BJP, however, somewhat moderated its antiminority stance once in office in order to further its longer-term political objectives. Chief Minister Kalyan Singh was anxious to prove that the party could be "responsible" while in state government, in order to win over Congress voters who associated the party with extremism and to maximize the chances of the BJP winning power in the future, including at the national level. Throughout the 1991 election campaign Singh had tried to reassure moderate voters that the party could guarantee a "riot-free state" in which law and order were paramount.[35] The Singh government even leaked figures to demonstrate that it had been very effective in reducing the number of riots compared with previous regimes.

The BJP interpretation of these figures was, not surprisingly, that "The BJP, which merely proclaims justice for all and appeasement of none...turns out to be the real savior of Muslims."[36] The BJP's opponents argued that the figures merely demonstrated that the BJP and its allies caused the riots in the first place in order to win political power by solidifying the "Hindu vote." As one opposition politician remarked, "When the thief is made the caretaker, he cannot steal, he won't steal. They [The Shiv Sena and the BJP] engineered the riots, now they are in charge of law and order. So there will be some peace."[37] The opposition point of view was supported by the fact that the Police Intelligence Department reportedly submitted a confidential report to the BJP government in May 1991 providing evidence that the BJP mobilization campaigns had led directly to communal riots in the state. The BJP government, not surprisingly, suppressed the report.[38]

But one serious riot did occur under the BJP regime, at Varanasi in November 1991. On Friday, November 8, 1991, in a move that went against the Singh government's official policy that there should be no large processions in connection with the temple movement, the Hindu nationalist VHP was allowed to conduct a religious procession and ceremony with only a light police escort in the sensitive city of Varanasi. This procession led directly to a serious Hindu-Muslim riot. At around 9:15 P.M. a VHP procession, carrying a statue of the Hindu goddess Kali, marched through the heavily Muslim Madanpura area of the old city. The Hindu processionists chanted slogans and a few set off fireworks, one of which hit and injured a Muslim. When the processionists refused to stop setting off

[35] One part of this law-and-order strategy, reported to be very popular among the upper castes, was the Anti Copying Act, which provided harsh penalties for students. The repeal of this act was the first act of the Mulayam Singh's government when in took office in early 1993. See "Good Riddance," *Sunday*, July 9–15, 1995, pp. 62–63.

[36] Source: B. P. Singhal, "Definition of Secularism," *Indian Express*, August 28, 1992.

[37] *Pioneer*, June 27, 1992; "Muslims: Fear and Distrust," *India Today*, May 31, 1996, pp. 42–43.

[38] *Pioneer*, October 1, 1992.

firecrackers, scuffles began and Muslims threw brickbats and then stabbed one of the processionists. Several processionists ran to the nearby predominantly Hindu area of Godaulia and told lurid tales of Muslim attacks. Hindu mobs in Godaulia then attacked and killed Muslims attending a cinema in Godaulia. These attacks sparked off four days of riots, in which 17 people were killed.[39]

After the initial incidents, several attacks were made on the properties of Muslim *kothidars* (merchants) in the Madanpura area of the old city. Many of these silk merchants are relatively recent entrants to the city's important sari trade, which traditionally has been dominated by Hindu middlemen who buy from the Muslim weavers. In Varanasi and in nearby villages an estimated 200,000 Muslims work making saris to supply the city's huge export industry. The *kothidars'* success in moving up from weavers to middlemen has been resented by some of the Hindu merchants. Resentment, according to a social scientist who has worked for fifteen years in the area, is especially strong among the less-established Hindu merchants.[40] Local Hindu politicians have claimed that Muslims, some of whom had been buying up land in the area before the riots, were trying to drive Hindus out of the trade.

How can we explain this riot and the failure of the government to ban the procession? The BJP, after all, was in power in Uttar Pradesh and apparently wanted to present a moderate face to north Indian voters in order to widen its electoral appeal. To understand why the Singh government allowed the procession that led to the riot, it is necessary to understand both the state electoral context and the internal tensions within the party by November 1991. By the autumn of 1991 there was substantial unease among the hard-line Hindu nationalist group within the Uttar Pradesh BJP over the party's pragmatic attempt to rein in Hindu nationalist mobilizations. The hard-liners represented around 15 of the party's 50 MPs in the state and 80 members of the 212-strong BJP contingent in the Vidhan Sabha. Singh's attempt to placate the hard-liners with the transfers of 67 policemen and civil servants (who had taken action against Hindu protesters during the Ayodhya campaign the previous year) was not successful.[41] In early September Vinay Katiyar, the local MP for Ayodhya and the state

---

[39] This information comes from interviews with several UP cadre officers in Lucknow, Delhi, Varanasi, and Bareilly, July and August 1995.

[40] For background on the structure of the Varanasi sari industry, see "A Matter of Pride," *Business India*, February 28–March 13, 1994, pp. 260–61.

[41] "Temple Talk," *India Today*, August 15, 1991.

secretary of the Bajrang Dal (the VHP's youth organization) stepped up the hard-line pressure when he demanded the removal of some police barricades at Ayodhya and warned that "I do not care whether the BJP Government stays or goes, but the barricades at the site have to go." The Kalyan Singh government removed the barricades, but it was becoming obvious that to reduce some of the internal party pressure on Ayodhya, which would bring the state government into direct conflict with the center, some temporary concessions might have to be made elsewhere in the state.

These internal ideological pressures were serious but would probably not have been enough on their own to force Singh to allow the procession in Varanasi. The key reason he allowed the anti-Muslim, pro-Hindu, procession to take place in one of the state's most religiously important and sensitive cities was that by-elections to 14 state assembly districts were due in two weeks and the BJP viewed those Hindu voters sympathetic to Hindutva and fearful of the alleged "Muslim threat" as the pivotal constituency his party needed to attract. The BJP leadership was worried that the party would lose its bare majority in the Assembly unless it could use these issues successfully to mobilize Hindu voters behind the party.[42] The BJP had only an eight-seat majority in the state assembly, and several of these constituencies in May 1991 experienced extremely tight races between the BJP and its rivals supported by backward castes and Scheduled Castes, the Samajwadi Party and the BSP. In Nawabganj constituency, for example, five candidates had received more than 10% of the vote in the May election, and the BJP had narrowly lost the contest, getting 21.43% of the vote compared with the Janata/Samajwadi alliance's 24.66%. It seemed possible to many that the BJP's failure to resolve the Ayodhya mosque issue, combined with more general antigovernment sentiment, might lead to a low Hindu turnout, which in turn would lead to BJP losses in at least some of the seats and the consequent fall of the BJP government.

The BJP's worries about losing its majority therefore persuaded it that allowing a planned VHP antiminority procession to take place in the sacred, symbolic city of Varanasi might help the party to mobilize Hindu voters for the forthcoming by-elections. The local district magistrate was against the procession, which would go through sensitive Muslim areas of the city normally off limits to processions. But the state government told the district magistrate unofficially that the procession should be allowed unless it would definitely cause a disturbance. He therefore rescinded the ban and allowed

---

[42] *Times of India*, November 16, 1991.

the November 8 procession that led directly to the riots. Once the riots broke out, there was a substantial delay on the part of the administration in intervening to stop the violence, and the local police refused to take any action against BJP and VHP activists murdering Muslims in the central Godaulia area.[43] Evidence of police partiality was clear when Varanasi's MP, Mr. S. C. Dixit of the BJP, an ex-senior policeman himself, stayed in the police control room for three days during the riots, offering advice on how best to keep law and order.[44]

In the short term, the BJP strategy to win over swing Hindu voters worked. The party won 8 of the 14 by-elections and held onto its precarious majority in the UP house.[45] The BJP allowed the 1991 Varanasi procession to go on and then did not intervene once violence broke out because, on the evidence of the 1991 state elections, it felt it could win an absolute majority in the UP Assembly by pursuing an antiminority agenda that appealed mainly to the upper castes and those voters prejudiced against and fearful of Muslims.

Mathura, 1995

The contrast between the riot at Varanasi and the riot that almost broke out in the town of Mathura in August 1995 provides a good example of the way in which the shift to a genuine multiparty system in Uttar Pradesh (a system that now increasingly requires coalition governments) has improved the state's effectiveness in preventing communal riots. Because the BJP's coalition partner in 1995 needed to attract Muslim votes in the next election, it forced the government to stop a mobilization in Mathura that would have probably led to a serious riot.

In the December 1993 elections, the Bharatiya Janata Party in Uttar Pradesh suffered what it initially regarded as a temporary setback when it failed to win an outright majority in the state legislature. The Samajwadi Party and the largely Scheduled Caste Bahujan Samaj Party formed an anti-BJP government coalition in January 1994, which then fell apart in May 1995, when the BSP unexpectedly formed a coalition of convenience with the BJP. Both the BSP and the BJP hoped to use their period in office in

[43] Interview with UP IAS cadre no. 5, July 14, 1995.
[44] A. A. Engineer, "Banaras Rocked by Communal Violence," *Economic and Political Weekly*, March 7–14, 1992, pp. 509–11.
[45] By-election results taken from *Journal of Parliamentary Information* (1992).

order to build support for the state elections that would follow once the two parties finally parted ways. But the two partners had very different views of the possibilities in the next election. The BSP, with 67 seats in a 425-seat house, and a social base (Scheduled Castes) of only 22% of the population, knew that its future lay in building coalitions with other Hindu castes and with the Muslims. The BJP, on the other hand, believed that by mobilizing a large segment of Hindus around antiminority issues as it had done in 1989–91, it could once again secure an overall majority in the UP assembly.

The BJP's chosen statewide symbol was the western UP town of Mathura. In August 1995 the BJP and its allied Hindu nationalist organization, the Vishwa Hindu Parishad (VHP), announced their attention to carry out a *Vishnu mahayagna* (religious offering to the Hindu god Vishnu) and a *parikrama* (circumambulation) around what it referred to as the "disputed" complex that houses both the Hindu Keshav Das temple and the Muslim Shahi Masjid Idgah.[46] The VHP timed the *parikrama* to coincide with the religious festival of Janamashthami, which draws thousands of pilgrims to Mathura every year. And it planned the *yagna* for a Friday, when it would coincide with large numbers of Muslim worshipers offering their afternoon prayers at the nearby Idgah.[47]

There was little local support for the *mahayagna* and *parikrama*. Mathura has not been the focus of intense Hindu-Muslim violence in the past nor has it been the focus of intense political competition. The only reported Hindu-Muslim violence near the site was in 1954, when a Krishna idol in the temple was broken by unknown intruders, leading to a brief scuffle during which three people were slightly injured and 25 people were arrested.[48] Local Hindus and Muslims had already come to a legal agreement, signed by the Muslim Trust and the Krishna Janmasthan Seva Sangh (Krishna's birthplace service organization) in 1968, about the boundaries and organization of what was now being claimed by the VHP as a "disputed site."[49] Excluding

---

[46] An Idgah is an enclosed site where the festival of Id (breaking the fast of Ramadan) is held. The VHP claimed a four and a half acre plot next to the Idgah as a hall for religious and cultural events. *India Today*, June 15, 1993.

[47] On August 4, some Muslim politicians from Aligarh visited Mathura to encourage Muslims there to turn out en masse for prayers at the Idgah on August 18. A proposed "peace march" to coincide with the VHP parikrama, planned by Muslim students from Aligarh Muslim University, was halted by authorities. *Hindu*, August 7, 1995; *Indian Express*, August 14, 1995.

[48] *Times of India*, August 23, 1954.

[49] The text of this agreement is reproduced by former supreme court justice V. R. Krishna Iyer in an article in *Hindu*, August 16, 1995.

the local VHP and BJP leaders in Mathura, the vast majority of the town's inhabitants seemed to oppose the VHP's *parikrama*. Because of the security precautions and worries about violence, the number of pilgrims in August 1995 was down sharply, ruining the town's most important tourist season. Those tourists who did make it through the security cordons found most of the hotel rooms occupied by civil servants and police officers.[50]

There were three reasons why Mathura rather than some other town was selected by the VHP for large-scale Hindu-Muslim mobilization in August 1995. First, Mathura is one of the most important Hindu religious sites in north India. Second, and more important, the Keshav Das temple–Muslim Idgah complex is one of several dozen disputed mosque-temple sites in Uttar Pradesh and, as such, a "natural" site for anti-Muslim mobilization. The third reason, and the one that led to the VHP choosing Mathura rather than one of the other possible sites, was that the VHP leaders knew that the BJP needed substantial backward-caste support if it was to win the upcoming assembly elections. The Keshav Das temple, and the city and district of Mathura are closely associated with the Hindu god Krishna, who is regarded as a Yadav (a backward caste), and the hope was that a campaign built around Krishna would win over large numbers of backward castes suspicious of the BJP's upper-caste image. As one Hindu nationalist leader put it, "As of now, the Yadavas, almost to a man, are with the S.P. [Samajwadi Party] led by Mulayam Singh Yadav. But when the call of a Yadava god comes, can they remain indifferent?"[51]

In backing the Mathura agitation, the BJP leaders knew that they were taking some risk of alienating their coalition partner in the UP government, the lower-caste Bahujan Samaj Party, and the state's chief minister, Ms. Mayawati. Mayawati and the BSP were looking to Muslims for political support in the upcoming elections, and there was a risk that she would disallow the Hindu agitation for this reason. However, the BJP-VHP leaders seemed to have gambled that Mayawati would acquiesce because of her wish to remain in power. Power means patronage, and Mayawati was not only making a great deal of money personally as chief minister but was also winning political supporters by dispensing state funds to important social groups. In addition, the BJP had taken great pains to win over Mayawati and drive a wedge between her and her national party leader, Kanshi Ram. For

---

[50] *Hindu*, August 16, 1995.
[51] *Frontline*, September 8, 1995, p. 8.

example, at one BJP function in Lucknow, Mayawati was praised effusively while Kanshi Ram was studiously ignored.

In late July, when the *mahayagna* was first mooted, Mayawati apparently did not wish to challenge it openly, and she gave her verbal permission for the *mahayagna*, as long as the festivities were not on too large a scale.[52] But Mayawati, whose party's ethnic support base was even smaller than the BJP's, quickly realized just how serious an electoral threat the Mathura *mahayagna* would be. During her period in office Mayawati had made great efforts to win over at least some of the Muslim vote from the Samajwadi Party.[53] Her government had created a new ministerial position for minority welfare and, at a meeting in Lucknow on July 10, the BSP national leader, Kanshi Ram, announced that the UP government would henceforth reserve 8.44% of government jobs for poor Muslims.[54]

If the BJP's mobilization campaign succeeded, Ms. Mayawati realized that the BSP stood to lose all the ground she had gained with Muslim voters, which could potentially block any hopes of increasing the BSP's share of the vote if state elections were to be called the next year. Mayawati had to weigh the advantages of remaining in government prior to the next year's elections against this likely loss of Muslim voters, and she ultimately decided there was more to be gained from taking a firm stance than for acquiescing in the Mathura mobilization. In early August, therefore, Mayawati took a public stance against the Mathura *mahayagna*. On August 4, in the UP Assembly, Mayawati announced "nobody will be allowed to start any new tradition for paying obeisance in the complex." Shortly afterward she announced that no VHP ceremony would be allowed within three kilometers of the complex.[55]

The hard-liners in the VHP held their ground, hoping that Mayawati would back down. On August 10, Acharya Giriraj Kishore, the joint general

[52] Venkitesh Ramakrishnan, "Angry in Mathura," *Frontline*, September 8, 1995, pp. 10–16.

[53] Meanwhile, the SP leadership was doing all it could to foment revolt among the BSP's Kurmi (Middle Caste) MLAs, who were unhappy over the allocation of ministries in the state government. Mayawati stemmed the revolt by immediately appointing four Kurmis as district magistrates and promising to appoint two Kurmis as ministers as soon as possible. For details, see *Sunday*, July 30–August 5, 1995, pp. 24–26.

[54] By reserving benefits for "backward Muslims" the BSP got round the constitutional provision that forbids employment discrimination on grounds of religion but allows it to relieve social backwardness. The BJP forced the BSP to withdraw this proposal, but it nonetheless helped establish Mayawati's credibility with Muslims. See "Looking for Support," *Sunday*, July 30–August 5, 1995, pp. 24–26, and "Growing Mandalisation," *Economic and Political Weekly*, July 22, 1995.

[55] "VHP's Mathura Plan Strains BJP-BSP Ties," *Indian Express*, August 7, 1995.

secretary of the organization, reiterated the VHP's determination to hold both events. The head of the VHP's national youth wing said on August 11 that the *parikrama* and *mahayagna* would go on as planned.[56] Meanwhile, BJP leaders were getting worried about the possible fall of the BSP-BJP coalition, which might open up the possibility of a more united opposition to the BJP in the forthcoming elections. Several senior leaders tried to broker a compromise in which the *parikrama* would be scrapped and the *mahayagna* held several hundred meters away from the complex.[57] Mayawati was prepared to make a few concessions. On August 12 she transferred Mr. Deen Dutt Sharma, the Mathura district magistrate and a man the VHP disliked for his firm commitment to law and order. But at a meeting on August in Lucknow, Mayawati again made it clear to the VHP leaders that she would not back down on the central issue of the *mahayagna*.

On August 14, VHP leaders met for an hour and a half with Mayawati in Lucknow. She refused to allow the *mahayagna* and threatened to resign if the BJP pushed the issue, unwilling to risk the long-term loss of Muslim votes for the short-term advantages offered by staying in power prior to the elections. Once it became obvious she would not back down, a BJP compromise plan was adopted. The VHP would scrap the *parikrama* and hold the *mahayagna* on August 18, but well outside the three-kilometer security cordon surrounding the temple-mosque complex.[58] This cordon prevented hundreds of Muslim and Hindu activists, who had traveled from throughout northern India, from getting near the site. This plan worked smoothly, and no Hindu-Muslim riot broke out, although many VHP cadres felt betrayed by their leadership and refused to participate in the VHP's face-saving "Vrat Hindu Sammelan," at which only 1,000 people turned up.

Conclusion

This chapter has examined how electoral incentives determine whether state governments will prevent communal violence. As party competition increases, especially if the new parties focus on redistribution from forward to backward castes, majority politicians will have greater incentives to appeal to Muslim voters who can provide them with the margin of victory. The

---

[56] Statement of All-India Bajrang Dal Chief, Jaibhan Singh Pawaiyya. *Indian Express*, August 12, 1995. For Kishore's statement, see *Hindu*, August 11, 1995.

[57] See the statement of BJP spokesman K. L. Sharma on August 11, 1995. *Hindu*, August 12, 1995.

[58] *Indian Express*, August 15, 1995.

effect of the decline of the dominant Congress Party and the resulting party competition in recent years has not, as some have argued, been to increase the level of communal violence. On the contrary, the increasing party competition for minority voters has led to a reduction in Hindu-Muslim violence, as politicians are forced by electoral incentives to take firm action to prevent Hindu-Muslim riots.

Greater political competition in the states leads, I have argued, to a greater degree of security for Muslims, who demand less for their votes than other significant groups of voters. Unfortunately, the growing leverage of Muslim voters has had negative consequences for India's 2% Christian minority. While Muslims are a large enough voting block to swing elections in most Indian states and have in recent years become a sought after support base for many backward-caste and Scheduled Caste parties, Christians, at least outside Kerala and the Northeast, are too small a community to "count" politically in most Indian states. In the late 1990s the Hindu right in many states therefore seems to have switched strategies and began polarizing Hindu voters against Christians rather than Muslims. For example, Dara Singh, the leader of the Bajrang Dal in the state of Orissa, reportedly organized attacks on missionaries in that state in the run-up to the 1999 parliamentary elections. Electorally, this strategy carries many of the benefits of the anti-Muslim strategy (with Christians, like Muslims, often being portrayed as tools of foreign powers bent on converting allegedly defenseless tribals and lower castes) and few of the electoral costs, because Christians are a much smaller proportion of the electorate.

One important question for the long term, however, is whether, as Muslims become more politically mobilized, wealthier, and make more demands for job reservations and economic benefits, they will become more "costly" and thus less attractive voters for majority parties to court, possibly even resulting in a resurgence of anti-Muslim polarization in state politics? One response to this worry is that Muslims in India are, given their poverty, a long way from being too costly to court compared with other groups of voters. But even if they do become wealthier and demand more, evidence from the South of India, where Muslims are already better off than in the North and have long enjoyed political clout, suggests that, after an initial electoral breakthrough is made by minorities, and majority parties all begin to court them as voters, it becomes difficult for majority parties to go back to scapegoating minorities overtly.

One plausible hypothesis is that, after an initial lengthy period in which minorities establish themselves as electorally pivotal, majority politicians over time try to neutralize the minority issue as a vote loser by accepting the need to protect minorities. In political science terms, supplying security to minorities moves from being a positional issue (with politicians taking different positions) to a valence issue (all politicians in public are for it) as politicians in competitive systems try to neutralize the issue as a vote loser.[59]

This tentative hypothesis seems to have some support from what has actually happened in some states in India, as well as in comparative cases (e.g., in Bulgaria and the United States) that we examine in Chapter 7. In the Indian state of Tamil Nadu, for example, Muslims are a highly urbanized and relatively well off community (63% live in towns) that has played an important role in politics ever since the 1967 DMK victory over the Congress, when Muslim support was important for the DMK's strong showing in Dindigul district and in electoral victories in the towns of Vaniyambadi, Ambur, Tiruvannamalai, and Tirupathur, a lesson that has not been lost on any of the main parties in the state in the succeeding decades.[60] Other political parties quickly began to court Muslims as well after this electoral breakthrough, and despite the community's relative wealth and political clout, it continues to be courted by all of the major parties in the state, and successive state governments have taken strong actions to prevent anti-Muslim polarization.

In Kerala too the Muslims have been a vital constituency ever since the formation of what became the Left Democratic Front (LDF) in the 1960s. Their pivotal role in 14–20 of the 140 seats in the State Assembly has allowed them to make or break the United Democratic Front (UDF) and LDF governments in the state. Muslim political leverage has allowed them to demand and get control of important ministries (such as Education) and force the removal of school textbooks that portrayed Muslims as disloyal Indians.[61] Yet this growing political clout has not led to Hindu voters in the state coalescing along the Hindu-Muslim cleavage or ceasing to appeal to Muslim parties and voters. Instead all the major parties and politicians accept the need to protect minorities in order to remain politically viable in the state.

---

[59] For the distinction between "valence" and "positional" issues, see Donald E. Stokes, "Spatial Models of Party Competition," *American Political Science Review* 57, no. 2 (June 1963), pp. 368–77.

[60] Muslims have also been a key swing vote in Madras corporation elections. Marguerite Ross Barnett, *The Politics of Cultural Nationalism in South India* (Princeton: Princeton University Press, 1976), p. 288.

[61] *India Today*, December 1–15, 1980, pp. 39–40; *Sunday*, February 27–March 6, 1994, p. 45.

6

Party Competition and
Hindu-Muslim Violence

THE INSTITUTIONAL ORIGINS
OF DIFFERENCES IN ELECTORAL
COMPETITION

Once we establish the existence of a relationship between party competition and levels of ethnic violence, an obvious question follows: if party competition is so important, then what explains states' different levels of party competition? Why do some states have party systems that reflect a greater degree of cohesion around backward-caste identities than others? Why, in particular, did some southern states in India such as Kerala and Tamil Nadu have an effective opposition to Congress by the early 1960s, well before states in the north such as Uttar Pradesh and Bihar?

My central argument in this chapter, laid out in Figure 6.1, is that an institutional difference going back to the 1920s – the implementation of job and educational reservations for backward and lower castes in the South but not in the North – is largely responsible for different state patterns of postindependence party competition and fractionalization. In the early 20th century, after the colonial state and several princely states in southern India grouped members of diverse castes together under a backward-caste identity, they provided political and economic incentives for Indians to mobilize around this identity, which has been sustained since then not only by government affirmative action programs but also by social and political organizations that grew up in response to the governments' willingness to reward claims made on the basis of "backwardness."[1]

In exploring the historical development of these caste cleavages, I show that, because the colonial state provided institutional incentives for

[1] The first preferences for "backward classes" were introduced by the government of the princely state of Mysore in 1918, and by the colonial governments in Madras and Bombay in the 1920s. Similar measures began to be adopted in a few northern states only in the 1980s. See Marc Galanter, *Competing Equalities: Law and the Backward Classes in India* (New Delhi: Oxford University Press, 1984).

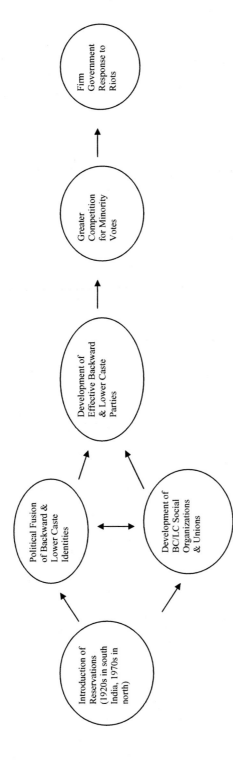

Figure 6.1 The institutional origins of state-level differences in party competition

backward-caste mobilization, substantial intra-Hindu party political competition emerged as early as the 1920s and 1930s in such southern states as Kerala and Tamil Nadu. Even after Congress's political victories in the south in the late 1930s and 1940s, these political movements retained their coherence, and they formed the basis of the Communist Party in Kerala and the Dravida Kazhagam in Tamil Nadu, parties that led the political opposition to Congress after independence. As a result of this strong backward-caste solidarity, political alternatives to Congress existed in the South, in the postindependence period creating a "market" for minority votes. To win Muslim votes away from their political rivals, Hindu parties here have had to offer security guarantees to Muslims and other minorities. Despite attempts to foment Hindu-Muslim conflict in Tamil Nadu and Kerala, governments in both states have effectively prevented or controlled most riots.

In the North, by contrast, large-scale mobilization around a backward-caste identity is a recent phenomenon. In previous decades, because of the weakness of opposition parties, the ruling Congress Party politicians had little incentive to woo Muslim voters at the expense of the Hindu nationalist swing vote (the Jana Sangh) and their core upper-caste constituents. The growing strength of similar lower- and middle-caste parties in northern India since the late 1980s, however, has shifted the balance. After experiencing a short-term increase in violence prompted by a Hindu nationalist countermobilization, the North has witnessed a similar overall decline in Hindu-Muslim violence.

Does Ethnic Fractionalization Explain Party Fractionalization?

Before beginning to analyze the effects of caste reservations on political fractionalization, we should first consider one alternative explanation that is often raised to explain why party fractionalization might be higher in some states than in others – that some states are more ethnically diverse than others and that their higher number of parties reflects a greater number of salient cleavages. Gary Cox, for example, has found that the effects of a first-past-the-post party system on party aggregation are always moderated by ethnic heterogeneity.[2] Pradeep Chhibber likewise argues that ethnic heterogeneity helps explain why there is more state-level party competition

---

[2] Gary W. Cox, *Making Votes Count: Strategic Coordination in the World's Electoral Systems* (Cambridge: Cambridge University Press, 1997), pp. 218–19.

in India than we would expect, given its first-past-the-post, single-member district electoral system.[3]

Although the link seems plausible, there is no clear relationship between a state's level of ethnic diversity (using Indian census data) and its number of parties. The measure for party competition (ENPV) is not highly correlated with the measures of ethnic heterogeneity, and regressions on ENPV using the same socioeconomic and ethnic variables used in Chapter 5 provide no ethnic fractionalization variables that explain the observed variation in states' levels of party competition (see Table 6.1). In fact, no socioeconomic variables whatsoever – including literacy and urbanization – seem to be significant in explaining a state's level of party competition.

One reason for the lack of a statistical finding may be because census data in India only imperfectly represent the underlying ethnic diversity of the country. For example, the Indian census, from which I calculate my indicator of linguistic fractionalization, lists "Hindi" as the dominant language in many states in the North. But since 1975 the census category "Hindi" has in fact aggregated 48 separate answers to the question "What language do you speak?" including such major regional languages as Bhojpuri (23 million speakers in 1971, or 7% of those identified as Hindi speakers), Chattisgarhi (10.6 million), Kumaoni (1.7 million in 1971), Pahari (2.2 million), and Garhwali (1.9 million). This 1975 decision to aggregate many language answers under the heading "Hindi" – presumably to bolster the position of Hindi as the national language – has had the effect of leaving unrecognized many languages that have been important both in politics and in party proliferation. For example, in 2000, after years of political mobilization, the new states of Chhattisgarh and Uttaranchal were carved out of Madhya Pradesh and Uttar Pradesh to accommodate political movements that represent people who speak Chhattisgarhi, Kumaoni, Garhwali, and Pahari, all of which are identified as "Hindi" in the census.[4]

Another obvious problem is that since 1931 the Indian census has not collected information on major caste identities, with the exception of the quarter of the population that composes the Scheduled Castes and Scheduled Tribes. In December 1949 the Indian government decided it would no

---

[3] Chhibber and Kollman find that party centralization as well as ethnic fractionalization has an effect on party fractionalization at the district level. Pradeep Chhibber and Kenneth Kollman, "Party Aggregation and the Number of Parties in India and the United States," *American Political Science Review* 92, no. 2 (1998), pp. 329–42.

[4] Personal communications from Dr. M. Vijayanunni, former census commissioner of India, November 3, 2002; March 27, 2003.

Table 6.1. *Do State-Level Differences in Ethnic Heterogeneity Explain Levels of Party Competition?*

	Number of Effective Parties	
	(1)	(2)
Population (log)	−0.144	−0.142
	(1.932)	(1.932)
Upcoming state election	−0.004	
	(0.011)	
Upcoming national election	0.001	
	(0.011)	
President's rule	0.001	
	(0.016)	
Literacy percentage	2.743	2.731
	(6.627)	(6.627)
Urbanization percentage	−5.570	−5.565
	(12.716)	(12.714)
Muslim percentage	2.351	2.385
	(21.286)	(21.285)
Urban Gini coefficient (World Bank)	−0.001	−0.001
	(0.011)	(0.011)
Religious fractionalization	−0.462	−0.430
	(11.572)	(11.573)
Linguistic fractionalization	−1.561	−1.534
	(11.921)	(11.921)
Ethnic fractionalization	3.827	3.751
	(33.186)	(33.187)
Riots in previous 10 years	0.000	0.000
	(0.002)	(0.002)
Constant	4.243	4.207
	(30.716)	(30.715)
Observations	5,472	5,472
Number of states	14	14

Notes: Standard errors in parentheses. * significant at 10%; ** significant at 5%; *** significant at 1%. For state dummy coefficients, see Appendix C.

longer publish caste data and cross-tabulate them with socioeconomic data because to do so would be to encourage further caste divisions within Indian society.[5] So the ethnic fractionalization data I use in the regression do not

---

[5] *Times of India*, December 5, 1949. This measure, of course, did not remove the influence of caste as an important social and political factor in Indian society.

reflect caste cleavages that are clearly politically important in explaining party competition and aggregation.[6]

Even if we were able to generate 1931-style caste data for the contemporary period, however, that would still not necessarily answer our problem, because a census-derived measure of the underlying number of castes does not necessarily tell us how castes will aggregate politically. Politicized ethnicity depends on a whole range of factors, such as federal boundaries and government policies, and not just on underlying census categories.[7] We know, for instance, that smaller ethnic groups in Nigeria identified themselves with the "big three" groups of Hausa-Fulani, Yoruba, and Ibo during the 1960s, when Nigeria had essentially a three-unit federation, because to do otherwise would have been politically suicidal for the small groups. But as the number of federal units has increased in Nigeria since the 1970s, politicians can now feasibly form political movements around ethnic identities that might include less than a million people, because the new smaller states make these identities potentially large enough to win a majority in state elections.[8]

Kerala: The Institutional Origins of Party Fractionalization

Preindependence Caste Mobilization in Travancore and Cochin

The present-day state of Kerala was created in November 1956 through the merger of the two former princely states of Travancore and Cochin together with the Malayalam-speaking areas of Madras state.[9] The new state, 39,000

---

[6] There was a major debate before the 2001 Indian census about whether caste categories should be reintroduced in the census (they were not). The main arguments for and against are outlined in Satish Deshpande and Nandini Sundar, "Caste and the Census: Implications for Society and the Social Sciences," *Economic and Political Weekly*, August 8, 1998, pp. 2157–59.

[7] Ethnofractionalization indices are frequently used in the comparative politics literature without considering the extent to which they are endogenous to the variables they are being used to explain. Gary Cox, for instance, interacts ethnic fractionalization data with a variable that measures the magnitude of the median legislator's district; he does not take account of how district magnitudes and other institutional factors affect underlying ethnic identifications over time.

[8] Donald A. Horowitz, *A Democratic South Africa: Constitutional Engineering in a Divided Society* (Berkeley: University of California Press, 1991), pp. 215–26. Dan Posner's excellent new study on Zambia explores in depth the whole issue of how the shifting size of the arena of competitive politics affects which ethnic identities become politicized.

[9] Travancore and Cochin became part of India in 1947 and were administered as a single unit after 1949.

square kilometers in area and with the country's highest population density, is one of the most linguistically homogenous in India, with around 94% of the population speaking Malayalam as its first language, and most of the remaining 6% speaking Tamil. Despite the fact that the state's per-capita income is below the national average, Kerala is by many social indicators highly advanced: the literacy rate, at 94.2% in 2001, is by far the country's highest, the proportion below the poverty line (25.4%) is well below the 36% national average, and life expectancy at birth is 70.7 compared with an all-India average of 62.4 years.[10]

Kerala is religiously diverse, and non-Hindu minorities are a larger proportion of the population than in any major state except Kashmir. Hindus, 82% of the overall Indian population, account for only 57% of Kerala's 29 million inhabitants. Muslims, with 23% of the population, are the next largest minority group, and Kerala is also home to a third of India's Christians, who account for 19% of the state population. Kerala is also home to the last 125 members – the rest having emigrated to Israel – of South Asia's oldest Jewish community. In contrast to most Indian states there are no significant religious differences in rates of urbanization; the rate for Hindus is 27%, for Muslims 27%, and Christians 24%.

At the turn of the 20th century the Hindu caste system in Travancore and Cochin, dominated by the 5% Brahmin minority, was harsher toward the middle-caste Nairs and lower-caste Ezhavas and Pulayas than in any other Indian states. While the *touch* of lower castes was regarded throughout India as polluting by high-caste Hindus, southern Indian upper castes practiced the concept of "atmospheric pollution," the idea that a lower caste could taint the upper by his mere presence within a specified distance. An untouchable who appeared on the scene while upper castes were engaged in an especially important religious rite therefore risked serious punishment for having "polluted" the ceremony. Ezhavas, though their situation was better than that of the lowest untouchables, also suffered from restrictions on social distance, and from sanctions that prevented Ezhava men and women from carrying umbrellas, covering their upper bodies, wearing certain kinds of cloth, and using some types of cooking utensils.[11]

---

[10] Figures from *Statistical Outline of India, 2000–2001* (Mumbai: Tata Services, 2001) and "Ranking of States and Union Territories by Literacy Rate and Sex: 2001," in *Census of India 2001 Provisional Population Totals: Paper 1 of 2001* (Delhi: Controller of Publications, 2001).

[11] Prema Kurien, "Colonialism and Ethnogenesis: A Study of Kerala, India," *Theory and Society* 23 (1994), pp. 393–94. A more detailed description of intrareligious differences

Lower-caste mobilization in Travancore and Cochin began much earlier than in states in the North, a development that had two main causes. First, Travancore and Cochin states were strongly influenced by politics and caste categorizations in the nearby Madras presidency (discussed later in this chapter), and therefore took a relatively benign attitude to lower-caste political mobilization compared with other princely states. Second, educated elites among the lower castes in Kerala arose much earlier than in the North, in part because a few Ezhavas were well placed to take advantage of growing economic opportunities in trade and agriculture in the 19th century. By the 1880s these Ezhava entrepreneurs wanted social recognition to go with their new wealth and began to press the government to admit their sons in elite educational institutions.[12]

In 1892, 10,000 Ezhavas, Christians, and Muslims in Travancore petitioned the Raja to protest against discrimination in access to education and government employment. This was followed in 1896 by a separate larger Ezhava petition complaining about discrimination against their caste. In 1903, in the most important single act of lower-caste mobilization, the Ezhava social reformer Sree Narayana Guru founded an Ezhava caste association, the Sri Narayana Dharma Paripalana Yogam (SNDP). By 1928 the SNDP, whose stated goal was to promote the "religious and secular education and industrious habits among the Elava [Ezhava] community," had over 50,000 members and hundreds of local branches throughout Travancore.[13] During the 1920s and 1930s the organization was active in fighting for Ezhava and untouchable access to Hindu temples, and held important nonviolent protests at Vaikom in 1924 and the Guruvayoor temple in 1931–32.[14] The regime responded favorably to many of these efforts. Frightened that the Ezhavas might convert to Christianity if their demands were not met, the government passed a path-breaking temple entry bill

---

among Kerala's religious communities is provided in V. K. S. Nayar, "Communal Interest Groups in Kerala," in Donald E. Smith, ed., *South Asian Politics and Religion* (Princeton: Princeton University Press, 1966), pp. 176–90. For a fuller description of caste among Kerala's Muslims, see Victor S. D'Souza, "Status Groups among the Moplahs on the South-West Coast of India," in Imtiaz Ahmed, ed., *Caste and Social Stratification among Muslims in India* (New Delhi: Manohar, 1978), pp. 41–56.

[12] T. J. Nossiter, *Communism in Kerala: A Study in Political Adaptation* (Berkeley: University of California Press, 1982), p. 30.

[13] Ibid., pp. 30–32.

[14] P. M. Mammen, *Communalism vs. Communism: A Study of the Socio-Religious Communities and Political Parties in Kerala, 1892–1970* (Calcutta: Minerva, 1981), p. 53.

in 1937 that guaranteed lower-caste access to all government-controlled religious sites.[15]

The Ezhava mobilization on behalf of lower castes and untouchables was matched by a process of middle-caste mobilization around a Nair caste identity. In 1914 several prominent Nairs, determined to reform their own community's personal laws, and worried about growing Christian and Brahmin dominance in education and government, followed the SNDP's lead and formed their own broad caste organization, the Nair Service Society (NSS), to press their community's interests. The NSS grew rapidly, and by independence in 1947 it had set up a network of local branches, hospitals, and educational institutions throughout Travancore and Cochin.

The Nairs' success as a lobbying group acted as a further spur to Ezhava mobilization in the state. The Ezhavas and several other castes feared that proposals in the early 1930s to introduce limited democratic government in Travancore would lead to the replacement of Brahmin rule by Nair rule, because the wealthier Nairs would dominate the proposed property franchise. The Ezhavas therefore joined together with Muslims and Christians and in 1932 successfully petitioned the Raja to moderate the plan so that each community had its own share of reserved seats. Spurred on by this success, the Muslim, Ezhava, and Christian "Joint Political Congress" then pushed for reservations in government employment for each religious and caste community, a demand that was conceded in 1936.

The Ezhava mobilization over political rights was matched by a corresponding agitation over the rights of the many Ezhava landless laborers, who worked on plantations owned by Brahmans, Nairs, and Christians. This labor movement forged a link between the Communists and the Ezhava community, because Communist members helped organize labor agitations and, in order to avoid detection and punishment by the Travancore and Cochin governments, concealed their Communist links by becoming active in Ezhava caste organizations.[16]

Postindependence Ethnic Politics in Kerala

The strong preindependence caste mobilization in Kerala and the political struggles between Nairs and Ezhavas led to the emergence of an effective backward-caste opposition party to Congress in the postindependence

---

[15] Nossiter, *Communism in Kerala*, p. 80.
[16] Bhabani Sen Gupta, *Communism in Indian Politics* (New York: Columbia University Press, 1972), pp. 175–83.

period much earlier than in north India. The Nair- and Christian-dominated Congress's harsh suppression of a Communist-organized labor strike on plantations between 1948 and 1952 helped cement the social and political division between the Nairs and Christians on the one side and the Ezhavas on the other.[17] According to one estimate, 1.2 million Ezhavas voted for the Communists in the 1957 elections, with only 200,000 voting for the Congress, whereas the Congress secured 1.25 million Christian votes compared to only 170,000 for the Communists.[18] In the 1950s the Ezhava's SNDP secretary estimated that his organization supplied the Communists with as many as 60,000 active party members.[19] The only polling data we possess on patterns of religious voting show that, just before Kerala's first election in 1957, the Hindu vote was split 27% to 42% between the Nair- and Christian-dominated Congress and the Ezhava-dominated Communist Party, with 28% of Hindus not expressing a preference. By comparison, in the northern state of Uttar Pradesh, 50% of Hindus expressed a preference for Congress before the 1957 elections, with those Hindus who opposed Congress dividing their votes among several smaller, weaker, caste-based parties.[20]

Kerala's state politics from 1957 to 1967 revolved around attempts by the Congress and Communists to win political power, either outright or through short-term coalitions with smaller parties. One major difficulty that both the Communists and Congress faced in trying to build coalitions was that their official stances against "communalism" made it politically very difficult to reach out to the Muslim League, which enjoyed solid support in Muslim majority areas in the north of the state. In the 1960 state elections, the Congress leadership became worried enough about its electoral prospects to make an informal electoral understanding with the Muslim League. After Congress did unexpectedly well in the 1960 elections, however, the Congress unceremoniously abandoned the league to form a government with a more acceptable "noncommunal" party.

In the mid-1960s the leaders of the Ezhava-dominated Communist Party finally realized that to win power they would need to form more lasting coalitions with explicitly ethnic parties. In September 1966 the Communist

[17] Ibid.

[18] Jitendra Singh, quoted in Sen Gupta, *Communism in Indian Politics*, p. 186.

[19] Mammen, *Communalism vs. Communism*, p. 103.

[20] Indian Institute of Public Opinion, *Monthly Public Opinion Survey* 16–19 (January–April, 1957).

leaders therefore met in Ernakulam with the leaders of six other parties, including the Muslim League, to discuss the possibility of a "United Front" alliance to contest the 1967 state elections. These negotiations were successful and the resulting alliance transformed Kerala politics: the United Front swept to power in the 1967 elections, gaining 117 of 133 seats. In response to their dramatic electoral defeat, the Nair- and Christian-dominated Congress Party quickly organized its own, multiethnic coalition. Congress made a particular effort to win over the Muslim League from the United Front. Mrs. Gandhi publicly moderated her earlier criticisms of the league and announced that the league was "not out and out communal" and was therefore an acceptable coalition partner.[21] Local Congress leaders assured the league that if it supported them in the future, there would be no repeat of Congress's 1960 postelection betrayal.

In the 1990s, though the names of the coalitions have changed, the two main competitors for political power in Kerala are still a Communist (Ezhava-led) coalition, now called the Left Democratic Front (LDF), and a Congress (Nair- and Christian-led) alliance, now called the United Democratic Front (UDF). Over the years, as party splits have occurred among all Kerala's ethnic parties, both coalitions have become genuinely multiethnic, although the majority of any one ethnic group usually votes with one coalition or the other. For example, from 1974 to 1986 a breakaway faction of the Muslim league supported the Ezhavas (Communists), while most Muslim representatives continued to vote with the Nairs and Christians in the Congress. The LDF and UDF coalitions in Kerala are so finely balanced and electoral margins so narrow that governments usually have a majority of only a few seats in what is now a 140-seat assembly. This outcome, of course, gives individual MLAs and minority parties a great deal of political leverage, which they can use if their group's interests are not being effectively addressed.[22]

The electoral demography of Kerala is especially favorable toward the Muslims, who are concentrated in the north of the state. Since the

---

[21] E. J. Thomas, *Coalition Game Politics in Kerala* (New Delhi: Intellectual Publishing House, 1985), p. 69.

[22] For example, in 1982, shortly before a crucial vote of confidence the house's only independent member demanded, and got, a new district (with the MLA's hometown of Patanamthitta as district headquarters) as the price for his support. "Kerala: Tightrope Act," *India Today*, February 28, 1982, pp. 33–34; "Rocking the Boat," *India Today*, November 30, 1982.

1960s this geographical concentration, combined with bloc voting on the part of the Muslims, has allowed the Muslim League to control 14 to 20 seats in the 140-seat Kerala Assembly. Given the continued strength of caste cleavages between the Nairs and Ezhavas, this puts the league in a very powerful position. Muslim politicians are not shy about broadcasting their importance as kingmakers. State Industries Minister E. Ahmad claimed in 1983 that "Without Muslim League support no one can rule Kerala for a day."[23] More recently C. H. Mohammed Koya, the longtime leader of the Kerala Muslim League, openly boasted that "We [the league] will decide who – the Congress or the Communists – should rule the state."[24]

These claims are only a slight exaggeration, and what Horowitz terms "multi-polar fluidity" – a situation where three or more ethnic parties exist, with shifting coalitions among them – has existed in Kerala since the 1960s.[25] On two occasions the league has brought governments down when it felt the Muslims were not being fairly treated: in the late 1960s, over the issue of Communist favoritism to Ezhavas, and then again in 1987, over what it saw as UDF (i.e., Nair-Christian) threats to Muslim employment preferences.[26] To avoid such defections, the prudent Congress or Communist coalition leader takes great care to appoint Muslims to important ministries such as Education (which Muslims held from 1967 to 1980) and to address all widely held Muslim concerns. In contrast to the North, for instance, Muslims in Kerala have been able to have textbooks that portray Muslims as disloyal Indians removed from the school system.[27] One indicator of Muslims' substantial political clout in Kerala is their control over government expenditure: at one point during the 1990s, Muslim ministers were reported to head departments responsible for 60% of the state budget.[28]

---

[23] *India Today*, January 15, 1983, p. 59.

[24] E. M. S. Namboodiripad, "Coming Full Circle," *Frontline*, November 3, 1995, pp. 93–94.

[25] Donald A. Horowitz, *Ethnic Groups in Conflict* (Berkeley: University of California Press, 1985).

[26] Nairs and Christians resent the fact that the richer sections of the Ezhavas and Muslims are eligible for state affirmative action programs, and have consistently tried to introduce economic criteria into these programs to exclude well-off Ezhavas and Muslims and include poorer Nairs and Christians. "Polarisation of Forces in Kerala," *Hindu*, February 23, 1991.

[27] *India Today*, December 1–15, 1980, pp. 39–40.

[28] *Sunday*, February 27–March 5, 1994, p. 45.

Hindu nationalist movements based in northern India have over the years tried to replace Kerala's caste cleavages with an overarching Hindu identity that would help them displace the Congress and Communists. In the early 1980s the BJP/RSS organized several events designed to bring Nairs and Ezhavas together around Hindu themes, including a mass ceremony in the port city of Cochin that attracted 500,000 participants.[29] The BJP also launched a campaign in 1992 to try to persuade Hindus in the UDF to throw out their Muslim cabinet members, who, it alleged – no doubt, tongue in cheek – were "religious fundamentalists."[30]

These Hindu nationalist mobilization efforts have failed. Even before independence Hindu nationalists found it extremely difficult to gain a foothold in Kerala, and Dilip Menon reports that Ezhavas, who "continued to see themselves as a community apart, rather than as Hindus," jeered the leader of the Hindu Mahasabha when he came south to address an SNDP meeting in 1930.[31] Since independence the caste cleavage has been sustained in Kerala by both state employment preferences for backward castes (extended in 1957) and the activities of strong social and political organizations that grew up in the preindependence era. The backward caste associations have dramatically expanded their scope and influence since independence. In the early 1980s, for example, the Nair Service Society had 4,000 branches throughout the state, large financial reserves, 1,125 schools, 23 colleges, and various hospitals and hostels. Access to these benefits was available to those who invested in a Nair identity.[32] Keralan voters, guaranteed access to numerous practical benefits on the basis of their caste affiliations, including large-scale affirmative action programs and access to credit unions and educational and health benefits, have unsurprisingly been unwilling to abandon these for membership in some ill-defined Hindu community. Keralan Hindus' generally low level of enthusiasm for a Hindu political identity is demonstrated both by their voting preferences (the Hindu nationalist BJP's share of the vote in Kerala has consistently been less than 1%) and by their tendency to tune out of national Hindu events such as the

---

[29] *India Today*, April 30, 1982, p. 49.

[30] *Malayala Manorama*, May 1, 1992, translated in *India Speaks through Its Regional Press*, May 27, 1992, p. 10.

[31] Dilip Menon, *Caste, Nationalism and Communism in South India: Malabar, 1900–1948* (Cambridge: Cambridge University Press, 1994), p. 107.

[32] *India Today*, January 15, 1983, p. 59.

televising of the Hindu epic Ramayana in Kerala (ratings were among the lowest in India).[33]

The Effects of Party Fractionalization in Kerala

The level of Hindu-Muslim violence in postindependence Kerala has been very low. From 1950 to 1995, according to the data I collected with Ashutosh Varshney, there were 19 reported Hindu-Muslim riots in Kerala in which 16 people died and 290 were injured. Controlling for population, Kerala has a moderate level of riots (0.65 riots per million) and an extremely low level of casualties (0.55 deaths per million in Hindu-Muslim violence since 1950), a rate far lower than that in states such as Gujarat, Maharashtra, Bihar, and Uttar Pradesh

This development cannot be explained, as is sometimes argued, by a long state tradition of religious syncretism or by the region's supposed culture of nonviolence.[34] The 1921 Mappila rebellion in Malabar was one of the worst outbreaks of communal violence ever in British India, with Muslim peasants attacking and murdering Hindu merchants and landlords. Recent research by Theodore Gabriel on ethnic conflict in North Malabar has also uncovered a considerable number of Hindu-Muslim riots in the 1920s and early 1930s: in 1932 Hindus attacked Muslims for not voting for their candidates in local board elections in Mattanur, and in March and November 1934 serious riots broke out near Cannonore.[35] Postindependence levels of general political violence in Kerala have also been high, with political party workers often attacking and murdering their rivals. In the early 1980s, for example, 138 people were killed in over 1,000 violent clashes between party workers.[36]

Nor can Kerala's low level of violence be explained by the absence of issues likely to precipitate violence. In states such as Andhra Pradesh and Gujarat, for example, Hindu-Muslim riots are often blamed on the recent influx of "Gulf Money," brought back by Muslims who work in the

---

[33] *India Today*, March 31, 1993, p. 45.

[34] C. Gouridasan Nair, for example, refers to "the Malayalee's cosmopolitan nature and religious tolerance . . . dating back to the millennium preceding the Christian era." *Frontline*, July 17, 1992.

[35] Theodore Gabriel, *Hindu-Muslim Relations in North Malabar, 1498–1947* (Lewiston, N.Y.: Edward Mellen, 1996), p. 293.

[36] *India Today*, August 31, 1983, pp. 30–31.

Persian Gulf, and who are then alleged to use their newfound wealth to try to dominate politics and build ostentatious mosques, which threaten the local Hindus. Yet no state has been so affected by this influx of money from the Gulf as Kerala. From 1975 to 1987, 1,100 new mosques were built in the state, and many of these were substantial *pucca* buildings that replaced small unobtrusive *niskara pallis* – prayer huts built in crowded market areas.[37]

Hindu nationalist organizations have also made many attempts to unify Kerala's Hindus against religious minorities, using exactly the same techniques that have led to riots elsewhere in India. In the past three decades, the RSS has organized major demonstrations against the creation of the Muslim-majority Malappuram district in 1969, attempted to use force to take control of the disputed Thali Temple/Mosque in 1968, and agitated against state expenditure during the visit of the pope to Kerala in 1986.[38] In 1992, during the height of the agitation over the Ayodhya mosque, both Hindu and Muslim extremist organizations from outside Kerala organized provocative marches throughout the state.[39]

The reason why the level of Hindu-Muslim violence has been so low, despite the existence in Kerala of antiminority mobilizations similar to those that have led to violence elsewhere in the country, is that high levels of party fractionalization have forced successive governments to order the Kerala police force to prevent attacks on minorities in the state at all costs. The Muslim minority's leaders in the state are well aware that they hold the balance of power between the UDF (Nair-Christian) and LDF (Ezhava) coalitions and are quick to demand action whenever they feel their security is in jeopardy. In 1992, as the Ayodhya mosque agitation was reaching dangerous levels throughout India, the Indian Union Muslim League under Sulaiman Sait threatened to bring the Congress-led UDF government down unless there was a speedy overhaul of the police and bureaucracy and strong action against those who sought to incite anti-Muslim riots in Kerala.[40]

---

[37] Some of these new mosques have shopping complexes attached, which raises suspicions that they may be built to circumvent zoning restrictions on shops. Since 1957, with the exception of religious buildings put up on government land, there have been virtually no building restrictions on mosques, churches, and temples in Kerala. "Petrodollar Mosques in Kerala," *Muslim India* 5, no. 60 (December 1987), p. 554; *India Today*, August 31, 1983, pp. 30–31.

[38] For details of these various agitations, see K. Jayaprasad, *RSS and Hindu Nationalism: Inroads in a Leftist Stronghold* (New Delhi: Deep and Deep, 1991), pp. 182–202.

[39] "A Flare-up in Kerala," *Frontline*, August 14, 1992, p. 122.

[40] *Frontline*, September 11, 1992, pp. 30–31.

After some clashes in Trivandrum in which the Muslim League felt the UDF government had not intervened firmly enough, the league invited leaders of the rival LDF coalition to a party dinner and warned that "We are taking stock of the situation. We may take a definite stand very soon."[41]

Given the importance of the Muslim swing vote in Kerala since the mid-1960s, such threats work. In Kerala, unlike in states in the North of India, police and local officials are left in no doubt that riots must be prevented if at all possible and quickly stopped if they do break out. On the very rare occasions where individual officers have not taken action to protect Muslims, they have been suspended or given punitive transfers. From 1967 to 1973, during which time 131 Hindu-Muslim riots (which led to 1,142 deaths) occurred throughout India, the only senior police official to be severely punished for negligence in connection with a communal riot was in Kerala. While police officials in states such as Gujarat were let off with written warnings for allowing hundreds to die, the Kerala government sharply criticized, then suspended a deputy superintendent of police for his negligence in the 1971 Tellicherry riots, in which no one was killed.[42]

Most Hindu mobilization efforts in Kerala do not turn into riots because they are met with a massive deployment of police, backed up where necessary by the Kerala Armed Police and Central Paramilitary forces. In Kerala, unlike most states (where riot-prevention instructions are issued only to district-level officers), detailed riot-prevention plans are given out to every station officer.[43] A book written by an author sympathetic to Hindu nationalists, reviewing the failure of the movement in Kerala, complains that the heavy-handedness of the police has prevented the RSS and Bharatiya Janata Party from effectively organizing in the state. During the Thali temple agitation in 1968, for example, district magistrates announced preventive curfews and restrictions on movement to prevent activists reaching the site, and during the following year the police arrested 1,500 RSS volunteers who were demonstrating against the creation of the Muslim Mallapuram district.[44]

On the rare occasions when Hindu-Muslim riots have broken out since Muslims became pivotal in Keralan politics, they have been met with swift

---

[41] *India Today*, August 15, 1992, pp. 29–30.

[42] *Lok Sabha Debates*, November 21, 1973, pp. 7–18; *Times of India*, December 11, 1973.

[43] *Ninth Annual Report of the Minorities Commission, 1-4-1986 to 31-3-1987* (New Delhi: Controller of Publications, 1989), p. 96.

[44] Jayaprasad, *RSS and Hindu Nationalism*, pp. 186–89.

and determined police action. In sharp contrast to states in the North, I have been able to identify no occasion where the Kerala police hesitated to break up anti-Muslim violence or intervened on the side of Hindus against Muslims. Most riots last only as long as it takes for the police to rush reinforcements to stop the violence. After riots broke out in Tellicherry in 1971 the police quickly cordoned off the town and then rushed in armed reinforcements.[45] In Trivandrum in 1985 the police opened fire to disperse large mobs that seemed to be on the brink of a riot.[46] News reports indicate that 80% of Hindu-Muslim riots in the state since the mid-1960s have been stopped within a single day, 95% within two days. In contrast to some riots in other states such as Bihar in the 1960s, or Gujarat, almost all the deaths in riots in Kerala occurred due to police firing rather than as a result of anti-Muslim pogroms. And almost all the deaths (88% of deaths in Hindu-Muslim riots) occurred on the first day of the riot, signaling that the police acted quickly and firmly rather than letting violence drag on for several days.

If anything, successive LDF and UDF governments have at times been accused of doing too much in order to retain Muslim political support, and we can point to several instances where Muslim attacks on Hindus have met with only a weak administrative response. In 1983 UDF Chief Minister K. Karunakaran ordered the police to withdraw from the capital city of Trivandrum just before Muslim organizations launched a demonstration that led to large-scale looting. Reports indicated that Karunakaran was worried because his Muslim League coalition partners were in discussions with the LDF, and so he overruled local police officers who argued that a strong police presence was necessary.[47] Another example of Muslim League influence over law enforcement came in 1991, when Ramesh Chandrabhanu, the deputy inspector general of police for northern Kerala, was transferred after only two months in the job for reprimanding some Muslim League activists involved in a clash in Kasargod.[48] And when in 1992 a commission of inquiry into incidents earlier that year at Palakkad (when Muslims attacked a BJP sponsored *ekta yatra*, or unity procession) indicted some politically connected Muslims, the ruling United Democratic Front, heavily reliant upon Muslim political support, quickly shelved the first report and

[45] *Times of India*, December 30, 1971.
[46] *Times of India*, December 23, 1986.
[47] *India Today*, January 31, 1983, p. 43.
[48] *India Today*, February 29, 1992, pp. 37–38.

announced a fresh "judicial probe" that was no doubt expected to come up with politically more acceptable answers.[49]

Tamil Nadu: Caste Polarization and Hindu-Muslim Peace

Caste Mobilization in Preindependence Madras

The southern state of Tamil Nadu, 130,000 square kilometers in area and with a 1991 population of 56 million, was created in 1956 after a lengthy and sometimes violent agitation by Telegu and Tamil speakers who wanted their own states to be carved out of the multilingual colonial-era boundaries of Madras state. Eighty-five percent of Tamil Nadu's population speaks Tamil as its mother tongue, with a further 9% speaking Telegu at home and Tamil outside. In 1991, 89% of the state's population was Hindu, with 5.5% Muslim and 3% Christian. Hindus are divided into several broad caste groups: the Brahmins (3%); the advanced backward castes and lower backward castes (51–67% depending on which figures one believes); and the Scheduled Castes (20%). The Muslim minority is concentrated in a few districts and highly urbanized, with 63% of Muslims living in towns compared with 32% of Hindus and 39% of Christians. Tamil Nadu's literacy rate of 73.7% in the 2001 census is better than the Indian average of 65.4%, while the proportion living in poverty (35%) in the state is around the Indian average.[50]

In Madras, as in Kerala, powerful backward-caste movements emerged in the first few decades of the 20th century. Their leaders complained about the existing Brahmin dominance of government employment and higher education. The Brahmins, 3% of the Madras population, held from 60% to 79% of the jobs in four major departments of the Madras government and accounted for around 70% of the graduates from the University of Madras.[51] Backward-caste leaders urged the government to guarantee political representation for the "non-Brahmins" in new provincial

[49] "Communalism Infects Kerala Too," Hindustan Times, May 25, 1992.
[50] Figures from Statistical Outline of India, 2000–2001, and Statement 32, "Ranking of States and Union Territories by Literacy Rate and Sex: 2001," in Census of India 2001 Provisional Population Totals: Paper 1 of 2001.
[51] S. Saraswati, Minorities in Madras State (Delhi: Impex, 1974), pp. 48–49. In 1912, according to figures provided by Irschick, Brahmins held 55% of deputy collector positions, and 82% and 73% of subjudge and Munsif positions. Eugene F. Irschick, Politics and Social Conflict in South India: The Non-Brahman Movement and Tamil Separatism, 1916–1929 (Berkeley: University of California Press, 1969), p. 13.

assemblies lest the Brahmins discriminate against them in politics as well as administration. Although there is today some doubt about the degree of government discrimination against non-Brahmins, given that few other communities were literate in English at the time, few question the skill of non-Brahmin leaders in adopting existing British administrative labels and using them to ask sympathetic senior officials for a larger share of the state's resources.

The concept of "non-Brahmin" was introduced by British administrators in Madras in the 1870s, as a way of lumping together a large number of Hindu castes against whom the Brahmins religiously discriminated, and which were believed at the time to be racially distinct in origin. In 1881, J. H. Nelson, in his influential book *The Madura Country* argued that it was "necessary to legislate separately for the non-Brahman castes, as being in all essential respects separate and distinct from, and incapable of association with, the Brahman." Nelson believed that the British had unwittingly supported the Brahmin version of caste relations when they had first arrived in Madras and recommended redressing the imbalance between the two categories by uncovering the "real" Hindu laws and customs. By 1900, Irschick argues, two beliefs had become entrenched in Madras government circles: the separateness of the majority "non-Brahmins" from Brahmins, and the unfair treatment of the non-Brahmins at the hands of the Brahmins, unfair treatment in which the colonial state had at times been an accomplice.[52]

When limited self-government for British India was discussed during the First World War, educated members of the Tamil-speaking Vellala caste and the Telegu-speaking Reddy and Kamma castes, together with Nairs from what would become northern Kerala, pressed for "fair treatment for the non-Brahmin majority," lest Home Rule mean Brahmin Rule. Since 1912 an association of non-Brahmin elites in Madras city had petitioned the government to provide jobs and scholarships for non-Brahmins. Now elite non-Brahmins formed the "Justice Party," skillfully playing on the British colonial government's desire to use the non-Brahmins as a political counterweight to the growing power of the Brahmin-dominated independence movement.[53] The colonial government in Madras met most of the

---

[52] This section draws on Eugene F. Irschick, *Tamil Revivalism in the 1930s* (Madras: Cre-A, 1986), chap. 1. J. H. Nelson, *A Prospectus of the Scientific Study of the Hindu Law* (London: C. Kegan Paul, 1881), p. 148, cited in Irschick, *Tamil Revivalism*, p. 23.

[53] On this issue, see Irschick, *Politics and Social Conflict in South India*, chap. 3.

Justice Party's demands and reserved 28 seats for non-Brahmins out of the 98 elected seats provided under the 1919 constitution. After the 1920 elections the government named the Justice Party the winner and invited it to form Madras's first elected provincial government.

Once in office, the Justice Party succeeded in passing or persuading the colonial government to pass a large number measures that gave government jobs, seats in the provincial Assembly, and places in educational institutions to non-Brahmins.[54] The 1922 employment rules it introduced, for instance, limited Brahmins to 2 positions in every 12 appointments, with non-Brahmins guaranteed 5 positions, Muslims 2, Anglo-Indians and Europeans 2, and others 1.[55] Although the rules allowed Brahmins to fill other communities' places if no qualified candidate from the other community was available, a system of checks ensured that Brahmins could not block the quotas completely, and their percentage of government employment therefore dropped substantially over the next two decades. By 1947 Brahmins occupied only 40.5% of the 2,876 senior government positions in the state and 27.7% of the 68,886 junior civil service jobs.[56]

The introduction of educational grants and preferences in government employment for non-Brahmins in the 1920s set off a process of caste fusion in politics, as many caste leaders petitioned for their castes to be recognized as part of the now advantageous "non-Brahmin" category. In some cases these were the same castes that had after 1901 fought to avoid the label of "backward." As a result of the success of these petitions the number of castes who received formal government recognition as "non-Brahmin" rose to 245 by the mid-1920s, compared with 45 castes before the reforms.[57] Non-Brahmin associations were also founded in Madras to fight for more concessions for the group. The most important of these was the Self Respect Association, founded in 1926 by E. V. Ramaswami Naicker (EVR). The association's Tamil-language newspaper *Kudi Arasu* (People's government)

---

[54] These measures included recommending the appointment of special "protectors of non-Brahmin subordinates in public services," whose job it was to protect the non-Brahmins from Brahmin discrimination. Andre Beteille, "Caste and Political Group Formation in Tamil Nadu," in Rajni Kothari, ed., *Caste in Indian Politics* (Hyderabad: Orient Longman Reprint, 1995), pp. 245–82.

[55] Scheduled Castes received a one-twelfth quota in 1927, at the expense of the "other" category. *Report of the Backward Classes Commission Tamil Nadu*, vol. 1, *1970* (Madras: Government of Tamil Nadu, 1974) [Chairman S. Sattanathan], p. 27.

[56] Ibid., p. 90.

[57] Irschick, *Tamil Revivalism in the 1930s*, pp. 36–37.

provided much of the ideological underpinning for the increasingly influential non-Brahmin movement.[58]

Postindependence Politics in Tamil Nadu

Politically the backward-caste movements were temporarily eclipsed in the 1930s. After the successes in the early 1920s, conflict began to sharpen between Telegu and Tamil speakers within the non-Brahmin movement over the ministerial appointments and patronage.[59] The Justice Party's opposition to the "Brahmin" Congress Party ultimately led to the party becoming too closely aligned with British colonialism.[60] As a result the Congress Party had a convincing victory in the 1937 Madras provincial elections. Crucially for the later development of politics in Tamil Nadu, however, the two key achievements of the non-Brahmin movement – government preferences for the backward castes and the aggregation of many small castes in strong backward-caste social organizations such as the Self Respect Association – remained intact into the postindependence period. As Atul Kohli puts it, this preindependence "development of a cleavage between the Brahman and anti-Brahman forces opened up the political space for later anti-Congress developments."[61]

Although Congress had originally condemned preferences for the backward castes as a colonial plot to "divide and rule," it found that the constituency for "backward castes" had become so well entrenched by 1947 as a result of two decades of preferences that it had to retain and then even extend the system.[62] In Tamil Nadu, 69% of government jobs and places in higher education are now set aside for members of disadvantaged castes, and the number of castes included under the "backward" label continues to rise.[63] And in 1944 the remnants of the Justice Party joined with the Self

---

[58] See also Irschick, *Politics and Social Conflict in South India*, chap. 8, "The Intellectual Background of Tamil Separatism."

[59] Irschick, *Politics and Social Conflict in South India*, pp. 257–58.

[60] Narendra Subramaniam, "Ethnicity, Populism and Pluralist Democracy: Mobilization and Representation in South India" (Ph.D. dissertation, MIT, 1993), p. 115.

[61] Kohli, *Democracy and Discontent*, p. 158.

[62] Irschick, *Tamil Revivalism in the 1930s*, pp. 68–70; P. Radhakrishnan, "Backward Class Movements in Tamil Nadu," in M. N. Srinivas, ed., *Caste: Its Twentieth Century Avatar* (New Delhi: Viking 1996), pp. 110–34. See my discussion in Chapter 4 for more details on the failure of the attempts to abolish reservations in postindependence Madras.

[63] Subramaniam, "Ethnicity, Populism and Pluralist Democracy," p. 67. According to press reports, the number of backward communities eligible for reservation in Tamil Nadu

Respect League to form the Dravida Kazhagam (DK), under the leadership of E. V. Ramaswami Naicker. Originally the DK operated very much like the SNDP or NSS in Kerala, as a social organization and political pressure group rather than as an organized political party. It railed against the influence of "Brahmanism" and the "North," forces it tended to conflate. After a major split within the organization in 1949, however, Naicker's heir apparent A. N. Annadurai took three-quarters of the party's members with him and founded the Dravida Munnetra Kazhigam (DMK), or "Progressive Dravidian Federation," which rapidly turned itself into a political party.

The DMK won 50 out of 234 seats in the 1962 state elections, a respectable second to Congress, which had 138 seats, but party leaders were frustrated that they had lost many close contests in constituencies where smaller parties such as the Swatantra Party and the Muslim League split the anti-Congress vote. In 1967, therefore, just before the election the DMK reached an agreement on seat adjustments with the Muslim League and a few other small parties.[64] The agreement with the Muslim League was possible because, from the very beginning of the Dravida Kazhagam in the 1940s, the organization had made an effort to seek Muslims as an ally in the greater battle against the Brahmins and northern domination. One of Annadurai's earliest political decisions, for example, was to distance his organization from Congress Party members who attacked Muslims in Tiruvannamalai town and a neighboring village in 1948. Muslims were welcomed into the reading rooms and local clubs organized in the 1950s by the DMK as part of the overall strategy to bring all Tamil-speaking non-Brahmins together into the same political movement.[65]

In the event the 1967 seat adjustments were unnecessary. The DMK, bolstered by a 1965 mass movement in Tamil Nadu against the imposition of Hindi as the only national language, won 40% of the vote and 138 seats, compared with Congress's 47 seats, and formed its first government. Since the 1967 elections, Tamil Nadu has been dominated by the DMK and

---

increased from 150 prior to 1970 to 310 in 1994. "Racketeering in Quotas," *India Today*, November 15, 1994, pp. 36–42.

[64] Marguerite Ross Barnett, *The Politics of Cultural Nationalism in South India* (Princeton: Princeton University Press, 1976), p. 136.

[65] Narendra Subramaniam points out that "EVR used the term 'Tamil' to exclude only Brahmins explicitly and the Schedule Castes implicitly. Such a notion of the Tamil community could be used to appeal to Muslims and Christians on the grounds that only the DK, not the Brahmin Congress party, would be truly tolerant of them." Subramaniam, "Ethnicity, Populism and Pluralist Democracy," p. 126.

(after the DMK split in 1972) its rival the AIDMK (All India AnnaDravida Munnetra Kazhagam). These parties tend to be divided between more advanced and less advanced backward castes, the DMK having excluded the lowest backward castes during its early years.

The DMK's short-term worries about losing three-way electoral battles during the 1967 elections led to what has ultimately become a more permanent interethnic alliance with the Muslims. From 1962 to 1974 the DMK was in a formal electoral alliance with the Muslim League, and, according to Subramaniam, "the two parties were so closely allied that their organizations became virtually indistinguishable."[66] Since that date there has been no formal alliance, but each of the two major parties in Tamil Nadu seeks Muslim votes and each has several Muslim Assembly members. Because Muslims are concentrated in a few towns and districts, Muslim support was the critical factor in the DMK's strong showing in Dindigul district and electoral victories in the towns of Vaniyambadi, Ambur, Tiruvannamalai, and Tirupathur. Muslims have also been a key swing vote in Madras corporation elections.[67] Subramaniam also argues convincingly that part of the DMK's success among Muslims lay in the fact that Tamil nationalism was not a religious ideology and thus, unlike Hindu nationalism in the North, allowed Muslims to retain their religious identity while integrating themselves politically with the dominant group.[68]

Hindu-Muslim Violence in Tamil Nadu

As in Kerala, the postindependence level of Hindu-Muslim violence in Tamil Nadu has been very low, despite a substantial number of Hindu-Muslim riots before independence, including the 1882 riots in Salem district, 1889 riots in Madras, an 1891 riot at Palakod, 1910 riots at Uthamapalayam, and a series of riots in the 1930s.[69] There have also been periodic attempts by Hindu nationalist organizations in recent years to mobilize Hindus around anti-Muslim issues. In the early 1980s, RSS activists, many from outside Tamil Nadu, launched a major anti-Muslim agitation after several hundred ex-untouchables, seeking to escape the economic and social

---

[66] Ibid., pp. 269–71.

[67] Barnett, *The Politics of Cultural Nationalism in South Korea*, p. 288.

[68] Subramaniam, "Ethnicity, Populism and Pluralist Democracy," pp. 269–71.

[69] See J. B. P. More, *The Political Evolution of Muslims in Tamilnadu and Madras, 1930–1947* (Hyderabad: Orient Longman, 1997), pp. 90–102, and "Formation of Conciliation Boards," UPSA GAD 413/1914.

194

constraints of their traditional Hindu status, converted to Islam in the village of Meenakshipuram. In 1989, 1991, 1993, and 1995 there were also organized attempts by both Hindu and Muslim militants to incite violence in the town of Nagore, the site of a famous Muslim shrine that attracts a large number of Muslim and Hindu worshipers. And in 1996 Hindu nationalists tried to take a Vinayaka Chaturthi procession past a sensitive mosque in Triplicane.

These various efforts at religious mobilization attempts have been unsuccessful because the continuing depth of cleavages around castes has lead to highly competitive party politics in which Muslims are a key swing vote. As a result, the parties in government ordered their state police forces to prevent Hindu-Muslim violence that might threaten their political coalitions. In 1982, for instance, when RSS supporters and Muslims and Scheduled Castes confronted each other near Meenakshipuram, large-scale violence was averted because of a massive deployment of police patrols through the affected villages and by the state government's threat to use the National Security Act to arrest those suspected of involvement in the clashes.[70] In the 1996 Triplicane mobilization, the police refused to allow the procession to go by the Ice House mosque and insisted on an alternate route. The police also banned a planned public meeting after the idol immersion ceremony on the grounds that it might lead to communal disturbances. When the Madras High Court turned down the Hindu Munnani's appeal against the alternate route and ban on the public meeting, the Munnani canceled the procession in protest.[71] In Nagore, the police managed to stop violence during attempts in 1989, 1991, and 1993 to cause violence in the town of Nagore and only failed in 1995 because many officers had been temporarily sent to Madurai in connection with the visit of the Chief Minister. The immediate spark for the violence was the assault by some Hindus upon an elderly Muslim man and a young Muslim woman outside the home of Thanga Muthukrishan, a prominent local Hindu activist. Muthukrishan later denied all responsibility and claimed he had only been trying to alert the Hindus about the dangers of "violent activities of Muslims with foreign help." As soon as the riot broke out, police officers were rushed into the town and quickly managed to stop the violence.[72]

---

[70] "Conversion Backlash," *India Today*, July 15, 1982, pp. 34–35.

[71] *Hindu*, September 20, 1996. The Hindu Munnani means "Hindu Front," and was founded in 1982 in Tamil Nadu to "defend Hinduism" by the RSS after conversions of low-caste Hindus to Islam.

[72] "Trouble at Nagore," *Frontline*, August 25, 1995, pp. 94–97.

Fifteen out of sixteen Hindu-Muslim riots (94%) in Tamil Nadu since the electoral breakthrough of the DK in the 1960s have been stopped within a single day, with all the casualties taking place on the first day of rioting, largely due to police firing. One example from 1979 illustrates the state's firm response to communal violence. In the early morning of June 4, 1979, a Hindu-Muslim dispute in the small town of Palacode led to the burning of 14 shops and 27 huts. By 10:00 A.M. the same morning, the local police had used rifles and tear gas four times, imposed a curfew, blocked outsiders' entrance to the town, and was rushing in units of both the Tamil Nadu Police and the Central Reserve Police. The violence stopped.[73]

Bihar: Delayed Lower-Caste Mobilization

Caste Mobilization before Independence

By almost any indicator, Bihar, with an area of 174,000 square kilometers and a population of 83 million (2001), is one of the most socially and economically backward states in India: its literacy rate is the lowest of any major state (47.5% compared with the national average of 65.4%); its percentage of the population below the poverty line (55%) in 2001 was the highest in India.[74] The proportion of Hindus in Bihar is exactly the same as India's, 82 percent. The state has long been dominated by powerful Brahmin, Bhumihar, Kshatriya, and Kayasth upper castes, who today account for around 16% of the population and as recently as 1951 owned 78% of the land. Numerically the largest group is the backward castes (c. 50%), dozens of castes whose traditional occupations were as cultivators and herders. The ex-untouchables or Scheduled Castes account for 14% of the population, around the same size as the state's substantial Muslim minority (15%). The state also has a large Hindu Tribal population (9%), almost all of which lives in the mineral-rich South.[75]

[73] "Report of Shri T. S. Venkataraman, Assistant Commissioner for Linguistic Minorities, Madras, on Communal Disturbances in Palacode, Dharmapuri District," in *Second Annual Report of the Minorities Commission (For the year ending 31st December, 1979)* (New Delhi: Government of India, 1980), pp. 62–69.

[74] Figures from *Statistical Outline of India 2000-2001*, and "Ranking of States and Union Territories by Literacy Rate and Sex: 2001," in *Census of India 2001 Provisional Population Totals: Paper 1 of 2001.*

[75] Ramashray Roy, "Caste and Political Recruitment in Bihar," in Rajni Kothari, ed., *Caste in Indian Politics* (Delhi: Orient Longman Reprint, 1995), pp. 215–41. While this book

Prior to independence, in sharp contrast to Tamil Nadu and Kerala, caste conflict in Bihar was largely a contest among the elite Kayasths, Rajputs, and Brahmins, rather than between upper and lower castes. There were several reasons for this. First, and most important, the colonial government in Bihar instituted no political reservations, employment preferences, or educational reservations for the backward castes. Politics therefore reflected the interests of the Hindu and Muslim upper castes that dominated the narrow property-based franchise (c. 5% of adults could vote before 1935 and c. 14% thereafter). The narrowness of the franchise meant that caste issues were overshadowed in the early part of the century by a quite different conflict: the fierce competition among Bihari and Bengali Hindus and Bihari Muslims for jobs in the administration. For a century before 1911 Bihar had been ruled from the state of Bengal, and well into the 20th century Bengali Hindus occupied many of highest positions open to Indians in the Bihar civil service and police, to the annoyance of the increasing number of English-educated Bihari Hindus. While governments in the 1930s in Madras, Travancore, and Cochin were concentrating on the division of jobs, political power, and educational scholarships between "non-Brahmins" and "Brahmins," politicians in Bihar were instead preoccupied with the relative gains and losses of "Bihari Hindus," "Bihari Muslims," and "Bengali Hindus." In the 1930s and 1940s, compared with perhaps 100 questions asked in the Bihar Legislative Assembly about these three groups, only a handful were concerned with the relative status of middle- and lower-caste Hindus.[76]

Postindependence Politics

The paradox of Bihar politics after independence, Paul Brass pointed out in the mid-1970s, was that although caste was the chief principle of political mobilization, "caste solidarity has not been pronounced at the state level and has not taken organized form." Some backward castes were mobilized within the Congress Party, but only as junior partners in what were essentially upper-caste faction fights. In the late 1960s for example the Congress Party in Bihar was divided between Kayasthas, Rajputs, and Bhumihars (all upper castes) on one side of Congress and a Brahmin–backward-caste

was being written, the southern part of the state was carved off to form the new state of Jharkhand.

[76] See, e.g., *Bihar Legislative Assembly Debates Official Report*, no. 1, March 5, 1938, pp. 220–22.

faction on the other.[77] The Congress Party, itself led by factions of upper-caste Brahmins, Kayasths, and Rajputs, dominated Bihar politics well into the 1980s not so much because it was strong as because the degree of middle- and lower-caste cohesion was so low that the opposition parties were weak. Parties such as the Communists, Janata Dal, and Praja Socialist Party disliked each other as much as they did the Congress. The anti-Congress vote in Bihar fluctuated between 65% and 70% of the total votes cast in elections to the state assembly held after 1967, but the fact that the opposition was divided along caste lines meant that Congress was still able to form almost all of Bihar's governments.[78]

Only on two occasions before the late 1980s was the Congress Party's dominance truly threatened. In 1967–68 and 1977–80 smaller parties put aside their disagreements to form coalition governments dominated by backward castes. Although these governments both collapsed under the weight of ethnic factionalism, they were nonetheless important because, especially in the case of the 1977–80 government of Karpoori Thakur, they helped to polarize Bihar around *backward-* and *forward-*caste identities. In 1979 Karpoori Thakur made a lasting impact on Bihar politics by introducing large-scale reservations for the backward castes, based on the southern model. The upper-caste backlash to Thakur's proposals and the countermobilization efforts by new backward-caste organizations in Bihar helped for the first time to bring some political cohesion to Bihar's backward castes. The government preferences that were instituted for backward castes in Bihar in the 1980s helped to encourage backward-caste political mobilization and a wider sense that "backwards" were a distinct social category.

In the late 1980s, many of the young backward-caste politicians who had been active in the 1979–80 agitations over the government preferences for the first time successfully forged a new Janata Party coalition in Bihar that combined the most important backward and Scheduled Castes. These castes, amounting to 25–30% of the electorate, allowed Janata to challenge the Congress, but the ethnic base of the party was still too small to

[77] Paul R. Brass, "Radical Parties of the Left in Bihar: A Comparison of the SSP and the CPI," in Paul Brass and Marcus F. Franda, eds. *Radical Politics in South Asia* (Cambridge, Mass.: MIT Press, 1973), pp. 326–27. Shree Nagesh Jha, "Caste in Bihar Politics," *Economic and Political Weekly*, February 14, 1970, pp. 341–44.

[78] The Congress share of the vote was 41.4% in 1962, 33.1% in 1967, 30.5% in 1979, 23.6% in 1977 (when the Janata Party won election after the emergency), and 34.2% in 1980.

guarantee electoral victory. Laloo Prasad Yadav, the Janata Dal's charismatic state leader, therefore made ultimately successful efforts to woo the Muslims from Congress. Muslims, disgusted with Congress after its weakness in protecting Muslims during the 1989 Bhagalpur riots, defected en masse to the Janata Dal in the 1989 elections. The Muslim votes were sufficient to give Yadav a stable majority in the Bihar Assembly. His Janata government was the first in 34 years to complete its full 5-year term; in 1995, again with Muslim support, it easily won reelection.[79]

Hindu-Muslim Violence in Bihar

Bihar has been one of the most violent states in India since independence, both in terms of the absolute and per-capita number of Hindu-Muslim riots and deaths. In several particularly large riots many hundreds of people have died in violence lasting perhaps a week or more. The common element in all these large riots, according to the independent inquiries that have been set up to investigate them, has been hesitation or outright negligence on the part of the police, especially an unwillingness to use firearms to shoot at Hindu rioters attacking Muslims. The inquiry into the 1979 Jamshedpur riots (in which 120 people were killed) found that in one incident, "Not a single Hindu could be identified as having been injured or killed as a result of the 108 rounds of firing by the Bihar Military Police in a Muslim *basti* [slum]."[80] The Balasubrahmaniam inquiry into the 1981 Biharsharif violence (48 dead) likewise concluded that "while goondas had a free time, burning and killing, only a single police bullet found a target, and that one was not aimed at anyone in particular but hit a wholly innocent person." Balasubrahmaniam found that the police had been negligent in posting police pickets, stopping traffic coming into the affected area, and in not firing against rioters.[81] He concluded that the senior police officers in the town had given no clear direction to their men during the first two days of the riot and that documents they produced that claimed to prove otherwise were fabricated.[82]

---

[79] "Laloo's Magic," *India Today*, April 30, 1995, pp. 26–35.
[80] *Times of India*, September 14, 1981, pp. 1, 9.
[81] Leaked extracts from the report, published in *Muslim India* 2, no. 21 (September 1984), pp. 425–26.
[82] Leaked extracts from the report, published in *Economic and Political Weekly*, February 18, 1984, pp. 266–67; *Muslim India* 2, no. 21 (September 1984), pp. 425–26.

What accounts for this hesitation and unwillingness to use force on the part of the police? The police delay action because it believes, often with good reason, that the rioters enjoy government protection. Behind all three of the largest riots in Bihar – Ranchi, Jamshedpur, and Biharsharif – there is evidence that the party in power interfered either directly – for example, by ordering a procession to go ahead when the local police pleaded for cancellation – or indirectly, by failing to give clear orders to the state police and local magistrates that violence had to be stopped as soon as it broke out.

This interference was because, prior to the mid-1980s, the depth of the division among Bihar's backward castes meant that it was often the upper-caste, Hindu nationalist Jana Sangh Party that was the swing vote in Bihar politics. In 1967, for example, the Jana Sangh was part of the United Front coalition in Bihar when Congress, intent on highlighting divisions within the coalition between the pro-Urdu Communists and the anti-Urdu Jana Sangh, introduced a bill that would have made Urdu the state's second official language. This bill provoked widespread and inflammatory anti-Muslim protests and demonstrations on the part of the Jana Sangh's main organizational backer, the Hindu nationalist RSS. The Jana Sangh refused to agree to tough action against these demonstrations, and the coalition government faced the prospect of losing political power to the Congress if it pushed the issue and the Jana Sangh left the government. Given the strong political backing enjoyed by the RSS, it is hardly surprising that when a Hindu-Muslim riot broke out after an RSS-led anti-Urdu procession in the town of Ranchi in August 1967, the local police hesitated. The commission of inquiry found that the local police delayed firing at the RSS and Jana Sangh rioters, and delayed calling in the army, because they were on the phone to Patna trying to get the Sinha ministry's permission to take action. In the meantime, dozens of Muslims were massacred.[83]

In Jamshedpur in 1979 the link between a Hindu swing vote and a weak state response to Hindu-Muslim violence was even more direct. The local district magistrate wanted to ban a Hindu nationalist procession planned through the town. But he was overruled – and only backed down after receiving written instructions from the chief minister's office – because the Janata government of Karpoori Thakur needed to retain the votes of

---

[83] *Report of the Commission of Inquiry on Communal Disturbances, Ranchi-Hatia (August 22–29, 1967)* (1968). See also Paul Brass, *Language, Religion and Politics in North India* (Cambridge: Cambridge University Press, 1974), pp. 260–69.

the Hindu nationalist Jana Sangh members of the Bihar Assembly in an upcoming vote of confidence.[84] Once violence broke out, the police reportedly did nothing because a Jana Sangh MLA from the ruling Janata coalition party, Dinanath Pandey, was alleged to be helping to organize the riot.[85]

Riot inquiries in Bihar, although often criticized for being cover-ups, have in fact made it abundantly clear that political backing for those doing the rioting is the main reason Hindu-Muslim riots continue. After the 1967 Ranchi-Hatia riots in Bihar, for example, the Dayal commission of inquiry recommended that, in order to avoid future riots the "State government should warn local officials of expected trouble, should not undermine local officers or attempt to interfere with them."[86] Because Bihar police officials and district magistrates know that many rioters enjoy political protection, they dither by comparison with their colleagues in Tamil Nadu and Kerala. In Bihar, riots in the 1960s, 1970s, and 1980s dragged on for five or six days or even longer, and the longer the riot, the higher the death toll. Half of all deaths in Hindu-Muslim violence since 1950 have taken place in a few large riots that lasted a week or more.

Only in the mid-1980s, as middle-caste parties began to provide real competition for Congress in Bihar, turning Muslims for the first time into a key swing vote, did the state's attitude to riot prevention begin to change. Laloo Yadav's government repaid Muslims for their votes in 1989 when it arrested the BJP leader Ram Krishna Advani the moment he set foot in the state on his "Rathyatra" procession to reclaim the Ayodhya mosque.[87] In 1992, when riots broke out throughout India after the destruction of the Ayodhya mosque, Bihar's Janata Dal government ensured that the state remained peaceful. Laloo Yadav, when asked why Bihar had had been so quiet despite its woeful record of past riots, explained how his government had arrested returning militants from Uttar Pradesh (the site of Ayodhya) before they could reach their towns and villages, and how he had threatened all district magistrates and station house officers with the loss of their jobs if they allowed any riots to break out in their towns. "The political will of the state government" he said, "was clear."[88]

---

[84] "Meddling Politicos, Inept Officials," *Times of India*, April 22, 1979.

[85] *India Today*, May 1–15, 1979, pp. 12–13.

[86] *Report of the Commission of Inquiry on Communal Disturbances, Ranchi-Hatia (August 22–29, 1967)*, pp. 102–3.

[87] "Laloo's Magic," *India Today*, April 30, 1995, pp. 26–35.

[88] Laloo Prasad Yadav, *Business India*, January 18–31, 1993, p. 44.

Yadav has also expressed his determination to stop riots in more personal ways. In 1992 he slapped a police officer he felt was negligent in not stopping anti-Muslim violence in the town of Sitamarhi and spent several days going round the town and neighboring villages reassuring local Muslims, disbursing relief, and reviewing security arrangements.[89] As soon as clashes broke out in the sensitive town of Biharsharif in July 1993, Yadav deployed two companies of central paramilitary forces and 32 fixed and 6 mobile police response teams to prevent further violence.[90] The chief minister has also brought a new openness to the discussion in the state parliament over the failings of the Bihar police and administration. He accepted the findings of an inquiry into the 1989 Bhagalpur riots (which took place before Yadav became chief minister) despite the fact it criticized a number of senior police officers and administrators, including the district superintendent of police and an inspector general of police.

Conclusion

In his fascinating study of why religious conflict between Muslims and Christians did not break out in the Yoruba region of Nigeria, though it did elsewhere in the country, David Laitin found the answer in the policies the colonial state followed in Yorubaland in the late 19th and early 20th centuries. The colonial government in Yorubaland – but not elsewhere in Nigeria – allocated political power and material resources to leaders from "ancestral cities." Local elites used these city identities to secure concessions from the colonial government, and in turn these leaders gave protection and access to land to those Yorubas who identified themselves with an "ancestral city" identity. The ancestral city identity, given new life because it served the interest of both the colonial state and Yoruba elites, came over time to have both practical value as well as what Laitin, borrowing from Gramsci, terms "ideological hegemony" over Yorubas.[91] The continuing strength of ancestral city identities in Yorubaland has inhibited the development of Muslim-Christian cleavages that have broken out with increasing frequency elsewhere in Nigeria.

[89] *Telegraph*, October 12, 1992.
[90] *Sunday Times of India*, July 4, 1993, p. 13.
[91] David D. Laitin, *Hegemony and Culture: Politics and Religious Change among the Yoruba* (Chicago: University of Chicago Press, 1986), especially pp. 150–60. Even as Muslim-Christian conflict has worsened in most of Nigeria the late 1990s and early 2000s, peaceful ethnic relations in the Yoruba region have continued.

In south India, as in Yorubaland, the colonial government's promotion of an identity ("non-Brahmin") that cut across religious boundaries has also had profound effects on postindependence ethnic politics and ethnic conflict. In south India the early strength of the backward movements helped reduce anti-Muslim violence in two ways. First, as I have explored in some depth in Chapter 4, the "non Brahmin" political movement (usually called backward caste today) has explicitly identified and mobilized many Muslim castes – such as Labbai Muslims in Tamil Nadu – as part of a larger "backward" community fighting for justice against the upper castes. Second, the colonial government's promotion of political, economic, and educational reservations for backwards in the 1920s was to have important effects on the postindependence pattern of party competition in the South. By instituting political, employment, and educational preferences for backward castes in the 1920s and 1930s, a full half century before these policies were introduced in the North, the colonial government encouraged the growth of social and political organizations around these identities. These organizations – the SNDP and Nair Service Society in Kerala, and the Dravida Kazhagam in Tamil Nadu – were crucial in explaining the early emergence of strong opposition parties to Congress after independence.

The fact that strong middle- and lower-caste parties have long existed in the southern states with the lowest levels of Hindu-Muslim conflict is not, as I have shown in this chapter, accidental. High levels of party competition combined with strong backward-caste movements that regard Muslims as acceptable and valuable coalition partners puts Muslims in an extremely good position to demand security as the price of their votes. In Kerala and Tamil Nadu, the Communists and the DMK were only able to win power by actively wooing Muslim voters. Similarly, in recent years, parties such as the Janata Dal in Bihar and the Samajwadi party in Uttar Pradesh have only been able to win power by building coalitions that include Muslims. Because these parties rely so heavily on Muslim votes, they have in turn taken strong action to protect Muslims from communal violence.

7

The Electoral Incentives for Ethnic Violence in Comparative Perspective

A full comparative test of the electoral explanation I have developed for explaining violence in India in the preceding chapters would require a blend of large-N research and case studies, together with detailed information on electoral competition, polarizing events, and ethnic violence in many countries since the 19th century. My goals in this chapter are more limited. My aim is to identify multiethnic states where we would expect increased political competition to lead to an increase in local ethnic polarization and then to examine how the level of government in charge of the police or army responds to this polarization and the threat of violence. When electoral competition increases in an ethnically divided society, do local politicians in close seats respond by organizing demonstrations and polarizing events in order to attract swing voters? If violence results from these mobilizations, how does the state respond? Does the state response depend as in India on the level of effective party competition in the state and on whether the state relies on the votes of the group doing the attacking or those being attacked?

I examine three cases where multiethnic societies moved from un-competitive party systems to competitive systems in a relatively short space of time: 19th-century Ireland, postindependence Malaysia, and post-Communist Romania. We therefore have one case from each of the three great waves of democratization identified by Samuel Huntington: the first wave, from 1828 to 1926, when the franchise was extended to 50% or more of adult males in many countries in Europe, the Americas, Australia, and New Zealand; the second wave, after World War II, when former colonies and many formerly authoritarian countries in Latin America became democratic; and the third wave, which began with the Portuguese Revolution of 1974 and continued with democratic liberalization in Eastern Europe, the former Soviet Union, and Africa.

In all three cases – Ireland, Malaysia, and Romania – as well as two additional cases I discuss in somewhat less detail (the United States and post-Communist Bulgaria) I argue that an electoral incentives theory does help us to explain both when and where polarizing ethnic events took place, and when and where states took action to prevent ethnic violence.[1] Violence in Ireland, Romania, and Malaysia was most likely to break out in those places where political competition was most intense, and one party – the Tories in 19th-century Ireland, the ex-Communists in Romania, and United Malays National Organization (UMNO) in Malaysia's Selangor state – stood to benefit from an increased identification with a majority ethnic identity.

Whether these local incidents would be prevented or quickly suppressed, however, was determined by the level of party competition and the support-base of the party in government. Figure 7.1 shows where each of these cases fits into the general typology of party competition and antiminority violence I introduced earlier in the book. I argue that the national-level situations in post-Communist Bulgaria and postindependence Malaysia best fit category A. In both these states there are 3 or more effective parties: Bulgaria for example had 4.4 effective parties in the crucial 1991 parliamentary election and 3.94 in its most recent election in 2001, while Malaysia had 5.2 effective parties in the most recent parliamentary election in 1999. The parties in power therefore have an incentive to protect minorities in order to keep their existing minority support and/or to preserve the option of forming a coalition with minority-supported parties in the future.[2]

In systems where there is two-party competition at the level of government that controls the police and army, there are two possible outcomes: strong government intervention to protect minorities if the government relies on minority voters (B_i) and a biased or weak government response that allows antiminority violence if the government does not rely on minority voters (B_{ii}). In the first category I would place the United States after 1948, when the growing political power of black voters in national elections prompted the federal government to intervene to protect minorities in the South. In the second category – states with two-party competition that do not rely on minority votes, and therefore that do not protect minority

---

[1] Samuel P. Huntington, *The Third Wave: Democratization in the Late Twentieth Century* (Norman: University of Oklahoma Press, 1991).

[2] The effective number of parties (ENPV) for Bulgaria was calculated from data available at the University of Essex Project on Political Transformation and the Electoral Process in Post-Communist Europe, downloaded May 14, 2003, from <http://www.essex.ac.uk/elections/>.

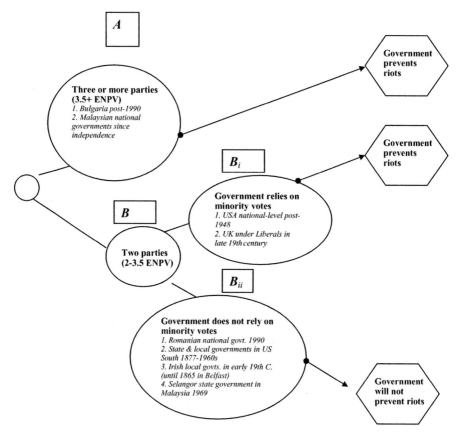

Figure 7.1 The relationship between party competition and a state's response to antiminority polarization and violence: Non-Indian examples

voters – I would place the U.S. federal government from 1877 to 1948, and state governments in the South from the 1870s until the 1960s. The fact that the federal government in the United States chose not to intervene in the South from 1877 to 1948 gave the southern state governments, which did not rely on minority voters, a free hand to tolerate or incite antiminority violence. Other cases I examine that fall into this most dangerous category for minorities are the Romanian national government in 1990 (only two effective parties, with the National Salvation Front (FSN) getting 66% of the total vote), Irish local governments in the early 19th century (until 1865 in Belfast), and the Selangor state government in Malaysia in 1969. In all these cases, I argue, we can best understand the biased state response to antiminority violence in terms of these three broad categories of electoral incentives.

Franchise Reform and Ethnic Riots in the First Wave

From the 1820s until the 1920s, large numbers of men and women in the Americas and Europe petitioned, protested, and in some cases fought for the right to vote. At the beginning of this period, only a small percentage of men in a handful of countries could vote; by the 1920s the majority of men could vote in most countries and in many states the franchise had also been extended to women. In the literature on this "first wave" of democratization, the expansion of the franchise is frequently portrayed purely in class terms, with middle and working classes pressing for the right to vote and the upper classes debating whether they should widen the franchise, and if they did so, how they could best compete for the support of new voters.[3]

Overlooked in the many class-based accounts of franchise reform is the fact that there was often an important ethnic dimension to democratization. At the beginning of the 19th century, political and financial elites in multiethnic states tended to be overwhelmingly drawn from one ethnic group rather than another, so electorates were highly unrepresentative of the ethnic composition of the country as a whole. For example, the approximately 12% Swedish minority dominated finance and the elected Landtag in Finland, the German minority played a similar role in the Czech-majority provinces of Bohemia (37% German) and Moravia (30% German), while the 12% Episcopalian Protestant minority dominated political life and (together with Presbyterians) the economy in Ireland.[4] Inevitably, in areas

---

[3] For a comprehensive class analysis of the history of the franchise in the United States, see Alex Keyssar's *The Right to Vote: The Contested History of Democracy in the United States* (New York: Basic Books, 2000). For an excellent article on the widening of the franchise in Europe in the 19th century that includes statistics on individual countries and a comprehensive guide to the literature on the subject, see Stefano Bartolini, "Enfranchisement, Equality and Turnout in the European Democratisation Process: A Preliminary Comparative Analysis," EUI Working Paper no. 121 (Barcelona, 1996).

[4] Cohen, for example tells us that in the mid-19th century "the highest Czech-speaking strata in Prague were the rich-millers, butchers, brewers, bakers, and soap-makers." Gary Bennett Cohen, "The Prague Germans, 1861–1914: The Problems of Ethnic Survival" (Ph.D. dissertation, Princeton University, 1975), p. 7. Population percentages are from Kenneth D. McRae, *Conflict and Compromise in Multilingual Societies: Finland* (Waterloo, Ont.: Wilfrid Laurier University Press, 1997), pp. 174–75; Alan O'Day, "Ireland's Catholics in the British State, 1850–1922," in Andrea Kappler, ed., *The Formation of National Elites* (New York: European Science Foundation/NYU Press, 1992), p. 45; and Jiří Kořalka, "The Czechs,

where an ethnic minority dominated a country's economy and politics, the possibility of franchise reform was a serious threat to the dominant ethnic group's hold on power.

Dominant ethnic elites responded to demands for democratization in different ways. Where members of a dominant group had complete autonomy to make constitutional rules within their region or state, the preferred strategy was often to block franchise reform that threatened their control. In Finland, for example, the 12% Swedish minority preserved a veto power over legislation after franchise reform in the 19th century by blocking changes to the "estates system" in which it controlled two of the four estates (Nobility and Burghers) in parliament.[5] In states where the population balance was changing rapidly in favor of the subordinate ethnic group, however, dominant ethnic groups had to do more than just preserve the existing constitutional system to keep their hold on power: they had to devise new institutions that would allow them to keep winning elections. In Rhode Island, for example, the Anglo-Protestants who controlled the state in the early 19th century worried that they would lose political power to the growing numbers of French Canadian and Portuguese immigrants. In 1842 they therefore introduced a new constitution that limited the political representation of the city of Providence (where most of the new immigrants had settled), overrepresented the rural areas and small towns where Protestants were dominant, and forced all naturalized Americans to meet additional property requirements in order to vote.[6] This move helped the Anglo-Protestant elite keep its grip on power for the next four decades.

1840–1900," in Andreas Kappeler, ed., *The Formation of National Elites: Comparative Studies on Governments and Non-Dominant Ethnic Groups in Europe, 1850–1940* (New York: New York University Press/Dartmouth, 1992), pp. 77–104.

[5] Osmo Jussila, "The Russian Government and the Finnish Diet: A Study of the Evolution of Political Representation, 1863–1914," in Geoffrey Alderman, ed., *Governments, Ethnic Groups and Political Representation*, vol. 6 of *Comparative Series of Governments and Non-Dominant Ethnic Groups in Europe, 1850–1940* (New York: European Science Foundation/ NYU Press, 1993), p. 170. The Swedes blocked reform of the house of the nobility (in which hereditary Swedish nobles dominated) and the house of burghers, in elections to which the richer Swedes could outvote the Finns because multiple votes were granted to voters, proportional to the taxes they paid. Anders Mattson Myhrman, "The Swedish Nationality Movement in Finland" (Ph.D. dissertation, University of Chicago, 1937; printed in a private edition by the University of Chicago Libraries, 1939), pp. 60–61.

[6] Providence was limited to one sixth of all seats in the assembly, although by 1850 Providence County had well over half (88,000 out of 148,000) of the state's entire population. For details of the constitution, see Charles Carroll, *Rhode Island: Three Centuries of Democracy* (New York: Lewis Historical Publishing Company, 1932), 1:499–500 and 2:643–44.

Where reforms could not be blocked outright, their impact could still be blunted if the dominant group controlled the electoral process. In Bohemia, the 1861 municipal franchise reform was pushed through against the wishes of the dominant German minority because the Austro-Hungarian government's desire to keep the peace between its many nationalities took political precedence over the Germans' wish to block reform in majority Czech areas. German officials in the town of Budweis, however, lessened their chances of losing power in the first years after the 1861 reform by manipulating voter registration and constituency delimitation so as to undercount Czechs.[7] This is similar to the response we see in India at an equivalent stage of franchise enlargement in the 1920s and 1930s, when Hindu and Muslim politicians used their control of local electoral rolls to undercount voters from the rival community.[8] Another method by which ethnic elites could maintain power even if franchise reform took place was through preventing secret ballots. In Connecticut, for instance, the assembly voted in 1801 to make voting public – the so-called Stand Up Law – a measure that preserved the white Protestant elite's control of politics for several decades after the electorate was expanded.[9]

So far in this chapter we have spoken of dominant ethnic groups as if there were no overlap between ethnic categories and little chance to pass from one group to the other. In fact, though, ethnic boundaries had never been solid, and dominant ethnic groups had long strengthened their numerical and political positions by assimilating individual members of the majority ethnic group: for centuries Finns had assimilated and become Swedish speakers; Catholics had become Protestant in Ireland; Czechs, no doubt mindful of the adage "You won't get far with Czech," had become Germans in Bohemia and Moravia;[10] and Flemish-speakers in Belgium had become French as they moved up in business or the bureaucracy.[11] Prior

---

[7] Jeremy King, "Loyalty and Polity, Nation and State: A Town in Hapsburg Central Europe, 1848–1948" (Ph.D. dissertation, Columbia University, 1998).

[8] See the complaints by C. S. Ranga Iyer about the undercount of Hindus in Najibabad in 1921 and 1931 at the behest of the Muslim-controlled Municipal Board. *India Central Legislative Assembly Debates*, III, 9, March 23, 1931, p. 2514.

[9] Robert Dahl, *Who Governs?* (New Haven: Yale University Press, 1961), p. 16. O'Day reports that the absence of secret voting before 1872 in Ireland also helped depress the Catholic nationalist vote there, because of Protestant intimidation. O'Day "Ireland's Catholics in the British State, 1850–1922," p. 49.

[10] Cohen, "The Prague Germans, 1861–1914: The Problems of Ethnic Survival," p. 24.

[11] Els Witte and Machteld de Metsenaere, "The Flemings in Brussels," in Max Engman, ed., *Ethnic Identity in Urban Europe*, vol. 8 of *Comparative Studies on Governments*

to the introduction of electoral institutions, the degree of elite openness to ethnic assimilation seems to have been related to the overall growth of the economy and availability of economic opportunities and land. Where these were plentiful and security concerns or the desire for labor were acute, ethnic elites were relatively accepting of those who wished to switch. Where they were not, elites often blocked admission to the favored group.[12]

In medieval Europe, German-, English-, Spanish-, French-, and Swedish-speaking elites often encouraged ethnic assimilation in order to increase the physical security of their dominant groups.[13] In the 19th and 20th centuries, the key was to assimilate sufficient voters to the dominant group so that it would feel politically secure in its control of the state. Where blocking electoral reforms or their implementation altogether was not possible, ethnic elites used either inducements or threats to persuade the many voters who had the option to identify with both the elites and the subordinate ethnic group to identify and vote with the dominant group. In Bohemia, for example, German and Czech politicians used their control of rapidly expanding municipal governments to persuade the substantial number of citizens whose family history and linguistic skills allowed them to select either identity (or the mixed identity of "Bohemian") to declare themselves as members of the locally dominant group. Jeremy King describes how in the German controlled town of Budweis "the Liberal-German faction in Town Hall handed out new jobs on the municipal payroll, demanding payment for the favor in multiple currencies: votes at the polls, membership in certain clubs, enrollment of one's children in a German-language school, and so on. Half-enticed, half-coerced, members of the municipal administration, police force, slaughterhouse, waterworks and other public corporations run by Town Hall toed the German and Liberal lines in order to hold on to their posts."[14]

Control of jobs and the local administration was one way to encourage voters to declare themselves as one ethnicity rather than another. But control over municipal employment was in most cases not sufficient to win over all the desired voters, especially as the franchise expanded. The other tactic

---

and Non-Dominant Ethnic Groups in Europe, 1850–1940 (New York: European Science Foundation/NYU Press, 1992), pp. 13–38.

[12] For examples of how this process worked on the German-Slav frontier in the Middle Ages, see Robert Bartlett's excellent *The Making of Europe: Conquest Colonization and Cultural Change, 950–1350* (Princeton: Princeton University Press, 1993), pp. 197–242.

[13] Ibid., pp. 197–242.

[14] King, "Loyalty and Polity, Nation and State," pp. 116–17.

to encourage swing voters to identify with one ethnic group rather than another was to use processions and ethnic violence to polarize people along one identity rather than another. This happened in many multiethnic societies in the 19th century – for example, in Ireland and some towns in western England and Scotland with large Irish populations in the 19th century, as local politics became more competitive, and Catholic and nonconformist Protestant support for Liberal candidates threatened the dominance of the Episcopalian Tories who had traditionally dominated politics and business in cities such as Derry, Liverpool, and Belfast.[15]

Protestant-Catholic Riots in 19th-Century Britain

Protestant-Catholic animosity had been a feature of life for decades in many parts of Ireland and in towns in western England and Scotland where Catholics had migrated in large numbers. But urban ethnic riots between the two communities were rare until the 1830s, when two institutional reforms – introduced because of the political imperatives of party competition in England, Scotland, and Wales – challenged the Episcopalian Protestant elite's domination of electoral politics in these ethnically mixed areas: property tax qualifications for all voters were lowered in a succession of national reforms, beginning with the 1832 Great Reform Act, and those Catholics who met the general property requirements were allowed to vote after 1829.[16] Even in Catholic-majority areas in Ireland, these reforms initially led to many more new Protestant voters than Catholics, because Catholics were as a whole a much poorer and more mobile community and therefore less able to meet property tax and residence requirements.

Tory politicians in Ireland had long shunned nonconformist Presbyterians and Methodists and viewed Catholics with even deeper suspicion. But

---

[15] According to O'Day, "Though relatively scarce [in Ireland] Protestants, especially those belonging to the Church of Ireland, exerted immense influence. They were preeminent in banking, large scale commerce, law, medicine, the state bureaucracy and other status occupations. They owned most of the land." O'Day, "Ireland's Catholics in the British State, 1850–1922," p. 45.

[16] Jonathan Bardon, *Belfast: An Illustrated History* (Dundonald: Blackstaff Press, 1982), p. 83. See also S. J. Connolly, "Mass Politics and Sectarian Conflict, 1823–30," in W. E. Vaughan, ed., *A New History of Ireland*, vol. 5, *Ireland under the Union, I, 1801–70* (Oxford: Clarendon Press, 1989), p. 80. The 1832 reform gave the vote to all owners or tenants of property worth 10 pounds per annum. Catholics in Ireland could vote before 1832 if they met the property qualification (which few did), but they could not stand for parliament or hold public office.

now, to their acute discomfort, within a few decades their Episcopal supporters were reduced to an electoral minority in some traditional strongholds. In the northern city of Derry, for example, Episcopalians constituted only 22.4% of voters after the second reform act in 1867, with Catholics 40.4% of the electorate and Presbyterians 37.2%.[17] These new Catholic and nonconformist Protestant voters were initially inclined to vote for the Liberals, who were both more moderate toward Catholics and more in tune with the ideology, economic interests, and religious affiliations of the Protestant middle classes. Although the relative contribution of religion and class interests to nonconformist political affiliations remains a subject of controversy, the fact that nonconformist Protestants England and Ireland were initially inclined to vote for the Liberals is by now well established. Phillips, summarizing recent research on towns in England, tells us that "Nonconformists were overwhelmingly Liberal, usually by ratios of between eight and twelve to one." His research on Colchester and Great Yarmouth found that 75% of nonconformists voted for the Liberals.[18] Nonconformist and Catholic voters helped the Liberals inflict some severe electoral defeats on the Tories in the 1830s: the Liberals won a number of Tory municipal seats in Derry and Belfast in the 1830s and control of the city of Liverpool in 1837.

In the many parliamentary seats with a majority of Protestant voters but a sizable Catholic minority, the Tory response to this electoral challenge was to play the anti-Catholic card in order to encourage Methodists and Presbyterians to identify themselves with the "Protestant party," the Tories, rather than what they tried to label the "Catholic party," the Liberals.[19] Tory politicians encouraged the foundation of new Protestant organizations and,

---

[17] K. Theodore Hoppen, *Elections, Politics, and Society in Ireland, 1832–1885* (Oxford: Oxford University Press, 1984), pp. 268–69.

[18] John A. Phillips, *The Great Reform Bill in the Boroughs: English Electoral Behaviour, 1818–1841* (Oxford: Oxford University Press, 1992), pp. 273–74, 287–88. For the link between nonconformism and liberalism in Ireland, see Bardon, *Belfast*, pp. 83–85.

[19] The British mainland cities with the largest proportion of Irish-born inhabitants in 1851 were Liverpool (22.3%), Glasgow (16.1%), Manchester and Salford (13.1%), Newcastle (8.1%), Gateshead (8.6%), and Newport (10.7%). The total size of the Irish community (i.e., including English-born people of Irish parentage) was probably nearer to 40% in Liverpool. Frank Neal, *Sectarian Violence: The Liverpool Experience, 1819–1914* (Manchester: Manchester University Press, 1988), pp. 9–10. For an account of election-related anti-Catholic violence in the nearby town of Stockport, see Pauline Millward, "The Stockport Riots of 1852: A Study of Anti-Catholic and Anti-Irish Sentiment," in Roger Swift and Sheridan Gilley, eds., *The Irish in the Victorian City* (London: Croom Helm, 1985), pp. 207–24.

for the first time, they forged links with the working- and middle-class Presbyterians and Methodists in the Orange Lodges they had earlier spurned. Belfast had virtually no Orange Lodge presence in 1800 but had 35 lodges with 1,335 members by 1851.[20] Tory politicians encouraged the lodges in their campaigns on behalf of presumed Protestant "rights" in education, employment, and the control of public space. They especially promoted new "July 12th" processions commemorating William of Orange's victory over the Catholic King James II at the Battle of the Boyne in 1690. These processions were deliberately taken through Catholic or mixed areas as a way of intimidating Catholics and sparking Catholic counterreactions (such as stonethrowing), which would rally more moderate Protestants – who might otherwise have voted with the Catholics for the Liberals – behind the "Protestant candidate."

In the north of Ireland and towns in western England and Scotland with an overall Protestant majority but a sizable Catholic minority, this Tory strategy was highly successful in enabling the party to hold off the Liberal challenge. In the western England port of Liverpool, where Irish Catholics had been a sizable minority since the 18th century, the Tories successfully used an anti-Catholic campaign to win the town council back from the Liberals, who had won the 1835 municipal elections with 58% of the vote after a massive expansion in the number of the city's middle-class voters.[21] Immediately after this setback the Liverpool Tories founded their own Protestant organization to appeal to middle-class voters and began to court the Operative Protestant Society and Orange Lodges that had already established strong links with the new Protestant voters. Tory politicians also made anti-Catholicism the central plank of their campaign in the 1837 election (which they won with 53% of the vote) and the 1841 parliamentary elections. The Tory candidates fiercely criticized the Liberal council for opening up two corporation schools to Catholics, which they claimed would open the door to greater Catholic influence. Episcopalian ministers actively supported the Tories' campaign, with one telling his flock "if any of these liberal councilors belonged to my congregation, I should feel it as my duty to refuse receiving them to the communion of the Lord's Supper. And I tell you farther, that if any man amongst you votes

---

[20] Bardon, *Belfast*, p. 116.
[21] The Great Reform Act enlarged the parliamentary franchise in 1832. But the town franchise in Liverpool was only enlarged after the passage of the Municipal Corporations Act in 1835. Neal, *Sectarian Violence*, p. 38.

for a Liberal candidate, let him be anathema, himself, his wife and children forever."[22]

In both these parliamentary contests and in the 1841 town council election (in which the Tories finally knocked the Liberals out of office), the campaign in Liverpool led to Protestant-Catholic riots. The fact that elections were held in the open with no secret ballot meant that much of the mobilization and intimidation went on during polling day. On Election Day in July 1837 for example, "young ship's carpenters went on the rampage, attacking anyone who wore Liberal colours and, more ominously, seeking out Irishmen for special treatment." And in 1841 Orangemen crowded the streets, playing Protestant songs and, in the south end of the city, "terrorising anyone wearing Liberal colours. In one incident a large group of carpenters attacked Irish homes, breaking all the windows, and late in the day gangs of Irish and carpenters clashed in the South End in a series of vicious fights."[23]

The strategy of polarization and violence to intimidate Catholic voters and solidify the Protestant vote was politically advantageous but often physically risky in areas where Protestants were a majority of the electorate but Catholics were the majority of the local population (until the second reform act in 1867 the number of Catholic voters in many towns remained small because of the £10 property qualification). In towns in the south of Ireland, for example, the absolute number of Protestants was simply too small to use anti-Catholic mobilization safely to solidify the Protestant vote unless the Protestants were in firm control of the local police, which became much less common after the police reforms of the 1830s. Protestants provoked riots in the south at Dublin, Portarlington, and Cork in the 1830s and 1840s, but after 1852, when Protestants in Roscrea and the counties of Cork, Clare, Tipperary, and Leitrim suffered badly from injuries inflicted by Catholics in election riots, southern Protestants abandoned their public anti-Catholicism. After these setbacks, Hoppen reports that "southern political life largely confined its rampant sectarianism to the prejudices of the parlour, the chapel, the club, and the employment office."[24]

In Belfast and other towns in the north of Ireland, where Protestants were a majority of the local population as well as the electorate, the use of

---

[22] Ibid., p. 49.

[23] Ibid., pp. 56–58.

[24] In the town of Roscrea, for example, the damage records for the 1852 riots report that 296 Protestant windows were smashed, but only 44 windows owned by Catholics. Hoppen, *Elections, Politics, and Society in Ireland*, pp. 386–87.

anti-Catholic campaigns was much safer for Protestants and just as successful in solidifying the Protestant vote. The first major Protestant-Catholic
riot in Belfast broke out, not by accident, just before the 1832 parliamentary
election, the first at which middle-class Protestants were eligible to vote.
Protestant-Catholic riots broke out in Belfast during eight of the next ten
elections.[25] In the 1857 campaign, Protestant processions on the boundary
between working-class Protestant and Catholic areas provoked Catholics to
fight back and in the ensuing violence "places of worship were reciprocally
destroyed to 'Three cheers for Dan O'Connell' and a whistled juxtaposition
of 'Croppies lie Down,' 'Kick the Pope before you,' and various Catholic
fighting songs."[26] These riots produced a string of Tory electoral successes,
including, in the aftermath of the 1841 riots, a clean sweep of the Belfast
town council in 1842.[27] The Tory strategy in Belfast was replicated with
similar success in Derry, Portadown, Drogheda, and in Monaghan, where
Orange marches were organized in 1865 to solidify the Tory candidate's
support in a tight race in which Catholic and Protestant voters were evenly
balanced.

The limited data that exist on ethnic voting patterns in 19th-century
Ireland lend strong support to the thesis that the frequent occurrence of
Protestant-Catholic riots led to declining Protestant support for the Liberals. In Derry, for example, 38% of the nonconformist Protestants voted
for the Liberals after the franchise expansion in 1867, but only 31% in
1870, following Protestant-Catholic riots that took place in the city in the
late 1860s. By 1872, when Tories finally won the Derry seat back from the
Liberals, Protestants accounted for only 16% of the Liberal vote.[28] Riots
in Belfast seem to have led to a similar erosion in the Liberals' Protestant
vote in that city: the Liberal candidate's agent calculated that Catholics, a
fifth of the city's electorate in the 1860s, were almost half his party's vote in
1865, and an even higher proportion by the end of the decade as Protestants
continued to abandon the party.[29]

Although the electoral incentive to mobilize Protestants using anti-
Catholic issues was strong in many towns in Ireland, it is striking that those
Protestant-Catholic riots that did break out led to very few deaths. Serious
riots at Derry, Drogheda, and Portadown ended quickly due to firm police

[25] Ibid., pp. 387–88.
[26] Ibid.
[27] Bardon, *Belfast*, p. 94.
[28] Hoppen, *Elections, Politics, and Society in Ireland*, pp. 268–69.
[29] Ibid., p. 268.

intervention, usually leaving only a few people with injuries. The speed and relative impartiality of the state response was due to the incentives facing the Irish government in Dublin. The administration in Dublin Castle was appointed by the Westminster Parliament, in which British rather than Irish Protestant interests were paramount. The main goal of the British administration was to avoid a mass Catholic uprising in Ireland and a repetition of the early 19th-century rebellions, not to help Irish Protestants. In a private letter written in 1852, British Home Secretary J. H. Walpole made it clear that the primary task of the British administration in Ireland was to "hold the scales even between the Protestants and Roman Catholics in all matters which lead to agitation."[30]

To achieve this goal, deliberate attempts were made to insulate local law-and-order forces from pressure by local Protestants to intervene in their disputes with Catholics. Local magistrates were appointed by the colonial government in Dublin (and hence by the London Parliament), and could therefore call in the police regardless of the wishes of the local elected representatives. These magistrates were given strong legal powers to regulate events likely to lead to Protestant-Catholic violence; a Party Processions Act that regulated sectarian displays was passed in 1850 and strengthened in 1860.[31] The magistrates were also left in no doubt by the British government that their job was to be evenhanded, rather than to support the Protestant Ascendancy. To this end large numbers of Protestant gentry magistrates were forcibly retired in the 1820s.[32] With a few exceptions, such as the biased actions of the local magistrate during the Monaghan election in 1865, local magistrates appointed by Dublin Castle were prepared to act against both communities to keep the peace. For example, magistrates refused Protestants permission to march through Catholic areas of Portadown in the 1860s and privately warned Catholics in Desertmartin in 1869

[30] Virginia Crossman, *Politics, Law and Order in Nineteenth-Century Ireland* (New York: St. Martin's Press, 1996), p. 102.

[31] An Act to Restrain Party Processions in Ireland, 14 & 14 Vict., c. 2 (March 12, 1850), allowed magistrates to ban "All assemblies of people meeting or parading together, or joining in procession, who have among them any firearm or offensive weapon, or any banner, emblem, flag, symbol, or display calculated to provoke animosity, or who are accompanied by any person or persons playing music or singing any song calculated to provoke animosity." Penalties were 5 pounds or one month in prison for a first offense, 10 pounds or two months for a second. Crossman, *Politics, Law and Order*, p. 218.

[32] Crossman, *Politics, Law and Order*, pp. 70–71.

that any attempt to attack a symbolic Protestant archway would be repulsed by cannons brought from Derry.[33]

The main government tool to hold the balance between Protestants and Catholics was a newly recruited national police force – the Irish Constabulary, founded in 1836 – that was much more ethnically representative than the old Protestant-controlled militias. This force, 8,000 strong in 1836 and with 12,392 officers by 1882, was well armed, well disciplined, ethnically representative (over 50% Catholic by 1854 and matching the ethnic composition of Ireland as a whole by the 1880s), and deliberately insulated from local sectarian and political squabbles. The force was under the control of centrally appointed magistrates rather than the (Protestant) local squires, Church of Ireland clergy, and absentee landlords who had been appointed to the magistracy earlier.[34] Its members were banned from joining the Orange lodges, and a policy was enforced that no constable could be "allocated to his native county or to any county in which he is connected by marriage."[35] In an effort to prevent the new force from being seen as the tool of the Protestant landlords, the new Irish Constabulary was forbidden from helping mainly Protestant landlords from extracting rents, tithes, or debts from their tenants unless the tenants had previously used violence.

The only massive Protestant-Catholic riot in the 19th century, the case that proves the rule about the importance of understanding the electoral incentives for the government that controls the local police, took place in Belfast in 1864, when the Protestants' burning of an effigy of the nationalist leader Daniel O'Connell sparked off 18 days of rioting in which 12 were killed and 100 injured. The reason the Belfast riot was so large and bloody was that, in all Ireland, only Belfast by 1864 still relied on a local police force controlled by a (Protestant) mayor and (Protestant-controlled) town council, rather than the Irish Constabulary.[36] The

---

[33] Frank Wright, *Two Lands on One Soil: Ulster Politics before Home Rule* (Dublin: Gill and MacMillan, 1996), pp. 271–72, 387, 401–3.

[34] See Oliver Macdonagh, "Ideas and Institutions, 1830–45," in W. E. Vaughan, *A New History of Ireland*, vol. 5, *Ireland under the Union, I, 1801–70* (Oxford: Clarendon Press, 1989), pp. 193–217.

[35] Hoppen, *Elections, Politics, and Society in Ireland*, pp. 408–10. Crossman, *Politics, Law and Order*, pp. 70–71.

[36] The Irish Constabulary was stationed just outside Belfast, at Ballymacarrett on the County Down side of the river, but could only be called in if the Protestant-controlled city police in Belfast asked it to do so. Wright, *Two Lands on One Soil*, pp. 245–47.

160-man Belfast police force, in a city that was 34% Catholic, employed only 6 Catholic constables and had over the years provided ample evidence of its anti-Catholic bias.[37] In 1864 the force refused to intervene to stop the Protestant demonstrations and then showed partiality to the Protestants during the riots, beating and arresting Catholics who resisted Protestant attacks. One town policeman threw stones at the Irish Constabulary trying to control the riot while another was seen encouraging a Protestant mob.[38] Dublin Castle's official investigation was in no doubt where the blame for the riots lay, and in 1865 the Castle forced the city to abolish the local force and replace it with the Irish Constabulary, which unlike the Belfast force proved willing to act against Protestant demonstrators and processions.[39]

After the abolition of the Belfast police, the pattern of Protestant-Catholic riots in the city was transformed, as Catholics became increasingly confident that the Irish Constabulary would intervene to protect them and thus felt less of a need to mobilize to confront Protestant mobs directly. Protestant politicians still sometimes played the anti-Catholic card, but given the changed circumstances, Protestant violence was often now directed against the police, who shielded the Catholics, rather than against the Catholics themselves. The massive 1886 riot in Belfast, which broke out in the context of Protestant mobilization in a close seat in anticipation of an imminent general election, was therefore very different from the 1864 riot. Catholics stayed in their houses throughout the riots, which were largely a battle of Protestants against the police (371 of whom were injured) and the army.[40] Militant Protestants complained bitterly in the aftermath of the riots about the fact that the force had protected Catholics, and they demanded a return to the pre-1865 system in which there was a separate Belfast police system under local (Protestant) control.[41]

---

[37] Bardon, *Belfast*, p. 116. For evidence of anti-Catholic bias by Belfast police officers prior to 1864, see Wright, *Two Lands on One Soil*, pp. 245–47, and *Report of the Commissioners of Inquiry into the Origin and Character of the Riots in Belfast in July and September 1857* (Dublin: Alex. Thom. and Sons, 1858), pp. 1–16.

[38] Bardon, *Belfast*, pp. 113–14.

[39] Wright, *Two Lands One Soil*, pp. 261–69.

[40] Bardon, *Belfast*, pp. 148–50.

[41] *Reports from Commissioners, Inspectors, and Others: Thirty-Five Volumes-(5.)-Belfast Riots Commission, 1887*, British Parliamentary Papers, vol. 18 (London: Her Majesty's Stationery Office, 1887), appendix D, especially p. 590.

Postcolonial Responses to Growing Interethnic Political Competition

In the two decades after 1947, British, French, and Belgian colonies in Asia and Africa attained independence in what Samuel Huntington refers to as the "second wave" of democratization. In most countries pressure for independence came from multiethnic coalitions such as the Congress in India, Kenya African National Union (KANU) in Kenya, or the Malay-Chinese-Indian UMNO-led coalition in Malaya. Despite the explicitly multiethnic character of these political movements, in practice one or perhaps two ethnic groups, typically those that had greatest access to civil service jobs and education under the colonial administration, dominated each party. The challenge for the leaders of the ethnic group that dominated these political parties was holding their multiethnic coalitions together in the face of pressure from their own group's members for more government jobs and benefits, and pressure from excluded ethnic groups for a fairer share of political power and the state's resources.

As in the first wave, dominant ethnic groups used several different strategies to prevent defections from the multiethnic coalitions that had won independence, especially through co-opting rival elites by offering them money or prestigious cabinet positions. But if this strategy failed and the loss of power was a real threat, politicians showed themselves willing to use ethnic polarization to depress the turnout of competing ethnic groups and to solidify their own group around the dominant party.[42] In 1992, for example, under political pressure from the newly legalized opposition – the multiethnic, though Kikuyu-led, Forum for the Restoration of Democracy (FORD) – Kenyan President Moi allowed, and probably planned, attacks on the Kikuyu, Luhya, and Luo tribes by well-organized bands of armed Kalenjin (Moi's own tribe, and the dominant group within the governing KANU Party).[43] In March 1992 Luo attacked by Kalenjin in Nyanza district reported that some of their attackers were wearing the uniforms of the governing party and that packed lunches were brought to them as they besieged the Luo.[44] In the first half of 1992, between 300 and 500 people were killed in these "ethnic riots." The riots solidified the Kalenjin behind

---

[42] Of course, the ultimate strategy was to avoid democratic competition altogether and establish an authoritarian regime, claiming that only this could save the new country from chaos.

[43] "Kenya, a Land That Thrived, Is Now Caught Up in Fear of Ethnic Civil War," *New York Times*, May 3, 1992, p. 3.

[44] *New African*, May 1992, p. 17.

Moi, because they sparked off revenge attacks by members of other tribes on Kalenjin: in April, Kikuyu in Molo killed seven Kalenjin and a Kalenjin couple was stoned by a Nairobi mob.[45]

Malay-Chinese Riots in Malaysia

Perhaps the most striking instance of the way in which postcolonial parties used ethnic violence to solidify their own support and divide that of their opponents was in Malaysia, where a threat to the dominance of the ruling UMNO coalition in the 1969 elections led to mass ethnic riots between Malays and Chinese. The Malay-Chinese riots that broke out in Kuala Lumpur in May 1969 are usually seen as the spontaneous reaction of Malaysia's largest ethnic community, the Malays (55%), to the national losses suffered in the 1969 general election by the ruling multiethnic coalition led by UMNO, the United Malays National Organization. This multiethnic alliance, formed in 1952 by a preelection agreement between UMNO and the main Chinese political organization, the Malaysian Chinese Association (MCA) Alliance, had ruled Malaysia since independence in 1957. But in 1969 its Malay and (especially) Chinese wings both lost ground to more nationalistic Chinese and Malay parties such as the Democratic Action Party (Chinese) and the Pan Malayan Islamic Party (PMIP). On the Malay side, the PMIP had very successfully played up the threat of the Chinese swamping Malaysia unless UMNO's "moderate" policies toward the 36% Chinese minority were stopped. The PMIP was particularly upset about the 1967 National Language Act, which satisfied the Chinese demand to keep English as an official language alongside Malay. During the election campaign the PMIP alleged that the prime minister, Tunku Abdul Rahman, was in reality a Buddhist from Thailand and circulated thousands of photographs of a Malay cabinet minister and his wife in Mandarin fancy dress as proof of their claim that UMNO was selling out the Malays to the Chinese![46]

Although the MCA Alliance still won a respectable majority in 1969, it failed for the first time to win the 50% of the popular vote and the two-thirds majority in parliamentary seats (see Table 7.1) that it needed to be able to amend the country's constitution. The UMNO alliance also suffered from

[45] "Kenya: Opposition in the Opposition," *Africa Confidential*, May 8, 1992.
[46] Tunku Abdul Rahman Putra Al-Haj, *May 13: Before and After* (Kuala Lumpur: Utusan Melayu Press, 1969), p. 30.

Table 7.1. *Election Results and Ethnic Cleavages in Malaysian Federal Elections, 1964–1969*

Party (Ethnic Support)	Seats Won in	
	1964	1969
Alliance	89	66
United Malays National Organization (Malay)	59	51
Malaysian Chinese Association (Chinese)	27	13
Malaysian Indian Congress (Indian)	3	2
Opposition		
Pan-Malayan Islamic Party (Malay)	9	12
People's Progressive Party (Malay)	2	4
Democratic Action Party (Chinese)	0	13
Gerakan (mainly Chinese/Indian)	0	8
Socialist Front	2	0
People's Action Party	1	0
United Democratic Party	1	0
Vacant	0	1

Source: Goh Cheng Tek, *The May Thirteenth Incident and Democracy in Malaysia* (Kuala Lumpur: Oxford University Press, 1971), p. 13.

some stunning individual defeats in Malay-dominated seats, which made it clear that the party was losing the support of many nationalist Malays. In Ampang, a constituency with a 52% Malay majority, 5% Indians, and 43% Chinese, large numbers of Malays defected to the Malay nationalist PMIP, enabling the Chinese Democratic Action Party (DAP) candidate to beat his Malay UMNO challenger by 1,000 votes.[47]

The usual description of the violence that broke out in May 1969 is as a *national* Malay reaction to this national electoral upset.[48] The majority Malay community, it is said, was angered by the Chinese opposition party's celebrations on May 11 and 12 and felt cheated of the two-thirds electoral victory. It therefore took out its anger on the Chinese minority in ethnic riots beginning on the evening of May 13. Over the next four days, according to official figures 196 were killed, 439 were injured, and 1,019 were reported

---

[47] The Malaysian population in the 1960s was 46% Malay, 36% Chinese, 10% Indians, 7% indigenous peoples and others. Goh Cheng Tek, *The May Thirteenth Incident and Democracy in Malaysia* (Kuala Lumpur: Oxford University Press, 1971), p. 16. The population balance in peninsular Malaysia (i.e., excluding Sarawak) in 1970 was 53% Malays, 35% Chinese, 11% Indians, and 1% others.

[48] Gordon P. Means, *Malaysian Politics: The Second Generation* (Singapore: Oxford University Press, 1991).

missing, but unofficial accounts estimate the death toll at between 300 and 700.[49]

What this generally accepted explanation overlooks is why, if the violence was truly a national Malay reaction to the strong Chinese showing in the elections, riots broke out only in Kuala Lumpur and elsewhere in Selangor state in May 1969 and not in other states with a similar ethnic mix and voting patterns? Penang, for example, was also very tense before the elections, but the state experienced no riots after the Chinese Gerakan party secured a solid majority in the state. And Parker reports that in states such as Johore and Kedah, "months after the initial violence visitors to these states were stunned by the contrast between their relaxed atmosphere and the prolonged tension in Selangor."[50]

The puzzle can be explained, I argue, if we examine the results in the state elections that took place at the same time as the 1969 federal elections. Kuala Lumpur, as well as being Malaysia's federal capital, is also the capital of Selangor state. And Selangor was, after the May 1969 elections, the only state in peninsular Malaysia in which it was unclear which party would form the government. The MCA Alliance had retained power in most states and clearly lost to Chinese parties in Perak and Penang. In Selangor, on the other hand, the opposition and the alliance had an equal number of MPs (see Table 7.2), and there was a strong possibility that the alliance might be displaced from power. The Chinese opposition parties, bolstered by their strong showing, were pressing for another election, on the grounds that 60% of the state's electorate had voted for the opposition. And it was unclear whether the moderate Chinese- and Indian-supported Gerakan Party would remain neutral, or join the antialliance opposition.[51]

The massive May 13 Malay demonstration that sparked the riots was planned against this backdrop of electoral uncertainty and backroom politicking. Malays from throughout Selangor state were encouraged by Malay chauvinist UMNO leaders to come to Kuala Lumpur for a mass procession. Although reluctant to grant the procession a permit, the state's chief minister did so on the evening of May 12 because chauvinist leaders within his party, whose position had been strengthened by the poor showing in

---

[49] Felix V. Gagliano, *Communal Violence in Malaysia 1969: The Political Aftermath* (Athens: Ohio University Center for International Studies Southeast Asia Program, 1970), p. 1.

[50] William Crego Parker, "Cultures in Stress: The Malaysian Crisis of 1969 and Its Cultural Roots" (Ph.D. dissertation, MIT, 1979), 1:183.

[51] Tek, *The May Thirteenth Incident and Democracy in Malaysia*, pp. 19, 23.

Table 7.2. *Selangor State Election Results, 1969*
(seats won by each party)

Alliance	
United Malays National Organization	12
Malaysian Chinese Association	1
Malaysian Indian Congress	1
Opposition	
Democratic Action Party	9
Gerakan	4
Independent	1
Pan-Malaysia Islamic Party	0

Source: Goh Cheng Tek, *The May Thirteenth Incident and Democracy in Malaysia* (Kuala Lumpur: Oxford University Press, 1971), p. 15.

the elections, threatened to hold a procession whether he gave permission or not.

> At 8.30 P.M. [on May 12] Haji Razali brought the leaders to see Dato Harun. Their grievances were forcibly stated. The Chinese had insulted their people and were determined to make pariahs of them in their own country. Was UMNO really spineless [*dayyus*] as the PMIP charged or castrated as Dr. Tan Chee Khoon asserted? If so, the Malay community would rise and set matters right. They could not stand the humiliation any longer. If the Chief Minister was telling the truth and the Alliance would remain in power in the state, they too deserved a demonstration. With the support of the government it could be a celebration. Otherwise, on their own they would present a show of power.[52]

The procession was devised partly to put pressure on the Gerakan Party to join the MCA Alliance, or at least to remain neutral, and also to demonstrate to the purely Chinese parties that UMNO's Malay supporters were determined not to see "their" state fall into Chinese hands. The procession and riots are therefore best understood not as a protest over a national electoral outcome but as a state-level strategy to solidify Malay support behind UMNO in Selangor and signal to the purely Chinese parties the dangers of a direct challenge to UMNO.

The May 13 riots began with reports that Chinese had attacked Malays on their way to the demonstration.[53] But even this spark does not explain

[52] Karl von Vorys, *Democracy without Consensus: Communalism and Political Stability in Malaysia* (Princeton: Princeton University Press, 1975), p. 322.
[53] Unlike most rumors that spark ethnic violence, these seem to have been true. Some fighting broke out in the Setapak area of Kuala Lumpur in the early evening between Malays going

the size and ferocity of the anti-Chinese pogrom that followed. The reason anti-Chinese violence assumed such proportions in a city whose population was 55% Chinese was that the UMNO-controlled central and state governments were unwilling to use federal and state police forces against the Malays who formed the core of their political support.[54] The federal and local UMNO leaders, who had been criticized by Malay nationalists since making some concessions to Chinese opinion over a 1967 language bill, now found their "moderate" policy discredited among Malays by their party's poor showing in the elections, and the Chinese support for the DAP and Gerakan. UMNO leaders made it clear that if they refused to take a strong line with the Chinese, and action to counter the threat from the Malay right, they would be replaced, and so they urged the replacement of the Chinese ministers of commerce and industry and finance to counter the Malay nationalist's charge that UMNO was soft on the Chinese. The so-called Ultras went even further and urged that the Malays go it alone and rule without the support of the Chinese in the MCA.[55]

In this environment, any minister who intervened to use state power to protect the Chinese from ethnic Malays risked his entire political career within UMNO, as well as further alienating those Malays who had defected to the nationalists. As a result, although it was widely known that Malays traveling to the demonstration were armed with *parangs* (machetes) and bamboo spears, and though armed police and soldiers were held in reserve, no orders were issued to state or federal forces to disarm the demonstrators.[56] The fact that anti-Chinese rioters believed that the state would not intervene to stop them is demonstrated by the fact that when a few policemen fired on some Malay rioters they rushed straight to the state's chief minister, Dato Harun, to express their shock and outrage.[57] In the case of the army, ethnically Malay and under the direct control of the central government, the rioters' faith in the state's pro-Malay bias was fully justified. UMNO's leaders, under pressure from Malay chauvinists within their own

to the UMNO procession and Chinese, after which some Malays rushed to the Malay crowd in the Kampong Bharu district of the city and told them what had happened. Parker, "Cultures in Stress," p. 156.

[54] Kuala Lumpur's ethnic balance in 1970 was 25% Malays, 55% Chinese, 19% Indians, and 1% others. Leon Comber, *13 May 1969: A Historical Survey of Sino-Malay Relations* (Kuala Lumpur: Heinemann, 1983), appendix 9, p. 99.

[55] Tunku, *May 13: Before and After*, pp. 117–57.

[56] Parker, "Cultures in Stress," p. 151.

[57] Von Vorys, *Democracy without Consensus*, p. 338. See also Means, *Malaysian Politics*, pp. 6–10.

party, made no effort to rein in the Royal Malay Regiment, which fired at Chinese mobs while ignoring or even assisting the Malays who were attacking them.[58]

Transitions from Communist Rule in Eastern Europe

In the transition from communism in Eastern Europe many political scientists expected multiethnic states such as Bulgaria, Romania, Latvia, and Lithuania to suffer from ethnic polarization and violence. Claus Offe, for example, argued that the combination of a weak civil society and bad economic prospects in Eastern Europe made playing the ethnic card the logical choice for ex-Communist politicians who wanted to retain or seize power and adopt a new "clean" identity.[59] This seemed especially likely given that in the Baltic States the large Russian minorities were identified with Communist persecution and that in Romania and Bulgaria Communist regimes had, during their final years in power, used periodic antiminority campaigns to bolster their own legitimacy among the majority ethnic group. A government campaign in Bulgaria in 1984–85 to assimilate the Turks was especially violent, leading to the deaths of hundreds and perhaps thousands of Turks and the expulsion or emigration of 350,000 more to Turkey.[60]

The reason why nationalist mobilization in the Baltics was muted was that nationalist leaders in Estonia and Latvia realized that harsh measures against their Russian minorities would draw a strong response, possibly a military response from neighboring Russia. Leaders in both countries referred often to the limitations this strategic situation placed on their freedom to take a more aggressive stance in encouraging Russians to leave or to pursue a strong assimilationist strategy. In both Romania and Bulgaria, however, with no superpower next door to stand up for the rights of the local minority, former Communist political leaders initially used campaigns against each country's main ethnic minority (the 8% Hungarian minority in Romania and the 10% Turkish minority in Bulgaria) in order to appeal to

[58] According to Gagliano, "The elite Royal Malay Regiment is entirely Malay; the armed forces senior officers (Division One) are 64.5 per cent Malay; at the lower ranks, the Malay proportion is much larger – these are 'areas of employment long avoided by non-Malays.'" Gagliano, *Communal Violence in Malaysia 1969*, p. 38.

[59] Claus Offe, "Strong Causes, Weak Cures: Some Preliminary Notes on the Intransigence of Ethnic Politics," *East European Constitutional Review* 1, no. 1 (1992), pp. 21–23.

[60] John T. Ishiyama and Marijke Breuning, *Ethnopolitics in the New Europe* (Boulder, Colo.: Lynne Rienner, 1998), chap. 2.

voters from the majority community. Although Romania experienced severe ethnic tensions, Bulgaria did not, even though in 1992 46% of Bulgarians polled by Gallup said that the country's minorities were a threat to national security. In fact, Bulgaria introduced a series of progressive minority rights measures in the 1990s – which included compensation for Turks who were expelled and had property seized in the 1980s – that were widely applauded by minority advocates.[61] The reason why Bulgaria escaped violence lies in the unexpected results of the transitional 1991 elections. The 1991 national elections were extremely close, with the Communists winning 44.2% of the vote (and hence 44.2% of the seats in the proportional representation system) and the reformist Union of Democratic Forces (UDF) winning 45.8% of the vote. The small Turkish party, the Movement for Rights and Freedoms (MRF), won 10% of the seats in parliament. The minority-supported MRF was therefore in a pivotal political position, and over the next few years its leader Ahmed Doggan switched his support first to the UDF and then to the Bulgarian Socialist Party (BSP) in a successful effort to secure legal protections for the Turkish minority. As a result of these institutional reforms, and the continuing high level of electoral fractionalization in Bulgaria (4.2 parties in the 1991 election, 3.8 in 1994, 3.3 in 1997, and 3.9 in 2001), the MRF has continued to play a pivotal role in Bulgarian politics since the early 1990s.[62] Successive central governments in Bulgaria have therefore acted to defuse antiminority sentiments and prevent local anti-Turkish mobilizations from turning violent. The situation in Romania was more difficult than Bulgaria however, and in the first years after independence the national government was unwilling to protect members of the large Hungarian minority because it seemed that doing so would be an electoral liability.

Romanian-Hungarian Violence in Post-Ceaucescu Romania

For centuries before the fall of the Hapsburg Empire in 1918, Transylvania was an integral part of the kingdom of Hungary, although more than two-thirds of the province's inhabitants were non-Hungarians, chiefly

---

[61] Petya Nitzova, "Bulgaria: Minorities, Democratization and National Sentiments," *Nationalities Papers* 25, no. 4, (1997), pp. 729–40.

[62] Calculated from Bulgarian election data available at the University of Essex Project on Political Transformation and the Electoral Process in Post-Communist Europe, downloaded May 14, 2003, from <http://www.essex.ac.uk/elections/>.

Romanians (54% in 1910), and Germans (11%).[63] After 1867, when Hungary achieved a large measure of autonomy within the Hapsburg Empire, Hungarian politicians began a highly unpopular campaign, complete with harsh language laws passed in 1879, 1883, and 1891, to Magyarize the kingdom's Romanians, Slovaks, and Ruthenes.[64] After World War I, when Transylvania became part of greater Romania, Romanian politicians took their revenge. Language tests in Romanian were used to remove Hungarians from the educational system and lower bureaucracy. And land reforms hit Hungarians harder than any other group, both because Hungarians owned more land than other groups to begin with and because they were especially targeted by Romanian officials. By 1930 Hungarian emigration and the fact that individuals who formerly identified themselves as Hungarian began to declare themselves as Romanians or Germans led to a fall in the Hungarian percentage of the Transylvanian population from 32% in 1910 to 27%.[65]

After the Second World War, the Romanian Communist Party under President Petru Groza was initially conciliatory toward ethnic minorities. The 1948 constitution guaranteed linguistic minorities (chiefly the Transylvanian Hungarians and Germans with 7.9% and 1.6% respectively of the total Romanian population in 1977), the right to use their own language in education and administration and for cultural purposes. In 1952 the government set up a Magyar Autonomous region in the Hungarian Szekler region. But even before this apparent high point of ethnic accommodation, the party had begun to expel prominent Jews and Hungarians, whom it saw as a potential fifth column that could be used by the Soviet Union.[66] By the late 1950s the Romanian government had completely abandoned its support for minority rights, and under Nicolae Ceaucescu, who led Romania from 1965 to 1989, Hungarian cultural institutions were progressively Romanianized. The Hungarian university in Transylvania's major city of Cluj, for example, was forcibly unified in 1959 with the city's Romanian university, after which Romanian language instruction began to displace

---

[63] Lazlo Sebok, "The Hungarians in East Central Europe: A Demographic Profile," *Nationalities Papers* 24, no. 3 (1996), p. 557.

[64] Keith Hitchins, *Rumania, 1866–1947* (Oxford: Oxford University Press, 1994), pp. 206–7.

[65] For a pro-Hungarian account of the post 1918 discrimination against Hungarians, see Robert Gower, *The Hungarian Minorities in the Succession States* (London: Grant Richards, 1937), especially pp. 27–33.

[66] Simona Schwerthoeffer, "The Nationalities Policy: Theory and Practice," in Vlad Georgescu, ed., *Romania: 40 Years (1944–1984)* (New York: Praeger, 1985), pp. 79–81.

Hungarian in many subjects. Middle-class Hungarians were also forced to find work in Romanian-language areas of the country, and professional jobs in traditionally Hungarian areas were effectively reserved for Romanians. In the late 1980s Ceaucescu announced a new policy of forced rural re-settlement that would, had it been fully enforced, have displaced half the country's Hungarians.[67]

The Ceaucescu regime fell in December 1989, spurred by mass protests in the Transylvanian town of Timisoara in which Hungarians played a prominent role. The new National Salvation Front (NSF) government, led by Ion Iliescu, announced that it would safeguard Romania's transition to democracy but take no active role in party politics. The NSF quickly announced that it would "observe the rights and freedoms of national minorities and ... ensure their full equality with those of the Romanians."[68] It backed up these promises in early January by including several prominent Hungarians in the cabinet and broadcasting 12 hours of Hungarian language programs each week from the radio stations in three major towns in Transylvania as well as in Bucharest.

Responding to this new environment, Hungarians began immediately to rebuild their cultural institutions, founding newspapers, magazines, and a Hungarian political organization, the Hungarian Democratic Union of Romania (HDUR), which operated initially as a subordinate part of the NSF. In January 1990 local NSF committees in overwhelmingly Hungarian areas began to put up Hungarian street names and signs alongside those in Romanian and to reclaim traditionally Hungarian schools and cultural institutions that had been Romanianized under Ceaucescu. These moves increased the insecurity of Romanians in Transylvania (despite the fact that Romanians now outnumber Hungarians three to one in the region), prompting large Romanian demonstrations and, at the end of January, the NSF's dismissal of the Hungarian minister for minority affairs in Bucharest.[69] The NSF, already under criticism because of its

---

[67] On the postwar maltreatment of the Hungarians, see Gyorgy Lazar's "Memorandum," in *Witness to Cultural Genocide: First-Hand Reports on Rumania's Minority Policies Today* (New York: American Transylvanian Federation, 1979), pp. 88–144.

[68] Martin Rady, *Romania in Turmoil* (New York: IB Tauris, 1992), p. 147.

[69] According to the January 1992 Romanian census, the ethnic balance in Transylvania is 72.3% Romanian, 23.9% Hungarian, 2.8% Roma, and 0.9% Germans. The national ethnic balance is 89.4% Romanian, 7.1% Hungarian, 1.8% Roma, with Germans, Ukrainians, and Russians accounting for most of the remainder. Romania's total population in 1992 was 22,760,449. Michael Shafir, "Preliminary Results of the 1992 Romanian Census," *RFE/RL Research Report* 1, no. 30 (1992), pp. 62–68.

decision to contest the May elections, decided to delay the pace of minority education reform until tensions cooled on both sides and announced that no more changes would be allowed until the following academic year.

Despite the widespread tensions in Transylvania over the education issue, the only place violent ethnic mobilization took place before the May 1990 elections was in the county and town of Tirgu Mures. Tirgu Mures was one of only two counties in all of Transylvania in which there was a rough balance between the various ethnic minorities (Hungarians, Germans, and Gypsies) and Romanians. The 1977 census, which Hungarians claim undercounts ethnic minorities, estimated the county's Hungarian minority at 43.6%. Of the remaining 14 counties, 2 have a solid Hungarian majority (Harghita 84.5% and Covasna 77.9%) and the rest have an overwhelming Romanian majority. Moreover, the city of Tirgu Mures, where free municipal elections were due to be held, had a population of 200,000, equally divided between Hungarians and Romanians.[70]

Given the closeness of the ethnic balance in both the county (the unit from which senators and assembly members are elected) and in the city, there were clear electoral incentives for Romanian politicians to promote issues that would rally Romanian voters and intimidate Hungarians. Local members of Vatra, a new nationalist organization set up in Romania in January 1990, planned a major demonstration in the town of Tirgu Mures on March 19 to demand the removal of a prominent Hungarian official and to protest against the Magyarization of a prestigious high school and the proposed creation of a Hungarian-language section in the local medical school. The protest was orchestrated by local Romanian mayors with the connivance of the local, overwhelmingly Romanian, police: "[C]ommittees in nearby factories and villages were asked to muster gangs of Romanians ready for transfer to Tirgu Mures. . . . In return for participating, Romanian workers and villagers were promised substantial sums of money; others were threatened by local mayors with fines if they did not join in. The group were issued with weapons and alcohol, and provided with coaches, lorries and police escorts. In the course of the descent on Tirgu Mures, various groups stopped off en route to attack Hungarian villages." After arriving in Tirgu Mures the "protesters" were issued more weapons and alcohol before they

---

[70] Helsinki Watch, *Struggling for Ethnic Identity: Ethnic Hungarians in Post-Ceaucescu Romania* (Human Rights Watch, 1993), appendix E, "Counties in Transylvania in Order of Size of Ethnic Hungarian Population."

began viciously attacking a group of protesting Hungarians and the local offices of the HDUR.[71]

A multiethnic Hungarian-Romanian protest against the violence was held the next day in the main square. Romanian thugs were again trucked in from surrounding villages to attack the protesters. The local police (virtually all Romanian) made halfhearted attempts to provide a security-cordon but they took no action against the Romanian attackers and, according to Martin Rady, provided "the 'Romanian side' with petrol for firebombs." The national government in Bucharest also refused repeated requests from Hungarians in Tirgu Mures to intervene, apparently for two reasons. First, the NSF had no real party organization of its own, and in order to win the May elections it needed the organizational help and votes of the former Communist Party officials throughout the country. In Transylvania, many of these party bosses had made their careers by baiting the minorities under Ceaucescu, and were now active in anti-Hungarian protests. If the state intervened against the Romanians in March 1990, it therefore faced the prospect of losing the support of the party organization it would need two months later in the national elections.[72]

Second, and probably more telling, the center refused to intervene because, with elections approaching and the size of the Romanian nationalist vote unknown (but on the basis of Vatra's claimed membership of 2 million and the size of the anti-Hungarian demonstrations in January and February 1990 certainly larger than the 7.1% of the vote the Hungarians could deliver), it did not want to be seen as taking the side of the Hungarians.[73] Doing so would not only ruin the chances of attracting the most ardent Romanian nationalists in Transylvania but might also alienate more moderate Romanian voters in the rest of the country. Polling data suggests that only one in five Romanians has a favorable opinion of Hungarians.[74] President Iliescu had already demonstrated in January 1990 that he was

---

[71] Tom Gallagher, *Romania after Ceaucescu: The Politics of Intolerance* (Edinburgh: Edinburgh University Press, 1995), pp. 80–81.

[72] Ibid.

[73] The September 1992 elections provide some indication of the strength of the Romanian nationalist vote. By 1992, even though the NSF had adopted many of the right's policies and had gone back on virtually all its promises to the Hungarian minority, Romanian nationalist parties got 12% of the vote, the Romanian National Unity Party 8%, and Romania Mare 4%.

[74] Mary McIntosh et al., "Minority Rights and Majority Rule: Ethnic Tolerance in Romania and Bulgaria," *Social Forces* 73, no. 3 (1995), pp. 939–68. A poll in 1995 found that 80% of Romanians regarded the Hungarian Democratic Federation of Romania (UDMR) as

prepared to play the anti-Hungarian card against critics of the NSF: the day after Romanian demonstrations against the NSF's decision to contest the May elections, Iliescu went on television to warn about the need for national unity in the face of the alleged separatist threat in Transylvania.[75]

The NSF therefore did nothing for two days. Only when Hungarians and Roma from the countryside surrounding Tirgu Mures began to move into the city to protect ethnic Hungarians from the Romanian thugs and the police did local Vatra officials call on the government to help and the NSF decide to intervene. On March 21, Romanian army tanks were finally ordered into Tirgu Mures to break up the violence, which by that time had claimed at least 3 dead and 269 injured. The police and army arrested and later prosecuted large numbers of Hungarians and Roma, but only a handful of Romanians. In the May 1990 elections, the center's anti-Hungarian stand was fully vindicated, and the NSF won 66% of the votes in the Assembly, 67% for the Senate, and 87% of the votes in the presidential elections. The only party to have taken a moderate stance on the anti-Hungarian actions in the previous months, Radu Campeanu's Liberal Party, saw its Romanian support collapse. In the presidential elections, election observers report that Campeanu's party won the Hungarian vote (7.1% of the total electorate) but only 2% or 3% of the Romanian vote.[76]

The interpretation of this delay as motivated by the upcoming election is also supported by Iliescu's similar decision not to intervene in tense interethnic scuffles over archaeological excavations in Cluj in June–July 1994, excavations that would have removed the statue of a famous Hungarian king. According to Michael Shafir, the government's month-long delay in stopping the dig was due to the fact that it needed the votes of the extreme nationalist Party of Romanian National Unity to defeat an impeachment resolution against Iliescu. This view seems to be borne out by the fact that the morning after Iliescu defeated the impeachment measure, it was announced that the excavation would be delayed.[77]

"anti-Romanian," a view shared by 8% of Hungarian-speaking Romanians. Open Media Research Institute, *Daily Digest*, July 20, 1995.

[75] International Foundation for Electoral Systems, *Romania in the Wake of Ceaucescu: An Assessment of the Romanian Electoral System on Election Eve* (Washington, D.C.: International Foundation for Electoral Systems, 1990).

[76] Joshua L. Dorosin, *Romania: A Dream Deferred, the 1990 Elections and Prospects for Future Democracy* (Washington, D.C.: International Foundation for Electoral Systems, 1990), p. 27.

[77] "Ethnic Tension Runs High in Romania," *RFE/RL Research Report* 3, no. 32 (1994), p. 24.

Conclusion

This chapter has shown the ways in which in Ireland, Malaysia, and Romania politicians from the dominant ethnic group have raised divisive symbolic issues and used violence – or allowed it to take place – in order to solidify their own support and depress the vote of their opponents in close races. In all three countries, as in India, the key to whether large-scale violence develops from these polarizing events is the attitude of the level of government that controls the police and the army. Governments, I suggest, decide whether to prevent antiminority violence by calculating whether doing so will help or hurt them politically. In Belfast, the town police in 1864 was unwilling to stop anti-Catholic riots because doing so would have involved attacking the politically dominant Protestants who controlled the police. In the rest of Ireland, on the other hand, the central government in Dublin controlled the police and ordered it to intervene to protect Catholics and prevent riots.

Another example of the way in which changes in electoral competitiveness at the national level can have a positive effect on the state's efforts to prevent ethnic violence at the local level comes from the United States. For almost a century, white Protestant politicians used political campaigns that baited African Americans and religious minorities such as Catholics and Jews in order to win elections. These campaigns were especially effective in breaking up multiracial political challenges to regional one-party dominance, such as the Progressive and Republican challenges to the Democrats in the South in the 1880s and 1890s. Research on patterns of lynching in Louisiana during this period has revealed a pattern of polarization and violence in election years remarkably similar to that we have seen for Hindu-Muslim riots in India in earlier chapters. Local politicians increased the supply of antiminority polarization in order to depress minority voting and maximize the majority community's identification with a "white" identity rather than with alternative political or economic identities. The three election years of 1892, 1894, and 1896 each saw a sharp upsurge in lynchings, with the greatest number of lynchings occurring in the campaign for the extremely close Louisiana gubernatorial race of 1896.[78]

The common thread in these incidents of antiminority violence was that locally controlled police forces in areas with a majority of white Protestant

[78] James M. Inverarity, "Populism and Lynching in Louisiana, 1889–1896: A Test of Erikson's Theory of the Relationship between Boundary Crises and Repressive Justice," *American Sociological Review* 41, no. 2 (1976), p. 214.

voters simply had no electoral incentive to help the ethnic group being attacked. In his study of violence in the 1830s and 1840s, Michael Feldberg has found that "The constabulary's reluctance to get involved in public disturbances became most pronounced when the victims of crime or disorder were unpopular minorities. Few constables would risk their re-election chances by trying to protect abolitionists, blacks, Mormons or other social outcasts from the righteous indignation of their constituents.... Philadelphia's mayor, sheriff, and other law enforcement officials stood by at the [anti-Catholic] burning of Pennsylvania Hall or during the sacking of Third Ward, Kensington."[79] Similar accounts of a partisan white police force standing by during attacks on minorities could be provided for almost every major riot in the United States up until the mid-20th century. During a wave of riots in 1919, for example, the police forces in major cities such as Washington and Chicago refused to intervene to protect blacks from white mobs.[80]

What changed? One important part of the picture is of course the action African Americans took themselves in their mass movement for civil rights during the 1950s and 1960s. But it is unclear – given that many previous civil rights campaigns had been brutally suppressed – that these campaigns could have succeeded as completely or as quickly as they did if the federal government had been unwilling to intervene to enforce federal antidiscrimination orders against the wishes of white-controlled southern state governments. Why then did the federal government choose to intervene after World War II when it had not done so earlier?

An electoral incentives model helps us to understand both why the federal government first abandoned black voters in the South in the 1870s, and why it was ready to intervene again after World War II. The explanation for the federal government's withdrawal lies in the disputed presidential election of 1877. In the aftermath of the election, white southern Democrats in Congress offered to cut a deal with the Republicans in Washington. In return for supporting (or more accurately not blocking) the election of the Republican presidential candidate Rutherford Hayes, they wanted the withdrawal of northern troops from South Carolina and Louisiana, where federal forces had been preventing militant whites from intimidating black

---

[79] Michael Feldberg, *The Turbulent Era: Riot and Disorder in Jacksonian America* (New York: Oxford University Press, 1980), p. 111.

[80] Arthur I. Waskow, *From Race Riot to Sit-In: 1919 and the 1960s* (New York: Doubleday, 1966).

233

voters. In order to win the presidency, the party of Lincoln agreed, in effect, to abandon blacks in the south, a decision that was not to be reversed by the federal government until the 1950s.[81]

What changed between the 1870s and the 1950s? The key difference, as Carmines and Stimson have explored in some detail, is that by the late 1940s and early 1950s both the Democratic Party and the Republicans needed to win large northern swing states such as Illinois and Michigan in order to defeat the other.[82] To win these states the Democrats in particular had to win heavily in the big cities, and by the 1940s, after several decades of black migration from the South to the manufacturing heartland of the North, this meant that Democrats needed to win the support of an increasingly black electorate, most of whom had relatives still living in the segregated South.[83] To win the support of these voters, the Democrats had to become more active on civil rights issues. In the 1948 presidential campaign, for example, the Democratic National Committee (DNC) advised Clark Clifford (who in turn advised President Truman) that the Democrats had to win the support of "working people, the veterans, and the Negroes" to win the election. To win black support the DNC suggested that President Truman "should speak out frankly and fully on his magnificent record as a fighter for Civil Rights – he should mention his votes in the Senate, his anti-poll tax and anti-lynching legislation, his support of the wartime FEPC [Fair Employment Practice Committee], and his orders to end discrimination in the government and the armed services to prove that he *acts* as well as talks Civil Rights. *The Negro votes in the crucial states will more than cancel out any votes he may lose in the South.*"[84] Black support was indeed crucial to Truman's reelection in 1948. McAdam shows how "Essential to Truman's victory that

---

[81] See C. Vann Woodward, *Reunion and Reaction: The Compromise of 1877 and the End of Reconstruction* (Boston: Little Brown, 1951).

[82] Edward G. Carmines and James A. Stimson, *Race and the Transformation of American Politics* (Princeton: Princeton University Press, 1989) p. 33.

[83] From 1910 to 1960 5 million blacks migrated from the South to other parts of the United States. This emigration was the main factor in the increase in the black population in the North from 1,027,674 in 1910 to 6,474,536 in 1960 (530%), and from 50,662 to 1,085,688 in the West (2043%). Doug McAdam, *Political Process and the Development of Black Insurgency, 1930–1970* (Chicago: University of Chicago Press, 1982), p. 78, table 5.1.

[84] Emphasis added. Memorandum to Mr. Clark Clifford from William L. Batt Jr., Director, Research Division Democratic National Committee, entitled "Notes on President's Campaign," August 11, 1948 (original in Clark M. Clifford Files, Truman Presidential Library, Independence, Mo.). Clifford sent Truman a virtually word-for-word version of this letter on August 17, 1948. Reprinted in Michal R. Belknap, ed., *Civil Rights: The White House and the Justice Department, 1945–1968* (New York: Garland, 1991), 1:56–62.

year were the electoral votes of California, Illinois and Ohio, three states which had absorbed 42 percent of all black net immigration between 1940 and 1950.... The fact that Truman's combined 57,000-vote margin of victory in these three states was barely one-tenth the total number of black votes he received in those same states emphasizes the crucial role played by the black electorate in the 1948 election."[85]

In the United States, electoral competition led to ethnic riots and state negligence in the 19th century, but national-level political competition also ultimately moderated ethnic violence in the mid-20th century, by giving the federal government and the national Democratic Party an electoral incentive to intervene to use federal power to protect minorities. As blacks moved to the North and Midwest, it became increasingly important for national parties to intervene to attract their support, as well as that of white moderates. An early sign of blacks' growing political influence in the North, as Douglas McAdam has noted, was the intervention by the National Association for the Advancement of Colored Peoples (NAACP) to block the 1930 Supreme Court nomination of John J. Parker, a staunch segregationist from North Carolina.[86] By 1954 the influence of minority voters in the North and Midwest had grown to be even more important, and Congressional Quarterly calculated that there were 61 districts outside the South where the percentage of blacks in 1950 was greater than the winning candidate's margin of victory in the 1954 congressional election.[87] In the United States as in India, the increasingly pivotal importance of the minority vote would have a huge effect in forcing often reluctant politicians in Washington to intervene during the 1950s and 1960s in the civil rights conflicts in the South.

---

[85] McAdam, *Political Process*, p. 81.
[86] Ibid.
[87] "Negro Vote Could Swing House to GOP," *Congressional Quarterly*, April 30, 1956, pp. 225–27.

8

Democracy and Ethnic Violence

Reading through the various accounts presented in this book of how local politicians in India and elsewhere foment ethnic riots in order to win elections, some readers might begin to feel pessimistic about the prospects for stability in multiethnic democracies. My findings about the relationship between political competition and communal violence in India might seem to lend empirical support to Rabushka and Shepsle's argument that "The plural society, constrained by the preferences of its citizens, does not provide fertile soil for democratic values or stability."[1] Much recent research in development economics and political science has indeed found that ethnic heterogeneity is generally associated with higher levels of political instability and violence, as well as lower levels of economic growth (which is in turn is linked to more instability and violence).[2]

However what this book ultimately shows, I believe, is that violence is far from being an inevitable by-product of electoral competition in plural

[1] See Alvin Rabushka and Kenneth A. Shepsle, *Politics in Plural Societies: A Theory of Democratic Instability* (Columbus: Charles E. Merrill, 1972), p. 92. The basic insight goes back to John Stuart Mill, who argued that democracy will not survive in multinational states where "the united public opinion necessary to the working of representative government can not exist." John Stuart Mill, *Considerations on Representative Government* (Buffalo, N.Y.: Prometheus Books, 1991), p. 310.

[2] See, e.g., Alberto Alesina, Reza Baqir, and William Easterly, "Public Goods and Ethnic Divisions," *Quarterly Journal of Economics* 114, no. 4 (November 1999), pp. 1243–84; Nicholas Sambanis, "Ethnic War: A Theoretic and Empirical Inquiry into Its Causes," World Bank, February 27, 2000; Edward Miguel, "Ethnic Diversity and School Funding in Kenya," December 2000, Working Paper, available at <http://emlab.berkeley.edu/users/emiguel/miguel_tribes.pdf>. Sambanis finds that ethnic fractionalization is related to the onset of "ethnic war," though interestingly the effect is less during periods and in regions of high democracy.

societies.[3] My central finding is that high levels of electoral competition can *reduce* as well as precipitate ethnic violence. This is consistent with other research that has found the interparty competition for minority votes (what Horowitz terms "vote-pooling" is the best guarantor of ethnic peace.[4] I have shown that in states with high levels of party fractionalization, such as Bulgaria, Malaysia, and the Indian states of Bihar and Kerala, governments will protect minorities in order to hold their existing coalitions together as well as preserve their coalition options for the future. In states with low levels of party fractionalization things become much more dangerous for minorities, but even here parties and governments that have substantial and pivotal minority support – such as the Democrats in the United States after the 1940s, and the Congress governments in Madhya Pradesh and Rajasthan in 2002 – have taken strong action to prevent antiminority violence. The fact that in recent years party fractionalization has increased in India is not as some have argued a bad thing but seems actually to have reduced Hindu-Muslim violence in many states, as we saw in my discussion in Chapter 5 of the many states where polarizing efforts *did not* lead to violence during the 2002 Gujarat riots. In substantive terms, moving from the lowest levels of party fractionalization found in Indian states (e.g., Gujarat) to the highest levels (e.g., Kerala) leads to a two-thirds

---

[3] In assessing the findings about the relationship between ethnic heterogeneity, violence, and growth, scholars have questioned the way in which ethnic heterogeneity is measured in most statistical studies. As Daniel Posner has shown, the indicator of ethnic heterogeneity (ELF, the ethnolinguistic fractionalization index) used in most cross-national studies – such as Cox's *Making Votes Count* and Easterly and Levine's studies (1999) – is highly suspect. The most serious problem is that the ELF index is primarily based on only one dimension of ethnic identity (language), which leads to clear anomalies – for example, Rwanda (85% Tlutu, 14% Tutsi, 1% Twa) being regarded as ethnically homogenous because almost all its inhabitants speak Banyarwanda. Another important issue is that the ELF index is based on data from only one period, the 1960s, even though we know that the salience and number of ethnic identities in many countries has changed since then in response to state policies, economic incentives, and ethnic conflicts. Daniel N. Posner, "Ethnic Fractionalization and Economic Growth in Africa," paper presented to the LiCEP working group, March 25, 2000.

[4] As Horowitz puts it, "The proliferation of parties must be accompanied by the rewards to moderation that accrue when parties are dependent, in part, on vote transfers from members of groups other than the groups they principally represent. Only coalitions that rest on intergroup vote-pooling, as well as seat pooling, have reason to be accommodative." See Donald L. Horowitz, *A Democratic South Africa: Constitutional Engineering in a Divided Society* (Berkeley: University of California Press, 1991), p. 177. Horowitz has extensively examined the potential of vote pooling for alleviating ethnic conflicts, as well as institutional ways to encourage vote pooling, in ibid., pp. 175–83, and *Ethnic Groups in Conflicts* (Berkeley: University of California Press, 1985), pp. 396–97, 425–26.

reduction in a state's level of communal riots, holding other factors constant. The reason, as we explored in Chapters 5, 6, and 7, is that politicians in highly fractionalized systems must provide security to minorities, in order to retain their electoral support today and preserve the option of forming coalitions with minority-supported parties tomorrow.

The fact that high levels of electoral fractionalization force even antiminority politicians to prevent ethnic violence raises what I think is a fundamental problem with the pessimistic work done by economists on ethnic heterogeneity, growth, and political instability over the past decade. The problem is the assumption that ethnic preferences are fixed, incompatible, and not amenable to compromise, and that sincere ethnic biases and preferences will always dictate politicians' public stances and policies. In fact, neither of these assumptions is correct. First, as the recent publication of several books with titles such as *How the Irish Became White* and *How Jews Became White Folks and What That Says about Race in America* indicates, ethnic identities, preferences, and individuals' publicly expressed sense of who represents the ethnic "other" and who is part of the in-group can and does change a great deal over time and from place to place.[5] Another good example of this is from southern India, as we saw in Chapter 6, where in political terms many Muslims have long been regarded as part of the "Dravidian" or backward-caste categories, in contrast to the Hindu-Muslim categorizations that have dominated in the North.

Second, it seems obvious to me that political necessity creates strange alliances and gives birth to unlikely ethnic moderates. We only need to look at the political careers of politicians such as former segregationist Senator Strom Thurmond in the United States or Home Minister L. K. Advani in India to see the ways in which political competition has at times forced politicians identified with hard antiminority stances to reverse previous policy positions, lessen their antiminority rhetoric, and even make trips to the symbolic sites and shrines of the groups they formerly railed against. Political competition not only forces people to compromise in

---

[5] I am not arguing that a politician's private prejudices change as quickly as his or her publicly expressed preferences. As the Indian press often reports, politicians who publicly decry casteism often practice it while arranging for the marriage of their children. Nonetheless, the fact that they must criticize casteism in public to be viable politically is not, I would argue, insignificant in determining the prospects for ethnic accommodation. For the recent U.S. literature, see Noel Ignatiev, *How the Irish Became White* (New York: Routledge, 1995), and Karen Brodkin, *How Jews Became White Folks and What That Says about Race in America* (New Brunswick, N.J.: Rutgers University Press, 2000).

public; there is also some evidence that it may even cause politicians to become more tolerant in their private beliefs. Sullivan, Walsh, and Shamir have found, for instance, that politicians are often personally more tolerant of "threatening" domestic groups (such as ethnic minorities) than members of the general public. In part, this is because politicians as a class are drawn from the wealthy, the cosmopolitan, and the well educated, those social groups most likely statistically to be tolerant. But Sullivan and his collaborators also argue that elite tolerance is the result of the practice of politics, the sine qua non of which is contact over time with diverse groups, with whom one must negotiate and compromise.[6] These arguments seem at least plausible when applied to India. Propelled by the need to survive politically and make alliances with politicians from many different castes, Indian politicians can no longer publicly express antiminority prejudices even if they might hold them privately, lest their statements be used against them during campaigns or foreclose future political alliances. And it is hard to believe that all the friendliness that we see when Indian politicians meet, negotiate, and drink tea together is just for the cameras and does not in at least some way reflect and perhaps cause a lessening of ethnic prejudices.

One question, of course, is how permanent changes toward minorities that are driven by party fractionalization are likely to be? Some might argue that what political competition gives toward minorities today, it might take away tomorrow. If party fractionalization declines in India (and elsewhere), will levels of violence automatically increase? I would argue that this is unlikely. The experience of Kerala in the 1960s – where the initial success of the Muslim League–Communist alliance led the Congress Party to quickly declare that the Muslims were now an acceptable coalition partner – seems to show that once major parties win an election by appealing to minorities the opposition political parties rapidly try to neutralize this threat by moderating their own stance toward minorities. As a result of parties simultaneously moving to defuse the "minority issue" in this way, it seems likely that supplying security to minorities will often quickly move from being a positional issue (i.e., an issue on which "candidates are free to select from a range of alternative positions and about which voters have varying views"), to that of a "valence issue," one on which virtually all voters and candidates agree, and on which no politically ambitious candidate can

[6] John L. Sullivan et al., "Why Politicians Are More Tolerant: Selective Recruitment and Socialization among Political Elites in Britain, Israel, New Zealand and the United States," *British Journal of Political Science* 23, no. 1 (1993), pp. 51–76.

afford to dissent.[7] Some areas of minority rights policy in India, such as support for job reservations for "backward" minorities, have already over the past decade moved from the status of positional issues to valence issues: electoral calculations have forced upper-caste politicians to give up fighting against job reservations for minorities, and they now instead demand that the reservations be expanded to include upper castes.[8]

One final issue that I have not considered very much in this book – largely because I have been explaining variation in communal violence within individual states – is the question of what factors *other* than levels of party competition might reduce ethnic violence? There is, for example, now a well-developed literature on how to moderate ethnic tensions through constitutional and electoral reforms. Arend Lijphart has advocated consociational power sharing that includes all the important ehnic groups (or other self-identified groups) within a country as a way to prevent violence. And Donald Horowitz's "incentives approach" advocates measures to encourage both intraethnic competition and interethnic cooperation in order to reduce ethnic conflicts.[9] Regional political and economic organizations such as the European Union (EU) and international organizations such as the World Bank are starting to insist – through instruments like the EU's 1993 Copenhagen political criteria for EU membership – that countries possess adequate safeguards for minority rights as the price (or at least part of the price) of admission to membership or access to financial aid.[10] These

---

[7] James E. Enelow and Melvin J. Hinich, "Non-Spatial Candidate Characteristics and Electoral Competition," *Journal of Politics* 44, no. 1 (1982), p. 117. The distinction was originally made by Donald E. Stokes, "Spatial Models of Party Competition," *American Political Science Review* 57 (1963), pp. 368–77.

[8] The BJP was at one time identified with opposition to reservations and remained decidedly lukewarm to them in the early 1990s, but in 2003 Vice President Gopinath Munde announced that his party supported a new 10% job reservation for "economically weaker Brahmins and other upper caste citizens." "Quota for Upper Castes Mooted," *Times of India*, May 25, 2003.

[9] Peter Harris and Ben Reilly have edited an excellent collection of articles that give an overview of electoral and constitutional options for ethnic conflict resolution in *Democracy and Deep-Rooted Conflict: Options for Negotiators* (Stockholm: IDEA, 1998). For Donald Horowitz's "incentives approach" to ethnic conflict resolution, see *Ethnic Groups in Conflict* and *A Democratic South Africa*. For Arend Lijphart's consociational approach, see the works cited in Chapter 4. For a good overview of the virtues of federalism in conflict resolution, see Daniel J. Elazar, "The Role of Federalism in Political Integration," in Elazar, *Federalism and Political Integration* (Jerusalem: Institute for Federalism, 1979), pp. 1–13.

[10] The European Union requires that countries wishing to join have "stability of institutions guaranteeing democracy, the rule of law, human rights and respect for and protection of minorities."

"requests" work. In response to the Copenhagen criteria, for example, the governments of Estonia and Latvia reformed some aspects of the electoral and language laws they had passed against the opposition of the Russian minority in the early 1990s, in return for which the EU has now moved toward formal negotiations on EU membership.[11] Frequently, the easiest way in which governments in Eastern Europe and elsewhere can prove that they are "doing something" about minority rights is to introduce formal consociational-style protections for minorities.[12]

My book will, I hope, help inject a note of caution into this urge to impose constitutional conditionality – especially of the consociational kind – in order to solve ethnic conflict. In the first place, my work shows that even within the same constitutional structure in India there is substantial intrastate variation in ethnic violence, due to different levels of political competition. The presence of such high levels of intrastate variation suggests that macroconstitutional innovations may take us only so far in preventing ethnic violence. Second, I would argue that we need many more studies that actually test the effectiveness of different approaches to conflict resolution before we encourage international organizations to force countries to adopt constitutional innovations that will allegedly moderate their ethnic conflicts. The need for such research is now acute. As far asf I am aware, Chapter 4 of this book is one of the first attempts to test systematically, albeit for one country, whether any of the policies associated with consociationalism actually work in reducing the level of ethnic violence (I found little evidence that they do). Perhaps EU bureaucrats, constitutional engineers, and political scientists should first investigate whether their proposals will really work before dictating policy "solutions" to states that in some ways have no real choice over whether to accept their recommendations.

---

[11] "EU Enlargement: A Historic Opportunity" available at <http://europa.eu.int/comm/enlargement/intro/criteria.htm>.

[12] See Steven I. Wilkinson, "Conditionality, Consociationalism and Ethnic Conflict Moderation," paper presented at the conference on From Power-Sharing to Democracy: Post Conflict Institutions in Ethnically Divided Societies, University of Western Ontario, November 8–10, 2002.

Appendix A: Data Sources for Hindu-Muslim Riots

Problems with the Existing Data

As with most ethnic conflicts, systematic information on where and when Hindu-Muslim riots have taken place is hard to find. For the preindependence period, the only widely available source is a British report that gives detailed information on Hindu-Muslim riots from 1923 to 1927.[1] And in the postindependence period, partly as a reaction to the colonial government's overemphasis on the Hindu-Muslim divide, Indian governments have not made information widely available. State governments keep riot commission reports secret or delay their publication for years. The central government instructs the state news media to provide no "inflammatory" information on riots, which in practice has sometimes meant no information at all. The government typically answers parliamentary questions about riots by placing the answers "on the table" of the house rather than publishing them in the parliamentary proceedings.[2] And in India's annual crime reports communal riots are not listed separately but included in the general category of "riot," together with union- and student-related violence.

Recognizing that these general "riot" data cannot be used to make inferences about the number of Hindu-Muslim riots, most scholars have turned instead to the Home Ministry figures on "communal incidents."[3]

[1] *Indian Statutory Commission*, vol. 4, *Memoranda Submitted by the Government of India and the India Office*, Part 1 (London, 1930), chap. 3, "Communal Disorders."

[2] See the response to a question about where and when riots took place from May 1971–February 1972, in *Lok Sabha Debates*, May 17, 1972, p. 110.

[3] See, e.g., the incomplete Home Ministry communal riot data cited by Paul Brass, *The Politics of India since Independence* (Cambridge: Cambridge University Press, 1990),

However, even though Home Ministry statistics provide an accurate picture of overall trends in Hindu-Muslim violence, they have three important limitations. First, they have only been published since 1954, making it impossible to test the claim that postindependence political and economic developments have led to an increase in communal violence. Second, they provide only the national and state-level totals of riots, deaths, and injuries, making it impossible to test the many important town-level theories of ethnic violence. Third, published Home Ministry statistics give the annual level of Hindu-Muslim violence not as the number of large riots (the phenomenon most people want to explain), but as a much larger figure, the total number of times the police have registered a criminal case of "riot."[4]

The third point is important because the number of cases of riot that are registered by different local police forces after a Hindu-Muslim riot of the same magnitude varies a great deal. Interviews with the officials who generate India's crime statistics confirm that four local factors influence the quality of riot statistics: the corruption of the local police (the police often demand bribes to register cases); the perceived power of those who initiated the riot (the greater the power, the greater the reluctance of the police to register a case); whether policemen were injured or fired their weapons (in which case the police must register a case to protect themselves or apply for compensation); and the level of financial compensation offered to riot victims by the state or central government (compensation rules require victims to register a case, and some states, such as Gujarat, offer higher levels of compensation than others).[5] And minority politicians claim that the police often refuse to register cases brought to their attention

---

p. 199. The Home Ministry figures are often printed in the Lok Sabha proceedings, which are somewhat easier to obtain than the Home Ministry's own reports. See, e.g., table on "*Sampradayik Dange*" (Communal riots), *Lok Sabha Debates*, July 11, 1979, pp. 164–65.

[4] Under Indian law, the crime of riot occurs "when an assembly of five persons or more uses force or violence in pursuit of a common aim." *The Indian Penal Code* (as on December 1, 1992) (Delhi: Manager of Publications, 1993), sec. 141–46. The Home Ministry apparently keeps confidential figures on "major incidents," defined as "Any incident with more than four deaths and involving [in 1970] loss of property worth Rs 50,000 or more." M. S. Prabhakar, "Of Hindus and Muslims," *Frontier*, February 28, 1970, pp. 8–13.

[5] Interviews with several serving members of the National Crime Records Bureau, New Delhi, and with S. K. Sharma, ex-IPS Rajasthan cadre and former director general of the bureau, New Delhi, August 9, 1995, and G. P. Shukla, IAS cadre, UP, Boston, December 15, 1994. The Muslim MP G. M. Banatwalla criticized the nonregistration of riot cases after the Meerut riots of September–October 1982. *Lok Sabha Debates*, October 7, 1982, pp. 471–72.

by Muslims.[6] All these factors make it impossible to transform Home Ministry "communal incidents" easily into the dependent variable we want to study, the Hindu-Muslim riot.[7]

The Indian Home Ministry in New Delhi does in fact collect town-level statistics on deaths, injuries, and property damage after each riot. It receives reports forwarded to New Delhi by each state's Home Ministry and by its own intelligence agencies. Although the full dataset is not publicly available, the Indian government has through the years been obliged to release some of the information it contains in response to parliamentary questions, government commissions, and the annual inquiries since 1979 of the Indian Minorities Commission.[8]

No scholar has yet tried to build a detailed picture of communal violence in India using these Home Ministry town-level statistics. Even if we were to do so, however, this would still not give us the comprehensive data we need to test our theories of ethnic violence. The problem is that the Home Ministry's own figures are sometimes incomplete and inaccurate. Many states do not send riot reports to New Delhi when they should; others send no data at all.[9] And even when figures are "complete" from Delhi's perspective, they still reflect state reports that are known to misrepresent the number of deaths and injuries.[10]

---

[6] G. M. Banatwala, MP, *Lok Sabha Debates*, October 7, 1982, p. 474; People's Union for Civil Liberties Investigation into the November 1989 Jaipur Riots, *Lokayan Bulletin* 7, no. 6 (1989), pp. 41–47.

[7] We have no information on the precise number of riot cases recorded after a Hindu-Muslim riot, but we do know that the comparable anti-Sikh riot in Delhi in 1984, which most people think of as one single riot, and human rights investigators have classified as no more than two dozen separate incidents, was registered by the local police (and hence in the Home Ministry figures) as 359 separate "riots." S. K. Ghosh, "The District Police and Public Order," in Jaytilak Guha Roy, ed., *Policing a District* (New Delhi: Indian Institute of Public Administration, 1992), pp. 19–20.

[8] The national Minorities Commission met for the first time in February 1978 under Muslim former justice Mirza Hamidullah Beg. Since 1979 the commission, which has the power to independently investigate communal violence, has published several detailed reports on communal riots. *Lok Sabha Debates*, March 7, 1979 p. 195.

[9] For example, four states sent no data to the government for the 1970–71 lists and eight states sent no data for 1987–88. Written Answer 1653, *Lok Sabha Debates*, June 7, pp. 76–78; *Tenth Annual Report of the Minorities Commission (for the period from 1-4-1987 to 31-3-1988)* (New Delhi: Controller of Publications, 1990), p. 38.

[10] The Indian Police Commission pleaded for more accuracy and openness in official riot statistics, pointing out that "In one recent riot, the official figures of the number of persons killed was [*sic*] given so low that no one believed it. . . . Not revealing the true facts gives rise to rumors. People start believing sources other than the administration and the government

Improving Our Data on Hindu-Muslim Riots

Because existing riot data are often inaccurate, incomplete, or otherwise unsuitable for testing our hypotheses on ethnic violence, this book relies on two new data sets. The first, compiled by Wilkinson, covers the period from 1900 to 1949. The second, jointly compiled by Wilkinson and Ashutosh Varshney, covers the period from 1950 to 1995.[11]

For the pre-1949 data on Hindu-Muslim riots, I turned to three sources. First, I examined the holdings in London's India Office Library (IOL). This library contains the reports and telegrams sent by the Government of India to the secretary of state for India on the most important riots that took place in "British India" after the 1890s. It also contains (for the period 1920–47) a complete set of the confidential government *Fortnightly Reports* on the main events that took place in each province. And the IOL possesses the 20th-century files on Hindu-Muslim riots in India's "Princely States," prepared by the British political officers assigned by the colonial government to supervise each state.[12]

Second, I read through riot reports published in Indian and British newspapers from 1850 to 1950. The Indian press, as we might expect, printed reports on many small riots not covered in the files kept by the India Office Library or in the annual Indian yearbooks such as *Mitra's Indian Register*.[13] The Lucknow paper, the *Pioneer*, is an excellent source for reports on communal violence in British and Princely India before 1950. Because the *Pioneer* and other Indian papers are not indexed, however, reading through all the pre-1950 issues would have been too great a task.[14] Instead, I read the *Pioneer* for every fifth year, and used it mainly as a cross-check on reports published in the British press, especially the *Times*, which I found to be an excellent source, except during World Wars I and II, for reports on large riots in India. Crosschecks confirm that the *Times* lists all the major

---

media." *Sixth Report of the National Police Commission* (New Delhi: Government of India, 1981), sec. 47.16, p. 27.

[11] These joint data are also used by Ashutosh Varshney in his book *Ethnic Conflict and Civic Life: Hindus and Muslims in India* (New Haven: Yale University Press, 2002).

[12] These files were transferred by the British from Delhi to London in 1947, over the objections of Congress, in order to avoid embarrassing disclosures after independence See, e.g., "Disturbances in Ajmer 1923" (IOR, R/1/1/1437); "Report on Communal trouble in the Hyderabad State during 1931–1933" (IOR, R/1/1/2526).

[13] *Mitra's Indian Annual Register* was published in Calcutta from 1919 to 1948 and has since been reprinted by Indian publishers. It is an invaluable source on the events and politics of the period.

[14] *The Indian Press Index* only began publication in April 1968.

communal riots. In fact, for information on Hindu-Muslim violence in India from 1946 to 1948, when press censorship was periodically enforced in many provinces and districts in India, the *Times* is actually a better source than the Indian press. In May 1947, for example, the Punjab government introduced local press censorship to try to prevent riots, but these restrictions did not apply to the Punjab riot reports sent to the *Times* by Ian Morrison, that paper's famous war correspondent.[15] Similarly, the Bengal government's October 1946 decision, in the aftermath of the August 1946 "Great Calcutta Killing," to ban the publication of detailed riot reports did not apply to the reports sent to London.[16]

Third, I read through the most important secondary sources on Hindu-Muslim riots before independence: year-end administration reports published by the eleven provincial governments, the main events from which were summarized, until the Indian constitutional reforms of 1935–36, in the secretary of state for India's annual reports to the British Parliament;[17] official gazetteers that describe the history of each of India's districts; published British government reports that addressed perceived crises in India's public order or possible changes in India's constitutional status;[18] inquiries into the partition violence conducted after 1947 by government and non-governmental organizations in India and Pakistan;[19] Indian political parties' reports on Hindu-Muslim violence, most of which were produced by the

[15] For details of the Punjab press restrictions, see *Pioneer*, May 11, 1947; *Times*, May 19, 1947. For similar restrictions in Delhi, see *Pioneer*, March 25, 1947.

[16] See *Times*, October 2, 1946. Only after independence did the Indian government began to censor British correspondents' reports on the communal situation. *Times*, September 13, 1947.

[17] By Independence in 1947 there were eleven provinces in British India: Assam, Bengal, Bihar, Bombay, Central Provinces, Madras, North West Frontier Province, Orissa, Punjab, Sind, and the United Provinces. Each province published annual reports on "general administration" (which summarize the most important communal riots) as well as reports on the administration of the police, which contain a much fuller account of communal riots in any particular year.

[18] For example, "Report on East India (Religious Disturbances)," *Parliamentary Papers* 63 (1893–94); *Indian Statutory Commission*, vol. 4, chap. 3, "Communal Disorders."

[19] For anti-Muslim violence, see the following reports compiled in Pakistan in 1948: *Note on the Sikh Plan* (Lahore: West Punjab Government Press, 1948); *RSSS (Rashtriya Swayam Sewak Sangh) in the Punjab* (Lahore: West Punjab Government Press, 1948); *The Sikhs in Action* (Lahore: West Punjab Government Press, 1948); *Intelligence Reports concerning the Tribal Repercussions to the Events in the Punjab, Kashmir and India* (Lahore: West Punjab Government Press, 1948); and *Kashmir before Accession* (Lahore: West Punjab Government Press, 1948). For anti-Sikh and anti-Hindu violence, see G. D. Khosla's 1951 book, *Stern Reckoning: A Survey of the Events Leading Up to and Following the Partition of India* (reprint, New Delhi: Oxford University Press, 1989), and S. Gurcharan Singh Talib's 1950 book,

Congress;[20] and a large number of theses, books and articles, some of whose authors were granted special access to still-confidential pre-1947 government and state records in India.[21]

For the postindependence era, the major source used was India's "paper of record," the Bombay edition of the *Times of India*. In collaboration with Ashutosh Varshney, every Hindu-Muslim riot reported in the paper from 1950 to 1995 was recorded and entered into a dataset.[22] In the post-1947 period, the Indian government and press often euphemistically label Hindu-Muslim riots as "group clashes," a term that can also apply to intrareligious or caste violence. To avoid including intrareligious and caste violence a protocol was developed that categorizes possible Hindu-Muslim riots as having a "definite," "strong," or "weak" likelihood. In this book I present only data from riots that I categorized as either "definite" or "strong."

Despite its reputation as India's best and most reliable newspaper, I was worried that the *Times of India* data we collected would give riots far from its place of publication no coverage unless they were large and particularly bloody. But I found that, for riots in which there was at least one fatality, the *Times of India* is a very accurate source. I cross-checked *Times of India* data against statistics in many other government and private sources: parliamentary reports and the annual reports of the Minorities Commission;[23]

Muslim League Attack on Sikhs and Hindus in the Punjab 1947 (reprint, New Delhi: Voice of India, 1991).

[20] The most famous Congress report was on the Kanpur riots of 1931. The Muslim League produced several reports of its own in 1938–39, most of which are reprinted in K. K. Aziz, ed., *Muslims under Congress Rule, 1937–1939: A Documentary Record*, vol. 1 (Islamabad: National Commission on Historical and Cultural Research, 1978). The Muslim League also put out a *Report on the Disturbances in Bihar and the United Provinces (October–November 1946)*.

[21] For accounts by scholars who have enjoyed privileged access to Indian government archives, see Y. B. Mathur, "Religious Disturbances in India," *Studies in Islam*, nos. 1–4 (January–October 1971), pp. 81–131; Vinita Damodaran, *Broken Promises: Popular Protest, Indian Nationalism and the Congress Party in Bihar, 1935–1946* (Delhi: Oxford University Press, 1992); Joya Chatterji, *Bengal Divided: Hindu Communalism and Partition, 1932–1947* (Cambridge: Cambridge University Press, 1995).

[22] Data for the period 1950–95 (Varshney-Wilkinson data) were collected with partial financial support from Harvard's Center for International Affairs and the Rajiv Gandhi Foundation, New Delhi.

[23] See, e.g., statements on riots in Madhya Pradesh and Bihar in *Lok Sabha Debates*, August 1, 1969, pp. 208–9; August 29, 1969, pp. 59–60. And for an example of the more detailed reports that were released in the 1980s and 1990s, see the table "*Jin Sthanon par Sampradayik Dange Hue...*" (in Hindi) which gives full town-by-town details on riots between September 1990 and June 1991. *Parliamentary Debates, Appendix CLIX Rajya Sabha– Official Report (11th July, 1991 to 7th August, 1991)*, Annexure nos. 1–56.

court records;[24] the report of the second Indian Police Commission[25]; official inquiries into specific riots;[26] and articles and books written by Indians granted access to confidential post-1947 Government of India riot data.[27]

The *Times of India* includes virtually all the riots cited in these other sources, and lists many other riots that they ignore (see the data provided in Table A.1). In a large crosscheck of 1970 to 1993 data from Uttar Pradesh, from the *Times of India* we added to our dataset 58 riots not covered in Government of India data, 37 riots covered by both sources, and only 7 riots listed in the parliamentary reports but not by the *Times of India*.

I consulted a much wider range of sources for the state of Uttar Pradesh, both to estimate the degree of underreporting in the pre- and post-1950 datasets, and to have more confidence in the town-level data I use to test theories of ethnic violence. In the State Archives in Lucknow, I read the pre-1947 riot files prepared by the UP General Administration and Police Departments. In India and London I also read through the annual General Administration and Police reports on Uttar Pradesh, which list the main riots that broke out in the province after the 1880s. And I reviewed most of the theses and books available on Hindu-Muslim violence in Uttar Pradesh in the 19th and early 20th centuries.[28] For the postindependence period, virtually all UP government riot files are off-limits to researchers. But in 1994–95 I showed the *Times of India* dataset to UP police officers and civil

---

[24] See, e.g., "Appeal of P. Abdul Sattar and Others against Conviction for Communal Rioting," *All India Reporter* 48, pt. 566 (1961), and "Appeal of Sherey and 24 Others vs State of U.P." (against charges of rioting and murder), *Criminal Law Journal*, no. 3289 (1991). Court records are one of the few sources for information on riot prosecutions and convictions.

[25] *The Sixth Report of the Police Commission* contains a chapter and an appendix on communal riots.

[26] For example, Justice Raghubar Dayal's *Report of the Commission of Inquiry on Communal Disturbances, Ranchi-Hatia (August 22–29, 1967)* (New Delhi: Government of India, 1968).

[27] See Gopal Krishna, "Communal Violence in India: A Study of Communal Disturbance in Delhi," *Economic and Political Weekly*, January 12, 1985, pp. 61–74.

[28] Some of the best sources are: Katherine Prior, "The Administration of Hinduism in British North India" (Ph.D. dissertation, University of Cambridge, 1990); Francis Robinson, *Separatism among Indian Muslims: The Politics of the United Provinces' Muslims, 1860–1923* (New Delhi: Oxford University Press, 1993); C. A. Bayly, *Rulers, Townsmen and Bazaars: North Indian Society in the Age of British Expansion, 1770–1870* (Cambridge: Cambridge University Press, 1988); C. A. Bayly, "The Pre-History of 'Communalism'? Religious Conflict in India, 1700–1860," *Modern Asian Studies* 19, no. 2 (1985), pp. 177–203; Gyanendra Pandey, *The Construction of Communalism in Colonial North India* (Delhi: Oxford University Press, 1992).

Table A.1. *Different Public Sources on Communal Violence Compared: Figures for Uttar Pradesh*

Year	Incidents (Deaths) in Aggregate Home Ministry Data	Deaths (Injuries) in	
		Lok Sabha/Rajya Sabha Data	*Times of India* Data
1982	45 (84)	Meerut –	Meerut 31 (28)
			Meerut 11 (40)
			Sardhana 0 (3)
			Aligarh –
1987	66 (32)	Meerut 10 (23)	Sarurpur Kila 2 (3)
		Meerut 141 (154)	Aligarh 2 (0)
			Faizabad 0 (2)
			Meerut 10 (40)
			Meerut 8 (12)
			Meerut 95 (134)
			Meerut 7 (4)
			Meerut 5 (7)
			Meerut 2 (6)
			Meerut 9
			Modinagar 2 (3)
1988	74 (28)	Aligarh 5 (52)	Aligarh (4) 27
		Muzaffarnagar 24 (80)	Muzaffarnagar 22 (70)
		Khatauli 2 (12)	Khatauli 2 (45)
		Faizabad 5 (10)	Faizabad 6 (50)
TOTAL	185 (144)	187 (331)[a]	218 (692)[b]

[a] 7 riots.
[b] 19 riots.

Sources: Aggregate Home Ministry data: *Rajya Sabha Debates Appendix CXXIX 23 Feb–23 March 1984*, pp. 60–61, Annexure no. 38; *Rajya Sabha Debates Appendix 151 July 18–August 18, 1989*, Annexure no. 75, pp. 259–60. Sources for Lok Sabha/Rajya Sabha town-level statistics: *Rajya Sabha Debates*, November 21, 1988, written answer 1545; *Lok Sabha Debates*, November 21, 1988; July 27, 1988, written answer 162.

servants familiar with these files, and asked them to point out possible gaps in my own data.

Database Sources Used in This Book

British Parliamentary Papers

Indian Statutory Commission, 1930 (this is the best single source on Hindu-Muslim riots prior to 1930).

Data Sources for Hindu-Muslim Riots

Parliamentary Debates (Commons), 1935–36, vol. 311, April 21 to Friday, May 8, 1936 (London, 1936), pp. 1113–14.
Parliamentary Debates (Commons), 1936–37, vol. 324, May 24 to June 11, pp. 1395–96.

India Office Records, London

Books/Official Publications

(IOR) V/10/135 *Report on the Administration of the N. – W Provinces for the Year 1871–72* (Allahabad: NWP Government Press, 1873)
(IOR) V/10/1273 *Annual Administration Report of the Janjira State for the Year 1877–78*, dated August 15, 1878

Manuscripts: Files on British India

(IOR) R/2/28/257 Note on the Agitation against Cow-Killing (1893)
(IOR) L/PJ/7/132 Information about Communal Riots during the Last 10–15 Years (1931)
(IOR) L/PJ/12/67 Local Government's Reports UP (1934)
(IOR) L/PJ/5/264 Governor's Reports UP (1937)
(IOR) L/PJ/5/265–6 Governor's Reports UP (1938)
(IOR) L/PJ/5/267 Governor's Reports UP (1939)
(IOR) L/PJ/269 Governor's Reports UP (1940)
(IOR) L/PJ/5/270 Governor's Reports UP (1941)
(IOR) L/PJ/5/271 Governor's Reports UP (1942)
(IOR) L/PJ/5/272 Governor's Reports UP (1943)
(IOR) L/PJ/5/273 Governor's Reports UP (1944)
(IOR) L/PJ/5/274 Governor's Reports UP (1945)
(IOR) L/PJ/5/275 Governor's Reports UP (1946)
(IOR) L/PJ/5/276 Governor's Reports UP (1947)

Manuscripts: Files on Princely States

(IOR) R/1/1/2323 Meo Disturbances in the Alwar State (1933)
(IOR) R/1/1/4282 Communal Disputes in Village Kalayat of the Patiala State (1945)
(IOR) R/1/1/4421 Hindu-Muslim riots in Gwalior (1946)
(IOR) R/1/1/4470 Communal Disturbances in Bikaner State (1946)
(IOR) R/1/1/4454 Pataudi Disturbances (1946)
(IOR) R/1/1/4487 Communal Disturbances in Baroda City (1946)
(IOR) R/1/1/4488 Disturbances in Alwar (1946)
(IOR) R/1/1/4509 Communal Disturbances in Gwalior City and Lashkar-Reported Exodus of Muslim Refugees to Bhopal (1946–47)
(IOR) R/1/1/4589 Communal Trouble in Baran (Kotan State) 1947
(IOR) R/1/1/4590 Loharu Disturbances (1947)
(IOR) R/1/1/4591 Disturbances in the Rewa State (1947)

(IOR) R/1/1/4592 Disturbances in Didwana-Jodhpur State (1947)

(IOR) R/2/721–56/57 Patan Riot (Junagarh) – Hindus and Mussalman's Commission (1893)

(IOR) R/1/1/2184 Junagadh Affairs: Communal Disturbances in the Junagadh State and the Proposed Abdication by His Highness the Nawab (1931)

(IOR) R/1/1/2687 Hindu-Muslim Trouble in Malerkotla State over Performance of "Katha" by Hindus in Malerkotla Town at the Time of Evening Prayers by Muslims (1934)

Uttar Pradesh State Archives, Lucknow

Miscellaneous Records

S#3/1868 Misc. Papers, box 1, Affray between the Mahomedans and Hindoos of the Town of Shahabad (1868)

General Administration Department Files (GAD)

GAD, box 138, file 214, Anti-Cow Killing Movement in UP (1893)

GAD, file 46c/1894, Disturbances in Connection with the Celebration of the Chelum Festival (1894)

GAD, file 255/1903, Muslim Disturbances in the Moradabad District (1903)

GAD, file 413/1914 Formation of Conciliation Boards to Settle Differences between Hindus and Muhammadans Regarding Their Religious Rites (1914).

GAD, box 119, file 72(14)/39, Communal Riot at Haldwani on Bhagat Singh Day (1939)

GAD, box 155A, file 438/1927, List of Riots in Response to Legislative Council Question on December 17, 1927

Indian Government Publications

Annual Reports of the Indian Minorities Commission, 1978–88

Indian and British Newspapers

Pioneer, 1933, 1935, 1940, 1948 (January–June)

Times, 1800–49, 1850–59, 1870–79, 1880–89, 1890–99, 1900–9, 1910–19, 1920–50

Times of India (Bombay) [collected jointly with Ashutosh Varshney], 1950–59, 1960–95

Secondary Sources

Copland, Ian. "Communalism" in Princely India: The Case of Hyderabad, 1930–40. *Modern Asian Studies* 22, 4 (1988): 356–89.

Damodaran, Vinita. *Broken Promises: Popular Protest, Indian Nationalism and the Congress Party in Bihar, 1935–1946.* Delhi: Oxford University Press, 1992.

Dar, Pandit Bishan Narayan. *An Appeal to the English Public on Behalf of the Hindus of the N.W. - P. and Oudh, with an Appendix Containing Full and Detailed Account of the Cow-Killing Riots in the United Provinces and All Public Documents upon the Same,* pp. 21–22. Lucknow: G. P. Varma and Brothers, 1893.

Das, Suranjan. *Communal Riots in Bengal, 1905–1947.* Delhi: Oxford University Press, 1993.

Mathur, Y. B. *Growth of Muslim Politics in India,* pp. 57–89. Lahore: Book Traders, 1980.

Majumdar, R. C., ed. *The History and Culture of the Indian People,* vol. 10: *British Paramountcy and Indian Renaissance,* pt. 2, p. 333. Bombay: Bharatiya Vidya Bhavan, 1965.

Pandey, Gyanendra. Encounters and "Calamities": The History of a North Indian Qasba in the Nineteenth Century. In Ranajit Guha, ed., *Subaltern Studies III: Writings on South Asian History and Society,* pp. 231–70. New Delhi: Oxford University Press, 1984.

Sharma, Ram. *The Religious Policy of the Mughal Emperors.* 1940; reprint, Asia Publishing House: New York, 1972.

The Siyar-ul-Mukhterin: A History of the Mahomedan Power in India during the Last Century, by Mir Gholam Hussein-Khan, revised from the translation of Haji Mustefa by John Briggs, 1: 214–20. London: John Murray, 1832.

Sleeman, W. H. *A Journey through the Kingdom of Oude in 1849–1850, with Private Correspondence Relative to the Annexation of Oude to British India,* 2:45–47. London: R. Bentley, 1858.

Verma, Rajendra. *The Freedom Struggle in the Bhopal State,* pp. 74–75. New Delhi: Intellectual Publishing House, 1984.

Dissertations

Gossman, Patricia. Riots and Victims: Violence and the Construction of Communal Identity among Bengali Muslims, 1905–1947. Ph.D. dissertation, University of Chicago, 1995.

Prior, Katherine. The British Administration of Hinduism in North India, 1780–1900. Ph.D. dissertation, Cambridge University, 1990.

Appendix B: Data-Entering Protocol for Riot Database

[The protocol reprinted here was originally developed by myself and Ashutosh Varshney for our 1950–95 dataset and was also used for the 1900–49 data I collected.]

Basic Entering Groundrules

The basic rule is to enter as much information as we can that a) will give us the information we need to fill in the boxes, and b) will allow us to check whether this information is an accurate reflection of the reported facts. So we should enter evidence of, e.g., different "final casualty" figures, the full range of "precipitating events" listed in the newspaper, together with a citation in the following form so we know exactly where the information in the notes comes from: "TOI 12/15/67." Unnecessary duplication of the facts is not needed: accurate reflection of the full range of the facts present in the *Times of India* is what we're after.

Fields and Entry Protocol

Definition of Event   What is a communal riot? Following Olzak's work on race conflict in the USA (1992:233–34) we might identify an event as a communal riot if a) there is violence, and b) two or more communally identified groups confront each other/members of the other group, at some point during the violence. In other words, Hindu riots against the police would not count. Nor would PAC or police shooting of Muslims if there was no Hindu-Muslim violence before or after. **If the event is police versus a single group, we should not enter the case as either probable or definite, but instead enter it in the <u>Police versus single group</u> box.**

In events involving one communally identified political group (Muslim League, BJP) and some group X, not necessarily the police (for example, violence between the Muslim League and Congress or violence between the Muslim League and CPM), unless we have reason to believe otherwise, the event *should* be classified as a probable (strong/small likelihood).

Town/City   Enter the name as given in the newspaper. Then check it later to see if the spelling conforms to the official spelling given in the index to the Oxford Atlas of India. We'll use the official spelling as standard, which will involve, e.g., changing "Ahmedabad" to "Ahmadabad."

Village

District   Enter when given.

State   Note the present-day state as well as the state name at the time of the riot. For example, a riot in 1968 in Mysore state should be marked "Karnataka, Mysore." Where there have been boundary changes or where there is general uncertainty about the name of the state in which a riot occurs mark "Yes" in the "Coding Question" category and mark the specific query next to an asterisk in the "Notes" section.

Population   These data will be entered later from census data.

Year   Year in which riot takes place. If a riot covers two years, enter as follows: "1971, 1972."

Month   Use the drop-down menu. Month in which riot takes place. If a riot covers two months, hit "other" category in drop-down down menu and enter as follows: "May, June."

Day   The day on which the riot was reported to have begun. As reports usually come out one or two days after the initial incident, it is important to count back to the original day.

Reported Cause   The purpose of this section is to specify general categories under which the causes of communal riots can be grouped. The list is self explanatory and hopefully comprehensive. When a reported cause does not fit any of the categories on the list, enter it as "other" and list the cause concisely in no more than five words. For example, Other: Forced Singing of Vande Mataram. We should be consistent as far as possible in the wording we use here, so that if the same event turns up more than once as a candidate for "other," we can later incorporate it as a new category without having to go back and standardize individual descriptions later.

Local Precipitating Events   If the local precipitating event is the same as the reported cause, enter it as such where the categories are identical. For example, if a land dispute is both the reported cause and precipitating event, the entry in both cases will be economic interest (land) and economic interest (land). In three cases, 1) **public ritual/festivities**, 2) **political**, and 3) **criminal**, the reported cause categories are not replicated in the list of precipitating events but broken down further. **Public ritual/festivitites** is broken down into a) Namaz/puja/aarti, b) religious procession, c) marriage procession, d) consecration of religious site. **Political** is broken down into a) bandh, b) demonstration, c) factional fight. There is one common category in the list of precipitating events that covers both public ritual and a political event: speech by political/relgious leader. Finally, **criminal** is broken down into a) gang violence, b) attack, c) theft. In these cases when reported cause and precipitating event are the same, the categories used to describe them will be different – the broader category will be used under reported cause and the more specific category under precipitating event. One example: when a tazia procession is both reported cause and precipating event, it will be entered as public ritual/festivities (other) in reported cause and as religious procession under local precipitating event. When a speech by Sadhvi Rithambara at a VHP rally is both the reported cause and precipitating event, it will be listed as *both* political (agitation) and public ritual/festivities (other) in the reported cause section and as speech by political/relgious leader under local precipitating event.

When the local precipitating event is different from the reported cause, there is no cause for worry. We just use the categories that seem most relevant in each case.

Hindu-Muslim   The purpose here is merely to identify whether an event involved Hindu-Muslim conflict, or alternatively, e.g., involved Shiah-Sunni or Hindu-Buddhist conflict. Unless specifically asked by Varshney or Wilkinson to list these conflicts, you should only mark "yes" in this box.

Probable Case   Your usual entry will be "Definite Case."

Coding Question If some information in a particular case is ambiguous, and the coder feels that a new category/term should be added to accommodate it, or some discussion is required before categorisation, then enter "Yes" here. Then in a note at the bottom state your question. Use the following example as guide: "*Event connected with state political conflict in Lucknow. Should I include within "Political conflict (state politics) or create a separate heading?"

Definite Case One where the following conditions apply: *If the riot was reported at the time of the event, or subsequently,* as "communal" in nature, **unless** there is good reason to believe that another competing mobilisation (such as caste, or ethnicity) may have been responsible for the violence. For example, in Ahmedabad in 1985, the violence was simultaneously seen as motivated by caste and communal identity. When this situation occurs (i.e., violence is reported as "communal" and as, e.g., "caste" "tribal") then we mark the event as *Strong Likelihood.*

As well as the above conditions where there is no room for ambiguity, all cases involving unspecified"group clashes" and the following precipitating events should also be regarded as "definite" **unless they occur in Punjab***:

- where "cow slaughter" is the precipitating event for the riot/group clash
- where "music in front of mosque" is the precipitating event for the riot/group clash
- where "music in front of religious building/place of worship" is the precipitating eventfor the riot/group clash

Strong-Likelihood Case The following conditions apply:

a) One where an event is reported as "communal" but there is good reason to believe that another competing mobilisation may have been responsible for the violence. For example, in Ahmedabad in 1985, the violence was simultaneously seen as motivated by caste and communal identity. When this situation occurs (i.e., violence is reported as "communal" and as, e.g., "caste" "tribal"), then we mark the event as *Strong Likelihood.*

---

* [In Punjab, because of the minuscule Muslim population, we assume all unspecified group clashes are Hindu-Sikh. In 1971 only 114,447 people out of 13,551,960 were Muslim, and of these only 42,306 were classified as "urban." In no place did Muslims account for more than 1% of a town's population. Source: *Census of India 1971 Series 17 – Punjab, Part II-C (i) and Part V-A, Distribution of Population by Religion and Scheduled Castes*, pp. 11–23.]

b) One where an event is not reported as "communal," but the group clash occurs in an area where "communal violence" was reported shortly before or after the event.

c) As well as the above conditions, all cases involving unspecified "group clashes" and the following precipitating events should also be marked as *Strong Likelihood*:

- where "Pig Slaughter" is the precipitating event for the riot/group clash
- where a more general phrase such as "animal slaughter" is the precipitating event for the riot/group clash
- where "Use of Public Space for Religious Ritual" is the precipitating event for the riot/group clash
- where "Procession" is the precipitating event for the riot/group clash
- where "Construction" is the precipitating event for the riot/group clash, and the construction *does* involve a building used for religious purposes
- where "Illegal Attack on Building" is the precipitating event for the riot/group clash, and the attack *does* involve a building used for religious purposes
- where "Demolition/Attempted Demolition" is the precipitating event for the riot/group clash, and the Demolition/Attempted Demolition *does* involve a building used for religious purposes

Weak Likelihood   If unspecified "group clashes" are mentioned in connection with the following events, they should always be entered as *Weak Likelihood*:

- where "Accident" is the precipitating event for the riot/group clash
- where "Fight" is the precipitating event for the riot/group clash
- where "Quarrels over Women (eve teasing)" is the precipitating event for the riot/group clash
- where "Quarrels over Women (rape)" is the precipitating event for the riot/group clash
- where "Quarrels over Women (inter-marriage)" is the precipitating event for the riot/group clash
- where "Construction" is the precipitating event for the riot/group clash, and the constuction does not involve a building used for religious purposes
- where "Illegal Attack on Building" is the precipitating event for the riot/group clash, and the attack does not involve a building used for religious purposes

- where "Demolition/Attempted Demolition" is the precipitating event for the riot/group clash, and the Demolition/Attempted Demolition does not involve a building used for religious purposes

Duration in Days   Count from the beginning of the riot to the last day on which violence was reported to have taken place. If there is a lull ("lull" defined as no reported incident of violence) in violence of a day or more separating incidents of violence in the same town (e.g., June 1–7, June 9–12), then enter this as two separate cases.

Killed, Injured, Arrested   The most accurate numbers available from the *Times of India*. In general these numbers will be the last figures quoted, which may be printed a week or even some months after a riot has actually ended (particularly if the figures are reported from the findings of a subsequent riot inquiry). In some cases, however, a specific figure will be quoted at the end of five days of rioting (e.g., "local officials report 43 killed, 128 injured, 405 arrests") but a week later only general figures will be given (e.g., "In the recent riots in x, an estimated 50 people were killed, and more than 500 injured"). In this case I would say that we should use the higher figures of 50 and 500 and make a note of the lower figures. Always list all "final" figures and their sources.

Source   Enter appropriate source from drop-down menus.

Source Dates   If more than one, enter using American-style notation, as follows: "3/8/71, 3/23/71."

Officials   The names of all the officials named in press accounts as being connected with the event in their official capacities, as well as their ranks, e.g., Mr. Ram Sharma (DM), Mr. J. N. Chaturvedi (SP). Information on any action these officials took (or didn't take) which may have alleviated or intensified the riot should be entered in the notes. The following abbreviations are acceptable: SP (Superintendent of Police), DM (District Magistrate), IG (Inspector General), and DIG (Deputy Inspector General). At present, all other ranks should be entered in full form in brackets after the name of the official. New abbreviations may be used only after consultation with the rest of the group.

Officials Transferred/Suspended   The rank of the official(s) should be listed, as well as the name(s), e.g., "SP Ram Sharma, SP Rahul Dwiwedi, DM Ashok Mitra" Abbreviation rules are as above.

Type of Policing Arrangement   Mark all police forces used, e.g., in a serious riot we may have "Police, PAC, BSF, Army." The term "police" is the default for local police. If a force was used in an area before the first day of violence (i.e., not ordered to an area but actually used in an area), enter it in this way: "PAC before, Army before." Normally the PAC, etc. only arrives after the outbreak of violence, so the default is simply "PAC" to save ourselves from typing "PAC after" every time. It is important for searching purposes that the space between, e.g., "PAC" and "before" is typed as option space rather than just a space.

Link Made to Outside Event   If a link is reported in the newspaper to events outside the city where a riot takes place (e.g., a communal riot nearby), then mark "Yes"; if not, then mark "No." After this write in the nature of the outside event, e.g., "Communal Riot" using the same terms (complete with option space entries) that are used for the "reported cause" section, complete with.

Police vs. Single Group   If an event fits only this category (i.e., the police do not attack Muslims after a Hindu Muslim riot has already broken out), then write, "Yes" in this space.

Dalit/Muslim   Mark "Yes" if an event fits this category, otherwise ignore.

Reported Cause   Use the causes in the drop down menu. If you have to use the "other" box in this menu, enter what you think is an appropriate category, then make sure to enter "Yes" in the "coding question" box, together with an asterisk and a note explaining the process by which you arrived at your decision.

Local Precipitating Event   Many times this will duplicate the "Reported Cause" category. The key point about this category is that it gives specific information about what sparked off the riot. This is not the same as cause. The object is not to label the cause as "Hindu Procession" or "Muslim Attack on Hindu Procession," but instead to decide if a "Procession" or

"Use of Public Space for Religious Ritual" is the key precipitating event or issue. The particular issue should always be noted in the "notes" section.

Notes   A specific citation should always be given after each note, e.g., "TOI, 3/24/78" The following information should always be entered when available: Hindu/Muslim residential and employment patterns, RSS/Jamaat involvement.

Appendix C: Additional Results from Statistical Tables

The following tables include state dummy variables not included in text.

Table C.4.4. *Congress, Consociationalism, and the Occurrence of Hindu-Muslim Riots*

	Riots		
	(1)	(2)	(3)
Andhra Pradesh	−2.487	0.417	96.970
	(1.120)**	(3.312)	(45.289)**
Bihar	−2.956	−4.774	128.717
	(2.058)	(5.259)	(86.163)
Haryana	−1.636	−1.745	−63.172
	(1.089)	(2.569)	(31.497)**
Karnataka	0.202	7.490	274.268
	(1.254)	(7.163)	(126.277)**
Kerala	8.003	10.114	−194.804
	(2.320)***	(8.502)	(127.997)
Maharashtra	−0.427	1.629	320.692
	(1.132)	(4.661)	(124.126)***
Madhya Pradesh	−3.153	1.461	55.143
	(1.465)**	(4.447)	(45.096)
Orissa	−3.500	3.298	
	(1.685)**	(6.299)	
Rajasthan	−2.471	−2.506	21.313
	(0.791)***	(1.979)	(20.638)
Tamil Nadu	−2.459	1.860	83.011
	(0.758)***	(2.491)	(27.808)***
Uttar Pradesh	−2.996	−5.926	53.280
	(2.049)	(4.887)	(52.698)
West Bengal	0.322	−4.644	
	(1.720)	(3.601)	

Notes: Standard errors in parentheses. * significant at 10%; ** significant at 5%; *** significant at 1%.

Table C.5.3. *Electoral Competition and Communal Riots in Major Indian States, 1961–1995*

	Riots		
	(1)	(2)	(3)
Andhra Pradesh	−1.397	−1.556	−0.805
	(1.291)	(1.302)	(1.294)
Bihar	−2.071	−2.372	−0.560
	(2.396)	(2.421)	(2.431)
Haryana	−2.219	−2.143	−2.767
	(1.352)	(1.355)	(1.370)**
Karnataka	1.761	1.745	2.125
	(1.401)	(1.405)	(1.397)
Kerala	6.870	6.492	8.126
	(3.376)**	(3.397)*	(3.352)**
Maharashtra	3.593	3.436	3.918
	(1.665)**	(1.669)**	(1.650)**
Madhya Pradesh	−2.517	−2.556	−1.955
	(1.729)	(1.735)	(1.724)
Orissa	−5.291	−5.212	−5.090
	(1.957)***	(1.963)***	(1.957)***
Rajasthan	−1.779	−1.817	−1.404
	(0.877)**	(0.878)**	(0.874)
Tamil Nadu	−0.738	−0.839	−0.962
	(0.858)	(0.862)	(0.846)
Uttar Pradesh	−2.267	−2.635	−0.515
	(2.500)	(2.531)	(2.546)
West Bengal	0.767	0.558	1.939
	(1.918)	(1.940)	(1.951)

Notes: Standard errors in parentheses. * significant at 10%; ** significant at 5%; *** significant at 1%.

Additional Results from Statistical Tables

Table C.6.1. *Do State-Level Differences in Ethnic Heterogeneity Explain Levels of Party Competition?*

	Number of Effective Parties	
	(1)	(2)
Andhra Pradesh	0.030	0.029
	(2.245)	(2.245)
Bihar	−0.062	−0.069
	(4.034)	(4.033)
Haryana	−0.136	−0.132
	(1.595)	(1.595)
Karnataka	0.204	0.198
	(2.723)	(2.723)
Kerala	−1.033	−1.042
	(5.249)	(5.248)
Maharashtra	0.446	0.443
	(2.104)	(2.104)
Madhya Pradesh	0.145	0.146
	(2.767)	(2.767)
Orissa	−0.457	−0.454
	(3.226)	(3.226)
Rajasthan	0.030	0.031
	(1.666)	(1.666)
Tamil Nadu	0.271	0.273
	(1.591)	(1.591)
Uttar Pradesh	−0.000	−0.007
	(4.367)	(4.366)
West Bengal	−0.249	−0.256
	(3.926)	(3.926)

Notes: Standard errors in parentheses. * significant at 10%; ** significant at 5%; *** significant at 1%.

References

Archives

India Office Library, London (IOR)

Governor's Reports, Punjab (IOR) L/PJ/249–L/PJ/250
Governor's Reports, United Provinces (IOR) L/PJ/5/276

Uttar Pradesh State Archives, Lucknow (UPSA)

Instructions Regulating the Height of Electric Wires So as Not to Interfere with the Passage of Tazias at the Time of Muharram. GAD, file no. 361/1929
Police Reorganisation Committee. U.P.S.A. Home Police, box 373, file 640/46
Inquiry made by the Government of India about the Employment of Members of the Minority Communities. GAD, file 49H/1958
Resolutions Passed by District Boards Regarding Stoppage of Cow Slaughter. Local Self Government Department, box 395, file 771(A) 1947

Private Collections

Report of the Punjab Police Commission, 1961–62
Report of the U.P. Police Commission, August 31, 1971, Office of the Secretary of the UP Police Commission, Lucknow

Published Government Documents

Damning Verdict. Reprinting of the Justice B. N. Srikrishna Commission Appointed for Inquiry into the Riots at Mumbai during December 1992–January 1993 and the March 12, 1993 Bomb Blasts. N.d. Mumbai: Sabrang.
East India (Cawnpore Riots). 1931. *Report of the Commission of Inquiry and Resolution of the Government of the United Provinces.* London: HMSO.

267

Government of Bihar. 1938. *Bihar Legislative Assembly Debates Official Report*, III, 1–6, 1, March 5.

Government of India. 1931. *India Central Legislative Assembly Debates*, III, 9, March 23.

1947–49. *Constituent Assembly Debates*. New Delhi: Government of India Press.

1948a. *Constituent Assembly of India (Legislative) Debates*, November 27, 1947.

1948b. *Constituent Assembly of India (Legislative) Debates*, August 11, 1948.

1955. *Census of India, 1951 District Census Handbook Uttar Pradesh*. Allahabad, 1954–55.

1988. *Commission on Centre-State Relations Report, Part 1* (Sarkaria Commission).

1989. *Eighth Annual Report of the Minorities' Commission* (for the period 1-4-1985 to 31-3-1986). New Delhi: Controller of Publications.

1995. *Census of India 1991, Paper 1 of 1995, Religion*. Delhi: Government of India.

2001. *Census of India 2001 Provisional Population Totals: Paper 1 of 2001*. Delhi: Controller of Publications.

Government of India. Commissioner for Linguistic Minorities. 1960. *Second Report of the Commissioner for Linguistic Minorities*. Ministry of Home Affairs. Delhi: Manager of Publications.

1965. *Seventh Report of the Commissioner for Linguistic Minorities*. Ministry of Home Affairs. Delhi: Manager of Publications.

1971. *Twelfth Report of the Commissioner for Linguistic Minorities in India, July 1969– June 1970*. Ministry of Home Affairs. Delhi: Manager of Publications.

1986. *Twenty Fifth Report of the Deputy Commissioner for Linguistic Minorities in India, 1984–85*. Ministry of Home Affairs. Delhi: Manager of Publications.

Government of India. Commissioner for Scheduled Tribes and Castes. 1964–65. *Fourteenth Report of the Commissioner for Scheduled Tribes and Castes*. Delhi: Government of India.

1982. *Report of the Commissioner for Scheduled Castes and Tribes, 1979–80 and 1980–1981*. Delhi: Government of India.

Government of India. Home Ministry. 1975. *Report of the One-Man Commission of Inquiry into the Sadar Bazar Disturbances, 1974*. New Delhi: Government of India Press.

Government of India. Law Commission of India. 1978. *Seventy-Seventh Report on Delay and Arrears in Trial Courts*. New Delhi: Government of India.

Law Commission of India, M. C. Setalvad, Chairman, Fourteenth Report (Reform of Judicial Administration). N.d. Delhi: Government of India, Ministry of Law.

Government of India. Ministry of Home Affairs. 1986. *Committee on the Welfare of Scheduled Castes and Scheduled Tribes (1985–1986) Eighth Lok Sabha, Sixth Report*. Delhi: Ministry of Home Affairs.

1993. *The Civil List of the Indian Police Service as of 1st January 1993*. New Delhi.

1995. *The Indian Administrative Service Civil List, 1995*. New Delhi.

Government of India. Minorities Commission. 1980. *Second Annual Report of the Minorities Commission (for the year ending 31st December, 1979)*. New Delhi: Government of India.

1989a. *Eighth Annual Report of the Minorities Commission (for the period 1-4-1985 to 31-3-1986)*. New Delhi: Controller of Publications.

References

1989b. *Ninth Annual Report of the Minorities Commission, 1-4-1986 to 31-3-1987.* New Delhi: Controller of Publications.

1990. *Tenth Annual Report of the Minorities' Commission (for the period 1-4-1987 to 31-3-1986).* New Delhi: Controller of Publications.

Government of India. National Commission for Minorities. 1997a. *National Commission for Minorities Second Annual Report* (FY 1994–95). New Delhi: Ministry of Welfare.

1997b. *National Commission for Minorities Third Annual Report* (FY 1995–96). New Delhi: Ministry of Welfare.

Government of India. National Police Commission. 1979. *Second Report of the National Police Commission.* New Delhi: Government of India.

1980 (November). *Fifth Report of the National Police Commission.* New Delhi: Government of India.

1981 (March). *Sixth Report of the National Police Commission.* New Delhi: Government of India.

Government of India. Reserve Bank of India. 1998. *Reserve Bank of India Bulletin,* February 1998 (Supplement: Finances of State Governments: 1997–98).

Government of Madras. 1947. *Madras Legislative Assembly Debates, 30 January–14th February 1947.* Madras: Government of Madras.

Government of Mysore. 1950. *Mysore Legislative Assembly Debates Official Report.* Vol. 1, *15 March to 4th April 1950.* Bangalore.

1953. *Mysore Legislative Assembly Debates, Official Report,* August 7, 1953. Banglore.

Government of Tamil Nadu. 1974. *Report of the Backward Classes Commission Tamil Nadu.* Vol. 1, *1970.* Madras: Government of Tamil Nadu. [Chairman S. Sattanathan].

1975. *Report of the Backward Classes Commission Tamil Nadu.* Vol. 2, *1970.* Madras: Government of Tamil Nadu. [Chairman S. Sattanathan].

Government of Uttar Pradesh. 1962. *Report of the Uttar Pradesh Police Commission, 1960–61.* Allahabad: Superintendent of Printing and Stationery, U.P.

Government of Uttar Pradesh. Bhasha Vibhag. 1966. *Facilities Provided for Linguistic Minorities in Uttar Pradesh.* Lucknow: Bhasha Vibhag.

Great Britain. 1928. *East India (Progress and Condition) Statement Exhibiting the Moral and Material Progress and Condition of India, during the Year 1926–27.* London: HMSO.

1937. *Government of India Act, 1935. Draft of Instrument of Instructions Which It Is Proposed to Recommend His Majesty to Issue to the Governors of Indian Provinces. House of Commons Accounts and Papers – 5- Session, 3 November 1936–22 October 1937.* Vol. 20, *1936–37.* London: His Majesty's Stationary Office.

Lok Sabha Secretariat. 1996. *President's Rule in the States and Union Territories.* New Delhi: Lok Sabha Secretariat.

Report into the Communal Disturbances at Ahmedabad and Other Places in Gujarat on and after 18th September 1969. Justice P. Jagmohan Reddy (Judge, Supreme Court of India). 1971. Gandhinagar: Gujarat Government Press.

Report of the Commission of Inquiry on Communal Disturbances, Ranchi-Hatia (August 22–29, 1967). 1968. Delhi.

269

Report of the Commissioners of Inquiry into the Origin and Character of the Riots in Belfast in July and September 1857. 1858. Dublin: Alex. Thom. and Sons.

Reports from Commissioners, Inspectors, and Others: Thirty-Five Volumes-(5.)-Belfast Riots Commission, 1887. Vol. 18. London: Parliamentary Papers.

Books and Articles

Ahluwalia, Montek S. 2001. State Level Performance under Economic Reforms in India. Stanford CREDR Working Paper, March.

Alesina, Alberto, Reza Baqir, and William Easterly. 1999. Public Goods and Ethnic Divisions. *Quarterly Journal of Economics* 114, 4 (November): 1243–84.

Allport, Gordon W. 1997. *The Nature of Prejudice.* 1954. Reprint, Boston: Addison Wesley.

Anifowose, Remi. 1982. *Violence and Politics in Nigeria: The Tiv and Yoruba Experience.* New York: Nok Publishers.

Bagchi, Amaresh. 1997. Fiscal Management: The Federal Dimension of Developing Countries. In Parthasarathi Shome, ed., *Fiscal Policy, Public Policy and Governance.* Symposium to commemorate the 20th Anniversary of the National Institute of Public Finance and Policy, December 5–6. New Delhi: Centax: 273–97.

1990. Predatory Commercialization and Communalism in India. In S. Gopal, ed., *Anatomy of a Confrontation.* New Delhi: Penguin: 193–218.

Banu, Zenab. 1980. Reality of Communal Riot: Class Conflict between the Haves of Hindus and Muslims. *Indian Journal of Political Science* 41, 1: 100–14.

1989. *Politics of Communalism.* Bombay: Popular Prakashan.

Bardon, Jonathan. 1982. *Belfast: An Illustrated History.* Dundonald: Blackstaff Press.

Barnett, Marguerite Ross. 1976. *The Politics of Cultural Nationalism in South India.* Princeton: Princeton University Press.

Bartlett, Robert. 1993. *The Making of Europe: Conquest Colonization and Cultural Change, 950–1350.* Princeton: Princeton University Press.

Bates, Robert H. 1983. Modernization, Ethnic Competition and the Rationality of Politics in Contemporary Africa. In Donald Rothchild and Victor Olorunsola, eds., *State versus Ethnic Claims: African Policy Dilemmas.* Boulder: Westview Press: 152–71.

Bartolini, Stefano. 1996. Enfranchisement, Equality and Turnout in the European Democratisation Process: A Preliminary Comparative Analysis. EUI Working Paper no. 121. Barcelona.

Bayly, C. A. 1988. *Ruler, Townsmen and Bazaars: North Indian Society in the Age of British Expansion, 1770–1870.* Cambridge: Cambridge University Press.

Beissinger, Mark R. 1996. How Nationalisms Spread: Eastern Europe Adrift the Tides and Cycles of Nationalist Contention. *Social Research* 63, 1: 97–146.

1998. Nationalist Violence and the State: Political Authority and Contentious Repertoires in the Former USSR. *Comparative Politics* 30, 4: 401–22.

References

Belknap, Michal R., ed. 1991. *Civil Rights: The White House and the Justice Department, 1945–1968*. New York: Garland.

Bernard, Cheryl. 1986. Politics and the Refugee Experience. *Political Science Quarterly* 101, 4: 617–36.

Bhattacharya, Mohit. 1997. Reservation Policy: The West Bengal Scene. In V. A. Pai Panandikar, ed., *The Politics of Backwardness: Reservation Policy in India*. New Delhi: Konark: 183–219.

Biographical Encyclopedia of Pakistan, 1960–61. 1961. Lahore: International Publishers.

Bohr, Annette, and Simon Crisp. 1996. Kyrgyzstan and the Kyrgyz. In Graham Smith, ed., *The Nationalities Question in the Post-Soviet States*. New York: Longman: 385–409.

Bohstedt, John. 1988. Gender, Household and Community Politics: Women in English Riots, 1790–1810. *Past and Present* 120: 88–122.

Brass, Paul R. 1973. Radical Parties of the Left in Bihar: A Comparison of the SSP and the CPI. In Paul R. Brass and Marcus F. Franda, eds., *Radical Politics in South Asia*. Cambridge, Mass.: MIT Press: 325–400.

1974. *Language, Religion and Politics in North India*. Cambridge: Cambridge University Press.

1990. *The Politics of India since Independence*. Cambridge: Cambridge University Press.

1991. Ethnic Conflict in Multiethnic Societies: The Consociational Solution and Its Critics. In *Ethnicity and Nationalism: Theory and Comparison*. London: Sage: 333–48.

1997. *Theft of an Idol: Text and Context in the Study of Collective Violence*. Princeton: Princeton University Press.

Bremmer, Ian, and Ray Taras, eds. 1993. *Nations and Politics in the Soviet Successor States*. Cambridge: Cambridge University Press.

Breuilly, John. 1994. *Nationalism and the State*. Chicago: University of Chicago Press.

Brodkin, Karen. 2000. *How Jews Became White Folks and What That Says about Race in America*. New Brunswick, N.J.: Rutgers University Press.

Brown, Judith. 1985. *Modern India: The Origins of an Asian Democracy*. Oxford: Oxford University Press.

Brown, Rupert. 1995. *Prejudice: Its Social Psychology*. Oxford: Blackwell.

Bunce, Valerie. 1996. From State Socialism to State Disintegration: A Comparison of the Soviet Union, Yugoslavia and Czechoslovakia. Paper presented at the conference on "Democracy, Markets and Civil Societies in Post-1989 East Central Europe," Harvard University, May 17–19.

Burg, Steven L., and Michael L. Berbaum. 1989. Community Integration and Stability in Multinational Yugoslavia. *American Political Science Review* 83, 2: 535–55.

Butler, David, Ashok Lahiri, and Prannoy Roy. 1995. *India Decides: Elections, 1952–1995*. New Delhi: Books and Things.

Carmines, Edward G., and James A. Stimson. 1989. *Race and the Transformation of American Politics*. Princeton: Princeton University Press.

Carroll, Charles. 1932. *Rhode Island: Three Centuries of Democracy*. New York: Lewis Historical Publishing Company.

Centre for Policy Studies. 1993. *Crying Peace Where There Is None? The Functioning and Future of Local Peace Committees of the National Peace Accord*. Research Report no. 31 (Transition Series). Johannesburg.

Chhibber, Pradeep, and Ken Kollman. 1998. Party Aggregation and the Number of Parties in India and the United States. *American Political Science Review* 92, 2: 329–42.

Cohen, Gary Bennett. 1975. The Prague Germans, 1861–1914: The Problems of Ethnic Survival. Ph.D. dissertation, Princeton University.

Comber, Leon. 1983. *13 May 1969: A Historical Survey of Sino-Malay Relations*. Kuala Lumpur: Heinemann.

Connolly, S. J. 1989. Mass Politics and Sectarian Conflict, 1823–30. In W. E. Vaughan, ed., *A New History of Ireland, 6 5, Ireland under the Union, I, 1801–70*. Oxford: Clarendon Press: 74–107.

Cook, S. W. 1978. Interpersonal and Attitudinal Outcomes in Cooperating Interracial groups. *Journal of Research and Development in Education* 12: 97–113.

Cox, Gary W. 1998a. Electoral Rules and the Calculus of Mobilization. Paper presented at the Shambaugh Comparative Legislative Research Conference, Iowa City, Iowa, April 16–19. Available at <http://gcox.ucsd.edu/iomob4.htm>.

Cox, Gary W. 1998b. *Making Votes Count: Strategic Coordination in the World's Electoral Systems*. Cambridge: Cambridge University Press.

Cox, Gary, and Michael C. Munger. 1989. Closeness, Expenditures, and Turnout in the 1982 U.S. House Elections. *American Political Science Review* 83, 1: 217–32.

Cribb, Robert. 1991. Problems in the Historiography of the Killings in Indonesia. In Robert Cribb, ed., *The Indonesian Killings, 1965–66: Studies from Java and Bali*. Melbourne: Centre for Southeast Asian Studies, Monash University: 1–44.

Crossman, Virginia. 1996. *Politics, Law and Order in Nineteenth-Century Ireland*. New York: St. Martin's Press.

Damodaran, Vinita. 1992. *Broken Promises: Popular Protest, Indian Nationalism and the Congress Party in Bihar, 1935–1946*. Delhi: Oxford University Press.

Das, Arvind S. 1992. *The Republic of Bihar*. New Delhi: Penguin.

Das, Durga. 1970. *India from Curzon to Nehru and After*. New York: John Day.

Das, Suranjan. 1993. *Communal Riots in Bengal, 1905–1947*. Delhi: Oxford University Press.

    2000. The 1992 Calcutta Riot in Historical Continuum: A Relapse into 'Communal Fury'? *Modern Asian Studies* 34, 2: 281–306.

Dayal, Rajeshwar. 1998. *A Life of Our Times*. Delhi: Orient Longman.

Deák, István. 1991. The One and the Many. Review of Aleksa Djilas's *The Contested Country: Yugoslav Unity and Communist Revolution, 1919–1953* (Cambridge, Mass.: Harvard University Press, 1991). *New Republic*, October 7: 29–36.

Desai, Mihir. 1990. The Need for Reservations: A Reply to Shourie and Others. *Lokayan Bulletin* 8, 4–5: 9–33.

References

Deshpande, Satish, and Nandini Sundar. 1998. Caste and the Census: Implications for Society and the Social Sciences. *Economic and Political Weekly*, August 8: 2157–59.

DiPasquale, Denise, and Edward L. Glaeser. 1996. *The L. A. Riot and the Economics of Urban Unrest*. NBER Working Paper no. W5456, February.

Diskin, Abraham. 1991. *Elections and Voters in Israel*. New York: Praeger.

Dorosin, Joshua L. 1990. *Romania: A Dream Deferred, the 1990 Elections and Prospects for Future Democracy*. Washington, D.C.: International Foundation for Electoral Systems.

D'Souza, Victor S. 1978. Status Groups among the Moplahs on the South-West Coast of India. In Imtiaz Ahmed, ed., *Caste and Social Stratification among Muslims in India*. New Delhi: Manohar: 41–56.

Easterly, William, and Ross Levine. 1999. Africa's Growth Tragedy: Policies and Ethnic Divisions. *Quarterly Journal of Economics* 114, 4: 1203–50.

Elazar, Daniel J. 1979. The Role of Federalism in Political Integration. In Daniel J. Elazar, ed., *Federalism and Political Integration*. Jerusalem: Institute for Federalism: 1–13.

Enelow, James M., and Melvin J. Hinich. 1982. Non-Spatial Candidate Characteristics and Electoral Competition. *Journal of Politics* 44, 1: 115–30.

Engineer, Ashgar Ali. 1984. The Causes of Communal Riots in the Post-Partition Period in India. In Ashgar Ali Engineer, ed., *Communal Riots in Post-Independence India*. Hyderabad: Sangam Books: 33–41.

1992a. Communal Riots in Ahmedabad. *Economic and Political Weekly*, August 1–8: 1641–43.

1992b. Banaras Rocked by Communal Violence. *Economic and Political Weekly*, March 7–14: 509–11.

1993. Bombay Riots: Second Phase. *Economic and Political Weekly*, March 20–27: 505–8.

1994. Communal Violence in Kanpur. *Economic and Political Weekly*, February 26: 473–74.

1995. The Bhagalpur Riots II. *Hindu*, June 23.

Feldberg, Michael. 1980. *The Turbulent Era: Riot and Disorder in Jacksonian America*. New York: Oxford University Press.

Forbes, H. D. 1997. *Ethnic Conflict: Commerce, Culture and the Contact Hypothesis*. New Haven: Yale University Press.

Gabriel, Theodore. 1996. *Hindu-Muslim Relations in North Malabar, 1498–1947*. Lewiston, N.Y.: Edward Mellen.

Gadgil, N. V. 1968. *Government from Inside*. Meerut: Meenakshi Prakashan.

Gagliano, Felix V. 1970. *Communal Violence in Malaysia 1969: The Political Aftermath*. Athens: Ohio University Center for International Studies Southeast Asia Program.

Gailus, Manfred. 1994. Food Riots in Germany in the Late 1840s. *Past and Present* 145: 157–93.

Galanter, Marc. 1991. *Competing Equalities: Law and the Backward Classes in India*. 2nd ed. Delhi: Oxford University Press.

Gallagher, Tom. 1995. *Romania after Ceaucescu: The Politics of Intolerance*. Edinburgh: Edinburgh University Press.

Ghosh, Partha S. 1989. *Cooperation and Conflict in South Asia*. New Delhi: Manohar.

Ghosh, Pratap Kumar. 1966. *The Constitution of India: How It Has Been Framed*. Calcutta: World Press.

Ghosh, S. K. 1972. *Riots: Prevention and Control*. Calcutta: Eastern Law House.

Ghosh, S. K., and K. F. Rustamji, eds. 1994. *Encyclopaedia of Police in India*. Vol. 2, sect. A. New Delhi: Ashish.

Glaser, James M. 1996. *Race, Campaign Politics and the Realignment in the South*. New Haven: Yale University Press.

Gomango, Giridhar. 1992. *Constitutional Provisions for the Scheduled Castes and the Scheduled Tribes*. Bombay: Himalaya Publishing.

Gopal, Sarvepalli. 1979. *Jawaharlal Nehru: A Biography*. Vol. 2, *1947–1956*. Cambridge, Mass.: Harvard University Press.

1983. *Jawaharlal Nehru: An Anthology*. Delhi: Oxford University Press.

1984. *Jawaharlal Nehru: A Biography*. Vol. 3. Cambridge, Mass.: Harvard University Press.

Gould, Harold A. 1994. *Grass Roots Politics in India: A Century of Political Evolution in Faizabad District*. New Delhi: Oxford & IBH.

Gower, Robert. 1937. *The Hungarian Minorities in the Succession States*. London: Grant Richards.

Gupta, Raghuraj. 1976. *Hindu-Muslim Relations*. Lucknow: Ethnographic and Folk Culture Society, U.P.

Gurr, Ted Robert, and Barbara Harff. 1994. *Ethnic Conflict in World Politics*. Boulder: Westview Press.

Gwyer, Maurice, and A. Appadorai, eds. 1957. *Speeches and Documents on the Indian Constitution*. Vol. 1, *1921–1947*. Bombay: Ernest Benn.

Hagerty, Devin T. 1996. Nuclear Deterrence in South Asia: The 1990 Indo-Pakistani Crisis. *International Security* 20, 3: 79–114.

Hardin, Russell. 1995. *One for All: The Logic of Group Conflict*. Princeton: Princeton University Press.

Harris, Peter, and Ben Reilly, eds. 1998. *Democracy and Deep-Rooted Conflict: Options for Negotiators*. Stockholm: IDEA.

Hasan, Mushirul. 1997. *Legacy of a Divided Nation: India's Muslims since Independence*. Delhi: Oxford University Press.

Helsinki Watch. 1993. *Struggling for Ethnic Identity: Ethnic Hungarians in Post-Ceaucescu Romania*. Human Rights Watch.

Hersh, Seymour M. 1993. On the Nuclear Edge. *New Yorker*, March 29: 56–73.

Hitchins, Keith. 1994. *Rumania, 1866–1947*. Oxford: Oxford University Press.

Hoppen, K. Theodore. 1984. *Elections, Politics, and Society in Ireland, 1832–1885*. Oxford: Oxford University Press: 268–69.

Horowitz, Donald L. 1985. *Ethnic Groups in Conflict*. Berkeley: University of California Press.

1991. *A Democratic South Africa: Constitutional Engineering in a Divided Society*. Berkeley: University of California Press.

2001. *The Deadly Ethnic Riot*. Berkeley: University of California Press.

References

Human Rights Watch. 1994. *We Have No Orders to Save You: State Participation and Complicity in Communal Violence in Gujarat.* 14, no. 3 (C).

1995. *Slaughter among Neighbors: The Political Origins of Communal Violence.* New Haven: Yale University Press.

Huntington, Samuel P. 1968. *Political Order in Changing Societies.* New Haven: Yale University Press.

1991. *The Third Wave: Democratization in the Late Twentieth Century.* Norman: University of Oklahoma Press.

Huntington, Samuel P., and Joan M. Nelson. 1976. *No Easy Choice: Political Participation in Developing Countries.* Cambridge, Mass.: Harvard University Press.

Ignatiev, Noel. 1995. *How the Irish Became White.* New York: Routledge.

Indian Annual Register. Calcutta: Annual Registar Office, 1919–47.

International Foundation for Electoral Systems. 1990. *Romania in the Wake of Ceaucescu: An Assessment of the Romanian Electoral System on Election Eve.* Washington, D.C.: International Foundation for Electoral Systems.

Inverarity, James M. 1976. Populism and Lynching in Louisiana, 1889–1896: A Test of Erikson's Theory of the Relationship between Boundary Crises and Repressive Justice. *American Sociological Review* 41, 2: 262–80.

Irschick, Eugene F. 1969. *Politics and Social Conflict in South India: The Non-Brahman Movement and Tamil Separatism, 1916–1929.* Berkeley: University of California Press.

1986. *Tamil Revivalism in the 1930s.* Madras: Cre-A.

Jaffrelot, Christophe. 1996. *The Hindu Nationalist Movement in India.* New York: Columbia University Press.

1998. The Politics of Processions and Hindu-Muslim Riots. In Amrita Basu and Atul Kohli, eds., *Community Conflicts and the State in India.* Delhi: Oxford University Press: 58–92.

Jayaprasad, K. 1991. *RSS and Hindu Nationalism: Inroads in a Leftist Stronghold.* New Delhi: Deep and Deep.

Jeffery, Roger, and Patricia M. Jeffery. 1994. The Bijnor Riots, October 1990: Collapse of a Mythical Special Relationship? *Economic and Political Weekly*, March 5: 551–58.

Jha, Shree Nagesh. 1970. Caste in Bihar Politics. *Economic and Political Weekly*, February 14: 341–44.

Jussila, Osmo. 1993. The Russian Government and the Finnish Diet: A Study of the Evolution of Political Representation, 1863–1914. In Geoffrey Alderman, ed., *Governments, Ethnic Groups and Political Representation*, vol. 6 of *Comparative Series of Governments and Non-Dominant Ethnic Groups in Europe, 1850–1940.* New York: European Science Foundation/NYU Press: 167–99.

Kabir, Humayun. 1968. *Minorities in a Democracy.* Calcutta: K. L. Mukhopadhyay.

Kaufmann, Chaim. 1996. Possible and Impossible Solutions to Ethnic Civil Wars. *International Security* 20, 4: 136–75.

Kaufman, Stuart. 1995. The Irresistible Force and the Imperceptible Object: The Yugoslav Breakup and Western Policy. *Security Studies* 4, 2: 281–329.

275

Keller, Stephen L. 1975. *Uprooting and Social Change: The Role of Refugees in Development*. Delhi: Manohar Book Service.

Keyssar, Alexander. 2000. *The Right to Vote: The Contested History of Democracy in the United States*. New York: Basic Books.

Khalidi, Omar. 1993. Muslims in Indian Political Process: Group Goals and Alternative Strategies. *Economic and Political Weekly*, January 2–9: 43–54.

1995. *Indian Muslims since Independence*. New Delhi: Vikas.

Khaliquzzaman, Choudhry. 1961. *Pathway to Pakistan*. Lahore: Longmans Green.

Khan, Dildar. 1992. Meerut Riots: An Analysis. In Pramod Kumar, ed., *Towards Understanding Communalism*. Chandigarh: Center for Research in Rural and Industrial Development: 455–70.

Khan, Kishwar Shabbir. 1991. *Brassware Industry of Moradabad and Its Muslim Artisans*. Interdisciplinary Centre of Development Studies, Aligarh Muslim University.

Kidwai, Anwar Jamal. 1993. An Unsung Hero of the Freedom Struggle: Rafi Ahmed Kidwai. *Islam and the Modern Age* 24, 2: 88–107.

King, Jeremy. 1998. Loyalty and Polity, Nation and State: A Town in Hapsburg Central Europe, 1848–1948. Ph.D. dissertation, Columbia University.

Kitschelt, Herbert, Zdenka Mansfeldova, Radoslaw Markowski, and Gábor Tóka. 1999. *Post-Communist Party Systems: Competition, Representation, and Inter-Party Competition*. Cambridge: Cambridge University Press.

Kohli, A. B. 1983. *Councils of Ministers in India, 1947–1982*. New Delhi: Gitanjali Publishing.

Kohli, Atul. 1990. *Democracy and Discontent: India's Growing Crisis of Governability*. Cambridge: Cambridge University Press.

Kooiman, Dirk. 1995. *Communities and Electorates: A Comparative Discussion of Communalism in Colonial India*. Amsterdam: VU University Press.

Koshy, M. J. 1971. *Constitutionalism in Travancore and Cochin*. Trivandrum: Kerala Historical Society.

Krishna, B. 1995. *Sardar Vallabhai Patel: India's Iron Man*. New Delhi: Indus.

Kumar, Nita. 1995. *The Artisans of Banaras: Popular Culture and Identity, 1880–1986*. New Delhi: Orient Longman.

Kurien, Prema. 1994. Colonialism and Ethnogenesis: A Study of Kerala, India. *Theory and Society* 23: 385–417.

Laitin, David D. 1986. *Hegemony and Culture: Politics and Religious Change among the Yoruba*. Chicago: University of Chicago Press.

Lambert, Richard D. 1951. Hindu-Muslim Riots. Ph.D. dissertation, University of Pennsylvania.

Lazar, Gyorgy. 1979. Memorandum. In *Witness to Cultural Genocide: First-Hand Reports on Rumania's Minority Policies Today*. New York: American Transylvanian Federation: 88–144.

Lemarchand, René. 1996. *Burundi: Ethnic Conflict and Genocide*. New York: Woodrow Wilson Center Press/Cambridge University Press.

Lijphart, Arend. 1977. *Democracy in Plural Societies: A Comparative Exploration*. New Haven: Yale University Press.

References

1985. *Power-Sharing in South Africa.* Institute of International Studies Policy Papers in International Affairs no. 24. Berkeley: University of California.

1995. Self-Determination versus Pre-Determination of Ethnic Minorities in Power-Sharing Systems. In Will Kymlicka, ed., *The Rights of Minority Cultures.* New York: Oxford University Press: 275–87.

1996. The Puzzle of Indian Democracy: A Consociational Interpretation. *American Political Science Review* 90, 2: 258–68.

1998. South African Democracy: Majoritarian or Consociational? *Democratization* 5, 4: 144–50.

Lipset, Seymour Martin, and Stein Rokkan. 1967. Cleavage Structures, Party Systems, and Voter Alignments: An Introduction. In Seymour Martin Lipset and Stein Rokkan, eds., *Party Systems and Voter Alignments: Cross-National Perspectives.* New York: Free Press: 1–67.

Long, J. Scott. 1997. *Regression Models for Categorical and Limited Dependent Variables.* Thousand Oaks, Calif.: Sage: 217–63.

Love, Mervyn T. 1995. *Peace Building through Reconciliation in Northern Ireland.* Avebury: Aldershot.

Lustick, Ian. 1979. Stability in Deeply Divided Societies: Consociationalism and Control. *World Politics* 31, 3: 325–44.

Macdonagh, Oliver. 1989. Ideas and Institutions, 1830–45. In W. E. Vaughan, *A New History of Ireland,* vol. 5, *Ireland under the Union, I, 1801–70.* Oxford: Clarendon Press: 193–217.

Malik, Ikram. 1984. *Hindu-Muslim Riots in the British Punjab, 1849–1900: An Analysis.* Lahore: Jamal Mahmud Press.

Mammen, P. N. 1981. *Communalism vs. Communism: A Study of the Socio-Religious Communities and Political Parties in Kerala, 1892–1970.* Calcutta: Minerva.

Manor, James. 1981. Party Decay and Political Crisis in India. *Washington Quarterly* 4, 3: 25–40.

Manshardt. Clifford. 1936. *The Hindu-Muslim Problem in India.* London: G. Allen & Unwin.

McAdam, Doug. 1982. *Political Process and the Development of Black Insurgency, 1930–1970.* Chicago: University of Chicago Press.

McIntosh, Mary, Martha Abele MacIver, Daniel G. Abele, and David B. Nolle. 1995. Minority Rights and Majority Rule: Ethnic Tolerance in Romania and Bulgaria. *Social Forces* 73, 3: 939–68.

Means, Gordon P. 1991. *Malaysian Politics: The Second Generation.* Singapore: Oxford University Press.

Menon, Dilip. 1994. *Caste, Nationalism and Communism in South India: Malabar, 1900–1948.* Cambridge: Cambridge University Press.

Midlarsky, Manus I. 1978. Analyzing Diffusion and Contagion Effects: The Urban Disorders of the 1960s. *American Political Science Review* 72, 3: 996.

Miguel, Edward. 2000. Ethnic Diversity and School Funding in Kenya. Working paper. Available at <http://iber.berkeley.edu/wps/cider/c01-119.pdf>, accessed December 31, 2003.

Mill, John Stuart. 1991. *Considerations on Representative Government*. Buffalo, N.Y.: Prometheus Books.

Millward, Pauline. 1985. The Stockport Riots of 1852: A Study of Anti-Catholic and Anti-Irish Sentiment. In Roger Swift and Sheridan Gilley, eds., *The Irish in the Victorian City*. London: Croom Helm: 207–24.

Misra, B. B. 1970. *The Administrative History of India, 1834–1947*. New Delhi: Oxford University Press.

Mohammed, U. 1995. Educational Problems of the Muslim Minority in Kerala. In Ashgar Ali Engineer, *Kerala Muslims: A Historical Perspective*. New Delhi: Ajanta: 147–56.

Moon, Penderel. 1961. *Divide and Quit*. London: Chatto and Windus.

More, J. B. P. 1997. *The Political Evolution of Muslims in Tamilnadu and Madras, 1930–1947*. Hyderabad: Orient Longman.

Mujahid, Sharif al-. 1970. *Indian Secularism: A Case Study of the Muslim Minority*. Karachi: University of Karachi Press.

Mukerjee, Radhakamal. 1941. Organization of Cottage Industries and Handicrafts. In Radhakamal Mukerjee and H. L. Dey, *Economic Problems of Modern India*. Vol. 2. London: Macmillan: 3–27.

Munshi, K. M. 1967. *Indian Constitutional Documents*. Vol. 1, *Pilgrimage to Freedom (1902–1950)*. Bombay: Bharatiya Vidhya Bhavan.

Murphy, Gardner. 1953. *In the Minds of Men: The Study of Human Behavior and Social Tensions in India*. New York: Basic Books.

Naidu, Ratna. 1990. *Old Cities, New Predicaments: A Study of Hyderabad*. New Delhi: Sage.

Nanda, B. R., ed. 1998. *Selected Works of Govind Ballabh Pant*. Vol. 11. Delhi: Oxford University Press.

Nandy, Ashish, Shikha Trivedy, Shail Mayaram, and Achyut Yagnik. 1995. *Creating a Nationality: The Ramjanmabhumi Movement and Fear of the Self*. Delhi: Oxford University Press.

National Police Commission: Its Relevance Today. 1997. Papers and discussions at seminar organized by Nehru Centre and Hindustani Andolan, April 19. Mumbai: Nehru Centre 1997.

Nayar, V. K. S. 1966. Communal Interest Groups in Kerala. In Donald E. Smith, ed., *South Asian Politics and Religion*. Princeton: Princeton University Press: 176–90.

Neal, Frank. 1988. *Sectarian Violence: The Liverpool Experience, 1819–1914*. Manchester: Manchester University Press.

Nitzova, Petya. 1997. Bulgaria: Minorities, Democratization and National Sentiments. *Nationalities Papers* 25, 4: 729–40.

Nossiter, T. J. 1982. *Communism in Kerala: A Study in Political Adaptation*. Berkeley: University of California Press.

O'Day, Alan. 1992. Ireland's Catholics in the British State, 1850–1922. In Andrea Kappeler, ed., *The Formation of National Elites*, vol. 6 of *Comparative Studies on Governments and Non-Dominant Ethnic Groups in Europe, 1850–1940*. New York: European Science Foundation/NYU Press: 41–76.

Offe, Claus. 1992. Strong Causes, Weak Cures: Some Preliminary Notes on the Intransigence of Ethnic Politics. *East European Constitutional Review* 1, 1: 21–23.

Olzak, Susan. 1992. *The Dynamics of Ethnic Competition and Conflict*. Stanford: Stanford University Press.

Ordeshook, Peter C., and Olga V. Shvetsova. 1994. Ethnic Heterogeneity, District Magnitude and the Number of Parties. *American Journal of Political Science* 38, 1: 100–23.

Parker, William Crego. 1979. Cultures in Stress: The Malaysian Crisis of 1969 and Its Cultural Roots. Ph.D. dissertation, MIT.

Parthasarathi, G., ed. 1985. *Jawaharlal Nehru Letters to Chief Ministers, 1947–1964*. Vol. 1, *1947–1949*. New Delhi: Oxford University Press.

ed. 1988. *Jawaharlal Nehru Letters to Chief Ministers 1947–1964*. Vol. 4, *1954–1957*. New Delhi: Oxford University Press.

ed. 1989. *Jawaharlal Nehru: Letters to Chief Ministers 1947–1964*. Vol. 5, *1958–1964*. New Delhi: Oxford University Press.

Pattie, Charles J., Ronald J. Johnston, and Edward A. Fieldhouse. 1995. Winning the Local Vote: The Effectiveness of Constituency Campaign Spending in Great Britain, 1983–1992. *American Political Science Review* 89, 4: 969–83.

Phillips, John A. 1992. *The Great Reform Bill in the Boroughs: English Electoral Behaviour, 1818–1841*. Oxford: Oxford University Press.

Posen, Barry. 1993. The Security Dilemma and Ethnic Conflict. *Survival* 35, 1: 27–47.

Posner, Daniel L. 2000. Ethnic Fractionalization and Economic Growth in Africa. Paper presented to the LiCEP working group, March 25.

2003. The Institutional Origins of Ethnic Politics in Zambia. University of California, Los Angeles. Unpublished manuscript.

Potter, David. 1987. IAS Mobility Patterns. *Indian Journal of Public Administration* 33, 4: 845–56.

1996. *India's Political Administrators: From ICS to IAS*. Delhi: Oxford University Press.

Prior, Katherine. 1993. Making History: The State's Intervention in Urban Religious Disputes in the North-Western Provinces in the Early Nineteenth Century. *Modern Asian Studies* 27, 1: 179–203.

Puri, Geeta. 1978. *The Jana Sangh*. Delhi: Sterling.

Rabushka, Alvin, and Kenneth A. Shepsle. 1972. *Politics in Plural Societies: A Theory of Democratic Instability*. Columbus: Charles E. Merrill.

Radhakrishnan, P. 1996. Backward Class Movements in Tamil Nadu. In M. N. Srinivas, ed., *Caste: Its Twentieth Century Avatar*. New Delhi: Viking: 110–34.

Rady, Martin. 1992. *Romania in Turmoil*. New York: IB Tauris.

Rai, V. N. 1995. A Case for Representation of Minorities in the Police. *Towards Secular India* 1, 2: 39–47.

Rajgopal, P. R. 1987. *Communal Violence in India*. New Delhi: Uppal Publishing House/Centre for Policy Research.

Ramachandran, R. 1992. *Urbanization and Urban Systems in India*. Delhi: Oxford University Press.

Rao, B. Shiva, V. K. N. Menon, Subhash C. Kashyap, and N. K. N. Iyengar. 1968. *The Framing of India's Constitution: A Study*. New Delhi: Indian Institute of Public Administration.

Rao Bahadur, M. Shama. 1936. *Modern Mysore*. Bangalore: Higginbothams.

Reddy, G. Ram. 1989. The Politics of Accommodation: Caste, Class and Dominance in Andhra Pradesh. In Francine Frankel and M. S. A. Rao, eds., *Dominance and State Power in Modern India: Decline of a Social Order*. Vol. 1. Delhi: Oxford University Press: 265–321.

Reilly, Benjamin, and Peter Harris. 1998. *Democracy and Deep-Rooted Conflict: Options for Negotiators*. Stockholm: International Institute for Democracy and Electoral Assistance.

Riker, William H. 1996. *The Strategy of Rhetoric: Campaigning for the American Constitution*. New Haven: Yale University Press.

Roy, Ramashray. 1995. Caste and Political Recruitment in Bihar. In Rajni Kothari, ed., *Caste in Indian Politics*. Delhi: Orient Longman Reprint: 215–41.

Rudolph, Lloyd I., and Suzanne Hoeber Rudolph. 1987. *In Pursuit of Lakshmi: The Political Economy of the Indian State*. Chicago: University of Chicago Press.

Rule, James B. 1988. *Theories of Civil Violence*. Berkeley: University of California Press.

Sachchidananda. 1997. Reservation and After: The Case of Bihar. In V. A. Pai Panandikar, ed., *The Politics of Backwardness: Reservation Policy in India*. New Delhi: Konark: 161–82.

Saiyed, A. R. 1995. Changing Urban Ethos: Reflections on Hindu-Muslim Riots. In A. R. Saiyed, *Religion and Ethnicity among Muslims*. Jaipur: Rawat: 321–43.

Saksena, N. S. 1987. *Law and Order in India*. New Delhi: Abhinav.

1990. *Communal Riots in India*. New Delhi: Trishul.

Saksena, R. N. 1961. *Refugees: A Study in Changing Attitudes*. London: Asia Publishing House.

Sambanis, Nicholas. 2000. Ethnic War: A Theoretic and Empirical Inquiry into Its Causes. World Bank, February 27.

Saraswathi, S. 1974. *Minorities in Madras State*. Delhi: Impex.

Saxena, N. C. 1984. The Nature and Origin of Communal Riots. In Ashgar Ali Engineer, ed., *Communal Riots in Post-Independence India*. Hyderabad: Sangam Books: 51–67.

Schwerthoeffer, Simona. 1985. The Nationalities Policy: Theory and Practice. In Vlad Georgescu, ed., *Romania: 40 Years (1944–1984)*. New York: Praeger: 79–92.

Sebok, Lazlo. 1996. The Hungarians in East Central Europe: A Demographic Profile. *Nationalities Papers* 24, 3: 551–62.

Sen Gupta, Bhabani. 1972. *Communism in Indian Politics*. New York: Columbia University Press.

Shafir, Michael. 1992. Preliminary Results of the 1992 Romanian Census. *RFE/RL Research Report* 1, 30: 62–68.

Shakir, Moin. 1983. *Islam in Indian Politics*. New Delhi: Ajanta Publications.

References

Shariff, Abusaleh. 1995. Socio-Economic and Demographic Differentials between Hindus and Muslims in India. *Economic and Political Weekly*, November 18: 2947–53.

Sharma, K. D. 1991. *Trials, Tribulations and Triumphs of the Police-Men*. Noida: Trishul Publications.

Shepsle, Kenneth M. 1972. *Politics in Plural Societies: A Theory of Democratic Instability*. Boston: Charles E. Merrill.

Sinha, M. K. 1981. *In Father's Footsteps: A Policeman's Odyssey*. Patna: Vanity Books.

Sisk, Timothy D. 1996. *Power Sharing and International Mediation in Ethnic Conflicts*. Washington, D.C.: United States Institute of Peace and the Carnegie Commission of Preventing Deadly Conflict.

Smelser, Neil J. 1962. *Theory of Collective Behavior*. London: Routledge and Kegan Paul.

Smith, Donald E. 1963. *India as a Secular State*. Princeton: Princeton University Press.

Spilerman, Seymour. 1971. The Causes of Racial Disturbances: Tests of an Explanation. *American Sociological Review* 36: 427–42.

Spilerman, Seymour. 1976. Structural Characteristics of Cities and the Severity of Racial Disorders. *American Sociological Review* 41: 771–93.

Srivastava, R. K. 1996. Sectional Politics in an Urban Constituency: Generalganj (Kanpur). *Economic and Political Weekly*, January 13–20: 111–20.

Stephens, Ian. 1967. *Pakistan*. London: Ernest Benn.

Stokes, Donald E. 1963. Spatial Models of Party Competition. *American Political Science Review* 57: 368–77.

Subramaniam, Narendra. 1993. Ethnicity, Populism and Pluralist Democracy: Mobilization and Representation in South India. Ph.D. dissertation, MIT.

Sullivan, John L., Pat Walsh, Michal Shamir, David G. Barnum, and James L. Gibson. 1993. Why Politicians Are More Tolerant: Selective Recruitment and Socialization among Political Elites in Britain, Israel, New Zealand and the United States. *British Journal of Political Science* 23: 51–76.

Talbot, Ian. 1996. Back to the future? The Punjab Unionist Model of Consociational Democracy for Contemporary India and Pakistan. *International Journal of Punjab Studies* 3, 1: 65–73.

Tambiah, Stanley. 1996. *Leveling Crowds: Ethnonationalist Conflicts and Collective Violence in South Asia*. Berkeley: University of California Press.

Tek, Goh Cheng. 1971. *The May Thirteenth Incident and Democracy in Malaysia*. Kuala Lumpur: Oxford University Press.

Thomas, E. J. 1985. *Coalition Game Politics in Kerala*. New Delhi: Intellectual Publishing House.

Tong, James W. 1991. *Disorder under Heaven: Collective Violence in the Ming Dynasty*. Stanford: Stanford University Press.

Tsebelis, George. 1990. *Nested Games: Rational Choice in Comparative Politics*. Berkeley: University of California Press.

Tunku, Abdul Rahman Putra Al-Haj. 1969. *May 13: Before and After*. Kuala Lumpur: Utusan Melayu Press.

Vaikunth, V. 2000. *An Eye to Indian Policing: Challenge and Response*. Madras: East-West.

Varshney, Ashutosh. 2002. *Ethnic Conflict and Civic Life: Hindus and Muslims in India*. New Haven: Yale University Press.

Vasquez, John A. 1988. The Steps to War: Towards a Scientific Explanation of Correlates of War Findings. *World Politics* 40, no. 1: 109–45.

Vijayagopalan, S. 1993. *Economic Status of Handicraft Artisans*. New Delhi: National Council for Applied Economic Research.

Vorys, Karl von. 1975. *Democracy without Consensus: Communalism and Political Stability in Malaysia*. Princeton: Princeton University Press.

Wadhwa, Kamlesh Kumar. 1975. *Minority Safeguards in India*. New Delhi: Thomson.

Ware, Robert Bruce. 1997. Political Stability and Ethnic Parity: Why Is There Peace in Dagestan? Paper presented at the American Political Science annual meeting, August 30.

Waskow, Arthur I. 1966. *From Race Riot to Sit-In: 1919 and the 1960s*. New York: Doubleday.

Weber, Max. 1978. *Economy and Society: An Outline of Interpretive Sociology*. Vol. 1. Ed. Guenther Roth and Claus Wittich. Berkeley: University of California Press.

Weiner, Myron. 1989. The Indian Paradox: Violent Social Conflict and Democratic Politics. In Ashutosh Varshney, ed., *The Indian Paradox: Essays in Indian Politics*. New Delhi: Sage.

Wilkinson, Steven I. 1995. U.P.'s "Riot-Prone" Towns. *Seminar* 432: 27–34.

　　1999. Ethnic Mobilization and Ethnic Violence in Post-independence India. Paper presented at American Political Science annual convention, Atlanta, September 2–4.

　　2002. Putting Gujarat in Perspective. *Economic and Political Weekly* (Mumbai), April 27: 1579–83.

Williams, R. M. 1964. *Strangers next Door: Ethnic Relations in American Communities*. Englewood Cliffs, N.J.: Prentice-Hall.

Wilson, Andrew. 1996. The Post-Soviet States and the Nationalities Question. In Graham Smith, ed., *The Nationalities Question in the Post-Soviet States*. New York: Longman: 23–45.

Witte, Els, and Machteld de Metsenaere. 1992. The Flemings in Brussels. In Max Engman, ed., *Ethnic Identity in Urban Europe*, vol. 8 of *Comparative Studies on Governments and Non-Dominant Ethnic Groups in Europe, 1850–1940*. New York: European Science Foundation/NYU Press: 13–38.

Wright, Frank. 1996. *Two Lands on One Soil: Ulster Politics before Home Rule*. Dublin: Gill and MacMillan.

Wright, Theodore P. 1966. The Effectiveness of Muslim Representation in India. In Donald E. Smith, ed., *South Asian Politics and Religion*. Princeton: Princeton University Press: 102–37.

Zaheer, M., and Jagdeo Gupta. 1970. *The Organization of the Government of Uttar Pradesh: A Study of State Administration*. Delhi: S. Chand.

Index

Andhra Pradesh, 2, 8, 48, 86, 128, 144
  ethnic proportionality, 134
  minority language rights in, 126
  party competition and minority support
    (2002), 158
  riot-prevention efforts (2002), 60, 61,
    158
Anglo-Indians, 141
Annadurai, A. N., 193
anti-Hindu violence after riots in India
  in Bangladesh, 16
  in Britain, 16
  in Dubai, 16
  in Pakistan, 13–16
  in Thailand, 16
Aurangabad
  attempts to foment violence (2002), 59
  riots in, 47
Ayodhya, 12, 164
Azad, Maulana, 120
  and Congress language policy, 121

Babri Masjid
  Bihar after destruction of, 86
  delay in preventing destruction of, 95
  See also Ayodhya
backward-caste mobilization pre-1947,
    172–174
Bahujan Samaj Party (BSP), 93, 144, 165
Bajrang Dal, 164, 170
Bakht, Sikandar and ethnic proportionality,
    134
Balasubrahmaniam Inquiry, 199
Bapat, S. K., 95

Bareilly, 32, 37
Bates, Robert, 1
Belfast, 9, 211
  causes of 1864 riots, 217
  elections and Protestant-Catholic riots,
    215
  locally controlled police force, 218
  police bias during 1864 riots, 217
  reduction in violence after 1864, 218
Belgium, 98
Bengal, 5
Bhagalpur
  1989 riots and Muslim voting, 199
  delay in stopping 1989 riots, 95
  inquiry into 1989 riots, 202
Bharatiya Janata Party (BJP), 103, 155,
    158
  alleged role in riots, 162
  effect of riots on elections, 47
  effect of rule on riots, 153
  electoral incentives and 1991 Varanasi
    riots, 164–165
  moderation in Uttar Pradesh (1991), 161
Bhiwandi, 56
  attempts to foment violence (2002),
Bhopal, 51
  1992 riots, 51
  attempts to foment violence (2002), 59
  riot-prevention efforts (2002), 60
Bhubaneshwar, and riot prevention (2002),
    160
Bihar, 5, 17, 65, 69, 85, 86, 94, 113, 153
  backward-caste mobilization and party
    competition, 172

Bihar (*cont.*)
  backward-caste mobilization (1980), 198
  backward-caste mobilization under
    Karpoori Thakur, 198
  ban on cow slaughter, 117
  Bihari-Bengali and Hindu-Muslim
    conflicts pre-1947, 197
  complicity in 1946 riots, 5
  Congress Party factionalism, 198
  economic and social indicators, 196
  electoral competition and Muslim vote in
    explaining violence, 199
  job reservations for backward castes, 198
  lack of pre-1947 backward-caste
    mobilization, 197
  minority language rights, 126
  police strength, 67
  political interference and response to
    riots, 200
  postindependence lack of caste
    aggregation, 197
  religious and caste breakdown, 196
  riot-prevention efforts (2002), 160
  Urdu as second official language, 200
Biharsharif
  political interference and 1981 riots, 200
  response to 1981 riots, 199
  state action after 1993 disturbances, 202
  See also Balasubramaniam Inquiry
Bodeli, 2002 riots in, 61
Bohemia-Moravia
  1861 franchise reform, 209
  19th-century politics and German
    minority, 207
Bombay (state), ban on cow slaughter, 117
Bosnia, 5, 46
Brass, Paul R., and "institutionalized riot
  systems," 52
Brodkin, Karen, and *How the Irish Became
  White* (2000), 238
Budweis
  German manipulation of franchise, 209
  German political power over Czechs, 210
  See also Bohemia-Moravia
Bulgaria, 205, 225
  ethnic violence in, 205
  low level of conflict (post-1990), 226
  Movement for Rights and Freedoms
    (MRF), 226
Burundi, 5

Calicut (Kozhikode), 53
Campeanu, Radu, and Liberal Party in
  Romania, 231
Canning (West Bengal), riot-prevention
  efforts (2002), 160
Carmines, Edward, 234
Carnegie Corporation, 99
caste politics, in Uttar Pradesh, 22
Ceaucescu, Nicolae, 227
Census of India
  ethnic identities, 175
  lack of caste data since 1931, 175
Central Bureau of Investigation, 72
Chandausi, 117
Chandrabhanu, Ramesh, 188
Chhattisgarh, 175
Chhibber, Pradeep, 174
Chicago, 19th-century antiminority riots,
  233
Christians, and political violence, 170
civic engagement and riots, 53–57
  systematic data, 54
Clare, Protestant-Catholic riots, 214
Clifford, Clark, 234
Cluj, ethnic character of university in,
  227
Cochin, 184
Communist Party (CPM), 198
  effect on riot deaths, 153, 154
  riot prevention in West Bengal (2002),
    160
Congress Party, 97, 98, 100, 103, 108, 110,
    117, 120, 143, 155, 158, 186
  complicity in riots, 153
  consociational power sharing, 97–98
  ethnic proportionality, 100
  Hindu-Muslim violence since partition,
    100
Congress Party rule
  effect on riot deaths, 154
  effect on riot occurrence, 153–54
  statistical relationship to riots, 132
Connecticut, Protestant elite in, 209
consociational power sharing, 17, 97–133
  abolition of structures after 1947 by,
    102–103
  assumption of fixed identities, 134
  in Colombia, 99
  in Crimea, 99
  criticism by Paul Brass, 99

Index

cultural autonomy after independence,
114–18
in Cyprus, 99
decline in India after independence, 98
definition of, 98
discrimination against minority
languages, 116
Hindu-Muslim violence, 97, 98
inability to explain ethnic violence,
126–33
increase since 1960s, 123–26
increase since 1970s, 98, 103
increased conflict and, 135–36
India as case for, 98–101
in India from 1919–47, 103–8
lack of Congress coalitions after 1947,
122–23
lack of consociationalism (1947–66),
108–23
in Lebanon, 99
in Malaysia, 99
minority opposition to dismantling after
1947, 119–22
miscoding of India as consociational,
102–3, 108–23
in Moldova, 99
policy prescription, 99
pre-1947 grand coalitions, 107
pre-1947 minority veto, 107
relation to ethnic violence, 127–33
in South Africa, 99
Urdu after 1947, 114–16
Constituent Assembly, 109
Constitution, Indian, 97
52nd Amendment, 149
Scheduled Caste and Tribe preferences,
113
constitutional reforms
premature implementation, 241
role of, 240
Cork, Protestant-Catholic riots, 214
Côte d'Ivoire, 2
cow slaughter, 103
Muslim opposition to ban, 118
restrictions after 1947, 116–18
Cox, Gary, 26, 174
criminalization of politics, 79

data on Hindu-Muslim violence, *see* ethnic
riots

Datta, Amal, 63
Dayal, Justice Raghubir, 46
causes of Ranchi-Hatia riots, 201
Deák, István, 36
Dehra Dun, 34, 54, 118
democracies, multiethnic, and violence,
236
Democratic Party (USA), 25
Derry (Londonderry), religious breakdown
of electorate, 211, 212
Doggan, Ahmed, 226
Dravida Munnetra Kazhagam (DMK)
anti-Hindi movement in 1965, 193
courting Muslim vote post-1967, 194
courting Muslim vote pre-1967, 193
founded in 1949, 193
success in 1967 elections, 193
Dublin, Protestant-Catholic riots,
214

East African whites, 141
Eastern Europe, antiminority campaigns
post-1990, 225
economic incentives for violence
in Bhiwandi, 27–28
in Bombay, Calcutta, and Ahmedabad,
27
census and survey data to test theories,
40
counterarguments to, 30–31
ethnic division of craft labor, 28–30
in Kanpur, Jabalpur, and Moradabad,
28–31
in Kyrgyzstan, 26
looting and economic causes, 46–47
in Lucknow, Varanasi, and Moradabad,
28–30
in Mau, 29
problems in testing theory, 40
in Rwanda, 27
in United States, 27
electoral effects of riots
comparative cases, 204
electoral incentives and violence, 237,
241
electoral incentives model of riot
occurrence, 21–26, 137
on turnout in Madhya Pradesh,
50–51
on turnout in Uttar Pradesh, 49–50

electoral incentives model of riot
occurrence
effect of electoral competition on riots,
152
in Ireland and Great Britain in 19th
century, 211
operationalization of, 41
party competition and riot prevention,
138–40
qualitative evidence for state-level theory,
160–69
qualitative evidence for theory, 47
statistical testing of, 146–54
electoral polarization
in Côte d'Ivoire, 26
in United States, 25
emigration, by Muslims after partition, 112
Estonia, reform of policy toward Russian
minority, 241
ethnic assimilation to dominant group
in 19th-century Belgium, 209
in 19th-century Bohemia and Moravia,
209, 210
in 19th-century Finland, 209
in Ireland, 209
in medieval Europe, 210
ethnic heterogeneity
assumption of fixed identities, 238
and growth, 236
levels of party competition, 174–77
political instability and violence, 236
preferences and political actions, 238
ethnic proportionality, 105, 113
abolition of in Bihar, 111
abolition of in Central Provinces, 111
abolition of in United Provinces, 111
in Assam Rifles, 124
in Bengal, 105
in Bihar, 105
and BJP, 134
in Bombay Province, 104
in Border Security Force, 124
in central and provincial governments
1919–47, 105–6
in Central Provinces, 104
in Central Reserve Police Force, 124
changes in Sind (1947), 111
in Cochin (Kerala), 105
dismantling after 1947, 108, 109–14
in Kerala, 113

Lucknow Pact (1916), 104
in Madras (Tamil Nadu), 105, 113
in Muslim-majority and Hindu-majority
states (1947), 111
Muslim representation in postpartition
India, 112
in Mysore (Karnataka), 105
in Punjab, 105
in Rapid Action Force, 124
in Rashtriya Rifles, 124
in Sind, 105
survival in southern states, 113–14
in Travancore, 105
ethnic proportionality and riots, 128–29
Bihar Special Police, 129
Central Reserve Police Force, 129
Uttar Pradesh PAC, 129
ethnic riots
data in FSU, 9
electoral incentives for state prevention,
5–9
electoral incentives for, 1
India data on caste riots, 147
India data on Hindu-Muslim riots, 11,
147
intrastate variation in riots, 3
pivotal swing constituencies, 21–23, 26
polarizing events, 3–4
precipitating planned events, 23–25
problems with explanations, 2–3
selection bias in study, 37
state prevention, 4–5
Varshney and Wilkinson riot data, 10–11,
38–40, 147
Wilkinson riot data, 10–11

Feldberg, Michael, 233
Finland
19th-century Swedish domination,
207
Swedish minority's veto over reforms,
208
franchise reform and ethnic riots, 207–11

Gandhi, Indira, 21, 64, 100, 182
Gandhi, Mahatma, 107, 116
Gangapur, 160
riot-prevention efforts (2002), 61, 160
Ganjdundwara, 1990 riot, 50
Gaon Hukumat bill (UP, 1947), 108

Index

Gehlot, Ashok, 158
Ghaziabad, 117
Glaeser, Edward, 64
Glancy, Sir Bertrand, and Unionist Party (1946), 108
Godhra, 34
  2002 riots, 59, 61
  See also Gujarat
Gorakhpur, 90, 119
Gramsci, Antonio, 202
Groza, Petru, 227
Gujarat, 2, 8, 87, 152, 154
  1969 riots, 101
  1970 riots, 21
  2002 violence, 8, 12, 61–62, 237
  political incentives and riot prevention (2002), 155
  transfers and riots, 94
Gulf, Persian, remittances from migrants, 185
Gupta, Raghuraj, 118

Hapur, 117
Harun, Dato, and 1969 Kuala Lumpur riots, 224
Haryana, 87
Hayes, Rutherford, 233
Himachal Pradesh, 87
Hindi
  aggregation of languages in census, 175
  See also Hindustani; Urdu
Hindu Mahasabha, 110
  opposition to Muslim reservations, 111
Hindu-Muslim riots
  casualties versus other violence, 12–13
  economic losses from, 13–15
  international dangers posed by, 16
  Muslim casualties in, 30
  riot data as imperfect measure, 38–40
  significance of, 12
  Varshney and Wilkinson riot data, 38–40
Hindustani versus Hindi, Congress support for, 106–7
Horowitz, Donald L., 10, 20, 90, 134, 183, 240
  See also vote pooling
Houphouet-Boigny, President, 2
Human Rights Watch, 2
Huntington, Samuel P., 204

Hyderabad, 53
  1981, 1983, 1984, and 1985 riots, 48–49
  attempts to foment violence (2002), 59
  electoral incentives for riots, 20, 48–49
  riot-prevention efforts (2002), 61, 158

Ibrahim, Hafiz Muhammad, and Congress language policy, 121
Ignatiev, Noel, *How Jews Became White Folks* (1995), 238
Iliescu, President, 230
Illinois, 234
India
  franchise manipulation (1920s–30s), 209
  local law enforcement, 68
Indonesia, complicity in 1960s riots, 5
Indonesian Chinese, 141
Indore
  attempts to foment violence (2002), 59
  riot-prevention efforts (2002), 60
International Institute for Democracy and Electoral Assistance (IDEA), 99
Ireland, 18, 204, 205
  1829 and 1832 reforms, 211
  electoral effect of riots on Tory vote, 215
  electoral explanation for ethnic violence, 205
  Episcopalian Protestant minority, 207
  ethnic balance, 217
  judicial reforms and Protestant bias, 216
  marches to solidify Protestant identity, 212–15
  nonconformists and Episcopalians, 212
  nonconformists and Liberals, 212
  police reforms and Protestant bias, 217
  riot-prevention efforts, 9, 215
Ismail, Muhammad, 120
Israel
  Agudat Yisrael Party, 140
  Degel Ha'Thora Party, 140
  Mapai Party, 140
  party competition and ethnic extremism, 140
  Shas Party, 140

Jaffrelot, Christophe, on electoral effects and riots, 21, 50–51

Jaipur, 37
  attempts to foment violence (2002), 59
  riot-prevention efforts (2002), 61, 158
Jalgaon, attempts to foment violence (2002), 59
Jamshedpur, response to 1979 riots, 199, 200
Jana Sangh
  in Bihar politics, 200
  See also Bharatiya Janata Party
Janata Dal, 198
Janata Party, coalition in Bihar, 198
Jaunpur, 37, 93
Jefferson, Thomas, 18
Jhansi, 117
judicial backlogs in courts, 81–82

Kannauj, 117
Karnataka (Mysore)
  ban on cow slaughter, 117
  See also reservations
Karunakaran, K., 188
Kasargod, 188
Kashmir, 101
Katiyar, Vinay, 163
Kaufmann, Chaim, 36
Kenya, 25
  ethnic violence (1992), 219
Kerala, 17, 70, 79, 85, 86, 92, 128, 152, 154
  Ayodhya agitation, 186
  backward-caste mobilization, 172
  caste mobilization and Congress Party, 180
  caste system, 178
  Communists and of Muslim vote in 1960s, 181
  economic and social indicators, 178
  electoral demography and Muslims, 182
  Ezhava and backward-caste mobilization, 179–80
  Ezhava and Communists, 180
  Hindu-Muslim violence prepartition, 185
  Hindu nationalist mobilization, 184–85, 186
  Indian Union Muslim League, 186
  job reservations in Travancore (1936), 180
  LDF, 186
  LDF and Muslim vote, 171, 182
  minority language rights, 126
  Muslim League and Assembly, 183
  Nair in caste mobilization, 180
  party competition and Hindu-Muslim violence, 185–89
  police action against riots, 187–88
  political incentives and low violence, 171, 186–88
  preindependence backward-caste mobilization, 177–89
  religious breakdown, 178
  seat reservations in Travancore (1932), 180
  UDF and Muslim vote, 171, 182, 186
  United Front and Muslim vote (1967), 181–82
Keshav Das Temple/Mathura Idgah agitation, 167
Khaliquzzaman, Choudhry, 111
Khan, Dildar, 28
Kher Commission on Official Languages, 115
Khopre, Suresh, 56
Khurana, Madan Lal, 35
Kidwai, Rafi Ahmed, 122
King, Jeremy, 210
Kishangarh, riot-prevention efforts (2002), 158, 160
Kishore, Acharya Giriraj, 168
Kohli, Atul, 69, 192
  and state weakness, 69–70
Kolkata (Calcutta)
  attempts to foment violence (2002), 59
  riot-prevention efforts (2002), 54, 61, 160
Koya, C. Mohammed, 183
Kuala Lumpur, 1969 riots, 220, 222, 224
Kumar, Nita, 29

Laitin, David D., *Hegemony and Culture*, 202
Lambert, Richard, 33
Lari, Z. H., and Congress language policy, 122
Latvia, 225
  reforms in response to EU, 241
Leitrim, Protestant-Catholic riots, 214
Lemarchand, René, 33
Lijphart, Arend, 97, 98, 99, 101, 102, 114, 126, 127, 129, 132, 135
Liverpool, 211
  anti-Catholic campaign, 213
  electoral effect of riots, 213
  riots in 1837 and 1841, 214

Index

Louisiana
  antiminority polarization (1890s), 232
  withdrawal of federal troops (1870s),
    233
Lucknow, 53, 54, 91

Madhya Pradesh, 2, 8, 21, 75, 76, 128,
    175
  ban on cow slaughter, 117
  party competition and minority support
    (2002), 158
  party competition and riot prevention
    (2002), 155
  political interference in law and order, 75
  riot-prevention efforts (2002), 59, 60,
    158
Madras
  backward-caste mobilization, 189–92
  Brahmin dominance, 189
  Brahmin employment, 191
  Dravida Kazhagam (1944), 192
  Justice Party, 190, 192
  Madras city (Chennai) riots (1889), 194
  non-Brahmin identities, 190
  non-Brahmin movement, 190
  Palakod riot (1891), 194
  political interference in law and order,
    75
  reservations and caste politics (pre-1947),
    191
  reserved jobs for backward castes (1922),
    191
  reserved seats for backward castes (1919),
    191
  riots in 1930s, 194
  Salem riots (1882), 194
  Self-Respect Association, 191, 192
  Uthamapalayam riots (1910), 194
  See also Tamil Nadu
Maharashtra, 13, 47, 87, 149
  party competition and riot prevention
    (2002), 155
  police strength, 67
Malaysia, 18, 204, 205
  1969 elections, 220–23
  Democratic Action Party (DAP), 220
  ethnic violence, 205
  Gerakan Party, 223
  Malaysian Chinese Association (MCA),
    220

Pan Malayan Islamic Party (PMIP), 220
  state variation in riots, 3, 222–25
  United Malays National Organization
    (UMNO), 220
Manor, James, 69
Manshardt, Clifford, 53
  civic engagement in preventing violence,
    53
Mathura, 117
  riots avoided in 1995, 165–69
  VHP mobilization in 1995, 166, 167
Mayawati, Ms., 93
  Mathura agitation (1995), 167, 168
McAdam, Doug, 234
Meenakshipuram conversions, 195
Meerut, 28, 34, 37, 117
  riots, 101
  riots (1987), 153
Menon, Dilip, 184
Michigan, 234
Mill, John Stuart, 18
Milošević, Slobodan, 2
minority veto, absence after 1947, 118–22
Mirzapur, 117
Mishra, D. P., 76
Mishra, Jagannath, 69
  and minority language rights, 126
Modasa, 2002 riots, 61
Modi, Narendra, 2, 94, 157
Moi, Daniel Arap, 25, 219
Moradabad, 32, 34, 37
  riots (1980), 153
Morley-Minto reforms, 104
Mumbai (Bombay), 54
  1992–93 violence, 14–15
  attempts to foment violence (2002), 59
  delay in stopping 1992–93 riots, 95
Munger, Michael, 26
Murphy, Gardner, and postpartition ethnic
    tensions, 54
Muslim League, 110, 111, 119
Muslim Personal Law, 126
Muslims, employment patterns of, 30
Mussoorie, 34
Mysore, see Karnataka

Nagore, police action, 195
Naicker, E. V. Ramaswami, 191, 193
Naidu, Chandrababu, 2
  Andhra Pradesh riot (2002), 158

Naidu, Ratna, 48
Nasik riots, 47
National Security Act, 60
Nehru, Jawaharlal, 100, 102, 107, 108, 109,
    111, 116, 121, 124
  on discrimination against minorities, 102
  and ban on cow slaughter, 117
  and discrimination against Muslims, 112
  and Urdu-speakers after 1947, 115, 116
Nelson, J. H., *The Madura Country* (1881),
    190
Netherlands, 98
Nigeria, 135
  changes in ethnic identities, 177
  Christians and Muslims in Yorubaland,
    202
Nixon, Richard, 1
Northern Ireland, 13, 103
  Good Friday Agreement, 135

Offe, Claus, 225
Olzak, Susan, 40
Organization for Security and Cooperation
    in Europe (OSCE), 99
Orissa
  anti-Christian violence, 170
  party competition and riot prevention
    (2002), 155, 160

Padmanabaiah, K., 84
Palakkad, Muslim-BJP clashes in, 188
Pandey, Dinanath, and Jamshedpur riots
    (1979), 201
Pant, G. B.
  and employment of Muslims, 111
  and state employment, 110
Parker, John J., 235
Partition of India, Hindu-Muslim violence
    during, 5, 13
party competition
  in Andhra Pradesh, 143
  backward-caste mobilization, 172–74
  competition in India states, 142
  effect of alliances on riots, 154
  effective number of parties (votes)
    measure, 147
  in Gujarat, 143
  in Himachal Pradesh, 143
  intra-Hindu competition in South India,
    17–18

  in Madhya Pradesh, 143
  in Rajasthan, 143
  state responses to 2002 violence, 154–60
party competition and ethnic moderation,
    141
  appeals to minority voters, 140–42
  Muslims and increased competition, 144
  rise of middle- and backward-caste
    parties, 144
  in United States, 141
party competition and riot prevention
    (2002), 157
party competition and reduced violence,
    237, 238
  in Bihar, 237
  in Bulgaria, 237
  in Kerala, 237, 239
  in Madhya Pradesh, 237
  in Malaysia, 237
  in Rajasthan, 237
  in United States, 237
Patel, Vallabhai, 76
  opposition to Muslim reservations, 111
Philadelphia
  19th-century antiminority riots, 233
police
  1979 nationwide strikes, 91
  capacity to prevent riots, 67–68
  diversion from duties, 80
  effect of transfers, 82–85
  political interference, 68
  weakness in 1970s, 80, 91
policies toward minorities, 239
political interference in law and order
  in Bihar, 78
  Congress Party and, 77–78
  Kerala Police Reorganization Committee
    (1959), 76
  police capacity to prevent riots, 70–71
  Punjab Police Commission (1961–62),
    75
  Second Uttar Pradesh Police
    Commission (1971), 76
  state inquiries, 75
  transfers, 71
  in Uttar Pradesh, 78
Protestant-Catholic riots, 214
Portugal, 204
Posen, Barry, 36
Potter, David, 92

Index

Praja Socialist Party, 198
President's Rule, 149
previous violence
    likelihood of violence, 35–37
    security dilemma, 36
Priyadarshi, Ashok, 56
proportionality in state employment
    increase since 1970s, 103
    to reduce ethnic violence, 101
Providence, 208
Punjab, 5, 87
    1946 elections, 108
    police strength in, 66
Punjab and Sind, refugees from, 34

Rabushka, Alvin, 236
Rahman, Tunku Abdul, 220
Rajasthan, 8
    ban on cow slaughter, 117
    party competition and riot prevention
        (2002), 60, 158
    riot-prevention efforts (2002), 61
Rajgopal, P. R., 27, 33
Ram, Jagjivan, and neutral administration,
    76
Ram, Kanshi, 167
Ramachandran, M. G., 85
Ranchi-Hatia, riots (1967) and response, 46,
    95, 153, 200
Rao, N. T. Rama, and ethnic
    proportionality, 134
Rapid Action Force (RAF), 60
Rashtriya Swayamsevak Sangh (RSS), 35
    anti-Urdu agitation, 200
    mobilization in Kerala, 195
Rasul, Begum Aizaz, 120–21
Reddy, G. Ram, 20
refugees and ethnic violence, 33
    in Bosnia, 33
    in Burundi, 33
    desire for revenge, 35
    economic motivation for riots, 34
    experiences during partition, 35
    in India, 33–35
    refugee theory, 41–42
refugees from Pakistan, and Indian
    Muslims, 34
reservations
    extension to Andhra Pradesh, 124
    extension to Assam, 124

extension to Bihar, 124
extension to Karnataka, 124
in Haryana, 123
implementation by Congress in 1970s,
    124
ineffectiveness in 1950s and 1960s, 113
in Karnataka, 123
in Kerala, 123
Nehru's opposition to, 109–10
for Scheduled Castes and Tribes, 103
in Uttar Pradesh, 123
Rhode Island, manipulation of franchise,
    208
Romania, 204, 205, 225
    ethnic violence, 205, 228–31
    Hungarian Democratic Union of
        Romania (HDUR), 228
    National Salvation Front (NSF), 228
    NSF anti-Hungarian campaign (1990),
        228
    Party of Romanian National Unity, 231
    Romanian-Hungarian relations, 226–28
Roorkee, 117
Roscrea, Protestant-Catholic riots, 214
Rwanda, 5, 33

Saharanpur, 34
    riot (1990), 50
Sahay, K. B., 153
Sait, Sulaiman, 186
Samajwadi Party, 144, 165
Scheduled Caste and Tribe, proportionality
    in 1970s, 124
security, and Muslim voters, 145
security/demographic balance hypothesis,
    32, 41
separate electorates, abolition of
    after 1947, 109
    by Constituent Assembly, 109
    after independence, 120
    in Uttar Pradesh, 109
    in West Bengal, 109
Setalvad, M. C., 82
Shafir, Michael, 231
Shahabuddin, Syed, 101, 129
Shakir, Moin, 33
Sharma, Deen Dutt, 169
Sharma, K. D., 75
Shastri, Lal Bahadur, 102, 111
Shepsle, Kenneth, 236

Shiv Sena, role in
  Aurangabad riots, 47
  Nasik riots, 47
  riots, 162
Singh, Arjun, 75, 77
Singh, Bijendra, 94
Singh, Charan, 76
Singh, Dara, 170
Singh, Digvijay, 2, 158
Singh, Gopal, and Commission on
  Minorities, 101
Singh, Kalyan, 161, 164
Singh, Khushwant, 101
Singh, Tara, and minority proportionality,
  119
Smelser, Neil, 63
South Africa, peace committees, 56
South Carolina, and federal troops, 233
South India, Muslims as backward castes in,
  238
Spilerman, Seymour, 27
Sri Lankan Tamils, 141
state autonomy from politicians, decline of,
  73
state capacity
  comparative data, 72–73
  Hindu-Muslim riots, 85–96
state-capacity explanations for violence
  in England, 63
  for Hindu-Muslim violence, 64–96
  in Mexico, 63
  in Ming China, 63
  in United States, 63
state finances, and deficits, 80
state intervention to prevent riots, 90
state-level incentives and riots
  outside Gujarat (2002), 59–61
  and town-level factors, 16–17,
  58
state response to ethnic violence and party
  competition, 207
  in Ireland, 206
  in Malaysia, 206
  in Romania, 206
  in United States, 205, 232–35
Stimson, James, 234
Subramaniam, Narendra, 194
Sullivan, John L., 239
Surat (2002), 53, 59
Switzerland, 98

Taldi (2002), 160
Tambiah, Stanley, 36
Tamil Nadu, 17, 85, 86, 92
  backward-caste mobilization, 172
  DMK and Muslim vote in 1960s, 171
  economic and social indicators, 189
  ethnic breakdown, 189
  Hindu-Muslim violence prepartition, 194
  Hindu nationalist mobilization, 194
  Muslim votes, 194
  police action against riots, 195–96
  political competition and violence,
  170–71, 195–96
Tandon, Purushottam Das, 121
Telegu Desam Party, 143, 144
  Andhra Pradesh riot prevention (2002),
  158
Tellicherry
  riots (1971), 187
  police action against riots, 188
Thakur, Karpoori
  backward-caste mobilization in Bihar, 198
  Jana Sangh votes and 1979 Jamshedpur
  riots, 200
Thurmond, Strom, 238
Tipperary, Protestant-Catholic riots, 214
Tirgu Mures
  1990 riots, 229–31
  electoral explanation for riots, 229, 230
Tiwana, Khizr Hyat, 108
Tong, James, 63
town-level incentives for riots, 16–17,
  19–62
  economic division of labor, 26
  electoral incentives for riots, 20–26
  and state-level factors, 58–62
  statistical analysis, 42–47
  statistical significance, 42–44
Travancore and Cochin, 177
  backward-caste mobilization, 179
  See also Kerala
Tripathi, Kamlapathi, 77
Triplicane, police action against riots in,
  195
Trivandrum (Thiruvananthapuram), 187
  police action against riots (1985), 188
Truman, Harry S., 234

Udaipur, 31
Unionist Party (Punjab), 108

Index

United Provinces (Uttar Pradesh)
political interference in law and order, 73
riot convictions, 87
United States, 18, 205
bias during antiminority riots, 233
black vote in Midwest, 234–35
electoral incentives and riot prevention, 8,
233–35
intervention to prevent riots, 8
minority voters during (1948), 234
Progressives and Republicans in 1890s,
232
Urdu language, 103
in police and administration pre-1947,
106
protected status pre-1947, 106–7
replaced by Hindi in Bihar, 116
replaced by Hindi in Central Provinces,
116
replaced by Hindi in Uttar Pradesh,
115
status in 1980s, 126
See also Hindi; Hindustani
Uttar Pradesh, 16, 65, 85, 86, 92, 93, 94,
119, 175
backward-caste mobilization and party
competition, 172
ban on cow slaughter, 117
electoral incentives and riot prevention in
Mathura (1995), 161, 165–69
electoral incentives and riot prevention in
Varanasi (1991), 161–65
and ethnic proportionality, 134
and minority language rights, 126
postindependence riot convictions, 90
Pradeshik Armed Constabulary (PAC),
91, 95
transfers and riots in, 93–94
Uttaranchal, 175

Vadodara (Baroda)
2002 riots in, 61
attempts to foment violence (2002), 59
delay in stopping 1969 riots, 95
Vaikunth, V., 75

Vajpayee, Atal Bihari, 21
Varanasi, 31, 117
1991 riots, 161–165
attempts to foment violence (2002),
59
ban on cow slaughter (1947), 117
economic motivations in 1991 riots,
163
role of traders in riots, 31
Varshney, Ashutosh, 10–16, 58, 147
civic engagement explanation, 52–53,
57
See also civic engagement; ethnic riots;
state-level incentives
violence, in multiethnic states, 236
Vishwa Hindu Parishad (VHP), 162, 166
vote pooling, Donald Horowitz and, 7, 138,
183, 237

Walpole, J. H., Protestant-Catholic riots,
216
Washington, 19th-century antiminority
riots, 233
West Bengal, 70, 86, 87, 94, 128, 240
minority language rights, 126
riot-prevention efforts (2002), 60, 61,
160
World Bank, 240
Wright, Theodore, 121

Yadav, Gangadin, 94
Yadav, Laloo Prasad, 86, 199
and action against police after Sitamarhi
riots, 202
and Hindu-Muslim riots, 201
and Muslim votes, 199
Yadav, Mulayam Singh, 93, 94
and ethnic proportionality, 134
and firing at Ayodhya 1989, 161
and minority language rights, 126
Yadav, Uma Kant, 93
Yorubaland
relevance for understanding India,
203
Yugoslavia, 36

Other Books in the Series (continued from page iii)

Roberto Franzosi, *The Puzzle of Strikes: Class and State Strategies in Postwar Italy*

Geoffrey Garrett, *Partisan Politics in the Global Economy*

Miriam Golden, *Heroic Defeats: The Politics of Job Loss*

Merilee Serrill Grindle, *Changing the State*

Anna Gryzymala-Busse, *Redeeming the Communist Past: The Regeneration of Communist Parties in East Central Europe*

Frances Hagopian, *Traditional Politics and Regime Change in Brazil*

J. Rogers Hollingsworth and Robert Boyer, eds., *Contemporary Capitalism: The Embeddedness of Institutions*

Ellen Immergut, *Health Politics: Interests and Institutions in Western Europe*

Torben Iversen, *Contested Economic Institutions*

Torben Iversen, Jonas Pontusson, and David Soskice, eds., *Unions, Employers, and Central Banks: Macroeconomic Coordination and Institutional Change in Social Market Economies*

Thomas Janoski and Alexander M. Hicks, eds., *The Comparative Political Economy of the Welfare State*

David C. Kang, *Crony Capitalism: Corruption and Capitalism in South Korea and Philippines*

Junko Kato, *Regressive Taxation and the Welfare State*

Robert O. Keohane and Helen B. Milner, eds., *Internationalization and Domestic Politics*

Herbert Kitschelt, *The Transformation of European Social Democracy*

Herbert Kitschelt, Peter Lange, Gary Marks, and John D. Stephens, eds., *Continuity and Change in Contemporary Capitalism*

Herbert Kitschelt, Zdenka Mansfeldova, Radek Markowski, and Gabor Toka, *Post-Communist Party Systems*

David Knoke, Franz Urban Pappi, Jeffrey Broadbent, and Yutaka Tsujinaka, eds., *Comparing Policy Networks*

Allan Kornberg and Harold D. Clarke, *Citizens and Community: Political Support in a Representative Democracy*

Amie Kreppel, *The European Parliament and the Supranational Party System*

David D. Laitin, *Language Repertories and State Construction in Africa*

Fabrice E. Lehoucq and Ivan Molina, *Stuffing the Ballot Box: Fraud, Electoral Reform, and Democratization in Costa Rica*

Mark Irving Lichbach and Alan S. Zuckerman, eds., *Comparative Politics: Rationality, Culture, and Structure*

Evan Lieberman, *Race and Regionalism in the Politics of Taxation in Brazil and South Africa*

Pauline Jones Luong, *Institutional Change and Political Continuity in Post-Soviet Central Asia*

Doug McAdam, John McCarthy, and Mayer Zald, eds., *Comparative Perspectives on Social Movements*

James Mahoney and Dietrich Rueschemeyer, eds., *Historical Analysis and the Social Sciences*

Scott Mainwaring and Matthew Soberg Shugart, eds., *Presidentialism and Democracy in Latin America*

Isabela Mares, *The Politics of Social Risk: Business and Welfare State Development*

Anthony W. Marx, *Making Race, Making Nations: A Comparison of South Africa, the United States, and Brazil*

Joel S. Migdal, *State in Society: Studying How States and Societies Constitute One Another*

Joel S. Migdal, Atul Kohli, and Vivienne Shue, eds., *State Power and Social Forces: Domination and Transformation in the Third World*

Scott Morgenstern and Benito Nacif, eds., *Legislative Politics in Latin America*

Layna Mosley, *Global Capital and National Governments*

Wolfgang C. Müller and Kaare Strøm, *Policy, Office, or Votes?*

Maria Victoria Murillo, *Labor Unions, Partisan Coalitions, and Market Reforms in Latin America*

Ton Notermans, *Money, Markets, and the State: Social Democratic Economic Policies since 1918*

Paul Pierson, *Dismantling the Welfare State?: Reagan, Thatcher, and the Politics of Retrenchment*

Marino Regini, *Uncertain Boundaries: The Social and Political Construction of European Economies*

Lyle Scruggs, *Sustaining Abundance: Environmental Performance in Industrial Democracies*

Jefferey M. Sellers, *Governing from Below: Urban Regions and the Global Economy*

Yossi Shain and Juan Linz, eds., *Interim Governments and Democratic Transitions*

Beverley Silver, *Forces of Labor: Workers' Movements and Globalization since 1870*

Theda Skocpol, *Social Revolutions in the Modern World*

Richard Snyder, *Politics after Neoliberalism: Reregulation in Mexico*

David Stark and László Bruszt, *Postsocialist Pathways: Transforming Politics and Property in East Central Europe*

Sven Steinmo, Kathleen Thelen, and Frank Longstreth, eds., *Structuring Politics: Historical Institutionalism in Comparative Analysis*

Duane Swank, *Global Capital, Political Institutions, and Policy Change in Developed Welfare States*

Sidney Tarrow, *Power in Movement: Social Movements and Contentious Politics*

Ashutosh Varshney, *Democracy, Development, and the Countryside*

Elisabeth J. Wood, *Forging Democracy from Below: Insurgent Transitions in South Africa and El Salvador*

Elisabeth J. Wood, *Insurgent Collective Action and Civil War in El Salvador*

Printed in the United States
60067LVS00002B/114